GLOBALIZATION AND EMERGING ISSUES IN TRADE THEORY AND POLICY

FRONTIERS OF ECONOMICS AND GLOBALIZATION

5

Series Editors:

HAMID BELADI
University of Texas at San Antonio, USA

E. KWAN CHOI
Iowa State University, USA

FRONTIERS OF ECONOMICS AND GLOBALIZATION VOLUME 5

GLOBALIZATION AND EMERGING ISSUES IN TRADE THEORY AND POLICY

Edited by

Binh Tran-Nam

Faculty of Law, University of New South Wales, Sydney, Australia

Ngo Van Long

Department of Economics, McGill University, Montreal, Canada

Makoto Tawada

Graduate School of Economics, Nagoya University, Nagoya, Japan

Emerald

United Kingdom – North America – Japan
India – Malaysia – China

Emerald Group Publishing Limited
Howard House, Wagon Lane, Bingley BD16 1WA, UK

First edition 2008

Copyright © 2008 Emerald Group Publishing Limited

Reprints and permission service
Contact: booksandseries@emeraldinsight.com

British Library Cataloguing in Publication Data
A catalogue record for this book is available from the British Library

ISBN: 978-1-84663-962-3
ISSN: 1574-8715

Printed and bound by MPG Books Ltd, Bodmin, Cornwall

Awarded in recognition of
Emerald's production
department's adherence to
quality systems and processes
when preparing scholarly
journals for print

INVESTOR IN PEOPLE

LIST OF CONTRIBUTORS

Eric W. Bond	Department of Economics, Vanderbilt University, VU Station B #351819, 2301 Vanderbilt Place, Nashville, TN 37235, USA
Chi-Chur Chao	Department of Economics, Chinese University of Hong Kong, Shatin, Hong Kong
Jai-Young Choi	Department of Economics and Finance, Lamar University, Beaumont, TX 77710, USA
E. Kwan Choi	Department of Economics, Iowa State University, Ames, IA 50011, USA; Department of Economics and Finance, City University of Hong Kong, Tat Chee Avenue, Kowloon, Hong Kong
Kai-Hsi Chu	Department of Economics, University of Washington, Box 353330, Seattle, WA 98195-3330, USA
Masahiro Endoh	Faculty of Business and Commerce, Keio University, 2-15-45, Mita, Minato-ku, Tokyo, 108-8345, Japan
Kenji Fujiwara	School of Economics, Kwansei Gakuin University, Uegahara 1-1-155, Nishinomiya, Hyogo, 662-8501, Japan
Koichi Hamada	Department of Economics, Yale University, P.O. Box 208269, New Haven, CT 06520-8269, USA
Bharat R. Hazari	Department of Economics and Finance, City University of Hong Kong, Tat Chee Avenue, Kowloon, Hong Kong
Arye Hillman	Department of Economics, Bar-Ilan University, Israel
Kazumichi Iwasa	Graduate School of Economics, Kobe University, Kobe, Japan
Murray C. Kemp	University of New South Wales, 6/77 Ocean St, Woollahra, NSW 2025, Australia
Toru Kikuchi	Graduate School of Economics, Kobe University, 2-1 Rokkodai-cho, Nada-Ku Kobe 657-8501, Japan

Jean-Pierre Laffargue   PSE-CNRS and CEPREMAP, University of Paris 1, 48 boulevard Jourdan, 75014 Paris, France

Ngo Van Long   Department of Economics, McGill University, 855 Sherbrooke St west, Montreal, H3A2T7, Canada

Michihiro Ohyama   Department of Economics, Toyo University, 5-28-20, Hakusan, Bunkyo-ku, Tokyo 112-8606, Japan

Masayuki Okawa   Department of Economics, Ritsumeikan University, Biwako-Kusatsu Campus, 1-1-1 Noji-Higashi, Kusatsu, Shiga 525-8577, Japan

Martin Richardson   School of Economics, Australian National University, H.W. Arndt Building (#25A), ANU, Canberra ACT0200, Australia

Raymond Riezman   Department of Economics, University of Iowa, Iowa City, IA 52242, USA

Koji Shimomura   Research Institute for Economics & Business Administration, Kobe University, Japan

Nobuhito Suga   Graduate School of Economics and Business Administration, Hokkaido University, Kita-9, Nishi-7, Kita-ku, Sapporo, 060-0809, Japan

Constantinos Syropoulos   Department of Economics and International Business, LeBow College of Business, Drexel University, 503-N Matheson Hall, 32nd and Market Streets, Philadelphia, PA 19104, USA

Makoto Tawada   Graduate School of Economics, Nagoya University, Furo-cho, Chikusa-ku, Nagoya 464-8601, Japan

Binh Tran-Nam   Atax, University of New South Wales, Sydney, NSW 2052, Australia

Henry Wan   Department of Economics, Cornell University, 470 Uris Hall, Ithaca, NY 14853-7601, USA

Niven Winchester   Department of Economics, University of Otago, P.O. Box 56, Dunedin, New Zealand

Kar-yiu Wong   Department of Economics, University of Washington, Box 353330, Seattle, WA 98195-3330, USA

Eden Yu   Department of Economics and Finance, City University of Hong Kong, Tat Chee Avenue, Kowloon, Hong Kong

Yinggang Zhou   Black Creek Global Advisors, 518 17th Street, Suite 1700, Denver, CO 80202, USA

CONTENTS

INTRODUCTION

Binh Tran-Nam[a], Ngo Van Long[b] and Makoto Tawada[c]

[a]*Atax, University of New South Wales, Sydney, NSW 2052, Australia*
E-mail address: b.tran-nam@unsw.edu.au
[b]*Department of Economics, McGill University, 855 Sherbrooke St west, Montreal,*
H3A2T7, Canada
E-mail address: ngo.long@mcgill.co
[c]*Graduate School of Economics, Nagoya University, Furo-cho, Chikusa-ku,*
Nagoya 464-8601, Japan
E-mail address: mtawada@soec.nagoya-u.ac.jp

This edited volume has its genesis in a conference entitled *New Paradigms in Economics of Welfare and Trade under Globalisation and Regionalisation.* Held at the Coogee campus of the Australian School of Taxation (Atax), University of New South Wales (Sydney, Australia) from 8th to 10th August 2006, this conference brought together economic theorists from around the globe to celebrate Murray Kemp's 80th birthday. Conference participants and presenters included a former teacher, colleagues, co-authors, senior academics and many former students of Murray. After a two-year gestation period, the volume has finally been published. Half of the chapters in this book are derived from papers presented at the conference. The remaining half of the book consists of invited papers completed after the conference. All chapters in this volume were subjected to a formal reviewing and revision process.

Murray Kemp is one of the world's most outstanding and prolific economic theorists. In a distinguished career spanning over five decades, he has made fundamental contributions to a range of economic subject matters, including exhaustible resources, welfare economics and international trade. He is perhaps best known for his pioneering work in the normative theory of international trade. Focusing on international trade, this volume pays tribute to Murray Kemp as a scholar, teacher, colleague, co-author and friend. In this sense, this volume can be regarded as a sequel to *Trade, Welfare and Economic Policies* edited by Horst Herberg and Ngo Van Long (in honor of Murray on the occasion of his 65th birthday) and *Economic Theory and International Trade* edited by Alan Woodland (in honor of Murray on the occasion of his 70th birthday). The present volume therefore not only provides recognition of Murray Kemp's numerous and important academic contributions but also serves as a testimony to his longevity as an economic theorist.

This book is a collection of latest research findings on topical issues in international trade theory and policy. These cover three broad areas of globalization and emerging issues in international trade. The book is accordingly divided into three parts. The first section of the volume, containing five chapters, deals with trade liberalization and outsourcing. The second section of the volume, also containing five chapters, examines trading clubs and preferential trading agreements. These chapters extend the famous Kemp–Wan proposition concerning customs unions in various directions. The final section of the book consists of six chapters on various aspects of trade and aid. Like previous edited books in honor of Murray, the topics considered here encompass a wide range of international trade issues and the techniques of analysis are firmly grounded in economic theory.

In Chapter 1 of Part I, Ohyama considers the role of the World Trade Organization (WTO) in a context where regional free trade agreements have proliferated to threaten the WTO's basic rule of multilateral and non-discriminatory tariff reduction, and where the international concern about labor and environmental standards has challenged its conventional practice of tariff negotiation. Wan and Zhou analyze trade liberalization as a game under uncertainty in the next chapter. They set out to explain a puzzle: while most countries realize the mutual benefit of tariff cutting, tariffs never become zero. In Chapter 3, Kikuchi and Shimomura employ a Chamberlinian–Ricardian model to show how technological differences between countries interact with the level of trade costs to determine trade patterns. Shifting to a more topical issue, Chu and Wong examine the welfare impact of a variety of import restriction policies in the presence of outsourcing. By contrast, in the last chapter of this section, Ngo Van Long studies the welfare effects of relaxing government restrictions on bidding by foreign firms for government procurement contracts.

Part II consists of a series of papers that were written to celebrate the 30th anniversary of the publication of the original Kemp–Wan proposition in 1976. Appropriately, it is Murray Kemp who, in Chapter 6, demonstrates that the Kemp–Wan proposition is valid for any form of free trade association. He also shows that sense can be made of the common conjecture that a customs union is more beneficial to the world economy than a comparable but distinct free trade association. In the next chapter, Endoh, Hamada and Shimomura employ the revealed preference approach to study the welfare effects of the formation of a free trade area (FTA) or a preferential trade agreement on non-member countries that are left without compensation. In a similar spirit but using a more conventional approach, Bond and Syropoulos examine how preferential liberalization between a pair of countries affects the terms of trade and welfare of the liberalizing member countries, as well as its impact on the rest of the world. In Chapter 9, Richardson and Winchester suggest that the value of the extension to an FTA of the Kemp–Wan proposition on how to construct welfare improving customs unions is undermined by its very rationale – they point to the greater popularity of FTAs over customs unions for "political" reasons. Returning to the issue of compensation, in the last chapter of Section II, Iwasa, Riezman and Shimomura study how far the Kemp–Wan result on Pareto-improving customs unions can hold without inter-country transfers.

Part III of the book commences with Tran-Nam's comprehensive and critical review of Murray Kemp's contributions to the discipline of international trade and welfare economics. In Chapter 12, Hillman discusses two paradigms, second-best and political economy, that have been used to explain instances of refusal to trade, in spite of the theorems on the gains from trade. Fujiwara, Suga and Tawada examine the pattern of trade and gains from trade in a two-country general equilibrium model with increasing returns to scale and oligopoly in the next chapter. Okawa in Chapter 14 examines whether a small open economy in the presence of a non-traded good produced under a monopolistically competitive market and foreign capital inflow can raise its national welfare by adopting trade liberalization coupled with foreign economic aid. Turning attention to aid and development, Choi and Choi determine the effect of infrastructure aid to developing countries on their national income and consumer welfare, and identify the condition for the Dutch disease. In the final chapter, Chao, Hazari, Laffargue and Yu show that in the presence of tourism, the traditional policy prescription, free trade in goods and the standard Pigouvian tax on pollution, is not optimal for a small open economy.

This volume is a joint product of many persons from around the world. First of all, we would like to thank all contributors who enthusiastically offered their research papers as a tribute to Murray Kemp. Their cooperation, fellowship and patience helped to bring this book into being without any major complication. Secondly, the authors and we are deeply grateful to the referees for willingly offering their valuable time and expertise to the important task of paper reviewing. Thirdly, a modern book typically comes into existence with the support of a capable editorial team. We are therefore indebted to Cindy Chan at Atax and the editorial staff at Emerald (Diane Heath, Emma Smith, Christine Ball and the production team of Macmillan Publishing Solutions) for cheerful, swift and efficient assistance. Fourthly, various institutions provided financial support to the organization of the 2006 Sydney conference as well as the preparation of this volume. In particular, the generous support of Kobe University, Nagoya University and Economic Design Network is greatly appreciated.

Finally, we wish to acknowledge our debt of gratitude to Koji Shimomura, a world-class economic theorist, who was also a former PhD student and prominent co-author of Murray Kemp. Due to illness, Koji could not attend the Sydney conference in 2006. He, however, more than made up for his absence by co-authoring five papers presented at the conference. Two of these plus a new joint paper appear in this volume. Koji's research grant at Kobe University also provided considerable support to both the conference and the publication of this book. Sadly, his untimely passing in early 2007 prevented him from assuming his rightful position as a co-editor of this volume. We will miss Koji.

PART I

Trade Liberalization and Outsourcing

CHAPTER 1

The WTO and The World Economy: A Welfare-Theoretic Perspective

Michihiro Ohyama

Department of Economics, Toyo University, Hakusan, Bunkyo-ku, Tokyo 112-8606, Japan
E-mail addresses: ohyama@toyonet.toyo.ac.jb; miohyama@nifty.com

Abstract

Purpose – This chapter reconsiders the role of the WTO in the world economy, where regional free trade agreements have proliferated to threaten its basic rule of multilateral and non-discriminatory tariff reduction and the deepening of globalization has developed international concern about labor and environmental standards to challenge its conventional practice of tariff negotiation.

Methodology/Approach – This chapter employs the general equilibrium approach of welfare economics in its analysis.

Findings – It is shown that the WTO should reconfirm its target of expanding and securing the market access property rights of member countries and engage in the international coordination of tariffs and other trade policy instruments to achieve this target, while leaving other policy targets such as propagating labor and environmental standards to other appropriate international organizations.

Practical implications – The steady move towards multilateral free trade has come to an end. This chapter offers a clear argument for economists and policy makers to regain confidence in the traditional role of the WTO/GATT.

Keywords: WTO, GATT, welfare, non-discriminatory tariff reduction, environmental and labor standards

Paper type: Research paper

1. Introduction

The World Trade Organization (WTO) and its predecessor, the GATT, have contributed to the liberalization of international trade and promoted the growth of the world economy. In recent years, however, WTO seems to

Frontiers of Economics and Globalization
Volume 5   ISSN: 1574-8715
DOI: 10.1016/S1574-8715(08)05001-X

stand at a turning point, confronted by new challenges. In this chapter, we shall consider the following two issues: First, regionally restricted free trade agreements (FTAs) have proliferated to threaten the basic principle of the WTO/GATT rules which advocates multilateral and non-discriminatory tariff reduction. As is well known, Article 24 of the GATT approves the formation of FTAs under certain conditions. With world-wide emergence of FTAs, it is getting more and more necessary to reconsider and even modify these conditions. Second, the globalization of international economies has advanced to the point that labor and environmental policies conventionally regarded as local or national problems are now becoming one of the central issues in the world economy. As the 1999 fiasco in Seattle eloquently showed, there are many groups of people regarding WTO as potentially dangerous to the attainment of sound environmental and labor standards. It is important to redefine the role of the WTO so as to ensure the compatibility of WTO-led liberalization of international trade with these new challenges.

Bagwell and Staiger (2001) argued convincingly that "the central purpose of the WTO rules is to create a negotiating forum where member governments can voluntarily exchange market access commitments, with the assurance that the property rights over negotiated market access commitments are secure against unilateral government infringement". They showed that this view of the WTO as a mechanism for expanding and securing market access property rights identifies how supporters of sound trade policies and sound labor and environmental standards can both benefit from the appropriate functioning of the WTO and serves to dissolve their attacks against the WTO. They did not consider, however, its implications for the GATT conditions for FTAs. We shall demonstrate that it is also effective as a key to reevaluate those conditions. Moreover, we shall provide a welfare-theoretic foundation of the view of the WTO as a market access securing mechanism, which Bagwell and Staiger did not elaborate in their 2001 paper.[1]

2. Preliminaries: Welfare comparison

Let us consider the economy of a single country (or a group of countries) engaging in external trade. The economy is assumed to be static in the sense that its technology, factor endowments and the preferences of its consumers are all given and fixed. There is a finite number of commodities produced and consumed in competitive markets.

The model is general enough to accommodate all kinds of commodities, final consumption goods and services, intermediate goods, factor services,

---

[1] Bagwell and Staiger (2002, Chapter 8) provides an alternative welfare theoretic treatment of the issue using a model different from ours.

any of which may be traded or non-traded. Consider two distinct open economic situations, S' and S'' and their general equilibria. For simplicity, we abstract from domestic distortions arising from external economies and diseconomies. In order to consider participation in FTAs, or labor and environmental policies, however, we need to assume that the government intervenes in the economy by means of tariffs, domestic taxes and subsidies (or other equivalent measures), which implies that consumers generally face commodity prices different from those producers face and from international prices.

Let p' and p'' denote the consumers' price vectors and let x' and x'' denote the aggregate equilibrium consumption vectors in situation S' and S'', respectively. Then, one can show that if

$$p''x'' \geq p''x' \tag{1}$$

situation S'' is potentially preferable to S' from the viewpoint of the country (or the union of the countries) in the sense that some consumers can be made better off with other consumers being kept as well off in situation S'' as in situation S'.[2] Note that if a commodity is a pure intermediate good, its consumption is identically zero in all situations. Suppose that the government imposes a tariff at *ad valorem* rate t_i'' on the trade of commodity i and provides a domestic production subsidy at *ad valorem* rate r_i'' in situation S''. For simplicity, we assume that there are no consumption taxes and subsidies. If we denote the consumers' price of commodity i by p_i'' and the corresponding international price and producers' price by q_i'' and p_i''', we obtain no arbitrage conditions:

$$p_i'' = (1 + t_i'')q_i'' \quad \text{and}$$

$$p_i''' = (1 + r_i'')p_i''.$$

In the absence of transportation costs, if t_i'' is positive, it represents an import tax or an export subsidy depending on whether commodity i is imported or exported in equilibrium. If t_i'' is negative, it represents an export tax or import subsidy. However, if r_i'' is positive (resp. negative), it represents a subsidy (resp. tax) on the production, or a tax (resp. subsidy) on the use in production of commodity i depending on whether commodity i is an output or an input in production. We can rewrite the above no arbitrage conditions in matrix form as

$$p'' = q''(I + T'') \quad \text{and} \tag{2}$$

$$p''' = p''(I + R''), \tag{3}$$

---

[2] This point is well recognized in the literature on the evaluation of real income. See Ohyama (1972) for a detailed explanation and discussion of the subject.

where T'' is a diagonal matrix with the ith diagonal element t_i'', R'' a diagonal matrix with the ith diagonal element r_i'', and I an identity matrix.

Let y' and y'' denote the equilibrium output vectors, a' and a'' the endowment vectors, e' and e'' the excess demand (or net import) vectors in situation S' and S''. By definition, we have

$$e' = x' - y' - a' \quad \text{and} \tag{4}$$

$$e'' = x'' - y'' - a''. \tag{5}$$

If a commodity is non-traded, its excess demand becomes identically zero in all situations. Let b' and b'' denote the net income transfers from the rest of the world in situation S' and S''. The current account payments is assumed to be in balance in both situations implying

$$q'e' = b' \quad \text{and} \tag{6}$$

$$q''e'' = b''. \tag{7}$$

Assuming that $a' = a''$, we obtain from Equations (2)–(6)

$$\begin{aligned} p''(x'' - x') = b'' - b' &+ (q' - q'')e' + q''T''(e'' - e') \\ &+ p''R''(y' - y'') + p'''(y'' - y'). \end{aligned} \tag{8}$$

The assumption of profit maximization under perfect competition implies $p'''y'' \geq p'''y'$. In view of (8), we have

THEOREM *(Welfare Comparison). Consider two distinct situations, S' and S'', with common initial endowment and production set. If*

$$(b'' - b') + (q' - q'')e' + q''T''(e'' - e') + p''R''(y' - y'') \geq 0, \tag{9}$$

situation S'' is potentially preferable to situation S'.

The first bracketed term on the left-hand side of condition (9) represents the difference in the net income transfer, the second term the difference in the terms of trade and the third term the difference in the tariff revenue index calculated by using tariffs in situation S'' and trade volumes in situation S' and S''. For brevity, they may be termed the "income transfer" effect, the "terms of trade" effect and the "tariff revenue" (or alternatively "trade volume") effect of transition from situation S' to S''. The first and the second effects are self-explanatory, but the third term may need some annotation. For instance, a positive tax on the import of a commodity implies that its domestic price exceeds the import price by the value of the tax. An increase in the volume of its import should increase the potential welfare of the country since its marginal domestic value signified by its domestic price is greater than its marginal cost measured by its import price. Similarly, if an import subsidy (or a negative tax) is given to the import of a commodity, a decrease of its import should be beneficial since its marginal domestic value signified by its domestic price is smaller than its marginal cost measured by its import price. Note also that condition (9) does not by itself ensure that S'' is *actually* preferable to S' unless income distribution realized in the former is judged to be not worse than income distribution realized in the latter.[3]

The WTO is designed to promote international trade via multilateral, non-discriminatory and reciprocal reduction of trade barriers. The following proposition loosely follows from our theorem of welfare comparison to endorse the welfare significance of this structure.

PROPOSITION 0. *(The significance of multilateral tariff reductions): Multilateral, non-discriminatory, and reciprocal tariff reductions negotiated at WTO are likely to increase the potential economic welfare of member countries.*

CIRCUMSTANTIAL EVIDENCE. Apply our theorem of welfare comparison to a member country of WTO. Let S' be the situation before the multilateral tariff reduction and S'' be the situation after that. Here, we simplify the world further by assuming away production taxes and subsidies. A multilateral tariff reduction in conformance with the reciprocity and MFN principles of WTO is likely to leave the terms of trade of participating countries largely unaffected and expected to increase the volumes of tariff-ridden international trade. Thus we may be allowed to presume $(q' - q'')e' \approx 0$ and $q''T''(e'' - e') \geq 0$ satisfying condition (9) of the theorem. ∎

3. WTO and FTA

Let us begin by showing that the Bagwell–Staiger view of the WTO as a market access securing mechanism is useful for clarifying the basic position of the WTO in dealing with FTAs proliferating all over the world. We already considered this problem elsewhere (Ohyama, 2003) and derived the following proposition demonstrating the conditions for a welfare-improving preferential tariff reduction (for brevity PTR). Here, we reproduce it with a rough proof.

PROPOSITION 1. *(a welfare-improving PTR): Consider a group of countries that agree to reduce or abolish tariffs on the imports of some commodities from member countries preferentially. The PTR improves world potential welfare if each member country adjusts its tariffs so as to keep its trade volumes of all commodities with non-member countries at their previous levels, not to decrease its trade volumes of commodities with member countries restricted by trade taxes and, not to increase trade volumes with member countries promoted by trade subsidies.*

---

[3] The assumption of competitive markets is employed here only for easy understanding. In fact, it is not necessary for the derivation of our theorem. Ohyama (1999) shows that a similar theorem can be established under imperfect competition if certain conditions are satisfied.

PROOF (sketch). Apply the theorem of welfare comparison to a country in the group. Let S' and S'', respectively stand for the situations before and after the PTR. Suppose that there are no production taxes and subsidies in situation S'', or that they are adjusted so as to maintain production structure in both situations, i.e., $y' = y''$. We then have $p''R''(y' - y'') = 0$ in condition (9). Under the conditions stipulated here, we also have $q''T''(e'' - e') \geq 0$ and the PTRs terms of trade against the rest of the world does not change from situation S' to S'', which implies that the terms of trade effects on the welfare of individual countries can be cancelled out under an appropriate intra-regional income transfer scheme to ensure $b'' - b' = (q'' - q')e'$. Condition (9) is thus satisfied. ∎

This proposition extends the celebrated Kemp–Wan theorem to cover PTRs or partial and incomplete FTAs or PTRs.[4] In short, it says that a PTR improves the potential welfare of the world provided that each participating country adjusts its tariffs (against member and non-member countries) so as to secure their previous market access property rights. This proviso is a natural requirement derived from the Bagwell–Staiger view of the WTO as the market access securing mechanism.[5]

Article 24 of the GATT approves the formation of FTAs provided that (1) trade barriers against non-member countries do not rise on average and (2) member countries eliminate all tariffs and other trade restrictions on 'substantially all' intra-regional exchanges of goods within a 'reasonable' length of time. Condition (1) may be reinterpreted to conform with the provisos of Proposition 1 (see below). Condition (2) is, however, economically questionable in the present set-up. Note that a further reduction of intra-regional tariffs in an "incomplete and partial" FTA may not be beneficial in general, given their tariffs against the rest of the world. For the rest of the world is likely to suffer from terms of trade deterioration as a result of the trade diversion effects of such a preferential tariff reduction. The FTA may also suffer as a whole through the adverse volume of trade effects. Proposition 1 provides a sufficient condition for avoiding such consequences.

Incidentally, condition (1) is often taken to mean that the FTA member countries should not raise the average rate of tariffs against non-member countries. This interpretation is inappropriate from the view of the WTO as a mechanism securing market access property rights. In fact, the formation of an FTA is likely to decrease a member country's volume of trade with non-member countries on account of trade diversion arising

---

[4] See Kemp and Wan (1976).

[5] In fact, any bilateral, or regional negotiation may infringe upon the market access property rights of non-participating nations implied by the existing tariff commitments made in the WTO. Bagwell and Staiger (2002) consider how the basic principles of GATT/WTO offer a "first-line of defense" against bilateral opportunism. Proposition 1 can also be interpreted to illustrate how to preserve the welfare of non-participants against such bilateral opportunism.

from intra-regional trade liberalization even if it maintains its pre-FTA rates of tariffs, thereby infringing on the market access property rights of non-member countries. In order to avoid such consequences, each member country must adjust its tariffs so as to keep its volume of trade with non-member countries at the pre-FTA level. In view of the Kemp–Wan theorem, McMillan (1993) proposed to modify Article 24 of the GATT clarifying condition (1) as the requirement that trade volumes with non-members do not fall on the average. We may take a further step forward and propose to rewrite condition (1) to conform with the conditions of Proposition 1 and abolish or alleviate condition (2) to accommodate an increasing number of partial and incomplete FTAs in the real world.

4. Labor and environmental policies

Bagwell and Staiger (2001) is an attempt to defend the WTO against the attacks of labor and environmental groups blaming the organization for hindering the realization of sound labor and environmental policies. In the eyes of these groups, the primary purpose of the WTO, or its predecessor, GATT, is to serve the interests of export industries. They argue that the reduction of tariffs negotiated there increases competitive pressures against domestic industries of member countries, which induce their government to resist the introduction of new labor and environmental standards (in a "regulatory chill") and even to lower the existing standards (in a race to the bottom"). Economists are largely in favor of the GATT/ WTO, but they had been apparently powerless against these attacks. Their traditional defense of the GATT/WTO that multilateral trade negotiations under the GATT/WTO have produced remarkable movements toward free trade is weak and even irrelevant.

What is missing from the attacks of the labor and environmental groups is the recognition that the important mission of the GATT/WTO is not only to negotiate over market access but also to secure the property rights over negotiated market access property rights. So long as the negotiated property rights are effectively maintained, there should indeed be no room for "regulatory chills" or "races to the bottom" to suffocating sound labor and environmental policies. If a country's new labor and environmental standards weaken the competitiveness of domestic industries giving larger market accesses to foreign competitors than previously negotiated, the WTO should authorize the government of the country to adjust (raise) its tariffs so as to maintain foreigner's market access rights at previous levels. However, a country's competitiveness may be threatened if its trading partners lower their labor and environmental standards. In such a case, the WTO should allow the government to secure its market access rights in domestic and foreign markets through the adjustment of tariffs or the introduction of export subsidies. As argued by Bagwell and Staiger (2001), these measures would be sufficient to circumvent "regulatory chills" and "races to the bottom" eroding labor and environmental policies. They did not elaborate, however, the welfare significance of securing market access property rights through such measures. The following proposition is an attempt to supplement their argument from the viewpoint of welfare economics.

PROPOSITION 2. *(Labor and Environmental Policies): Suppose that a country wishes to introduce new labor and environmental standards which restrict the outputs or inputs of certain goods and services while securing market property rights of trading partners negotiated at the WTO. Given these policy targets, the policy instruments most efficient from the viewpoint of world economic welfare are taxes and subsidies on outputs and inputs appropriately designed to achieve new standards, combined with readjustment of taxes and subsidies on imports and exports to secure the market access property rights of trading partners.*

PROOF. Let S' stand for the situation where the country introduces appropriate taxes and subsidies on production and readjusts its tariffs so as to achieve the given policy targets and let S' represent any other situation where the country achieves the same targets employing a different set of policy instruments. If output of product j (or input of factor j) is restricted to a certain level $\overline{y}_j$ by new standards, $y'_j = y''_j = \overline{y}_j$ and if good k is not affected by new standards, $r'_k = r''_k = 0$. Thus we have $p'' R''(y' - y'') = 0$. By hypothesis, tariff-restricted trades with trading partners are maintained at the same negotiated level in both situations to ensure $q'' T''(e'' - e') = 0$. Furthermore, the country's gains or losses resulting from any possible change in its terms of trade can be compensated through international income transfer without affecting welfare of the rest of the world. Thus we may also set $b'' - b' + (q' - q'')e' = 0$. Thus condition (9) of our welfare comparison theorem is satisfied implying that situation S'' is potentially preferable to situation S' from the country's viewpoint while the rest of the world is kept indifferent between them under such an arrangement. ∎

Perhaps some comments on our formulation of labor and environmental standards are in order here. First, Proposition 2 extends the theory of well-known optimal policy instruments for given policy targets discussed by many authors such as Corden (1957), Johnson (1964), and Ohyama (1972). They considered only the case of a price-taking small country where the terms of trade effects are absent and compared the effects of alternative policy instruments on the country's economic welfare. In such a case, what is optimal for the country is also unconditionally optimal for the world as a whole, but generally only on the condition that appropriate international income transfers are made to compensate and cancel out the terms of trade effects as in Proposition 2.

Second, note that the government is assumed here to employ production taxes and subsidies as policy instruments to achieve given environmental and labor standards. Labor or environmental standards are, however, usually introduced in the form of direct restriction of the outputs or inputs of productive activities which may cause labor or environmental problems. Their effects are equivalent to those of indirect restriction by means of production taxes and subsidies under the present assumption of perfect competition, but they may differ from each other under alternative market structures.

Third, labor and environmental standards are actually related to consumption activities such as use of polluting materials in households or use of air conditioners at workplaces. Clearly, we can extend Proposition 2 to cover standards pertaining to such consumption activities.[6]

Proposition 2 implies that given certain labor and environmental standards and market access property rights negotiated at the WTO, it is desirable from the viewpoint of world economic welfare to employ trade taxes and subsidies for the maintenance of market access property rights, while assigning production taxes and subsidies to the achievement of labor and environmental standards. This perspective sheds light to the role that the WTO should play in the world economy: It should specialize in the international coordination of trade policies for the purpose of reducing trade barriers and securing the negotiated market access property rights in full view of the changing labor and environmental standards which individual countries introduces either voluntarily or as a result of negotiations at the other international organizations.

5. Concluding remarks

Tinbergen (1952) emphasized the distinction between target variables and instrument variables of the government in his theory of economic policy. It is important to understand this distinction especially in the discussion of international policy coordination or policy assignment. In view of welfare analysis developed in the present chapter, the first and foremost condition for any international coordination is an agreement on the policy targets which individual countries should pursue. They dictate the optimal choice of instrument variables they should employ for that purpose. The first condition of the GATT's Article 24 for approving FTAs is that they should not raise trade barriers against non-member countries. It is notoriously ambiguous admitting multiple interpretations. The most popular interpretation is that it requires them not to raise the average rate of tariffs and tariff-equivalent trade barriers. This interpretation may,

---

[6] See Ohyama (1972) for welfare comparison in the presence of consumption taxes and subsidies.

however, interfere with the obligations of the WTO to secure market access property rights since the member country's volume of trade with the rest of the world is likely to decrease on account of the trade diverting effects of the preferential arrangement under the same average tariff rates as before. According to Proposition 1 in the present chapter, the requirement for welfare improving FTAs is that they keep the volume of all commodity trades with the rest of the world at the level prior to their formation, providing an alternative interpretation of the GATT condition. This alternative interpretation accords perfectly with the recent character-ization of the GATT/WTO as a mechanism for securing market access property rights advocated by Bagwell and Staiger (2001).[7] Proposition 1 also reveals the economic irrelevance of the second condition of Article 24 that the members of FTAs eliminate all tariffs and other trade restrictions on "substantially all" intra-regional exchanges of goods within a "reasonable" length of time. If the condition is to be abode by faithfully, it virtually rules out most of the promising FTAs under negotiation since every country has some politically strong industries clamoring for continued protection. From the viewpoint of economic welfare, however, the important requirement is that they do not reduce the imports of the commodities they continue to protect against other member countries.

In case of labor and environmental standards, policy targets are usually expressed in terms of hours of labor (especially of female and child labor), or emission of polluting materials, to be achieved by the policy instruments such as penalty taxes or pollution taxes. Apparently, there is little room here for confusing policy targets with policy instruments. In order to deal with trade problems and labor and environmental problems at the same time, however, it is important for the government correctly to assign appropriate policy instruments to the given policy targets. For instance, if new labor and environmental standards are introduced, relevant policy instruments are taxes and subsidies on the specific production activities to be controlled, but they would affect international trade activities infringing upon the market access property rights agreed at the WTO, were there not for appropriate readjustment of taxes and subsidies on the affected trade activities. Similarly, if further reduction of tariffs is negotiated at the WTO to expand market access rights of member countries, they would affect production activities leading to the violation of established labor and environmental standards were it not for appropriate readjustment of taxes and subsidies on the affected production activities. Proposition 2 shows how the governments should supplement the use of production taxes and subsidies to realize their new labor and environmental standards by the use of trade taxes and subsidies for the purpose of securing their market access

---

[7] McMillan (1993) argued for the revision of Article 24 along the line of the Kemp–Wan theorem. By virtue of Proposition 1, a similar case can be made for the extension and revision of Article 24 covering any preferential tariff arrangement among WTO members.

commitments agreed at the WTO. This assignment of policy instruments is not only effective in eliminating "regulatory chills" and "races to the bottom," but also efficient from the viewpoint of world resource allocation.

Acknowledgement

I wish to thank an anonymous referee for helpful comments on an earlier draft.

References

Bagwell, K., Staiger, R.W. (2001), The WTO as a mechanism for securing market access property rights: implications for global labor and environmental issues. *Journal of Economic Perspectives* 15 (3), 69–88.

Bagwell, K., Staiger, R.W. (2002), *The Economics of the World Trading System*. MIT Press, Cambridge, MA.

Corden, M.M. (1957), Tariffs, subsidies and the terms of trade. *Econometrica* 24 (95), 235–242.

Johnson, H.G. (1964), The cost of protection and the scientific tariff. *Journal of Political Economy* 68 (4), 327–345.

Kemp, M.C., Wan, H.Y. (1976). An elementary proposition concerning the formation of customs unions. *Journal of International Economics* 6 (1), 95–97. Reprinted with an addendum in Kemp, M.C. (2001), *The Gains From Trade and the Gains From Aid*. Routledge, London, pp. 37–46.

McMillan, J. (1993), Does regional integration foster open trade? Economic theory and GATT's Article XXIV. In: Anderson, K., Blackhurst, R. (Eds.), *Regional Integration and the Global Trading System*. Harvester Wheatsheaf, New York, pp. 292–309.

Ohyama, M. (1972), Trade and welfare in general equilibrium. *Keio Economic Studies* 9 (2), 37–73.

Ohyama, M. (1999), Market, trade and welfare in general equilibrium. *Japanese Economic Review* 50 (1), 1–24.

Ohyama, M. (2003), Free trade agreements and economic welfare: Beyond the Kemp–Wan theorem. KUMQPR Discussion Paper Series, DP2003–11, Keio University, Tokyo.

Tinbergen, J. (1952), *On the Theory of Economic Policy*. North-Holland, Amsterdam.

CHAPTER 2

Trade Liberalization as a Game of Decision Under Uncertainty

Henry Wan Jr.[a] and Yinggang Zhou[b]

[a]*Department of Economics, Cornell University, 470 Uris Hall, Ithaca New York 14853-7601, USA*
E-mail address: hywl@cornell.edu
[b]*Black Creek Global Advisors, 518 17th Street, Suite 1700, Denver, CO 80202, USA*
E-mail address: zhou.yinggang@gmail.com

Abstract

Purpose – This study explains a puzzle: most countries realize the mutual benefit of tariff cutting, but tariffs never become zero.
Approach – The method is decision-theoretic, and proves the results by example.
Findings – The Johnson tariff-ridden equilibrium may be unique, but not the free-trade equilibrium, and tariff cutting may cause a 'decision problem under uncertainty' (d.p.u.u.) of Luce, R.D., Raiffa, H. (1989), in which mutual tariff-cutting benefits both parties only up to some point.
Originality/value – This approach addresses a pragmatic problem with global analysis and suggests institutional rearrangement to avoid such conundrum.

Keywords: Trade liberalization, tariff-cutting, game, uncertainty

Paper type: Research paper

1. Overview

Samuelson (1938) reminded us that trade theory and economic theory shared common roots, when Smith and Ricardo deployed their deductive power, against challenging policy issues in their days. In its modern form, international welfare economics started when Samuelson (1962) and Kemp (1962) generalized the gains from trade study of Samuelson (1939), beyond the small country case. One of the lasting teachings in Professor Kemp's work is his relentless quest for Truth. Going beyond marginal analysis, he

Frontiers of Economics and Globalization
Volume 5 ISSN: 1574-8715
DOI: 10.1016/S1574-8715(08)05002-1

employs the global approach, to study the gains from trade and investment (Kemp, 1966). Having developed his theory, he cares greatly for the consistency of its predictions with reality. In our work on customs unions (Kemp and Wan, 1976), he questions why the entire world has not evolved into a 'grand customs union' of free trade. In studying trade issues with theory, he has balanced relevance with rigor, and carried forth the torch of Ricardo and Smith.

Today, in celebrating his 80th birthday, we seek to follow the trail he blazed. We note that our era of the GATT–WTO exhibits a triplet of stylized facts:

(a) The negotiation begins from a tariff-ridden status quo.
(b) Out of hesitancy, negotiation is aimed at tariff reduction, not tariff abolition.
(c) Tariff rates have come down around the world as a result of negotiations.

From the theoretical point of view, the core paradox is highlighted in Bagwell and Staiger (2002, p. 47), the standard reference on the world trading system, today. On the one hand, substantial mutual reduction of tariffs and trade barriers has been recognized as beneficial in the Preamble of GATT, but on the other the term 'free trade' is nowhere mentioned as the objective of GATT.

A model is constructed below to show how far such observations can be explained in terms of economic theory, before the deployment of considerations from political economy, as in Bagwell and Staiger. As an intellectual exercise, a full appreciation of the strength of the non-traditional explanations ought start, only after the implications of traditional economic theory ends.

2. The model

In an exchange model with two goods, the following assumptions are adopted for Country X and Country Y:

A1 (Endowment). Each country is endowed with the entire supply of a particular good. Both endowments are assumed to be 1 unit. They consume portions x and y of their respective endowments, and export the rest, $1-x$ and $1-y$, to each other in exchange of their imports.

For simplicity, we assume that

A2 (Preferences). The utility functions of the two countries are

(a) symmetric to each other,
(b) having the quasilinear form, linear in one's own endowed good and (concave) quadratic in the good imported, and

(c) with such specific parameters values, so that the utility indices are:

$$U^X = x + 4(1 - y) - 2(1 - y)^2 = x + 2(1 - y^2) \quad \text{and}$$
$$U^Y = y + 4(1 - x) - 2(1 - x)^2 = y + 2(1 - x^2). \tag{1}$$

Denote:

p and q as the unit prices of the two goods and
t^X and t^Y as the ad valorem tariff rates of the two countries.

The budget equation of each country shows that:

$$B^X = [p + qt^X(1 - y)] - [px + q(1 + t^X)(1 - y)] = 0 \quad \text{and}$$
$$B^Y = [q + pt^Y(1 - x)] - [p(1 + t^Y)(1 - x) + qy] = 0. \tag{2}$$

(*Total expenditure equals the value of endowment plus tax revenue*) – One now obtains.

2.1. The behavioral rules

Both countries maximize their utilities in (1), subject to their respective tariff-ridden budget lines in (2). The export offered by each country becomes a function of the export level of the other (or, what each country imports). So that given the two tariff rates, the pair of (Marshallian) offer curve (Marshall and Marshall, 1881) takes the parabolic form:

$$(1 - x) = F^X(1 - y; \ t^X) = 4[1 - (1 - y)](1 - y)/(1 + t^X)$$
$$\text{for Country } X$$
$$(1 - y) = F^Y(1 - x; \ t^Y) = 4[1 - (1 - x)](1 - x)/(1 + t^Y) \tag{3}$$
$$\text{for Country } Y,$$

or,

$$(1 - x) = 4y(1 - y)/(1 + t^X) \quad \text{for Country } X$$
$$(1 - y) = 4x(1 - x)/(1 + t^Y) \quad \text{for Country } Y. \tag{4}$$

LEMMA 2.1 *(Transformation)*.

(a) Equation (3) (or (4)) defines two families of offer curves, parametrically dependent upon the tariff parameters, (t^X, t^Y).

(b) Each point (x, y) in the unit square, $[0, 1] \times [0, 1]$, is now associated with a specific ordered pair of utility levels (U^X, U^Y) on the one hand, and belongs to the intersection set of a unique ordered pair of offer curves, as indexed by the tariff rate pair, (t^X, t^Y), on the other hand.

(c) Corresponding to some tariff rate pair, the intersection set may not be a singleton.

Consider now,

2.2. The game of tariff war: Johnson (1953–1954)

One now specifies

(a) (Information) Each country $i = X$ or Y takes as given, the tariff rate
   (equivalently, the offer curve in (3)) of the other country, $t^j = t^Y$ or t^X.
(b) (Objective) Each country seeks to maximize one's own utility in (1).
   The target is a point (x, y) where the other country's offer curve in (3)
   (or (4)) is tangent to the highest attainable indifference curve of one's
   own. Specifically,

   Slope of the offer curve of the = The own tariff ridden price
   other country   ratio
                                   = Slope of the highest own
                                     indifference locus,

   or,

$$4(2x - 1)/(1 + t^Y) = p/q(1 + t^X) = 1/4y \quad \text{for Country } X$$
$$4(2y - 1)/(1 + t^X) = q/p(1 + t^Y) = 1/4x \quad \text{for Country } Y \tag{5}$$

(The *tangency conditions*)

(c) (Choice) To achieve the above objective, one chooses a tariff rate, t^i, of
   one's own so that one' corresponding offer curve would intercept the
   offer curve of the other at precisely the desired point (x, y).
(d) (Best response) For each country, the above discussion defines the *best
   response*:

$$t^i = R^i(t^j), \quad i = X, Y; \ j = Y, X.$$

The equilibrium concept for the Johnsonian tariff war, one now identifies
the *best response* mapping, from the non-negative pair of tariff rates into
itself.

$$R(\cdot) = (R^X(\cdot), R^Y(\cdot)), \tag{6}$$

so that the equilibrium of the game of Johnsonian tariff war is identified
with the fixed point under mapping, $R(\cdot)$,

$$t^* = (t^{X*}, \ t^{Y*}). \tag{7}$$

That is to say,

$$t^{X*} = R^X(t^{Y*}) \text{ and}$$
$$t^{Y*} = R^Y(t^{X*}). \tag{8}$$

Equation (8) corresponds to an ordered pair (t^X, t^Y) which implies
a point (x^*, y^*), where the utility levels in (1) are simultaneously

maximized with respect to the offer curves of the other countries in (4).

LEMMA 2.2 *(Symmetric equilibrium)*. *In the intersection set of a symmetric, equilibrium tariff pair (t^X, t^Y), there corresponds a symmetric point on the ray, $x^* = y^*$. By symmetry, the equilibrium prices satisfy the condition:*

$$p^* = q^*. \tag{9}$$

PROPOSITION 2.1 *(Existence and Uniqueness)*. *There exists a symmetric, unique equilibrium for:*

$$t^{X*} = 3/2 = t^{Y*}, \tag{10}$$

$$p^* = 1 = q^*, \tag{11}$$

$$x^* = 5/8 = y^* \quad and \tag{12}$$

$$U^{X*} = 59/32 = U^{Y*}. \tag{13}$$

Proof by verification.

Step 1. Assuming (10) is the equilibrium pair, then the system in (4) has only two solutions, either

$$x = 1 = y, \tag{14}$$

which is the autarkic case, with the result of:

$$U^X = 1 = U^Y \tag{15}$$

(and it is irrelevant, as each country can do better), or, (12)

$$x = 5/8 = y.$$

Thus, if this is *the solution*, the solution is unique.

Step 2. Using (10), straightforward computation verifies that *the tangency conditions* in (5) are satisfied. Q. E. D.

COROLLARY 2.1. *The equilibrium solution of the game of Johnsonian tariff war is inefficient.*

This is so since,

The price ratio for Country X, $2/5 <$ The price ratio for Country Y, $5/2$. The above discussion may be illustrated graphically in Figure 1.

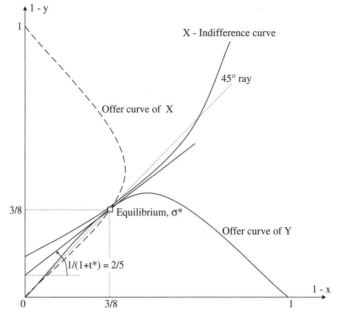

Fig. 1.   The game of tariff war of Johnson.

3. Tariff reform as a decision problem under uncertainty?

Formally, in the model of Johnsonian tariff war, two types of agents are recognized:[1]

(a) the classes of identical individuals in each of the two countries, who take prices, incomes (including any shared tariff revenue) as given and
(b) the two governments who take for granted the offer curve of the other country and the behavior of the individuals in one's own country.

The individuals are strategic dummies; to the governments who set their tariff rates, there is no objective probability about the chance of occurrence over the alternative market equilibria, unless the equilibrium is unique. This situation is neither deterministic, nor 'risky', and hence referred to as 'uncertain', by default, in view of the Knightian trichotomy. Note this provisional usage differs from 'Knightian uncertainty' (or 'ambiguity', as used in the literature) where decision makers do not know well the true probabilities they face. There is not even any probability one can ever know, by logic!

The point to be emphasized here is the time sequence of such events. This is highlighted with the time line in Figure 2. At tariff negotiations in

---

[1] See further discussion in the penultimate paragraph of the concluding section.

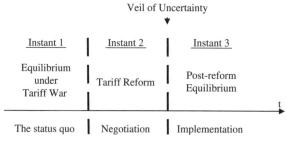

Fig. 2. The time line of tariff reform.

Instant 2, both countries must concur on the extent of tariff reduction, if any. The decision must be reached, both before the market equilibrium is determined at Instant 3 in the *future*, and under the influence of the status quo of Instant 1, in the *past*.

We take the unique equilibrium for the symmetric, Johnsonian game of tariff war as the status quo, where $t^{X*} = 3/2 = t^{Y*}$. Tariff reform becomes the negotiation between the two countries over the (t^X, t^Y) pair. Given that the two countries have engaged in a symmetric Johnsonian tariff war, and given our present purposes, it suffices to consider equal tariff reductions. This implies:

$$t^X = t^Y = t \in [0, 3/2). \tag{16}$$

Corresponding to each such t, there exists a specific pair of offer curves, one for each country as in (4). Their intersection marks the realization of a market equilibrium. The relevance of both the past and the future are captured in the following two assumptions.

A3 (Paretian Principle). No country would agree to an arrangement that brings about an equilibrium in which its future utility is lower than what was enjoyed in the past.

A4 ('Safety First Principle'[2]). No country would agree to an arrangement that brings about any equilibrium in which its future utility is lower than what was enjoyed in the past.

A4 pertains to the case of multiple equilibria where some outcome(s) may be better than the status quo, yet there is the distinct possibility that a worse outcome may obtain.

Roy (1952) asserted that minimizing the probability of disaster is a fundamental tenet in human behavior. By extension, a decision-maker facing the multiplicity of equilibrium would focus on the 'worst outcome',

---

[2] See, Roy (1952).

bearing in mind that there is no rational basis to assign probabilities over the different equilibrium outcomes.

Two questions now suggest themselves in the present context:

(1) Would tariff reform lead to situations of *uncertainty*, where there exists no objectively decidable probability measures over alternative outcomes?
(2) Would the prospect of reform become affected by such *uncertainty*?

Our finding is stated as,

PROPOSITION 3.1 *(Reform may fail due to uncertainty). It is possible that:*

(1) some reform plan gives rise to uncertainty and
(2) some such reform plan may fail to be accepted as a consequence.

Proof by construction.

For illustration, we focus on the case of free trade where $t = 0$. In our example, from the parameter values we adopt, the interested readers can verify.

LEMMA 3.1. *For free trade, there exist three equilibria, namely*

(a) The symmetric solution σ_0, with:

$$x_0 = 1/4 = y_0; \quad U_0^X = 17/8 = U_0^Y \tag{17}$$

and

(b) a pair of asymmetric solutions, σ_1 and σ_2, with:

$$
\begin{aligned}
x_1 &= [3 - (5)^{1/2}]/8, & y_1 &= [3 + (5)^{1/2}]/8, \\
U_1^X &= [31 - 5(5)^{1/2}]/16, & U_1^Y &= [31 + 5(5)^{1/2}]/16 \ and \\
x^2 &= [3 + (5)^{1/2}]/8, & y^2 &= [3 - (5)^{1/2}]/8, \\
U_2^X &= [31 + 5(5)^{1/2}]/16, & U_2^Y &= [3 - 5(5)^{1/2}]/16.
\end{aligned}
\tag{18}
$$

The positions of these equilibria are shown in Figure 3.

Define:

$$
\begin{aligned}
\Delta U^X &= \text{Min } \{U_0^X, \ U_1^X, \ U_2^X\} - U^{X*}, \\
\Delta U^Y &= \text{Min}\{U_0^Y, \ U_1^Y, \ U_2^Y\} - U^{Y*}.
\end{aligned}
\tag{19}
$$

Since,

$$[31 - (5)^{1/2}]/16 - 59/32 = [3 - 2(5)^{1/2}]/32$$
$$= [(9)^{1/2} - (20)^{1/2}]/32 < 0,$$

$$\Delta U^X = \Delta U^Y < 0,$$

the proposal for free trade will not be accepted. Q.E.D.

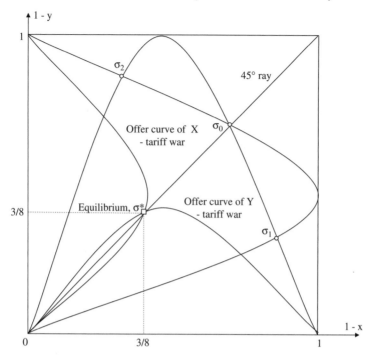

Fig. 3. The free trade equilibria.

From the above discussion, the failure of a proposal for mutual tariff reduction under the Safety First Principle only happens when there is a multiplicity of equilibrium. The latter phenomenon depends upon the proposed tariff rate. One can readily verify for the present example,

PROPOSITION 3.2 *(The range of uncertainty).*

(a) *The number of equilibria is* 3 *when* $t \in [0, 1/3)$ *and*
(b) *The number of equilibria is* 1 *when* $t \in [1/3, 3/2]$.

REMARK 1. There is a bifurcation at $t = 1/3$, under which the offer curves of the two countries become tangent to each other, with slope -1, at the intersection point on the ray, $x = y$. This is illustrated in Figure 4.

One can derive by routine computation,

COROLLARY 3.1.

(a) *Tariff reduction yields a unique equilibrium outcome if and only if* $t \in [1/3, 3/2]$.
(b) *Over this range* [1/3, 3/2] *for* t, *one has:*

$$1 - x(t) = (3 - t)/4 = 1 - y(t) \quad and \tag{20}$$

$$U^X(t) = (17 - t^2)/8 = U^{Y*}(t). \tag{21}$$

*(c) Over the same range, both trade and utility increases monotonically
     with tariff reduction.*

COROLLARY 3.2.

  (a) For $t \in [0, 1/3)$, tariff reduction yields three equilibrium outcomes,
  *(b) For each such t, the three equilibrium outcomes are tabulated below in
       Table 1 and*

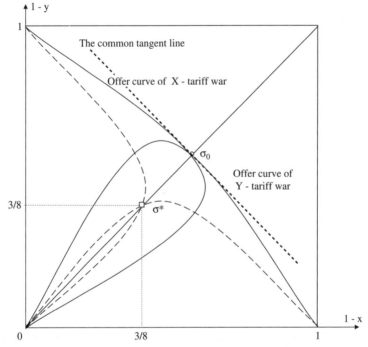

Fig. 4.   The critical, unique tariff-ridden equilibrium.

Table 1.   Solutions over the range of uncertainty

	σ_0	σ_1	σ_2
x	$(1+t)/4$	$[(3-t)+(5+t)^{1/2}(1-3t)^{1/2}]/8$	$[(3-t)-(5+t)^{1/2}(1-3t)^{1/2}]/8$
y	$(1+t)/4$	$[(3-t)-(5+t)^{1/2}(1-3t)^{1/2}]/8$	$[(3-t)+(5+t)^{1/2}(1-3t)^{1/2}]/8$
U^X	$(17-t^2)/8$	$[31+8t+t^2+(5+t)^{3/2}(1-3t)^{1/2}]/16$	$[31+8t+t^2-(5+t)^{3/2}(1-3t)^{1/2}]/16$
U^Y	$(17-t^2)/8$	$[31+8t+t^2-(5+t)^{3/2}(1-3t)^{1/2}]/16$	$[31+8t+t^2+(5+t)^{3/2}(1-3t)^{1/2}]/16$

(c) *In addition,*

$$(d/dt)U_0^X < 0, \quad (d/dt)U_1^X < 0, \quad (d/dt)U_0^X > 0 \text{ and}$$

$$(d/dt)U_0^Y < 0, \quad (d/dt)U_1^Y > 0, \quad (d/dt)U_0^X < 0.$$

One can conclude by direct computation.

PROPOSITION 3.3 *(Characterization over the uncertainty range).*

(a) There exists $t° \approx 0.29$, *such that,* $\forall \ t \in [t°, 1/3]$,

$$U_m^X(t) = \text{Min} \{U_i^X(t) : i = 0, 1, 2\} \geq U^{X*},$$

$$U_m^Y(t) = \text{Min}\{U_i^Y(t) : i = 0, 1, 2\} \geq U^{Y*} \text{ and}$$

$$\text{Max}_t \ U_m^X(t) = U_m^X(1/3) = U_m^Y(1/3) = \text{Max}_t \ U_m^Y(t).$$

Because of symmetry, one can show that $U_m{}^X(t) = U_m{}^X(t) = U_m(t)$, say. All these are graphically shown in Figure 5. It is clear that under the assumption adopted, the negotiated equilibrium tariff reduction implies a value $t = 1/3$, yielding a maxmin value of utility, $2 \ 1/9 = 19/9$ for each country. This is marked b in Figure 5.

Here the functions $U_m{}^X(t)$ and $U_m{}^Y(t)$ define the minimum attainable utility for X and Y, for each t.

COROLLARY 3.3. *Even within the range of uncertainty, plans of tariff reform, with a target rate* $t \geq t°$, *can be considered by both countries, in the sense that the plan does not violate Assumptions A3 and A4.*

REMARK 2. If one can adopt the lumpsum compensation of the Grandmont–McFadden–Grinols type,[3] then each country can enjoy a utility level of $2 \ 1/8 = 17/8$ at a in Figure 5.

4. Concluding remarks

Although the focus of attention in this chapter is negotiated tariff reduction, the discussion is obviously relevant to the comparison of lumpsum versus nonlumpsum compensations, mentioned in Wan (1997), and applicable to the works like Hammond and Sempere (1995). In the tradition of the nonlump compensation, redistributive tax rates have to be decided at Instant 2 in Figure 2, leaving completely to the market force to decide what the actual equilibrium price will be at Instant 3. Suppose the situation resembles what is depicted in Figure 5, with three distinctive branches of possible equilibria. If one can be sure which of the three is

---

[3] See, for example, Kemp and Wan (1999).

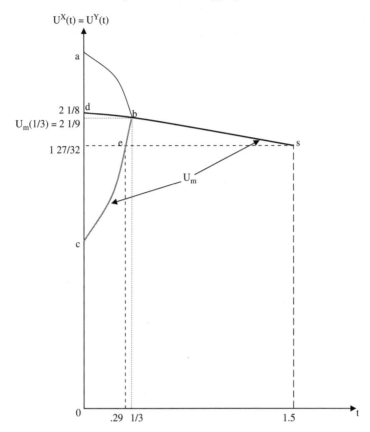

Fig. 5.   The maxmin criterion.

going to happen in Instant 3, there exists one suitable redistributive tax
for it. But then what suits one contingency need not do for others, and
there exists no objective probability about the occurrence of these possible
outcomes.

In real life, decisions are generally made by rational agents endowed
with foresight. Agreement made today reflects the awareness of the
alternative outcomes these arrangements imply for the future, and no
objective probability can be assigned over such future alternatives. This
holds true for the Game of the Battle of Sexes, no less than a general
equilibrium model blessed with a diversity of market-clearing terms of
trade. In principle, the presence of such possibilities is relevant in other
fields such as financial economics as in trade theory. Much remains to be
explored in the future.

The specific assumptions adopted for the model are chosen for simplicity.
But the resulting model is far from being a knife-edge curiosum. Effort is
being made to extend the analysis to broader classes of cases.

There is however a related 'cognitive' issue. If one focuses on a variation of the study of the CES preference case by Chipman (2008), there can be two classes of individuals in each country, so there is no representative agent in either country. In each country, both classes share that same homothetic preference but differ between each other in endowment. Now, by the aggregation theorem of Chipman (1974), all results in this chapter essentially go through, just as if there is only one type of individual in each country, and there still can be multiple equilibria. But in this new model, the doubt on how would countries with representative agents behave in Kemp and Shimomura (1995) should not arise.

At this juncture, we should all emulate Professor Kemp, securing long, robust and productive research careers, with full engagement in life-energizing sports.

Acknowledgements

The authors are grateful for discussions with Larry Blume, David Easley and Ani Guerdjikova, as well as comments by John Chipman, Robert Staiger and an anonymous referee. They also benefited from interactions with the audience when an earlier version was presented both at the Conference on New Paradigms in Economics of Welfare and Trade under Globalization and Regionalization at Sydney, Australia, August 2006, and earlier seminars given at Cornell University, Ithaca, NY, and Institute of Economics, Academia Sincia, Taipei. All remaining shortcomings fall under the residual claim of the authors.

References

Bagwell, K., Staiger, R.W. (2002), *The Economics of the World Trading System*. MIT Press, Cambridge, MA.

Chipman, J.S. (1974), Homothetic preferences and aggregation. *Journal of Economic Theory* 8 (1), 26–38.

Chipman, J.S. (2008), Multiple equilibria under CES preferences. Manuscript University of Minnesota, Minneapolis, MN.

Hammond, P.J., Sempere, J. (1995), Limits to the potential gains from economic integration and other supply side policies. *Economic Journal* 105 (432), 1180–1205.

Johnson, H.G. (1953–1954), Optimal tariffs and retaliation. *Review of Economic Studies* 21 (2), 142–153.

Kemp, M.C. (1962), The gains from international trade. *Economic Journal* 72 (288), 803–819.

Kemp, M.C. (1966), The gains from international trade and investment: A neo-Heckscher-Ohlin approach. *American Economic Review* 56 (4), 788–809.

Kemp, M.C., Shimomura, K. (1995), The apparently innocuous representative agent. *Japanese Economic Review* 46 (3), 247–256.

Kemp, M.C., Wan, H., Jr. (1976), An elementary proposition concerning the formation of customs unions. *Journal of International Economics* 6 (1), 95–97.

Kemp, M.C., Wan, H., Jr. (1999), On lumpsum compensation. In: Melvin, J.R., Moore, J.C., Riezman, R.G. (Eds.), *Trade, Theory and Econometrics: Essays in Honor of John Chipman*. Routledge, London, UK, pp. 185–205.

Luce, R.D., Raiffa, H. (1989), *Games and Decisions: Introduction and Critical Survey*. Dover Publications, New York.

Marshall, A., Marshall, M.P. (1881), *Economics of Industry*. MacMillan, London, UK.

Roy, A.D. (1952), Safety first and the holding of assets. *Econometrica* 20 (3), 431–449.

Samuelson, P.A. (1938), Welfare economics and international trade. *American Economic Review* 28 (2), 261–266.

Samuelson, P.A. (1939), The gains from international trade. *Canadian Journal of Economics and Political Science* 5 (2), 195–205.

Samuelson, P.A. (1962), The gains from international trade once again. *Economic Journal* 72 (288), 820–829.

Wan, H., Jr. (1997), A note on compensation schemes. *Japanese Economic Review* 48 (2), 147–155.

CHAPTER 3

Comparative Advantage and Trade Liberalization in a Chamberlinian–Ricardian Model

Toru Kikuchi[a] and Koji Shimomura[b]

[a]*Graduate School of Economics, Kobe University, 2-1 Rokkodai-cho, Nada-Ku Kobe 657-8501, Japan*
E-mail address: kikuchi@econ.kobeu.ac.jp
[b]*Research Institute for Economics & Business Administration, Kobe University, Japan*

Abstract

Purpose – The present note shows the interaction between technological differences between countries and the level of trade costs as a determinant of trade patterns.
Methodology/approach – It takes the work of Kikuchi *et al.*'s (2008) Chamberlinian–Ricardian model as its point of departure, and extends the analysis to include both a continuum of industries, as did Dornbusch *et al.* (1977), and iceberg transport costs.
Findings – It will be shown that trade liberalization drastically changes the nature of trade patterns, particularly the emergence of intra-industry trade.
Originality/value – This present model extends the Chamberlinian–Ricardian model to include positive trade costs.

Keywords: Trade liberalization, comparative advantage, Chamberlinian–Ricardian model

Paper type: Research paper

1. Introduction

Over the last several decades a vast literature has developed on the emergence of intra-industry trade (i.e., two-way trade of differentiated products). Among several competing models of intra-industry trade, Chamberlinian monopolistic competition models of trade have been extensively investigated since the groundbreaking work of Krugman (1979). Helpman's (1981) influential work on the integration of the monopolistic competition trade model into a neoclassical framework,

Frontiers of Economics and Globalization
Volume 5 ISSN: 1574-8715
DOI: 10.1016/S1574-8715(08)05003-3

which has been extended and made popular by Helpman and Krugman (1985), has led to the widely held belief that neoclassical and new trade theories are complementary in nature.[1] Those models are very successful in explaining the emergence of intra-industry trade.

To focus on the role of increasing returns and imperfect competition, a standard one-factor model assumes cross-country technical homogeneity: each firm in the monopolistically competitive sector incurs an identical fixed cost and a constant marginal cost. As a result, there has been little investigation into the role of technical heterogeneity among countries. However, the Ricardian comparative advantage, which plays a basic role in the traditional international-trade context, is worthy of more attention. To address this point, Kikuchi *et al.* (2008) explored cross-country technical heterogeneity in both fixed costs and marginal costs as a determinant of trade patterns. Within a two-country, many-industry framework, they showed that the extent of cross-country technical differences among industries plays an important role as a determinant of trade within each industry. However, they assumed away any trade costs between countries.

The present note takes the work of Kikuchi *et al.* (2008) as its point of departure, and extends the analysis to include both a continuum of industries, as did Dornbusch *et al.* (1977), and iceberg transport costs. In each industry, fixed costs can differ between countries. It will be shown that the equilibrium specialization pattern is determined by the interaction between technical heterogeneity (i.e., the differences in fixed costs) and the level of iceberg transport costs. It will also be shown that trade liberalization drastically changes the nature of trade patterns, particularly the emergence of intra-industry trade.

This note is closely related to the research of Venables (1999), which explored the division of industries between countries in a multi-industry framework with cross-country technical differences. However, he used a framework in which there are both transport costs and linkages through intermediate inputs: his focus was on the interaction between technical differences and agglomeration forces via input-output linkages. In contrast, in this note, we assume away such aspects (e.g., sources of agglomeration forces such as input–output linkages) and focus on the interaction between cross-country technical differences and trade liberalization.

This chapter is organized as follows. Section 2 provides the basic setup of the model of monopolistic competition. Section 3 examines the impact of trade liberalization.

---

[1] See Wong (1995) for the comprehensive surveys of the relevant literature.

2. The model

Suppose there are two countries in the world, Home and Foreign. Each country is endowed with L units of labor and the only source of income is the wage, w ($\tilde{w}$). We assume that there is a continuum of industries on the unit interval. Industry-specific variables will be indexed by industry label i ($i \in [0, 1]$). Consumers have Cobb–Douglas preferences and purchase equal values of the output of all industries. The market structure of each industry is monopolistically competitive. Each industry is modeled as a Dixit-Stiglitz (1977) monopolistically competitive industry, so the quantity index of industry i takes the form

$$X^i = \left(\sum_{k=1}^{n^i} (d_k^i)^{(\sigma-1)/\sigma} + \sum_{\tilde{k}=1}^{\tilde{n}^i} (d_{\tilde{k}}^i)^{(\sigma-1)/\sigma} \right)^{\sigma/(\sigma-1)} , \quad \sigma > 1 \tag{1}$$

where n^i ($\tilde{n}^i$) is the number of products produced in industry i in Home (Foreign), d_k^i ($d_{\tilde{k}}^i$) the quantity of product k ($\tilde{k}$) in the Home market, and $\sigma > 1$ the elasticity of substitution between every pair of products. Trade between countries is costly. We assume that, for every t units shipped, only one unit arrives. Thus, the price of imported differentiated product to the home consumers will be $t\tilde{p}$, where $\tilde{p}$ is the producer's price for the Foreign product. The price index of industry i can be obtained as:

$$P^i = \left(\sum_{k=1}^{n^i} (p_k^i)^{1-\sigma} + \sum_{\tilde{k}=1}^{\tilde{n}^i} (t p_{\tilde{k}}^i)^{1-\sigma} \right)^{1/(1-\sigma)} , \tag{2}$$

where p_k^i ($p_{\tilde{k}}^i$) is the price of the k ($\tilde{k}$)th differentiated product produced by industry i in Home (Foreign).

There is cross-country technical heterogeneity: fixed costs are assumed to differ across countries: each Home (Foreign) firm in industry i has α^i ($\tilde{\alpha}^i$) units of labor as a fixed input. We assume, however, that marginal costs are the same for all industries and for both countries, being equal to β units of labor. With the number of firms being very large, the elasticity of demand for each product becomes σ. Thus, each product is priced at a markup over marginal cost:

$$p_k^i = \frac{\sigma \beta w}{\sigma - 1}, \quad p_{\tilde{k}}^i = \frac{\sigma \beta \tilde{w}}{\sigma - 1}.$$

We chose units so that $\beta = (\sigma - 1)/\sigma$, which implies that $p^i = w$. Free entry ensures that the equilibrium output per product is constant, but differ across countries, and independent of the level of trade costs:

$$x^i = \alpha^i \sigma, \quad \tilde{x}^i = \tilde{\alpha}^i \sigma.$$

For cross-country differences in fixed costs, we would like to employ the following specification.[2]

$$\alpha^i = 1 + i \quad \text{and} \tag{3}$$

$$\tilde{\alpha}^i = 2 - i. \tag{4}$$

The production technologies are mirror images of each other. By virtue of market symmetry, factor prices will be the same in all markets, thus w is identical across all countries; henceforth we set $wL = \tilde{w}L = 1$. The symmetry assumptions imply that trade yields a relative wage of one.

Product market equilibrium requires that supply equal demand for each product. By substituting the zero-profit condition into this equilibrium condition and denoting $\tau \equiv t^{1-\sigma}$ yields the following equilibrium condition for a home product and its foreign counterpart in industry i:

$$\alpha^i \sigma = \left(\frac{1}{n^i + \tau \tilde{n}^i} \right) + \left(\frac{\tau}{\tau n^i + \tilde{n}^i} \right) \quad \text{and} \tag{5}$$

$$\tilde{\alpha}^i \sigma = \left(\frac{\tau}{n^i + \tau \tilde{n}^i} \right) + \left(\frac{1}{\tau n^i + \tilde{n}^i} \right). \tag{6}$$

Its solution is

$$n^i = \frac{1}{\sigma(\alpha^i - \tilde{\alpha}^i \tau)} - \frac{\tau}{\sigma(\tilde{\alpha}^i - \alpha^i \tau)} \quad \text{and} \tag{7}$$

$$\tilde{n}^i = \frac{1}{\sigma(\tilde{\alpha}^i - \alpha^i \tau)} - \frac{\tau}{\sigma(\alpha^i - \tilde{\alpha}^i \tau)}. \tag{8}$$

If trade cost τ is small enough so that

$$\tau < \min \left[\frac{\alpha^i}{\tilde{\alpha}^i}, \frac{\tilde{\alpha}^i}{\alpha^i} \right]. \tag{9}$$

Then all the denominators are positive. The difference in the number of firms in ith industry is

$$n^i - \tilde{n}^i = \frac{(\tilde{\alpha}^i - \alpha^i)(1 + \tau)^2}{\sigma(\alpha^i - \tilde{\alpha}^i \tau)(\tilde{\alpha}^i - \alpha^i \tau)}.$$

It is positive when $\tilde{\alpha}^i > \alpha^i$ and (7) are satisfied. The degree of specialization will depend on both (a) the level of trade cost t and (b) the level of difference in fixed (or comparative advantage).[3]

---

[2] See Yi (2003) and Neary (2003).
[3] Since marginal costs levels differ quite a lot across countries, it is more natural to include those differences. In order to make analysis tractable, however, we concentrate on the technical differences in fixed costs and downplay differences in marginal costs. This kind of extension needs further consideration.

3. The impact of trade liberalization

By combining (5)–(7), we can obtain two cutoff points determining specialization patterns: $\underline{i}\,(\alpha^i/\tilde{\alpha}^i = \tau)$ and $\bar{i}\,(\tilde{\alpha}^i/\alpha^i = \tau)$.

For $0 \leq i \leq \underline{i}$, only Home will produce those products, while only Foreign firms are active for $\bar{i} \leq i \leq 1$. Within the range of $\underline{i} < i < \bar{i}$, both countries' firms are active and intra-industry trade occurs between countries. These trade patterns are summarized in Figure 1: the vertical axis shows both the relative fixed costs and the freeness of trade (τ), while the horizontal axis shows the index of industries. In contrast to the findings in the previous literature, we found that intra-industry trade occurs in the middle range of industries.

It is important to note that this result is crucially dependent on the assumption of the monopolistically competitive industries. If firms in each industry produce *homogeneous* products as in Dornbusch *et al.* (1977), there are few incentives of intra-industry trade between countries. In our model, intra-industry trade occurs since each firm produces *differentiated* products and those firms are distributed between countries.

Now we turn to the impact of trade liberalization, which is captured by a decrease in t (i.e., an increase in τ). Reducing trade costs has two effects. First, trade liberalization intensifies import competition: a fall in t reduces the industry price index due to the extra firms competing for a share of a limited domestic market demand (2). This leads to a fall in domestic demand for domestically produced products in each country. The industry price indices fall more greatly in less competitive industries (i.e., industries

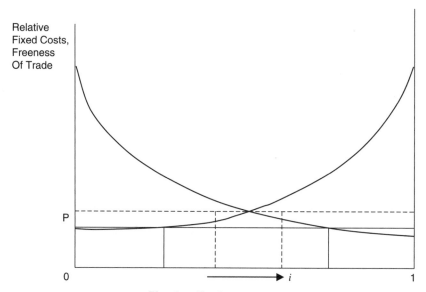

Fig. 1. Trade patterns.

with relatively higher fixed costs) since firms with larger fixed costs are exposed to more import competition compared to firms with lower fixed costs. Second, trade liberalization makes it easier to gain access to the export market: a fall in t leads to an increase in exports to each country. The relative strength of the two effects determines equilibrium trade patterns: the import competition effect dominates since sales in the domestic market are more significant than exports in the presence of positive trade costs.[4] Firms with relatively higher fixed costs find the gain in exports does not offset the sales lost in the domestic market so the amount of output they can sell is insufficient to cover (higher) fixed costs and this leads to the exit of some firms in the sectors with comparative disadvantage. The reverse is true for the firms with relatively lower fixed costs, so there is entry in the sectors with comparative advantage. Summarizing these changes, due to trade liberalization, Foreign (resp. Home) firms will be wiped out in the sectors around $\underline{i}$ ($\overline{i}$): the range of sectors with intra-industry trade will become narrower (see Figure 1).

PROPOSITION. *Due to trade liberalization, the range of sectors with intra-industry trade becomes narrower.*

This result cannot be obtained under the assumption that technologies are identical across both countries. This implies that it is important to extend the standard model of monopolistic competition to include both technological heterogeneity and many sectors. The present note must be regarded as very tentative. Hopefully it provides a useful paradigm for considering how trade liberalization works as a driving force for industrial reformulation.

Acknowledgements

We would like to express our gratitude to the editors, Dao-Zhi Zeng and the anonymous referee for constructive comments. We acknowledge financial support from the Ministry of Education, Culture, Sports, Science and Technology of Japan (the Grant-in-Aid for the 21st Century COE Program 'Research and Education Center of New Japanese Economic Paradigm'). Professor Koji Shimomura and I derived some of the basic results in this chapter when I was attending his seminar in 2004. But the co-authorship was interrupted when Koji died of cancer on February 24, 2007. Koji was a fine scholar and a very kind teacher. He is greatly missed (Kikuchi).

---

[4] See Amiti (1998) for the similar argument in the two-sector setting.

References

Amiti, M. (1998), Inter-industry trade in manufactures: does country size matter? *Journal of International Economics* 44 (2), 231–255.

Dixit, A.K., Stiglitz, J.E. (1977), Monopolistic competition and optimum product diversity. *American Economic Review* 67 (3), 297–308.

Dornbusch, R., Fischer, S., Samuelson, P. (1977), Comparative advantage, trade and payments in a Ricardian model with a continuum of goods. *American Economic Review* 67 (5), 823–829.

Helpman, E. (1981), International trade in the presence of product differentiation, economies of scale and monopolistic competition: a Chamberlin-Heckscher-Ohlin approach. *Journal of International Economics* 11 (3), 305–340.

Helpman, E., Krugman, P.R. (1985), *Market Structure and Foreign Trade*. MIT Press, Cambridge, MA.

Kikuchi, T., Shimomura, K., Zeng, D.-Z. (2008), On Chamberlinian-Ricardian trade patterns. Forthcoming in Review of International Economics.

Krugman, P.R. (1979), Increasing returns, monopolistic competition, and international trade. *Journal of International Economics* 9 (4), 469–479.

Neary, J.P. (2003), Competitive versus comparative advantage. *The World Economy* 26 (4), 457–470.

Venables, A.J. (1999), The international division of industries: clustering and comparative advantage in a multi-industry model. *Scandinavian Journal of Economics* 101 (4), 495–513.

Wong, K.-Y. (1995), *International Trade in Goods and Factor Mobility*. MIT Press, Cambridge, MA.

Yi, K.-M. (2003), Can vertical specialization explain the growth of world trade? *Journal of Political Economy* 111 (1), 52–102.

CHAPTER 4

Outsourcing and Import Restriction Policies

Kai-Hsi Chu and Kar-yiu Wong

Department of Economics, University of Washington, Box 353330, Seattle,
WA 98195-3330, USA
E-mail addresses: kaihsi@u.washington.edu; karyiu@u.washington.edu

Abstract

Purpose – The purpose of this chapter is to examine the issues of outsourcing and corresponding policy interventions by the government.
Design/methodology/approach – This chapter begins with a situation in which no government interventions are allowed, and examine the government of the North, when it is allowed to intervene, can choose one of the three options: (a) to limit the quantity of each type of variety of the foreign intermediate inputs to be imported; (b) to limit the number of varieties of the foreign intermediate inputs to be imported; and (c) to impose a tariff on the imported intermediate inputs.
Findings – For each policy, the optimal intervention is derived.
Originality/value – The analysis can be used to examine the argument for restricting outsourcing.

Keywords: Outsourcing, varieties, import restriction, trade policy, welfare

Paper type: Research paper

1. Introduction

Outsourcing has become a very important feature of the ongoing process of globalization, and a centerpiece of the many policy debates and protectionist arguments. On the one hand, many people recognize the rising significance of outsourcing and the growing reliance of multi-national corporations on it as a way to gain international competitiveness, and on the other, many people are viewing it as a threat to their jobs and earnings and are using it as a reason to argue for protectionist measures.

Outsourcing is the transfer of parts of a production process, which are initially done within the local plant or factory, to other firms in the same

Frontiers of Economics and Globalization
Volume 5   ISSN: 1574-8715
DOI: 10.1016/S1574-8715(08)05004-5

country or in other countries.[1] Recently, it is getting more and more common to have final products consisting of components made in different countries. For example, computer companies such as Dell outsource many of their components, and footwear firm Nike only keeps R&D and coordination at home while outsources most of its production to Southeast Asia. Grossman and Helpman (2005) cite from recent annual report of the World Trade Organization (1998) describing the production of a particular "American" car:

> *Thirty percent of the car's value goes to Korea for assembly, 17.5 percent to Japan for components and advanced technology, 7.5 percent to Germany for design, 4 percent to Taiwan and Singapore for minor parts, 2.5 percent to the United Kingdom for advertising and marketing services, and 1.5 percent to Ireland and Barbados for data processing. This means that only 37 percent of the production value ... is generated in the United States. (p. 36)*

Why would firms choose to outsource? One argument offered is based on the existence of incomplete contracts (see, e.g., Antras and Helpman, 2004; Grossman and Helpman, 2005). Feenstra and Hanson (1996) argue that the difference in endowments is the fundamental reason for comparative advantage and international outsourcing: Companies in industrialized countries shift labor-intensive stages of their production process to labor abundant countries with lower wage rates. However, Ethier (1979) and Hummels *et al.* (2001) use a Ricardian model to explain the pattern of vertical specialization in intermediate inputs.

The purpose of this chapter is to analyze several issues related to outsourcing. It begins with the choice of a local firm in terms of outsourcing. It then examines the impacts of several policies available to a local government, and derives the optimal use of each of these policies. In particular, it will look at the wisdom of restricting outsourcing, which was raised in recent discussion about the appropriate response of a local government to outsourcing. In analyzing outsourcing, this chapter takes the convenient approach of considering the use of intermediate inputs by a local firm, some from a local market and some from other countries.[2] Outsourcing in the present chapter refers to the increase in the use of

---

[1] A variety of terms have been used in the literature or the media to refer to this or related phenomena: for example, the "slicing of the value chain", "international outsourcing", "fragmentation of the production process", "vertical specialization", "global production sharing", "disintegration of production", "multi-stage production", "intra-product specialization", "offshoring" (for the transfer of the production activity to a firm in another country), and so on.

[2] There is a large literature on trade in intermediate inputs (see, for example, Ethier, 1982; Jones, 2000; Feenstra and Hanson, 2001). Many papers have focused on the volume of trade in intermediate inputs (see, for example, Yeats, 2001; Hummels *et al.*, 2001; Kleinert, 2003).

foreign intermediate inputs.[3] The framework constructed here allows us to examine the impacts of three different government policies: (a) to restrict the quantity of import of each type of intermediate inputs to be used by a local final-product firm; (b) to restrict the number of types of intermediate inputs to be used by a local final-product firm; and (c) to impose a tariff on the imported intermediate inputs.

The rest of the chapter is organized as follows. Section 2 describes the model to be used in the present chapter. It consists of three countries (the North, the South, and the Rest of the World), a final product, and intermediate inputs. The section explains the technology to produce the final product and the market structure in the North. Section 3 focuses on the production and technologies of the intermediate inputs in the North and the South. The equilibrium under free trade is derived. Section 4 explains how the welfare of the North is measured. It then analyzes the impacts of each of the three policies described earlier. Whether it makes sense to restrict outsourcing using these policies is examined. Section 5 presents some concluding remarks.

2. The model

Consider three countries and a final product. The countries are labeled N (North), S (South), and R (rest of the world). The final product is produced only in country N by a single firm using two types of hetero-geneous intermediate inputs, one of which comes from the local economy and the other type is imported from country S. All transport costs are negligible. For the time being, free trade is assumed with no government intervention. The demand for the final product exists in country R only, and thus the output of the firm in country N will be exported to country R. The demand can be represented by $p = p(y)$, where p is the market price and y is the output, which is equal to the level of export. Using a prime to denote a derivative, we assume that $p' < 0$, and p'' is less than a sufficiently small positive number. There are N^n varieties of intermediate inputs in country N and N^s varieties of intermediate inputs in country S, where N^n and N^s are to be determined endogenously but are taken as given by the final-product firm. The production function of the final product is given by[4]

$$y = \sum_{i=1}^{N^n} \gamma^n(x^{in}) + \sum_{i=1}^{N^s} \gamma^s(x^{is}),$$
(1)

where x^{ij} is the quantity of intermediate input of variety i from country j, $j = n, s$ and function $\gamma^j(x^{ij})$ satisfies the following conditions: $\gamma^{j\prime} > 0$, $\gamma^{j\prime\prime} < 0$,

---

[3] Feenstra and Hanson (1999) focus on vertical specialization with goods being made in multiple stages located in different countries.

[4] The production function is simplified by assuming no primary inputs.

and $\gamma^{j'''}$ is less than a sufficiently small positive number. Intermediate inputs from each country enter the production function in a symmetric way.

The profit of the final-product firm can be defined as

$$\Pi = py - \sum_{i=1}^{N^n} r^{in} x^{in} - \sum_{i=1}^{N^s} r^{is} x^{is}, \tag{2}$$

where r^{ij} is the price of variety i from country j. Taking the numbers of varieties and their prices as given, the firm chooses the intermediate inputs to maximize its profit, subject to the production function defined in (1).[5] Define $\varphi \equiv \varphi(y) \equiv p + p'y$ as the marginal revenue of the final product, which falls with y, $\varphi' < 0$.[6] The first-order conditions are (assuming an interior solution):

$$\varphi(y)\gamma^{j'}(x^{ij}) = r^{ij}. \tag{3}$$

Equation (3) represents an inverse derived demand for intermediate input x^{ij}, and can be written as $r^{ij} = r^{ij}(x^{ij}, y)$. Differentiate (3) to give

$$dr^{ij} = \varphi\gamma^{j''}dx^{ij} + \varphi'\gamma^{j'}dy, \tag{4}$$

which shows that r^{ij} depends negatively on x^{ij} and y. We assume that the number of varieties of intermediate inputs in each country is sufficiently large so that a small change in one of the input prices will not affect much the total output. As a result, each intermediate-input firm takes the value of y in Equation (3) as given, implying that Equation (3) can be regarded as the derived demand for an intermediate input, with a slope equal to (evaluated at a given level of y):

$$\frac{dx^{ij}}{dr^{ij}} = \frac{1}{\varphi\gamma^{j''}(x^{ij})} < 0. \tag{5}$$

3. Intermediate sectors

The intermediate good sector in each country is characterized by monopolistic competition, heterogeneous products, and increasing returns. Each variety is produced by a firm using a technology that exhibits increasing returns, with the labor input required to produce x^{ij} units of variety i in country j, $j = n, s$, given by

$$\ell^{ij} = \alpha^j + \beta^j x^{ij}, \tag{6}$$

---

[5] For simplicity, we assume that the final-product firm exploits the monopoly power on the output side but not the monopsony power on the input side because of a large number of intermediate inputs.

[6] This is due to the assumption that p'' is less than a sufficiently small positive number.

where α^j, $\beta^j > 0$. The profit of the firm producing variety i in country j is

$$\pi^{ij} = r^{ij}x^{ij} - w^j(\alpha^j + \beta^j x^{ij}), \tag{7}$$

where w^j is the wage rate in country j. The assumption of a large number of varieties of intermediate inputs in each country implies that the two intermediate input sectors can be solved separately, and in the same way.

The profit of each intermediate-input firm is maximized by choosing the optimal output, taking the inverse demand function, final-product output level y, and the wage rate as given. The first-order condition is

$$\frac{d\pi^{ij}}{dx^{ij}} = r^{ij} + r^{ij}_x x^{ij} - w^j\beta^j = 0. \tag{8}$$

Let us denote the marginal revenue by $\theta^{ij} \equiv r^{ij} + r^{ij}_x x^{ij} = \varphi(\gamma^{j\prime} + x^{ij}\gamma^{j\prime\prime})$, where a subscript for r^{ij} represents a partial derivative. The derivative of the marginal revenue is $\theta^{ij\prime} = 2r^{ij}_x + r^{ij}_{xx}x^{ij} = \varphi(2\gamma^{j\prime\prime} + x^j\gamma^{j\prime\prime\prime})$, which is assumed to be negative.[7] Note that all input firms in the same country are symmetric both on the demand side and on the cost side. Thus in equilibrium they must make the same production decision. This allows us to drop the subindex "i" for each firm unless confusion may arise. Thus, using (3), the profit-maximization condition can be written as

$$\varphi(\gamma^{j\prime} + x^j\gamma^{j\prime\prime}) = w^j\beta^j. \tag{9}$$

Condition (9) can be illustrated in Figure 1. The demand D^j is obtained from (3), which yields the marginal revenue function θ^j, or MR^j, which is assumed to be declining with x^j. The marginal cost is equal to $w^j\beta^j$. Point E, the intersection point between the MR^j curve and the horizontal line at $w^j\beta^j$, gives the equilibrium output that satisfies condition (9). Since it is assumed that $\theta^{j\prime} < 0$, the second-order condition holds.

Condition (9) gives a relation between w^j and x^j, which can be illustrated by curve PP in Figure 2. The slope of PP is

$$\left.\frac{dw^j}{dx^j}\right|_{PP} = \frac{\varphi(2\gamma^{j\prime\prime} + x^j\gamma^{j\prime\prime\prime})}{\beta^j} < 0. \tag{10}$$

Note that in the region left (right) of curve PP, $\theta^j > (<) \, w^j\beta^j$.

Free entry and exit exists drives the profit of each existing firm to zero. From (7), zero profit implies

$$\varphi\gamma^{j\prime}x^j = w^j(\alpha^j + \beta^j x^j), \tag{11}$$

which gives another relation between w^j and x^j, and can be illustrated by curve ZZ in Figure 2. The slope of ZZ can be obtained by differentiating

---

[7] The derivative $\theta^{ij\prime}$ involves the third derivative of γ^j and thus its sign is ambiguous, but we assume that it is less than a sufficiently small positive number. This guarantees that the second-order condition for the input firm's profit maximization is satisfied.

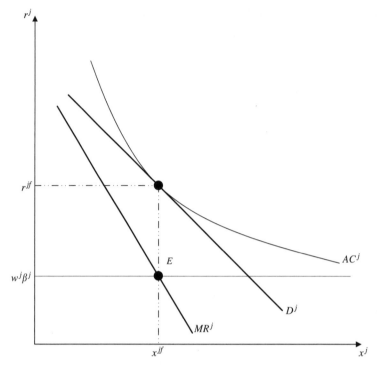

Fig. 1.   Zero profit and profit maximization.

condition (11) and rearranging terms:

$$\left.\frac{dw^j}{dx^j}\right|_{ZZ} = \frac{\theta^j - w^j\beta^j}{\alpha^j + \beta^j x^j}. \tag{12}$$

As explained above, $\theta^j - w^j \beta^j$ is the derivative of the profit function with respect to output, and is positive (negative) in the area left (right) of curve PP and condition (12) implies that curve ZZ is positively (negatively) sloped, as shown in Figure 2. Curve ZZ reaches a maximum at the intersection point with PP. The region below (above) curve ZZ represents positive (negative) profit.

The intersection between curves PP and ZZ in Figure 2, point F, represents the free-trade equilibrium (x^{jf}, w^{jf}), where the superscript "f" denotes the value of a variable under free trade. This equilibrium is also shown in Figure 1. The AC^j curve represents the average cost, $w^j(\beta^j + \alpha^j/x^{ij})$. Zero profit means that the demand for the firm's output D^j will be such that it touches AC^j at the equilibrium input price r^{jf}. Equations (9) and (11) are solved for the input production level and wage rate in country j, x^{jf}, and $w^{jf} = w^{jf}(y)$. Note that the value of x^{jf} is

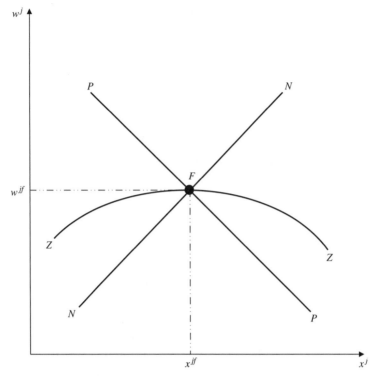

Fig. 2.   Equilibrium under free trade.

independent of the value of y, but that of w^{jf} is not.[8] From the profit-maximization or zero-profit condition, it is easy to get

$$w^{jf\prime} = \frac{\mathrm{d}w^{jf}}{\mathrm{d}y} = \frac{\varphi'\gamma^{j\prime}x^j}{\alpha^j + \beta^j x^j} < 0. \tag{13}$$

From (3), we can write the corresponding input price as

$$r^j = \tilde{r}^{jf}(x^{jf}, y) = \varphi(y)\gamma^{j\prime}(x^{jf}).$$

To explain how the number of varieties is determined, suppose that labor for the intermediate input production is withdrawn from other parts of the economy according to the following function,

$$L^j = L^j(w^j), \tag{14}$$

where $L^{j\prime}(w^j) > 0$. Thus w^j can be interpreted as the opportunity cost of using one extra unit of labor in this market. Function (14) can be inverted to give

$$w^j = \omega^j(L^j), \tag{15}$$

---

[8] Note that when (9) is divided by (11) both $\varphi(y)$ and w^j are cancelled out, leaving x^j to be determined. Thus with no government intervention, x^j is independent of y.

which can be interpreted as the minimum wage rate required to attract an amount of L^j labor from the rest of the economy. The derivatives of functions $L^j(\cdot)$ and $\omega^j(\cdot)$ depend on the cost of attracting labor from the rest of the economy. If the market considered is only a small part of the economy so that the wage rate is not too much affected by the employment in the market, $L^{j\prime}$ is very large (or $\omega^{j\prime}$ very small). Using the production function in (6), the equilibrium of the labor market is

$$L^j = N^j \ell^j = N^j(\alpha^j + \beta^j x^j).$$

Using the free-trade equilibrium described above, the number of varieties in country j under free trade is

$$N^j = N^j(w^j, x^j) = \tilde{N}^{if}(y) = \frac{L^j(\tilde{w}^{if}(y))}{(\alpha^j + \beta^j x^{if})}. \tag{16}$$

Differentiation gives

$$\tilde{N}^{if\prime} = \frac{L^j \mathrm{d}\tilde{w}^{if}/\mathrm{d}y}{(\alpha^j + \beta^j x^{if})} < 0. \tag{17}$$

The number of varieties can also be shown in Figure 2, which shows the contour NN representing $\tilde{N}^{if}(y)$ passing through point F. Contours below (above) NN represent smaller (larger) number of varieties. We now close the model by explaining how the final-product output is determined. Making use of the production function:

$$y = N^n(y)\gamma^n(x^{nf}) + N^s(y)\gamma^s(x^{sf}), \tag{18}$$

which can be solved for the free-trade output of the final product, y^f. The corresponding values of the intermediate-input markets are $w^{if} = \tilde{w}^{if}(y^f)$ and $N^{if} = \tilde{N}^{if}(y^f)$. It should be noted that the derivative of the right-hand side of (18) is assumed to be less than unity. This assumption is needed for normal comparative-static results, as will be shown later.

4. Policies to control outsourcing

We now examine the following policies for the government of country N to control outsourcing. We will derive the optimal policy parameter under each of the policy options under the assumption that the governments of countries S and R remain passive in policy choice. The policy options analyzed in the present chapter are:

1. to restrict the quantity of each of the imported intermediate inputs;
2. to restrict the number of varieties of the imported intermediate inputs;
3. to impose a tariff on all the imported intermediate inputs.

4.1. Welfare of country N

The social welfare of country N can be defined as follows:

$$W^n = \Pi + N^n \pi^n + \left(w^n L^n - \int_0^{L^n} \omega^n(v) dv \right). \tag{19}$$

In (19), the first term is the profit of the final-product firm, and the second term is the total profit of the intermediate-input firms. The term inside the parentheses is the surplus generated by hiring L^n from the rest of the economy: $w^n L^n$ is the income generated and $\int \omega^n(v) dv$ the total opportunity cost of hiring L^n.

Substitute the firms' profit functions in (2) and (7) into (19) to get

$$W^n = py - N^s r^s x^s - \int_0^{L^n} \omega^n(v) \, dv. \tag{20}$$

Condition (20) can be used to evaluate the social welfare level at different equilibria. For example, under free trade, the social welfare level is

$$W^{nf} = p^f y^f - N^{sf} r^{sf} x^{sf} - \int_0^{L^{nf}} \omega^n(v) dv. \tag{21}$$

The welfare level in (21) will be used as the benchmark, with which the welfare levels under different policies are compared. The three policies mentioned above are now analyzed one by one.

4.2. Quantitative restriction

The first policy for country N we examine is quantitative restriction. Suppose that government N imposes a ceiling $\bar{x}^s < x^{sf}$ on the quantity of each of the imported intermediate inputs, i.e., $x^{is} \leq \bar{x}^s$ for all i. This policy will likely create a gap between the price of each input in country S and that in country N. We assume that it is the producers, not the local government, who pick up this quota premium.

Let us first examine the impacts of this policy. Because the output of each intermediate-input firm in country S goes to country N, the restriction on import means a direct restriction on the output of the intermediate-input firms in country S. As a result, the firms may not be able to maximize their profits. This implies that condition (9) and curve PP for country S are no longer applicable. However, because of free entry and exit, the profit of each of the firms in country S will be zero at the new equilibrium. This means that Equation (11) and curve ZZ still hold. Treating x^s as a parameter, write the wage rate in country S as $w^s = \tilde{w}^{sq}(y; x^s)$. As Figure 3 shows, a drop in x^s, when given y, will lower w^s, measured along curve ZZ:

$$\frac{\partial \tilde{w}^{sq}}{\partial x^s} = \frac{\theta^s - w^s \beta^s}{\alpha^s + \beta^s x^s} > 0, \tag{22}$$

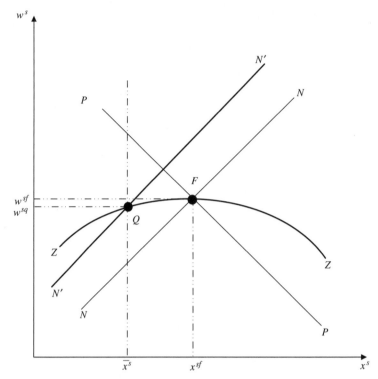

Fig. 3.   Quantity restriction.

where for $x^s < x^{sf}$, $\theta^s > w^s \beta^s$. The derived demand implies that a quantitative restriction will lower the wage rate, when y is given. The effect of a change in the final-product output on the wage rate is

$$\frac{\partial \tilde{w}^{sq}}{\partial y} = \frac{\varphi / \gamma / x^s}{\alpha^s + \beta^s x^s} < 0, \tag{23}$$

where x^s is evaluated at $\bar{x}^s$. The number of varieties in country S is given by (16), and we can write $N^s = \tilde{N}^{sq}(y; x^s)$. When taking y as given, the effect of the policy is

$$\frac{\partial \tilde{N}^{sq}}{\partial x^s} = \frac{(\alpha^s + \beta^s x^s)L^{s\prime}\partial \tilde{w}^{sq}/\partial x^s - L^s \beta^s}{(\alpha^s + \beta^s x^s)^2}. \tag{24}$$

The sign of the expression in (24) is ambiguous, but if the current market is a small part of the economy so that $L^{s\prime}$ is sufficiently large and if $\partial \tilde{\omega}^{sq}/\partial x^s$ is finite, then $\partial \tilde{N}^{sq}/\partial x^s > 0$. The effect of a change in y on the number of varieties is

$$\frac{\partial \tilde{N}^{sq}}{\partial y} = \frac{L^{s\prime}(\partial \tilde{w}^{sq}/\partial y)}{\alpha^s + \beta^s x^s} < 0. \tag{25}$$

We now examine the effects of the policy on country N. Refer back to Equation (18), except that x^s is now treated as a parameter. Differentiate it and rearrange the terms to give

$$\frac{dy}{dx^s} = \frac{N^s \gamma^{s\prime} + \gamma^s \partial \tilde{N}^{sq}/\partial x^s}{1 - \gamma^n dN^n/dy - \gamma^s \partial \tilde{N}^{sq}/\partial y} > 0, \tag{26}$$

where the denominator is positive.[9] Condition (26) means that a restriction on x^s for each of the intermediate inputs imported from country S will lower the output of the final product. Using Equations (24)–(26), the total effects of a change in x^s on the number of varieties in country S is

$$\frac{dN^s}{dx^s} = \frac{\partial \tilde{N}^{sq}}{\partial x^s} + \frac{\partial \tilde{N}^{sq}}{\partial y}\frac{dy}{dx^s}.$$

Equation (26) can also be used to examine the effects of a change in x^s on the wage rate in country N,

$$\frac{dw^n}{dx^s} = \frac{dw^{nf}}{dy}\frac{dy}{dx^s} < 0. \tag{27}$$

We now examine how the policy may affect the welfare of the market. Again, treating x^s as a parameter, differentiate the welfare function in (20) with respect to x^s:

$$\frac{dW^n}{dx^s} = -r^s x^s \frac{dN^s}{dx^s} - N^s x^s \frac{dr^s}{dx^s} - w^n L^{n\prime} w^{nf\prime} \frac{dy}{dx^s}, \tag{28}$$

where $L^{n\prime} = dL^n/dW^n$ and $w^{nf\prime} = dw^{nf}/dy$. Conditions (23), (24), and (27) can be used to simplify (28). In general, the sign of the derivative in (28) is ambiguous. However, we can evaluate it in two special cases. First, consider the small region near the free-trade equilibrium. As Figure 2 shows, the zero-profit curve, ZZ, has a horizontal tangent, which means that a small change in x^s will marginally not affect the wage rate. Condition (24) reduces to

$$\frac{dN^s}{dx^s} = -\frac{L^s \beta^s}{(\alpha^s + \beta^s x^s)^2} < 0. \tag{29}$$

Similarly, Equation (28) reduces to

$$\frac{dW^n}{dx^s} = -r^s x^s \frac{dN^s}{dx^s} - N^s x^s \frac{dr^s}{dx^s} > 0. \tag{30}$$

Equation (30) implies that a small restriction on the volume of import is detrimental. This result is not surprising, as the policy severely restricts the choice of the local final-product firm and the use of labor.

---

[9] See the explanation given above.

Second, assume that x^s is very small so that only small amounts of intermediate inputs are allowed from country S. Equation (28) reduces to

$$\frac{dW^n}{dx^s} = -w^n L^{n'} w^{nf'} \frac{dy}{dx^s} > 0. \tag{31}$$

Equation (31) implies that in the small region with small trade volume, allowing more import of intermediate inputs benefits country N. Another way to put it is that (at least a small volume of) trade is good.[10]

The above results are summarized by the following propositions:

PROPOSITION 1. *In the present framework, the gain from (at least a small) trade is positive for country N.*

PROPOSITION 2. *With the government N collecting none of the quota premium, the market is hurt by the following quantitative restriction: (i) a small restriction; (ii) a large restriction so that the imported quantity of each type of intermediate input is small.*

4.3. Variety restriction

We now turn to the second policy option for country N, namely, restricting the number of types of intermediate inputs imported from country S, i.e., the government of country N setting the maximum number of the varieties to be less than the free-trade number, $\bar{N}^s < N^{sf}$.

The restriction on the number of varieties of intermediate inputs in country S prevents free entry and exit, and thus zero profit is not guaranteed. In other words, condition (11) and curve ZZ in Figure 2 are no longer applicable. Firms, however, can still maximize their profits by choosing the optimal outputs, and Equation (9) holds:

$$\theta^s(x^s, y) = w^s \beta^s, \tag{32}$$

recalling that firms take the output level y as given. Because of the constraint, condition (16) can be written as

$$\bar{N}^s = \frac{L^s(w^s)}{(\alpha^s + \beta^s x^s)}. \tag{33}$$

---

[10] Equation (31) assumes that with small import of intermediate inputs the profit of the final-product firm is positive. If the profit of the firm is zero so that it chooses not to produce when no or a small volume of intermediate inputs are allowed, then $dW^n/dx^s = 0$ as the welfare of the market is zero.

Conditions (32) and (33) can then be solved for $x^s = \tilde{x}^{sv}(y; \bar{N}^s)$ and $w^s = \tilde{w}^{sv}(y; \bar{N}^s)$. Keeping N^s as a parameter, differentiate (32) and (33) to give:

$$\begin{bmatrix} 2r_x^s + x^s r_{xx}^s & -\beta^s \\ N^s \beta^s & -L^{s\prime} \end{bmatrix} \begin{bmatrix} dx^s \\ dw^s \end{bmatrix} = -\begin{bmatrix} r_y^s \\ 0 \end{bmatrix} dy - \begin{bmatrix} 0 \\ \alpha^s + \beta^s x^s \end{bmatrix} dN^s, \qquad (34)$$

which are solved to give

$$dx^s = \frac{r_y^s L^{s\prime} dy - \beta^s(\alpha^s + \beta^s x^s) dN^s}{\tilde{D}} \qquad (35)$$

$$dw^s = \frac{N^s \beta^s r_y^s dy - (2r_x^s + x^s r_{xx}^s)(\alpha^s + \beta^s x^s) dN^s}{\tilde{D}}, \qquad (36)$$

where $\tilde{D} = -(2r_x^s + x^{sv} r_{xx}^s)L^{s\prime} + N^s(\beta^s)^2 > 0$. From (35) and (36), we have the following signs of the partial derivatives: $\tilde{x}_y^{sv} < 0$, $\tilde{x}_N^{sv} < 0$, $\tilde{w}_y^{sv} < 0$, and $\tilde{w}_N^{sv} > 0$.

The equilibrium is illustrated in Figure 4. Point F is the free-trade equilibrium point, through which the number-of-variety contour NN

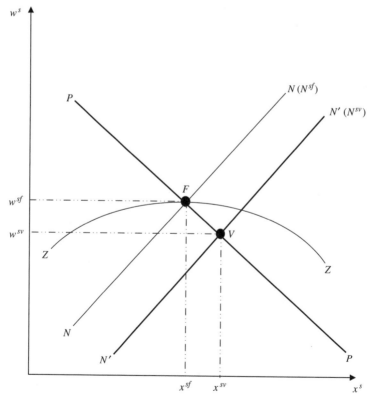

Fig. 4. *Variety restriction.*

representing N^{sf} passes. The present constraint can be illustrated by contour $N'N'$, which is lower than contour NN. The intersecting point V between curve PP and contour $N'N$ gives the new equilibrium, representing a rise in x^s but a drop in w^s.

The market in country N can be solved in the same way as before. The determined functions of intermediate outputs and number of varieties are then substituted back to the production function:

$$y = N^{nf}(y)\gamma^n(x^{nf}) + N^s\gamma^s(\tilde{x}^{sv}(y; \tilde{N}^s)), \tag{37}$$

which can be solved for the final-product output. With N^s treated as a parameter, differentiate both sides of (37) totally and rearrange terms to give

$$\frac{dy}{dN^s} = \frac{\gamma^s + N^s\gamma^{s\prime}\tilde{x}_N^{sv}}{B^y}, \tag{38}$$

where $B^y = (1 - \gamma^n N^{nf\prime} - N^s\gamma^{s\prime}\tilde{x}_y^{sv}) > 0$. Consider the following condition

$$\gamma^s + N^s\gamma^{s\prime}\tilde{x}_N^{sv} < 0. \tag{C}$$

Condition (C) is satisfied if the number of varieties in country N is sufficiently large, and if it is satisfied, the total effect of N^s on y is negative. So if and only if condition (C) is satisfied, $dy/dN^s < 0$. Making use of (38), the total effects of a change in N^s are as follows:

$$\frac{d\tilde{x}^{sv}}{dN^s} = x_N^{sv} + \tilde{x}_y^{sv}\frac{dy}{dN^s} \tag{39}$$

$$\frac{d\tilde{w}^{sv}}{dN^s} = w_N^{sv} + \tilde{w}_y^{sv}\frac{dy}{dN^s}. \tag{40}$$

If condition (C) is not satisfied, then $d\tilde{x}^{sv}/dN^s < 0$, or if condition (C) is satisfied, then $d\tilde{w}^{sv}/dN^s > 0$.

We now try to examine the welfare impacts of this policy for country N. The welfare function is still given by Equation (20), with $N^s = \bar{N}^s$. Treating N^s as a parameter, differentiate the welfare function:

$$\frac{dW^n}{dN^s} = -r^s x^{sv} - N^s x^{sv}\left(r_x^s\frac{dx^{sv}}{dN^s} + r_y^s\frac{dy}{dN^s}\right) - w^n L^{n\prime} w^{nv\prime}\frac{dy}{dN^s}. \tag{41}$$

The sign of the derivative in (41) is in general ambiguous. If we consider a small drop in the number of varieties from the free-trade level, $w^{nv\prime}$ would be very small.[11] Equation (41) reduces to

$$\frac{dW^n}{dN^s} = -r^s x^{sv} - N^s x^{sv}\left(r_x^s\frac{d\tilde{x}^{sv}}{dN^s} + r_y^s\frac{dy}{dN^s}\right). \tag{42}$$

---

[11] Recall that the free-trade equilibrium occurs at a point on the zero-profit curve with a zero slope. See Fig. 2.

Thus either (i) if condition (C) is not satisfied and if r_y^s is sufficiently small or (ii) if condition (C) is satisfied and if $dx^{sv}/dN^s < 0$, then the derivative in (42) is negative, which means that a small drop in N^s is beneficial to country N. However, we showed earlier that the gain from free trade is positive. This means that the welfare of the market when $N^s = 0$ is lower than that when the economy is under free trade. Thus there exists an optimal number of imported varieties that will maximize the local welfare, where the optimal number is obtained by solving the following equation:[12]

$$-r^s x^{sv} - N^s x^{sv}\left(r_x^s \frac{dx^{sv}}{dN^s} + r_y^s \frac{dy}{dN^s}\right) - w^n L^{n\prime} w^{n\nu\prime} \frac{dy}{dN^s} = 0. \tag{43}$$

The above results are summarized by the following proposition:

PROPOSITION 3. *If either (i) condition (C) is not satisfied and if r_y^s is sufficiently small, or (ii) condition (C) is satisfied and if $dx^s/dN^s < 0$ then a small cut in the number of imported varieties benefits country N. The optimal number of varieties to be imported from country S is the one that solves Equation (43).*

4.4. The tariff policy

We now examine the use of a tariff on the imported intermediate inputs. Denote the per unit tariff by $t > 0$, which can drive a wedge between the price of the Southern intermediate input in country N, r^s, and that in country S, $\hat{r}^s$. In equilibrium, we have

$$r^s = \hat{r}^s + t. \tag{44}$$

Despite the tariff, for the intermediate-input firms in country S, the profit-maximization and zero-profit conditions are still satisfied. More specifically, for country S,

$$\theta^s = w^s \beta^s + t \tag{45}$$

$$r^s x^s = w^s(\alpha^s + \beta^s x^s) + tx^s, \tag{46}$$

where (45) describes profit maximization and (46) represents zero profit. These two equations are solved for the output and wage rate in country S, $x^{st} = x^{st}(t, y)$ and $w^{st} = w^{st}(t, y)$. It should be noted that x^s is now generally a function of t and y. Differentiate (45) and (46) totally and rearrange terms to give

$$\begin{bmatrix} 2r_x^s + x^{st}r_{xx}^s & -\beta^s \\ 0 & -(\alpha^s + \beta^s x^{st}) \end{bmatrix} \begin{bmatrix} dx^{st} \\ dw^{st} \end{bmatrix} = \begin{bmatrix} 1 \\ x^{st} \end{bmatrix} dt - \begin{bmatrix} r_y^s \\ x^{st}r_y^s \end{bmatrix} dy,$$

---

[12] The second-order condition for a maximum is assumed.

which are solved to give

$$dx^{st} = \frac{-(\alpha^s + \beta^s x^{st})dt + \alpha^s r_y^s dy}{D''} \tag{47}$$

$$dw^{st} = \frac{\theta^{s'} x^{st} dt - \theta^{s'} x^{st} r_y^s dy}{D''}, \tag{48}$$

where $D'' = -\theta^{s'}(\alpha^s + \beta^s x^{st}) > 0$ and $\theta^{s'} = 2r_x^s + x^{st}r_{xx}^s < 0$. Note that all intermediate-input firms take y as given. Equations (47) and (48) imply that an increase in the tariff rate or the output of the final product will lower both x^{st} and w^{st}. The dependence of the variables on the tariff rate can be illustrated in Figure 5. A rise in the tariff rate will shift curves PP and ZZ to the left (to P'P' and Z'Z', respectively), resulting in a drop in both x^{st} and w^{st}. The resulting change in the number of varieties is

$$N^{st} = N^{st}(t, y) = \frac{L^s(\tilde{w}^{st}(t, y))}{\alpha^s + \beta^s \tilde{x}^{st}(t, y)}. \tag{49}$$

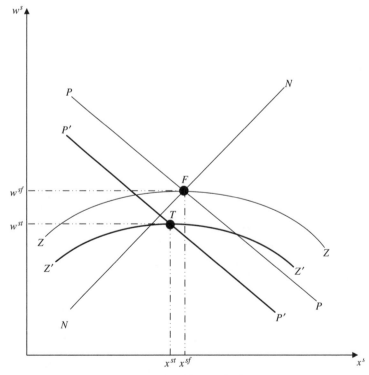

Fig. 5.   *Tariff restriction.*

Differentiate (49) totally to give:

$$dN^{st} = \frac{(\alpha^s + \beta^s x^{st})L^{s'}(\tilde{w}_t^{st}dt + \tilde{w}_y^{st}dy) - L^s\beta^s(\tilde{x}_t^{st}dt + \tilde{x}_y^{st}dy)}{(\alpha^s + \beta^s x^{st})^2}. \tag{50}$$

The sign of the term on the right-hand side of (50) for each country is ambiguous. If the labor market is not too wage sensitive so that $L^{s'}$ is sufficiently large, then N^{st} will react negatively to an increase in t or y.

The effect of the tariff on the final-product output can be obtained by making use of (18):

$$y = N^n(y)\gamma^n(x^{nf}) + \tilde{N}^{st}(t, y)\gamma^s(\tilde{x}^{st}(t, y)),$$

which can be differentiated to give

$$\frac{dy}{dt} = \frac{N^{st}\gamma^{s'}\tilde{x}_t^{st} + \gamma^s\tilde{N}_t^{st}}{B^t} < 0. \tag{51}$$

where $B^t = 1 - \gamma^n N^{n'} - N_y^{st}(\gamma^s + \gamma^{s'}\tilde{x}_y^{st}) > 0$, where $(\gamma^s + \gamma^{s'}\tilde{x}_y^{st}) > 0$ is the marginal revenue faced by an intermediate-input firm in country S, and where the number of varieties in each country depends negatively on y. Condition (51) implies that an increase in t will lower the final product output level.

We now examine the welfare impact of the tariff policy for country N. The welfare function of the country is still given by condition (20). Differentiate the welfare function with respect to the tariff rate to yield:

$$\frac{dW^n}{dt} = -r^s x^{st}\frac{d\tilde{N}^{st}}{dt} - N^s x^{st}\left(r_x^s\frac{d\tilde{x}^{st}}{dt} + r_y^s\frac{dy}{dt}\right) - w^n L^{n'}w^{n\prime}\frac{dy}{dt}. \tag{52}$$

In general, the sign of the derivative in (52) is ambiguous. We can examine two special cases. First, consider the case in which t is zero or small. This is close to the free-trade equilibrium and the change in w^n is small. Then (52) reduces to

$$\frac{dW^n}{dt} = -r^s x^{st}\frac{d\tilde{N}^{st}}{dt} - N^s x^{st}\left(r_x^s\frac{d\tilde{x}^{st}}{dt} + r_y^s\frac{dy}{dt}\right). \tag{53}$$

If, furthermore, the resulting change in the price of the intermediate inputs from country S is small, then the small tariff is beneficial. Second, consider the case when t is near prohibitive. Then the volume of import, x^s, is small. Equation (52) reduces to

$$\frac{dW^n}{dt} = -w^n L^{n'}w^{n\prime}\frac{dy}{dt} < 0. \tag{54}$$

Equation (54) means that when t is near prohibitive, a small reduction in the tariff rate is beneficial. This result confirms Proposition 1, i.e., (at least a small) trade is gainful. Equations (53) and (54) imply that if a small tariff imposed by country N does not change much the price of the intermediate inputs from country S, there exists an optimal tariff that maximizes the welfare of country N.

The above results are summarized by the following proposition:

PROPOSITION 4. *If a small tariff imposed by country N does not change much the price of the intermediate inputs from country S, it is beneficial. Then there exists a positive optimal tariff that maximizes country N's welfare.*

5. Concluding remarks

In this chapter, we constructed a model to analyze the phenomenon of outsourcing. We explained the production of a final product by a firm and its use of intermediate inputs from the local market and those from a foreign market. We then used the model to analyze three policy options for the local government to restrict outsourcing. In the present model, the welfare of the local economy depends mainly on the profit of the final-product firm. While the firm is able to maximize its own profit, subject to certain conditions, externality arises because the firm does not take into consideration the effects of its decision on the price and the number of varieties of the imported intermediate inputs. Our analysis suggests that general restrictions on outsourcing are not the right policies to remove the externality. In many cases, restricting outsourcing could hurt the welfare of the economy.

One main reason why in the present model restricting outsourcing could be damaging is that all the policies considered will lead to a rise in the price of the imported intermediate inputs. In the case of a tariff, both the price of the imported inputs that the final-product firm is facing and the price of the inputs in the foreign country rise. This means that outsourcing restriction could jack up the cost of the imported intermediate inputs, and it will not be optimal unless it can substantially raise the profit of the final-product firm.

Acknowledgement

Thanks are due to Judith Thornton, Philip Brock, Hyun-Hoon Lee, and an anonymous reviewer for very useful and constructive comments. All remaining errors and shortcomings are the responsibilities of the authors.

References

Antras, P., Helpman, E. (2004), Global sourcing. *Journal of Political Economy* 112 (3), 552–580, http://www.journals.uchicago.edu/doi/abs/10.1086/383099

Ethier, W.J. (1979), Internationally decreasing costs and world trade. *Journal of International Economics* 9, 1–24, http://www.sciencedirect.com/science/article/B6V6D-45KNK2S-P/1/29625d5439b7f0aa83a782032a67081e

Ethier, W.J. (1982), National and international returns to scale in the modern theory of international trade. *American Economic Review* 72 (3), 389–405, http://www.jstor.org/stable/1831539

Feenstra, R.C., Hanson, G.H. (1996), Globalization, outsourcing, and wage inequality. *American Economic Review* 86 (2), 240–245, http://www.jstor.org/stable/2118130

Feenstra, R.C., Hanson, G.H. (1999), The impact of outsourcing and high-technology capital on wages: estimates for the United States, 1979–1990. *Quarterly Journal of Economics* 114 (3), 907–940, http://www.mitpressjournals.org/doi/abs/10.1162/003355399556179

Feenstra, R.C., Hanson, G.H. (2001), Global production sharing and rising inequality: a survey of trade and wages. NBER Working Papers No. W8372. http://ssrn.com/abstract = 276002

Grossman, G.M., Helpman, E. (2005), Outsourcing in a global economy. *Review of Economic Studies* 72 (1), 135–159, http://www.blackwell-synergy.com/doi/abs/10.1111/0034-6527.00327

Hummels, D., Ishii, J., Yi, K-M. (2001), The nature and growth of vertical specialization in world trade. *Journal of International Economics* 54 (1), 75–96, http://www.sciencedirect.com/science/article/B6V6D-45FK025-5/2/51c662c289fb7eb1cb5c5993e9dc672c

Jones, R.W. (2000), *Globalization and the Theory of Input Trade.* MIT Press, Cambridge, MA.

Kleinert, J. (2003), Growing trade in intermediate goods: outsourcing, global sourcing, or increasing importance of MNE networks? *Review of International Economics* 11 (3), 464–482, http://www.blackwell-synergy.com/links/doi/10.1111/1467-9396.00396/enhancedabs

World Trade Organization. (1998), *The WTO Annual Report 1998.* World Trade Organization, Geneva.

Yeats, A.J. (2001), Just how big is global production sharing? In: Arndt, S.W., Kierzkowski, H. (Eds.), *Fragmentation: New Production Patterns in the World Economy.* Oxford University Press, London.

CHAPTER 5

Liberalization of Government Procurements: Competition from Foreign Firms

Ngo Van Long

Department of Economics, McGill University, 855 Sherbrooke St west, Montreal, H3A2T7, Canada
E-mail address: ngo.long@mcgill.co

Abstract

Purpose – In this chapter we study the welfare effects of relaxing government restrictions on bidding by foreign firms for government procurement contracts.

Methodology – We use a modified version of the Tullock model of rent contests. Firms spend resources to influence decisions of awarding contracts. We consider the case where firms are heterogeneous in terms of lobbying effectiveness.

Findings – The opening of the bidding opportunities to foreign firms can, under certain conditions, improve social welfare of the liberalizing country. The gain partly comes from reduced aggregate domestic lobbying efforts, which implies lower social waste, and partly from tax revenue on the profits of winning foreign firms.

Practical implications – Our analysis indicates that when negotiating on opening up trade in services, governments should take into account the effects of foreign entry on domestic lobbying costs.

Keywords: Trade liberalization, government procurements, rent-seeking contest, lobbying, welfare

Paper type: Research paper

1. Introduction

Although the liberalization of goods trade has been going on for several decades, there has been very slow progress on liberalization of trade in services, especially when the services relate to government contracts. Governmental procurements are quite substantial in modern economies: the OECD estimates that public procurement by governments and by

Frontiers of Economics and Globalization
Volume 5   ISSN: 1574-8715
DOI: 10.1016/S1574-8715(08)05005-7

state-owned enterprises amounts to about 15% of GDP in OECD countries (OECD, 2005). Governments seem to have strong preferences for domestic firms (Trionfetti, 2000). The WTO had established a Working Group on Transparency in Government Procurement in order to enhance transparency in public procurement. However, due to lack of support, the WTO General Council decided in 2004 that this issue would be deferred and would not form part of the Doha Round. Hence countries are free to set up their own rules and procedures unless they are in conflict with supranational provisions, such as rules set up by the European Union, or bilateral agreements with other countries.

An important feature of government procurements is that bidding for a government contract is not quite the same as a private auction, because government officials take into account many additional factors beyond the bids. Quite often governments declare from the outset that the contract is not necessarily awarded to the highest bidder, because there are other relevant dimensions that are not easily quantifiable; these include concerns such as whether a bidder has sufficient financial resources or expertise to carry out the project, whether it has a good safety record, or whether there is some shadow of doubt about its possible links with organized crimes, etc. A recent survey shows that firms often have to offer a substantial share of the contract value as additional illicit payments to secure procurement contracts (Transparency International, 2007, p. 320.) These observations suggest that governmental procurement decisions may be strongly influenced by partisanship or even corruption. Although this practice is discouraged by the OECD Anti-bribery Convention, this convention seems to lack enforcement power. As Thomas Hobbes put it, covenants without the sword are but words. According to a World Bank report, about USD 200 billion are spent on public procurement bribery per year, which amounts to about 3.5% of public procurement spending (Auriol, 2006).

Evenett and Hoekman (2005) give a good overview of government procurements. From a theoretical perspective, procurement has been modeled in an asymmetric information framework: Mougeot and Naegelen (2005) consider a foreign and a domestic firm whose costs are private information and discuss preferential treatment under alternative assumptions about political processes.

In this chapter, we model government procurement as an imperfectly discriminating contest in which firms lobby for winning (Tullock, 1980; Hillman and Riley, 1989; Nitzan, 1994). The winner is awarded a project, which generates a surplus. The size of this surplus, however, may depend on the type of the winning firm. In particular, foreign firms may have different abilities to run the project compared to domestic firms. We will explore conditions under which the inclusion of foreign firms will improve domestic welfare.

In Tullock's view, the lobbying efforts by individuals or firms constitute a social waste: resources are used in an attempt to transfer money from one person's pocket to another's agents. Tullock's basic model assumes that agents are homogeneous: they have equal valuations of the prize, and their efforts have equal effectiveness. We relax these assumptions, and introduce heterogeneity in both (a) valuations of the prize and (b) comparative advantage in lobbying, in order to capture more adequately the real world features of rent seeking, in particular in the context of government procurements. The rent associated with winning a procurement contract depends on the firm's production cost. If foreign firms have lower production costs than domestic firms, their valuations of the "prize" will be higher. However, foreign firms' rent-seeking efforts may not be as effective as those of domestic firms, because the latter group is better informed about the channels by which a government's decisions can be influenced. In this chapter, we develop an index of comparative disadvantage in lobbying, and model liberalization as a decrease in this index for foreign firms.

The evaluation of social welfare gain for a liberalizing country is complicated, and should take into account several factors. First, while the profit of foreign firms should not be counted in the social welfare of the liberalizing country, if a domestic bidder wins, its after-tax rent should be included as part of the welfare gain. Second, while all the resource costs in rent seeking by domestic firms should be subtracted from the social welfare, in contrast, the resource costs in rent-seeking incurred by foreign firms, whether in their own countries, or in the host country, are not part of the social cost of the host country. This is because either the foreign firms use lobbying resources from the source countries which are irrelevant for the host country, or hire the host country's capital and labor for lobbying, in which case the earnings of these factors of production should be considered as the host country's export revenue. Third, when a foreign firm is allowed to bid for government procurements, this will change the equilibrium lobbying effort levels of all domestic firms: some domestic firms will intensify their lobbying activities, while other domestic firms will scale them down. Finally, the probability that a given firm wins will be affected by adjustments in lobbying intensities of all domestic firms in response to foreign entry.

In this chapter, we show that opening the bidding to foreign firms can, under certain conditions, improve social welfare of the liberalizing country, even when the foreign firms are less efficient in production than some domestic firms. The gain partly comes from reduced aggregate domestic lobbying effort, and partly from the tax revenue on the profit of the winning foreign firm.

In our model, rents are partially dissipated by contests for rents. Dissipation is not complete because each contestant has some power: it can influence the probability of winning of other firms. Even though there is free entry, equilibrium is not determined by zero rent of the marginal firm: under the assumption of a discrete distribution of firm types, with a finite number of firms of each type, the intra-marginal firms enjoy positive rents.

2. The model

For concreteness, consider a government that wants to establish a theme park with the aim of attracting a flow of foreign tourists that would result in increased employment of the home country's unskilled workers. Each candidate firm must submit a plan on how the site will be developed and operated. Government officials are supposed to choose as winner the firm whose submitted development-cum-operation plan is judged to be most likely to achieve the desired level if tourist flow. The winning firm's obligation is to develop and operate the site according to its winning plan, and to pay profit tax at the exogenous rate. We assume that the actual profit is observable and verifiable once the firm starts its operation.

Following Tullock (1980) and Hillman and Riley (1989), we do not explicitly model how government officials make their decision, and simply specify that any candidate firm that undertakes some lobbying effort has a positive chance of winning the contract. Hillman and Riley refer to this model as "imperfectly discriminating contests" model. We assume at the lobbying stage, each firm has perfect knowledge of its own profitability, and knows the lobbying strategies of its rivals. Government officials receive "documents" (sent by the firms) that supposedly influence their perception of the relative merits of the plans of the candidate firms.

In our welfare calculation, we do not count the enjoyment of power by government officials. The "ego rents" earned by officials when they receive and evaluate documents are not counted in social welfare; this is in keeping with the tradition that envy and the like should not be counted in cost–benefit analysis.

2.1. Domestic firms, foreign firms, and domestic welfare

Suppose there are two groups of firms that are permitted to bid for government procurements: m_d domestic firms and m_f foreign firms. We define $m = m_d + m_f$. Let D denote the set of domestic firms and F the set of foreign firms. Assume there are at least two domestic firms. Let M be the union of the two sets D and F. It is the set of all potential rent-seekers in the game.

After evaluations of "documents" by bureaucrats, one firm will be selected as the winner. (This is a winner-takes-all game.) The probability that firm i wins is assumed to be

$$p_i = \frac{s_i/\beta_i}{\sum s_j/\beta_j},$$

where s_i is firm i's expenditure on lobbying (which includes preparation of documents, formal and informal meetings, etc.) and β_i the effectiveness parameter of its lobbying expenditure. If the contract (often called "prize" in the rent-seeking literature) is awarded to firm i, it generates R_i dollars of profit for the firm. Let t be the exogenous tax rate on profit. Each firm takes the lobbying expenditure of other firms as given, and chooses s_i to maximize its expected net gain:

$$\pi_i = \frac{s_i/\beta_i}{\sum s_j/\beta_j} tR_i - s_i.$$

A Nash equilibrium of the game is a strategy profile such that for each firm i, the strategy s_i is its best response to the strategies of other firms. Formally, the outcome of the game is the assignment to each firm i a probability p_i that it will be the winner.

From the home country's point of view, social welfare, denoted by W, is the sum of (a) expected government revenue and (b) domestic firms' expected net gains. In this social welfare expression, the foreign contribution is only through tax revenue. Notice that the lobbying costs of domestic firms are subtracted from social welfare, because we assume that the costs are real resource costs, not money transfers (such as bribes). For example, if a domestic firm hires a lobbyist to prepare and transmit a document, the lobbyist's time is withdrawn from socially useful activities (such as production of intermediate or the final goods) and re-allocated to a socially useless rent-contest activities (transferring money from one pocket to another).

2.2. Optimization by individual firms

It is convenient to transform variables by defining the "effective effort" of player i as

$$g_i = s_i/\beta_i.$$

The parameter β_i may be interpreted as player i's cost (in money terms) of achieving one unit of g_i. Define "aggregate effective effort" as the sum of the effective efforts of all rent-seekers:

$$G = \sum_{j \in M} g_j.$$

The probability of success of firm i can now be expressed as

$$p_i = \frac{g_i}{g_i + G_{-i}}.$$

Firm i's problem is now transformed into the following format: choose lobbying effort level to maximize

$$\pi_i \equiv \beta_i F_i(g_i) \equiv \beta_i \left[\frac{g_i}{G_{-i} + g_i} \left(\frac{(1-t)R_i}{\beta_i} \right) - g_i \right].$$

We define firm i's "effective valuation" as

$$v_i = \frac{(1-t)R_i}{\beta_i}.$$

Without loss of generality, let us order firms so that $v_1 \geq v_2 \geq v_3 \ldots \geq v_m > 0$. It is also useful to define

$$y_i = \frac{1}{v_i}.$$

We will refer to y_i as firm i's "comparative disadvantage in lobbying".

ASSUMPTION A1. Before liberalization, foreign firms have strong comparative disadvantage in lobbying. In the list of m firms that are ordered in terms of comparative disadvantage in lobbying the first m_d firms are domestic firms, and the remaining firms are foreign firms.

Let us denote, for any positive integer $k \leq m$ the sum of the comparative disadvantage levels of the first k firms by $Y_k \equiv \sum_{i=1}^{k} y_i$. Assumption A1 implies that $my_m \geq Y_m$.

ASSUMPTION A2. (Strong heterogeneity of comparative disadvantage in lobbying) The following inequality holds $(m-1)y_m \geq Y_m$.

As will seen below, this assumption implies that firm m, the foreign firm with the greatest comparative disadvantage level, will not be an active rent-seeker. (Note that our specification that $m > 2$ ensures that Assumption A2 can be satisfied.)

Firm i chooses g_i to maximize its expected profit. Let us note the following properties of the objective function of firm i:

(i) It is zero if g_i is zero, given that the aggregate lobbying of the rivals is positive.
(ii) Its derivative at zero is positive if and only if $v_i > G_{-i}$.
(iii) The objective function is strictly concave in g_i, and its derivative is negative if g_i is sufficiently large.

From the above observations, we obtain the following lemma:

LEMMA 1. *The maximization problem of firm i has a unique solution. The firm will be active in lobbying if and only if the sum of effective efforts of its rivals is strictly less than its own valuation of the prize. It follows that if $v_i > G_{-i}$ then $g_i = 0$; otherwise $g_i = \sqrt{G_{-i}v_i} - G_{-i} > 0$.*

2.3. Properties of Nash equilibriums of the lobbying game

We say that that firm i is an active rent-seeker if his equilibrium lobbying effort is strictly positive.

LEMMA 2. *In any Nash equilibrium there are at least two active rent-seekers.*

PROOF. Suppose there were a Nash equilibrium where firm i is the only active rent seeker. Then $G_{-i} = 0$ and firm i would choose $g_i = 0$, but this would make firm j's marginal benefit of lobbying equal infinity. Thus firm j would choose a strictly positive effort level, contradicting $G_{-i} = 0$.

Consider a Nash equilibrium in which n rent-seekers are active. Let A denote the set of active rent-seekers in that Nash equilibrium. Let us define

$$Y_A \equiv \sum_{i \in A} y_i \quad \text{and}$$

$$G_A \equiv \sum_{i \in A} g_i.$$

Then, for all $i \in A$ the following first-order condition holds:

$$G_A^2 = [G_A - g_i] v_i.$$

Thus the following equation holds in equilibrium, for all $i \in A$,

$$g_i = G_A \left[1 - \frac{G_A}{v_i} \right].$$

Summing over all $i \in A$, we get

$$G_A = n G_A - Y_A (G_A)^2$$

where n is the number of elements of set A, i.e., the number of active rent-seekers in the Nash equilibrium, and Y_A the sum of comparative disadvantage indices of all active rent-seekers.

Dividing by G_A to get

$$1 = n - Y_A (G_A).$$

DEFINITION 1. *The "modified average comparative disadvantage in lobbying" of a group of firms A that consists of n firms is*

$$\frac{Y_A}{n - 1}.$$

We obtain the following result.

PROPOSITION 1. *In a Nash equilibrium with n active rent-seekers, their aggregate effective lobbying effort is equal to the inverse of their modified average comparative disadvantage in lobbying:*

$$G_A = \frac{n-1}{Y_A}.$$

REMARK 1. This proposition is equivalent to the Hillman–Riley result that total outlays closely approximate the harmonic mean of individuals' valuations as the number of participants increases.

We now turn to the question of uniqueness of Nash equilibrium. We will show below that Nash equilibrium is unique. Before doing so, we must state a few results.

LEMMA 3. *Let A be the set of active firms in a Nash equilibrium. If firm $i \in A$, then any firm j with $y_j \leq y_i$ also belongs to A. Hence, if there are exactly n active firms in a Nash equilibrium, they must be the first n firms.*

It follows that $A = \{1, 2, 3, \ldots, n\}$, and $Y_A = Y_n$.

LEMMA 4. *Under Assumption A2, there exists a unique integer $n \in \{2, 3, \ldots, m-1\}$ such that*

$$y_n < \frac{Y_n}{n-1} \quad \text{and}$$

$$y_{n+1} \geq \frac{Y_n}{n-1}.$$

PROPOSITION 2 *(Uniqueness of Nash equilibrium). Let M be the set of permitted rent-seekers. Given Assumption A2, only $n < m$ rent-seekers are active, where n is uniquely determined by the two inequalities in Lemma 4 above. Their equilibrium aggregate effective effort in lobbying is equal to*

$$G_A = \frac{n-1}{Y_A}$$

and the equilibrium pure strategies are as follows. For $i < n$

$$g_i = G(1 - Gy_i) = \left(\frac{n-1}{Y_n}\right)\left[1 - \frac{(n-1)y_i}{Y_n}\right],$$

where Y_n satisfies the cut-off condition

$$y_{n+1} \geq \frac{Y_n}{n-1} > y_n.$$

For all firm $i > n$, the equilibrium lobbying effort is zero.

PROOF. The uniqueness of the set of active firms follows from Lemma 4. To show the uniqueness of equilibrium, suppose there are two different equilibrium strategy profiles, $g = \{g_1, g_2, \ldots, g_n, 0, 0, 0 \ldots, 0\}$ and $q = \{q_1, q_2, \ldots, q_n, 0, 0, 0 \ldots, 0\}$. Then, for all $i \in \{1, 2, \ldots, n\}$

$$\frac{G - g_i}{Q - q_i} = \frac{G^2}{Q^2} \equiv \omega.$$

Thus, for all $i \in \{1, 2, \ldots, n\}$

$$(Q - q_i)\omega = G - g_i.$$

Summing over all active firms, we obtain

$$(n - 1)Q\omega = (n - 1)G.$$

Thus

$$(n - 1)Q\frac{Q^2}{G^2} \equiv (n - 1)G.$$

Hence $Q = G$ and thus $q_i = g_i$.

3. Properties of equilibrium strategies

PROPOSITION 3. *For any active firm i, the following properties hold:*

(i) *(monotonicity of lobbying effort in own comparative advantage)* *Suppose y_i increases by a small amount (while all other y_j stay unchanged), such that n remains unchanged and the cut-off condition remains valid at n. The firm that suffers an increase in its index y_i will reduce its equilibrium lobbying effort.*

(ii) *(non-monotonicity of lobbying effort in rival's comparative advantage)* *Suppose for some $j < n$, where $j \neq i$, y_j increases by a small amount, such that n remains unchanged and the cut-off condition remains valid at n. Then firm i will decrease its lobbying effort if and only if*

$$y_i < \frac{Y_n}{2(n - 1)}.$$

PROOF. Available upon request.

4. Entry of a foreign firm

Suppose initially there are n active domestic firms, and all foreign firms are inactive because their β_f are too high. We let

$$Y_n^d \equiv \sum_{i=1}^n y_i^d.$$

Here the superscript d is used to remind us that the sum is over n *domestic* firms. Then

$$y^d_{n+1} \geq \frac{Y^d_n}{n-1} > y^d_n$$

and the equilibrium aggregate effort is, from Proposition 1:

$$G = \frac{n-1}{Y^d_n}$$

Suppose now a foreign firm f experiences a sufficiently big fall in its β^f, so that y^f falls below the threshold level, that is,

$$y^f < \frac{Y^d_n}{n-1}.$$

This inequality implies that

$$ny^f < Y^d_n + y^f.$$

There are two cases to be considered.

Case A: The foreign firm's comparative disadvantage in lobbying, while satisfying the condition that it is below the threshold level, is still at least as great as that of the most lobby-inefficient domestic firm, i.e.,

$$y^f \geq y^d_n,$$

so that at the new equilibrium, there are $n+1$ active rent seekers.

Case B: The foreign firm's comparative disadvantage in lobbying is lower than that of a non-empty subset of domestic firms. In this case, only k domestic firms remain active (the possibility that k is equal to n is admitted). Then

$$y^d_{k+i} \geq \frac{y^d_1 + \cdots + y^d_k + y^f}{k}$$

while

$$y^f < \frac{y^d_1 + \cdots + y^d_k + y^f}{k}.$$

EXAMPLE 1 (Case A). Initially, $n = 3$ with $y^d_1 = 1$, $y^d_2 = 2$ and $y^d_3 = 2.4$. Then

$$y^d_3 < \frac{1+2+2.4}{n-1} = 2.7.$$

Now, after the fall in β^f, let $y^f = 2.4$. At the new equilibrium, all four firms are active, since

$$y^d_3 = y^f < \frac{1+2+2.4+2.4}{4-1} = 2.6.$$

EXAMPLE 2 (Case B). Initially, $n = 3$ with $y_1^d = 1$, $y_2^d = 2$ and $y_3^d = 2.4$. Assume that after the fall in β^f, we have $y^f = 1$. Then the domestic firm 3 ceases to be active because

$$y_3^d > \frac{1 + 1.5 + 2}{2} = 2.25.$$

PROPOSITION 4. *In both cases A and B, total effective lobbying effort increases after the entry.*

PROOF. Consider first Case B. Before entry, there are n active firms. After entry, there are $n - (n - k) + 1 = k + 1$ active firms, of which k are domestic firms. Let G^b and G^a denote the before-entry and after-entry aggregate efforts (the superscripts b and a refer before-entry and after-entry, respectively). We now show that $G^a > G^b$. This inequality holds if and only if

$$\frac{k}{Y_k^d + y^f} > \frac{n - 1}{Y_n^d}.$$

That is, if and only if

$$k Y_n^d > (n - 1)\left(Y_k^d + y^f\right).$$

Consider the left-hand side of the above inequality

$$k Y_n^d \equiv k Y_k^d + k\left(y_{k+1}^d + \cdots + y_n^d\right) \geq k Y_k^d + (n - k)k y_{k+1}^d$$
$$\geq k Y_k^d + (n - k)\left(Y_k^d + y^f\right)$$
$$= n Y_k^d + (n - k)y^f > (n - 1)Y_k^d + (n - 1)(y^f),$$

where the last strict inequality follows from

$$y^f < \frac{Y_k^d + y^f}{k}.$$

It follows that

$$k Y_n^d > (n - 1)\left(Y_k^d + y^f\right).$$

Next, consider Case A. Simply set $k = n$ and the above proof applies to this case.

PROPOSITION 5. *(Entry of a foreign firm leads to decreased lobbying by inefficient domestic firms)*
Suppose that before entry, there are n active firms. The before-entry equilibrium lobbying effort of domestic firm i, denoted by g_i^b, is given by

$$g_i^b = G^b\left(1 - G^b y_i^d\right) = \frac{n - 1}{Y_n^d}\left[1 - \left(\frac{n - 1}{Y_n^d}\right)y_i^d\right] \equiv X^b\left(1 - X^b y_i^d\right).$$

After entry, there are $k + 1$ active firms, where $k = n$ in case A, and $k < n$ in case B. The after-entry equilibrium lobbying effort of domestic firm i, *denoted by g_i^a, is given by*

$$g_i^a = G^a\left(1 - G^a y_i^d\right) = \frac{k}{Y_k^d + y^f}\left[1 - \left(\frac{k}{Y_n^k + y^f}\right)y_i^d\right] \equiv X^a\left(1 - X^a y_i^d\right).$$

There exists a critical level y_c, such that domestic firm i will intensify its lobbying effort upon the entry of the foreign firm if and only if $y_i^d < y_c$.

PROOF. Define

$$Y^a \equiv Y_k^d + y^f.$$

We want to find a value y_c such that if $y_i^d < y_c$ then

$$\frac{g_i^b}{g_i^a} < 1.$$

Now, consider the ratio

$$\frac{g_i^b}{g_i^a} = \frac{X^b\left(1 - X^b y_i^d\right)}{X^a\left(1 - X^a y_i^d\right)}.$$

Note that $g_i^b < g_i^a$ if and only if the following critical inequality is satisfied:

$$y_i^d\left(X^a + X^b\right)\left(X^a - X^b\right) < X^a - X^b.$$

Observe that

$$X^a - X^b = \frac{k}{Y^a} - \frac{n-1}{Y_n^d} > 0 \quad \text{and}$$

$$X^a + X^b = \frac{(2n-1)Y_n^d + (n-1)y^f}{Y^a Y_n^d} > 0.$$

It follows that the above critical inequality is satisfied if and only if

$$y_i^d < \frac{1}{X^b + X^a} \equiv y_c.$$

EXAMPLE 3. There are two domestic firms, with $y_1^d = 0.10$ and $y_2^d = 0.20$. Firm 3, the foreign firm, has high comparative disadvantage before liberalization, say $y_3^f = 4/10$. Then, before liberalization, only the two domestic firms are active:

$$Y_n^b < \frac{1}{10} + \frac{1}{5} = \frac{3}{10}$$

$$G^b = \frac{n-1}{Y_n} = 3.333$$

$$g_1^b = G^b\left(1 - G^b y_1^d\right) = 2.222 \quad \text{and}$$

$$g_2^b = G^b\left(1 - G^b y_2^d\right) = 1.111.$$

After liberalization, suppose β^f falls so that $y_3^f = 1/5 = y_2^d$. Entry is then profitable to the foreign firm. After entry

$$Y_{n+1}^a = \frac{1}{10} + \frac{1}{5} + \frac{1}{5} = \frac{1}{2}.$$

It follows that

$$y_c = \frac{1}{X^b + X^a} = \frac{Y_n^b Y_{n+1}^a}{(2n-1)Y_n^b + (n-1)y^f} = 0.11538.$$

Thus $G^a = 4$, $g_1^a = 2.43 > g_1^b$ and $g_3^a = g_2^a = 0.8 < g_2^b$.

REMARK 2. This example shows that the sum of lobbying efforts of the two domestic firms falls after the foreign entry.

We now state a necessary and sufficient condition for aggregate domestic lobbying to fall. Observe that the aggregate domestic lobbying falls if and only if

$$G^a - g^f - G^b < 0.$$

Now

$$g^f = G^a - y^f(G^a)^2$$

So the necessary and sufficient condition is

$$y^f(G^a)^2 - G^b < 0.$$

That is,

$$y^f < \left(\frac{n-1}{Y_n^b}\right)\left(\frac{Y_k + y^f}{k}\right)^2.$$

A sufficient condition for this inequality to be satisfied is that y^f is close to zero. Thus we have proved:

PROPOSITION 6. *If the foreign entrant is very efficient, total aggregate domestic lobbying effort will fall (but remains positive).*

5. Effects of foreign entry on welfare

Consider two scenarios. In the first scenario, all rent-seekers are domestic firms. The foreign firms are not permitted to bid, so their β^f is infinity. Social welfare of the home country, before liberalization, is the sum of expected tax revenue and expected net gains by domestic firms:

$$W^b = \sum_{i \in D} \left(p_i^b R_i - s_i^b \right).$$

In the second scenario, foreign firms are allowed to bid, i.e., some of the β^f falls. Suppose n^f foreign firms cross the threshold and become active rent-seekers. Social welfare of the home country, after liberalization, is then

$$W^a = \sum_{i \in D} \left(p_i^a R_i - s_i^a \right) + \sum_{j \in F} p_j^a t R_j.$$

The second sum, being tax revenue from foreign profits, is positive. Thus there is a net welfare gain, if and only if the (before-tax) expected net gain to domestic firms fall by less than the expected tax revenue collected from the foreign firms. We will show below that the (before-tax) expected net gain to domestic firms does fall as a result of foreign entry, i.e.,

$$\sum_{i \in D} \left(p_i^b R_i - s_i^b \right) > \sum_{i \in D} \left(p_i^a R_i - s_i^a \right).$$

PROPOSITION 7. *The probability of success of any active domestic firm falls after entry of a foreign firm.*

PROOF.

$$p_i^b = \frac{g_i^b}{G^b} = 1 - G^b y_i > 1 - G^a y_i = \frac{g_i^a}{G^a} = p_i^a.$$

PROPOSITION 8. *Expected profit (whether before or after tax) of each active domestic firm falls after a foreign entry.*

PROOF. The change in expected after-tax net profit is

$$(p_i^a - p_i^b)\frac{1}{y_i} + (g_i^b - g_i^a).$$

The first term is negative. The second term is clearly negative if $y_i < y_c$, i.e., if firm i is very efficient. For less efficient domestic firms, the second term is positive. However, we still can show that the first term dominates, so that expected profit falls after entry. The proof consists of noting the following inequalities:

$$\pi_i^a = g_i^a \left[\frac{1}{y_i G^a} - 1 \right] < g_i^b \left[\frac{1}{y_i G^a} - 1 \right] < g_i^b \left[\frac{1}{y_i G^b} - 1 \right] = \pi_i^b.$$

EXAMPLE 4. We continue with example 3 in the preceding section. Suppose $\beta_1 = \beta_2 = 1$ and $R_1 = 10$ $R_2 = 5$

Before entry,

$$p_1^b = \frac{g_1^b}{g_1^b + g_2^b} = \frac{2}{3}$$

$$\sum_{i=1}^{2} p_i^b R_i = \frac{25}{3}$$

$$\sum_{i=1}^{2} s_i^b = 3$$

$$W^b = \frac{16}{3} = 5.33.$$

Suppose that only one foreign firm enters. After entry,

$$p_1^a = \frac{2.4}{0.8 + 0.8 + 2.4} = 0.6,$$

$$p_2^a = \frac{0.8}{0.8 + 0.8 + 2.4} = 0.2, \quad \text{and}$$

$$s_1^a + s_2^b = 2.4 + 0.8 = 3.2.$$

It follows that $W^a > 5.33$ if and only if $tR_3 > 7.66$. Suppose $t = 0.5$. Then the net social gain is positive if and only if $R_3 > 15.33$. Since we have assumed that $y_3 = \frac{1}{v_3} = (\beta_3^f/(1-t))R_3 = \frac{1}{5}$, the condition that $R_3 > 15.33$ implies that $\beta_3^f = ((1-t)R_3/5) > 1.533$.

Thus, if the domestic firm's lobbying effort is about 50% more effective than the foreign counterpart, and the foreign firm's operating net revenue is about 50% more than that of the most efficient domestic firm, there will be a net gain in social welfare when the foreign firm is permitted to lobby for government procurement.

6. Mean-preserving spreads

Given the set of values $\{y_1, y_2, ..., y_m\}$ let $n < m$ be the equilibrium number of active rent seekers. Then the equilibrium total effective lobbying expenditure is

$$G^b = \frac{n-1}{Y_m}$$

and the equilibrium effective lobbying expenditure of player i is

$$g_i^b = G^b(1 - G^b y_i) = \frac{n-1}{Y_n}\left[1 - \frac{(n-1)y_i}{Y_n}\right].$$

Firm $n+1$ will enter as an active player if and only if y_{n+1} is lower than the threshold level $Y_n/(n-1)$:

$$y_{n+1} < \frac{Y_n}{n-1}.$$

He would not enter if $y_{n+1} \geq Y_n/(n-1)$.

Given n active agents, consider a mean-preserving spread (MPS) in the distribution $\{y_1, y_2, \ldots, y_m\}$ Such a MPS does not encourage entry of the player $n + 1$. This holds, as long as the new y_n remains lower than y_{n+1}.

PROPOSITION 9. *(i) A mean-preserving spread of the distribution of the y_i's of the domestic firms will not encourage entry of the foreign firms.*

(ii) A mean-preserving spread of the distribution of the v_i's of the domestic firms may encourage foreign entries.

PROOF. Part (i) is obvious. For part (ii), suppose that n is an even integer, and the first $n/2$ active players have effective valuation $v_i = v + \varepsilon$ (where $v > \varepsilon > 0$) and the remaining $n/2$ active players have effective valuation $v_i = v - \varepsilon$. A small increase in ε represents a mean-preserving spread of the distribution $\{v_1, v_2, \ldots, v_m\}$. Such a MPS increases Y_n, because

$$Y_n = \sum_i \frac{1}{v_i} = (n/2)\frac{1}{v + \varepsilon} + (n/2)\frac{1}{v - \varepsilon} = \frac{n}{2}\left(\frac{2v}{v^2 - \varepsilon^2}\right)$$

and

$$\frac{\partial Y_n}{\partial \varepsilon} > 0.$$

7. Concluding remarks

We have shown that a relaxation of rules that restrict foreign firms from participating in contests for government procurements can increase domestic welfare. Several factors contribute to this result. First, the aggregate lobbying efforts of all domestic firms may fall. Second, foreign lobbying that uses host country's resources is not a social waste (from the point of view of the host country). Third, the foreign firm may be more profitable, which contributes more to the tax revenue of the host country.

There are a number of questions that can be raised. Suppose all domestic firms are identical, what is the optimal number of foreign firms that should be allowed to bid? What is the effect of foreign entry on global welfare? What are the welfare implications of reciprocal opening up of government procurements?

Acknowledgement

Constructive comments from a referee are gratefully acknowledged.

References

Auriol, E. (2006), Corruption in procurement and public purchase. *International Journal of Industrial Organization* 24 (5), 867–885.

Evenett, S.J., Hoekman, B.H. (2005), Government procurement: market access, transparency, and multilateral trade rules. *European Journal of Political Economy* 21 (1), 163–183.

Hillman, A.L., Riley, J. (1989), Politically contestable rents and transfers. *Economics and Politics* 1 (1), 17–39.

Mougeot, M., Naegelen, F. (2005), A political economy analysis of preferential public procurement policies. *European Journal of Political Economy* 21 (2), 483–501.

Nitzan, S. (1994), Modelling rent-seeking contests. *European Journal of Political Economy* 10 (1), 41–60.

OECD. (2005), *Fighting Corruption and Promoting Integrity in Public Procurement.* OECD, Paris.

Transparency International (2007). Global Corruption Report 2007, Cambridge University Press, Cambridge, UK.

Trionfetti, F. (2000), Discriminatory public procurement and international trade. *World Economy* 23 (1), 57–76.

Tullock, G. (1980), Efficient rent seeking. In: Buchanan, J., Tollinson, R., Tullock, G. (Eds.), *Toward a Theory of Rent Seeking Society.* Texas A&M University Press, College Station, TX.

PART II

Trading Clubs and Preferential Trade Agreements

CHAPTER 6

Normative Comparisons of Customs Unions and Other Types of Free Trade Association

Murray C. Kemp

University of New South Wales, 6/77 Ocean St, Woollahra, NSW 2025, Australia
E-mail address: murraykemp@bigpond.com

Abstract

Purpose – The chapter examines whether the well-known Kemp–Wan proposition about customs unions is valid for free trade associations (FTAs).
Methodology/approach – The chapter employs the assumption of perfect competition but with considerable generality.
Findings – It is shown that the Kemp–Wan proposition is valid for any form of FTA. It is also shown that sense can be made of the common conjecture that a customs union is more beneficial to the world economy than a comparable but distinct FTA.
Originality/value – The findings are of significance in view of the recent tendency of governments to prefer FTAs to customs unions.

Keywords: Trade gains, customs unions, free trade associations

Paper type: Research paper

1. Introduction

Free trade associations (FTAs) are the best known and have been the most closely examined of all preferential trading arrangements (PTAs); and, in the general class of FTAs, special attention has been focussed on customs unions (CUs), in each of which the member countries share a common tariff vector. Perhaps the most widely accepted proposition concerning CUs is the so-called Kemp–Wan proposition; see Kemp (1964, p. 176) and Kemp and Wan (1976, 1986), also Vanek (1965, pp. 160–165) and Ohyama (1972). Indeed, for a long time, it was the only available proposition of any generality; its only competitor was the rather vague Vinerian proposition that a CU might be either 'trade diverting' or 'trade creating'; see Viner (1950). In quite recent times, however, there has

Frontiers of Economics and Globalization
Volume 5   ISSN: 1574-8715
DOI: 10.1016/S1574-8715(08)05006-9

developed an interest in two normative questions closely related to each other and to the Kemp–Wan proposition.

(i) Can we find a result parallel to the Kemp–Wan proposition but applying to FTAs that are not also CUs?
(ii) Can it be shown that a CU is more beneficial or less harmful to the world economy than a comparable but distinct FTA that is not also a CU?

The first of the above questions has already been addressed by Ohyama (2002) and Panagariya and Krishna (2002). They answered the question in the affirmative. However, in both papers it was assumed that each member country chooses its tariffs so that the vector of that member's aggregate trades with non-member countries remains unchanged at its pre-FTA level.

PROPOSITION 1. *(Ohyama and Panagariya–Krishna): An FTA in which each member country adjusts its tariffs so as to keep the quantity of its trade with non-member countries at the pre-FTA level is beneficial to the world as a whole.*

Evidently the assumption in Proposition 1, that the country-specific FTA tariffs maintain the pre-FTA trade vector of *each member country* with the rest of the world, is much more restrictive than is the assumption of Kemp and Wan, that the *aggregate* trade vector of member countries is maintained at its pre-FTA level. Thus the results obtained by Ohyama and by Panagariya and Krishna for FTAs are not parallel to or closely similar to the Kemp–Wan proposition.[1] Whether it is necessary to assume that each member country chooses its tariffs to preserve its pre-FTA trade vector with the rest of the world remains an open question.

It is often implicitly assumed that the second question also can be answered in the affirmative. However, standing in the way of effective analysis of the question has been vagueness about the *constituency* (whose welfare is at issue?) and about the sense in which a CU and an FTA may be described as *comparable*. The question has been formally addressed only in a very brief note by Kemp (2000). However Kemp's method of attack on the second question throws new light on the first question. In the present chapter, then, I offer a coordinated re-examination of both questions. It will be shown in Section 2 that if the compensated excess demand functions of member countries are differentiable then, except in a singular case, there always exists a Pareto-improving FTA in which the pre-FTA aggregate trade vectors of member countries with non-member countries are preserved: The more restrictive condition imposed by Ohyama and by Panagariya and Krishna is unnecessary. It will be shown also that

---

[1] For a contrary opinion, see Raimondos-Møller and Woodland (2006, p. 80).

corresponding to each FTA there is a Pareto-preferred and feasible CU (strongly preferred if the FTA is not also a CU).

In Section 3 and in the Appendix it will be shown that the new proposition is valid whether or not excluded countries respond to the formation of an FTA by adjusting their own tariffs. And, finally, Section 4 summarizes the findings of the chapter and provides several cautionary remarks, technical as well as political-economic, concerning the interpretation of the findings.

2. *Analysis*

Consider an Arrow–Debreu (Arrow and Debreu, 1954) world economy containing N, $N > 2$, countries which trade in two or more commodities. (Since each commodity is distinguished by its date of delivery, international borrowing and lending are implicitly accommodated.) Let $N \equiv \{1, ..., N\}$. Initially, each country maintains an arbitrary tariff vector and there is a tariff-distorted world equilibrium (TWE), not necessarily unique. Sontheimer (1971) has provided sufficient conditions for the existence of equilibrium; see also Kemp and Wan (1995).

The initial TWE is disturbed by the formation of a Kemp–Wan CU comprising a subset N' of the trading countries. Among the defining characteristics of the CU is a common tariff vector and a scheme of lump-sum compensation, restricted to households in the CU, such that (a) the pre- and post-CU equilibrium aggregate net import vectors of the member countries are identical and (b) no household, whether inside or outside the CU, is worse off after the formation of the CU. Kemp and Wan (1986) have provided sufficient conditions for the existence of a post-CU equilibrium and have shown that, in that equilibrium, (c) the net tariff revenue of the CU can be made at least as large as the net compensation accruing to individual households in the CU.

Let us now assume explicitly that, in the Kemp–Wan equilibrium, at least one member country is strictly better off than in the initial TWE, so that the Kemp–Wan CU is strictly Pareto-preferred to the TWE. Let us assume also that the compensated excess demand functions of member countries are differentiable. Given these assumptions, it is possible to disturb the Kemp–Wan CU by marginally manipulating the tariff vectors of individual member countries, abandoning the common tariff vector but leaving unchanged the aggregate import vector of the CU and the equilibrium world price vector.[2] The new trading association obtained in this way is an FTA. Some member countries may be worse off in the FTA than in the TWE. However, any changes in the wellbeing of members are

---

[2] The N vectors of marginal tariff changes are, of course, not uniquely determined by this requirement.

of the second order; and at least one member of the Kemp–Wan CU is strictly better off in the union than in the TWE. Hence, losing members can be compensated to ensure that all members remain better off in the FTA than in the TWE. However, it is not possible to ensure that all members are better off than in the Kemp–Wan CU. Indeed in *no* compensated FTA with the property that its aggregate net imports remain at their TWE levels (that is, in *no* Kemp–Wan FTA) is it possible to ensure that outcome; for to suppose the contrary is to suppose that a *tariff-distorted* compensated equilibrium of the economy which comprises the subset N' of countries, with the aggregate factor endowment of those countries adjusted by the addition of their (unchanging) aggregate TWE net import vector, exists and is Pareto-preferred to an *undistorted* equilibrium of the same economy. Moreover, each Kemp–Wan FTA which is not a Kemp–Wan CU is Pareto-inferior to at least one Kemp–Wan CU. Thus we arrive at the following proposition.

PROPOSITION 2. *Consider any TWE and an associated strictly Pareto-preferred Kemp–Wan CU. Corresponding to the TWE there is a strictly Pareto-preferred and feasible Kemp–Wan FTA; and corresponding to each feasible Kemp–Wan FTA there is a Pareto-preferred and feasible Kemp–Wan CU.*

From the first part of Proposition 2 we learn that a Pareto-improving FTA need not retain the pre-FTA member-specific vectors of net imports from the rest of the world: Proposition 1 *can* be extended. That part of Proposition 2, added to the original Kemp–Wan proposition, establishes the existence of both Pareto-improving Kemp–Wan FTAs and Pareto-improving Kemp–Wan CUs.

To Proposition 2 I now add an incidental result: corresponding to each Ohyama–Panagariya–Krishna FTA there is a Pareto-preferred Kemp–Wan CU; for in the former, but not in the latter, commodity prices differ from one member country to another.

We note also that Proposition 2 is valid for *partial* FTEs, that is, for FTEs that allow each member country to maintain by subsidy its output of each of a subset of commodities at its TWE level.[3] To accommodate partial FTAs one need only assign to each member country its TWE production set restricted by the constancy of the subsidized outputs at their TWE levels. In other words, the member's assigned production set is the projection of its TWE production set on the hyperplane defined by the constant subsidized outputs; see Kemp (2001, p. 67).

In deriving Proposition 2 I have relied on the assumption that the compensated excess demand functions of member countries are

---

[3] Ohyama (2002) has noted that the Ohyama–Panagariya–Krishna result also can be extended to accommodate partial *FTAs*.

differentiable. The assumption is not trivial. Without it, I can establish the second part of the proposition but not the first: I can construct particular examples in which Pareto-improving Kemp–Wan FTAs exist but I cannot obtain a general result valid for all examples.[4]

3. Extensions of Theorem 2

Kemp and Wan (1976) assumed that countries excluded from a CU are completely passive; in particular, they do not adjust their own tariffs in response to the common external tariff (CET) of the CU. Similar assumptions have been implicit in the analysis of Section 2. Evidently, the assumptions are quite restrictive. However, they can be relaxed.

3.1. Non-passive non-members

It has recently been shown by Kemp and Shimomura (2001a) that, even if those countries excluded from a CU are alert to the possibility of modifying their tariffs in response to the union's choice of CET, the union may thwart non-members by revealing to them not a specific CET but a formula which describes how the CET is determined for each set of non-member tariff vectors and which provides adequate incentives for excluded countries to refrain from retaliation. Proposition 2 can be protected in a similar way. Confronted by non-members which respond to its choice of tariff vector, each member of a Kemp–Wan FTA may reveal to non-members not a specific tariff vector but a formula which describes how that vector is determined for each set of non-member tariff vectors and which provides adequate incentives for excluded countries to refrain from retaliation. A detailed demonstration may be found in the Appendix.

---

[4] This becomes apparent if we attempt to reconstruct the detailed Panagariya–Krishna proof of Proposition 1 on the basis of Kemp–Wan assumptions. For then their Equation (2) must be revised: m^o and M^o must be replaced by m^f and M^f, respectively. This adds a new term $(p^f + P^f)(M^o - M^f)$ to the right-hand side of their crucial Equation (5) and minus that term must be added to their Equation (7). Thus the Ohyama–Panagariya–Krishna assumption can be replaced with the Kemp–Wan assumption only if we are prepared to place some restrictions on the response of the individual member-country excess demand vectors to the formation of the *FTA*. In deriving Proposition 2, I did not need to explicitly introduce extra restrictions of this kind. Nevertheless, such restrictions were already implicit in my reliance on the differential approach; that approach ensured that the term $(p^f + P^f)(M^o - M^f)$ is sufficiently small.

3.2. Public goods

It is now known also that the Kemp–Wan proposition (Kemp and Wan, 1976) can accommodate public goods, whether or not they are internationally tradable, provided that each member country holds its production of each public good at its pre-union level; see Kemp (2001, pp. 61–62). Proposition 2 can be extended in the same way. A Kemp–Wan FTA with the output of public goods set in this way displays the essential properties of fiscal federalism; see Hillman (2003, pp. 567–573) and Buettner and Wildasin (2007).

4. Summarizing and cautionary remarks

In the present chapter, it has been shown that if there exists a strictly Pareto-improving Kemp–Wan CU and if the compensated excess demand functions of member countries are differentiable then Proposition 1 can be freed of the restrictive Ohyama–Panagariya–Krishna assumption that the initial TWE trade vector of each member country with the rest of the world is maintained when an FTA is formed. The first of my assumptions is innocuous; it simply rules out limiting special examples of the initial TWE. The second assumption is standard but substantial. Moreover, it is essential to the reasoning of Section 2; without it, it is not certain that a parallel to the Kemp–Wan proposition exists.

I have focussed on a particular question of existence: Does there always exist a Pareto-improving and feasible Kemp–Wan FTA? I found that question interesting because the Kemp–Wan assumptions are analytically less restrictive than the alternative Ohyama–Panagariya–Krishna assumptions. However, I readily agree with Professor Ohyama's remark (in correspondence) that assumptions that are analytically more restrictive might be politically more acceptable. Governments of the world have revealed a clear preference for FTAs over CUs, possibly because the former offer to each member country greater freedom of choice of tariffs and are therefore less objectionable from the viewpoint of highly sensitive domestic industries (e.g., agriculture in Japan) and from the viewpoint of equally sensitive non-member countries with rights of market access negotiated in the past under the GATT (one recalls the expansion of the EEC to the south and its effect on the trade in agricultural products of the United States). On occasion, and for similar reasons, governments may be found to prefer Ohyama–Panagariya–Krishna FTAs to Kemp–Wan FTAs. However, in practice, political choices are invariably made from alternative FTAs and CUs none of which is of the fully compensated Ohyama–Panagariya–Krishna or Kemp–Wan type.

In establishing Proposition 2, it has been convenient to follow Kemp and Wan (1976, 1986) in assuming that trading countries excluded from a

PTA passively accept the new tariffs of member countries. As noted in Section 3, however, that assumption is unnecessary: In any competitive, tariff-ridden context it is possible for a subset of trading countries to form a PTA that enhances the wellbeing of each member country without hurting non-member countries *even when the latter seek to retaliate by manipulating their own tariffs.* This extended proposition, like the parent Kemp–Wan proposition, confirms the possibility of improving world wellbeing by forming a *single* PTA. In the real world, however, there are many PTAs, most of them FTAs. The policy-relevant question therefore takes a new form: Given any two (or more) non-overlapping subsets of the trading countries, do there always exist two (or more) PTAs that together ensure an improvement in world welfare? The answer is in the negative: The reasoning employed in Kemp and Shimomura (2001a) (and in Section 3 and the Appendix of the present chapter) cannot be applied to this question for it is not possible for each of two (or more) PTAs to behave as Stackelberg price leaders.[5]

Finally, we recall that the analysis of Section 2 has been conducted in terms of straightforward extensions of the Arrow–Debreu model of a closed economy. In that model, all households and firms are price takers. However, the model is finite in all respects, implying that all households and firms possess market power. The apparent incompatibility of these features is considered in detail by Kemp (2005a, 2005b). Here we note only that internal consistency in the model can be preserved only by adding the assumption that each household is incompletely informed (about the economy of which it is a member) or incompletely rational (unable to appreciate the implications of membership for its market power) or both. With that additional assumption, and perhaps paradoxically, the familiar existence theorem and the fundamental welfare propositions of Arrow and Debreu (1954) remain intact and so do the several propositions of Section 2. Thus a little carefully delineated ignorance and/or irrationality can serve as a helpful preservative. But if the assumption of imperfect knowledge and/or irrationality is unacceptable then one must fall back on the model proposed by Kemp and Shimomura (2001b), excluding non-convex production sets while continuing to admit market power on the part of households. Appeal might then be made to the single-economy existence result of Nishimura and Friedman (1981, Theorem 1). However, it must be borne in mind that the Nishimura–Friedman result rests on assumptions unlike those of Arrow and Debreu in that they are imposed on households' best responses to the strategies of other households, which are normally viewed as endogenous variables, not directly on the customary defining elements of an economy (preferences, technologies and

---

[5] A similar remark applies to the analysis of *non*-preferential trading arrangements of the type examined by Raimondos-Møller and Woodland (2006).

endowments (including information)). For an unsympathetic discussion of the widespread resort to restrictions on endogenous variables, see Kemp and Wan (2005).

Acknowledgements

An earlier version of this article appeared in the *European Journal of Political Economy* 23: 416–422. I am grateful to Elsevier Science Publishers for permission to recycle the article. I acknowledge with gratitude the stimulating comments of Michihiro Ohyama.

Appendix: The extended Kemp–Wan FTA

N countries trade in $M+1$ commodities, labelled $0, 1, \ldots, M$. Commodity 0 is the numéraire and remains free of duty in each country. In Section 2 it was supposed that initially, before the formation of an FTA, each country $n, n \in N$, imposes an *arbitrary* vector of tariffs $(0, \tau_1^n, \ldots, \tau_M^n) \equiv (0, \tau^n)$. The N country-specific tariff vectors then determine the TWE price vector $p(\tau^1, \ldots, \tau^N)$, not necessarily uniquely.

In this appendix, however, we focus on the particular case in which, both initially and after the formation of an FTA, all countries impose Bertrand-optimal tariff vectors. Let us suppose for the time being that the TWE is uniquely determined and let us indicate both the country-specific tariff vectors and the TWE price vector by asterisks: $\tau_*^n, n \in N; p_*(\tau_*^1, \ldots, \tau_*^N)$. The domestic TWE price vectors are then $p_* + \tau_*^n, n \in N$.

The TWE is disturbed when the first N' countries form a Kemp–Wan FTA (defined in Section 2). Let us indicate by $\Delta \equiv (\Delta^1, \ldots, \Delta^{N'})$ the balanced or self-financing scheme of lump-sum transfers in the FTA. Then, since non-member countries are passive in a Kemp–Wan FTA, member country n imposes a tariff vector $\tilde{\tau}^n(p(\tau_*^1, \ldots, \tau_*^N), \tau_*^{N'+1}, \ldots, \tau_*^N, \Delta) \equiv \hat{\tau}^n(\tau_*^1, \ldots, \tau_*^N, \Delta), n \in N'$. In view of Proposition 2, world prices remain at their TWE levels and all member countries are better off in the new world equilibrium.

If, as we now suppose, non-member countries are prepared to adjust their tariff vectors so that they are optimal in the post-FTA situation, Proposition 2 is no longer directly relevant to a member's choice of tariff vector. However, member countries may reveal to non-member countries the *tariff* functions

$$
\tilde{\tau}^n \left(p \left(\tau_*^1, \ldots, \tau_*^{N'}, \tau^{N'+1}, \ldots, \tau^N \right), \tau^{N'+1}, \ldots, \tau^N, \Delta \right)
$$
$$
\equiv \hat{\tau}^n \left(\tau_*^1, \ldots, \tau_*^{N'}, \tau^{N'+1}, \ldots, \tau^N, \Delta \right), \quad n \in N,
$$

thus inducing each non-member country l to choose its optimal tariff vector on the Bertrand assumption that the tariffs of other non-members are given and on the non-Bertrand assumption that member country n's choice of tariff vector responds to l's choice of tariffs and no longer takes world prices as constant at their TWE levels. It is then optimal for l to retain its TWE tariff vector if all other non-member countries do so. For country l knows that the post-FTA world price vector is $p\left(\tau_*^1, \ldots, \tau_*^{N'}, \tau^{N'+1}, \ldots, \tau^l, \ldots, \tau^N, \varDelta\right)$ so that, by definition of a Nash equilibrium, if $\tau^k = \tau_*^k$ $(k > N', k \neq l)$ then country l will retain its TWE tariff vector τ_*^l.

That almost completes our analysis. It remains only to recall that, throughout the appendix, it has been assumed that the TWE is based on the search by each government for an optimal tariff vector and on the assumption of uniqueness. The same assumptions were made by Kemp and Shimomura (2001a). However, Kemp and Shimomura showed that, for their purposes, neither assumption is needed. By reasoning similar to theirs, it can be shown that the assumptions are not needed in the present context either.

Finally, throughout the appendix it has been implicitly assumed that in each country factors of production (including profit-maximizing producers) are perfectly (costlessly) mobile between occupations. That this assumption is unnecessary has been argued in a companion paper; see Kemp (in press).

References

Arrow, K.J., Debreu, G. (1954), Existence of an equilibrium for a competitive economy. *Econometrica* 32 (3), 265–290.

Buettner, T., Wildasin, D.E. (2007), Symposium on new directions in fiscal federalism: an introduction. In: Buettler, T., Wildasin, D.E. (Eds.), *Symposium on New Directions in Fiscal Federalism*. CESifo Economic Studies, Vol. 53(4), pp. 491–636.

Hillman, A.L. (2003), *Public Finance and Public Policy*. Cambridge University Press, Cambridge, MA.

Kemp, M.C. (1964), *The Pure Theory of International Trade*. Prentice Hall, Englewood Cliffs, NJ.

Kemp, M.C. (2000), Welfare comparisons of customs unions and other free trade associations. *Pacific Economic Review* 5(1), 1–3. Reprinted in corrected form in Kemp, M.C. (2001), *International Trade and National Welfare*. Routledge, London, pp. 63–65.

Kemp, M.C. (2005a), Price taking in general equilibrium. *American Journal of Applied Sciences* 2 (Special Issue), 78–80.

Kemp, M.C. (2005b), Trade gains: the end of the road? *Singapore Economic Review* 50 (Special Issue), 361–368.

Kemp, M.C. (in press), Non-competing factor groups and the normative propositions of trade theory. *International Review of Economics and Finance*.

Kemp, M.C., Shimomura, K. (2001a), A second elementary proposition concerning the formation of customs unions. *Japanese Economic Review* 52 (1), 64–69.

Kemp, M.C., Shimomura, K. (2001b), Gains from trade in a Cournot–Nash general equilibrium. *Japanese Economic Review* 52 (3), 284–302.

Kemp, M.C., Wan, H.Y. (1976), An elementary proposition concerning the formation of customs unions. *Journal of International Economics* 6 (1), 95–97.

Kemp, M.C., Wan, H.Y. (1986), The comparison of second-best equilibria: the case of customs unions. In: Bös, D., Seidl, C. (Eds.), *Welfare Economics of the Second Best, Supplementum 5 of Zeitschrift für Nationalökonomie*. Springer-Verlag, Vienna, pp. 161–167.

Kemp, M.C., Wan, H.Y. (1995), The gains from free trade. In: Kemp, M.C. (Ed.), *The Gains from Trade and the Gains from Aid*. Routledge, London, pp. 21–36.

Kemp, M.C., Wan, H.Y. (2005), On the existence of equivalent tariff vectors – when the status quo matters. *Singapore Economic Review* 50 (Special Issue), 345–359.

Nishimura, K., Friedman, J.W. (1981), Existence of Nash equilibrium in n person games without quasi-concavity. *International Economic Review* 22 (3), 637–648.

Ohyama, M. (1972), Trade and welfare in general equilibrium. *Keio Economic Studies* 9 (2), 37–73.

Ohyama, M. (2002), The economic significance of the GATT/WTO rules. In: Woodland, A.D. (Ed.), *Economic Theory and International Trade*. Edward Elgar, Cheltenham, pp. 71–85.

Panagariya, A., Krishna, P. (2002), On necessarily welfare-enhancing free trade areas. *Journal of International Economics* 57 (2), 353–367.

Raimondos-Møller, P., Woodland, A.D. (2006), Non-preferential trading clubs. *Journal of International Economics* 68 (1), 77–91.

Sontheimer, K.C. (1971), On the existence of international trade equilibrium. *Econometrica* 39 (6), 1015–1036.

Vanek, J. (1965), *General Equilibrium of International Discrimination: The Case of Customs Unions*. MIT Press, Cambridge, MA.

Viner, J. (1950), *The Customs Union Issue*. Carnegie Endowment for International Peace, New York.

CHAPTER 7

A Free Trade Area and its Neighbor's Welfare: A Revealed Preference Approach

Masahiro Endoh[a], Koichi Hamada[b] and Koji Shimomura[c]

[a]Faculty of Business and Commerce, Keio University, Mita, Minato-ku, Tokyo, 108-8345, Japan
E-mail address: endoh@fbc.keio.ac.jp
[b]Department of Economics, Yale University, New Haven, CT 06520-8269, USA
E-mail address: koichi.hamada@yale.edu
[c]Research Institute for Economics & Business Administration, Kobe University, Japan

Abstract

Purpose – A free trade agreement (FTA) or a preferential trade agreement (PTA) is almost always negotiated without concessions to the non-member countries. This chapter studies the welfare effects of such an FTA or PTA on the non-member countries.

Methodology/approach – This chapter employs the revealed preference approach (e.g., Ohyama, 1972; Kemp and Wan, 1976; Deardorff, 1980).

Findings – Under such conditions that the initial levels of the tariffs are small, or that the effects on production efficiency dominate the effects on tariff revenue, or that the tax-subsidy scheme proposed by Bhagwati, Ramaswami, and Srinivasan is employed in all the countries, the formation of a PTA without any tariff concessions to the outside countries will harm the welfare of the outside countries.

Practical implications – In order to make a PTA beneficial not only for member countries but for the rest of the world, member countries need to grant some tariff concessions to the imports from the non-member countries.

Keywords: PTA, FTA, CU, GATT Article XXIV, revealed preference, Pareto-improving FTA

Paper type: Research paper

1. Introduction

The world is in a mode of forming preferential trade agreements (PTA's) and free trade agreements (FTA's). In most cases, the member countries that negotiate tariff reductions between them in an FTA or a PTA, neglect

Frontiers of Economics and Globalization
Volume 5   ISSN: 1574-8715
DOI: 10.1016/S1574-8715(08)05007-0

the adjustments in tariffs on the imports from the non-member countries. Literally speaking, this is a violation of the most favored nation (MFN) principle. GATT Article XXIV, however, allows this practice as an exception with respect to the formation of FTAs and customs unions (CU's).

For the sake of discussions below, let us define in this chapter an FTA as an agreement between two or more countries to give reciprocal tariff concessions so that tariffs are at zero. A PTA by definition includes a CU and an FTA; a CU is an agreement where the member countries share common tariff levels for the import of goods from the rest of the world, while an FTA does not have such common external tariffs. We distinguish an FTA from an "interim" PTA, which does not reduce members' tariffs to zero.

Under what conditions can a PTA benefit the rest of the world, namely the country outside the PTA, without any tariff concessions or transfers to the rest of the world? [1] This question is worth attention because few FTA's or CU's, which are serious exceptions to the MFN principle, are negotiated with adjustments in tariffs on imports from the rest of the world, or in transfers to the rest of the world, taking into account the welfare of the rest of the world. We address this question by appealing to the global, revealed preference approach. We show that if the initial levels of tariffs are sufficiently small, if the effect on production efficiency over the world dominates the effect on tariff revenues, or if the tax-subsidy scheme in the fashion of Bhagwati and Ramaswami (1963) and Bhagwati *et al.* (1969) (BRS hear after) prevails in the countries, then the formation of an FTA will deteriorate the welfare of the outsider countries in the world. The welfare deterioration will occur unless concessions in tariffs are made towards the products of the rest of the world by the participating countries.

The following approach using the revealed preference apparatus does not rely on a local or infinitesimal calculus approach, and the strength of this approach is to allow rather general assumptions on consumption, production, and trade behavior. This approach is effectively employed by Ohyama (1972), in a celebrated paper by Kemp and Wan (1976), and by Deardorff (1980). Ohyama (1972) explores sufficient conditions for a welfare outcome after trade. In contrast, Deardorff (1980), as well as Bernhofen and Brown (2004, 2005), derive necessary conditions by appealing to the weak axiom of the revealed preference. We follow the latter tradition. We slightly extend the weak axiom of the revealed preference in such a way that, when a government negotiates for a situation that allows a consumption bundle for its citizens, then the particular bundle was not available for the economy before the negotiation. We conclude that under a certain set of conditions, the welfare of the rest of

---

[1] The same question is asked for the trade model with differentiated products and monopolistic competition in Goto and Hamada (1998, 1999).

the world cannot possibly increase. Thus, there will be no Pareto-improving PTA formation in the world under these conditions.

Panagariya and Krishna (2002) and Iwasa *et al.* (2008) also employ a revealed preference approach in order to show the possibility of a Pareto-improving PTA formation. Both of them require tariff concessions or transfers to the rest of the world for Pareto improvement. Their results do not present essential contradictions to the main messages of this chapter, since our approach differs from theirs in the sense that we are primarily interested in characterizing the necessary conditions for the Pareto-improving PTA formation without any additional side payments and concessions.

As Kemp and Wan (1976) rightly pointed out, there must be certain changes in outside tariffs for the PTA in order to keep the welfare of the countries outside the PTA constant and, under normal circumstances, those changes should be tariff concessions to the outside countries. This chapter is accordingly a confirmation of the statement in Kemp–Wan, "there exists a common tariff vector which is consistent with pre-union world prices and, therefore, with pre-union trade patterns and pre-union levels of welfare for nonmembers (Kemp and Wan, 1976, p. 95)." Their results apply mainly to CUs, but are also effective for the welfare assessment of a PTA by considering the state where the terms of trade remain unchanged to each country in the rest of the world. This state that preserves the terms of trade can be called the "terms of trade preserving state" (TTPS), and works as the key concept in the demonstration of the Kemp–Wan theorem. Our results suggest that, in order to achieve the state of the TTPS, most likely PTA members should give tariff concessions to the rest of the world. The ongoing practice of keeping the initial tariff levels for the rest of the world does violate the criterion of a Pareto-improving PTA for the world.

2. Model

Suppose, for simplicity, that there are three countries, $K = 0$, 1, 2. These two countries form an FTA by abolishing tariff barriers between them or an interim PTA by reducing tariff barriers between them. Those countries that engage in the FTA (or in the interim PTA) are indexed by superscripts, $K = 1$, 2, and the country that remains outside the FTA (interim PTA), which is sometimes called the rest of the world country, is indexed by superscript $K = 0$. There are m commodities numbered by subscripts $J = 1, ..., m$, and we impose the Armington assumption that a particular commodity is produced in only one country. The commodities that may have the same physical quality but are exported from different countries are treated as different commodities. This assumption is, as Panagariya and Krishna (2002) convincingly argue, the assumption most congruent to the practice of the rules of origin in the WTO. Country 0 produces goods indexed by subscripts from $J = 1$ to m_0, Country 1 produces goods indexed from $J = m_0+1$ to m_1, and Country 2 produces goods indexed from $J = m_1+1$ to $m_2 (= m)$.

Let us assume that each country has a well-defined social utility function or the policy preference function defined on available consumption bundles of commodities.[2]

There are two states, $S = I$ before the formation of an FTA (an interim PTA) and $S = II$ after its formation. In the following, let $T^K(S)$ be the vector of specific tariffs on m commodities imposed by Country K in state S, such that

$$T^0(S) = (0, 0, \ldots, 0; T^0_{m_0+1}(S), T^0_{m_0+2}(S), \ldots, T^0_{m_1}(S);$$
$$T^0_{m_1+1}(S), T^0_{m_1+2}(S), \cdots, T^0_{m_2}(S)), \tag{1}$$

$$T^1(S) = (T^1_1(S), T^1_2(S), \ldots, T^1_{m_0}(S); 0, 0, \ldots, 0;$$
$$T^1_{m_1+1}(S), T^1_{m_1+2}(S), \ldots, T^1_{m_2}(S)), \tag{2}$$

$$T^2(S) = (T^2_1(S), T^2_2(S), \ldots, T^2_{m_0}(S);$$
$$T^2_{m_0+1}(S), T^2_{m_0+2}(S), \ldots, T^2_{m_1}(S); 0, 0, \ldots, 0). \tag{3}$$

Let also $C^K(S)$, $X^K(S)$, and $M^K(S)$ denote the column vector (with m elements) of consumption, production and net import, respectively, for Country K in state S. Let $P^K(S) = (P^K_1(S), P^K_2(S), \ldots, P^K_m(S))$, the domestic price vector for country $K = 0, 1, 2$, at state $S = I$ and II. Under the Armington Assumption a commodity is exported only from one country. We denote the international price, or the export price of a commodity at an exporting country, in state S as $P^*(S) = (P^*_1(S), P^*_2(S), \ldots, P^*_m(S))$. By definition,

$$P^K(S) = P^*(S) + T^K(S), \quad K = 0, 1, 2; S = I, II. \tag{4}$$

When we consider the effect of a formation of an FTA, *and not in an interim PTA*, the tariffs will be abolished *in State II* for the commodities that are mutually traded between Country 1 and Country 2. We also assume that Country 0, the rest of the world, does not change tariff rates on the goods exported from Country 1 and Country 2, and that neither Country 1 nor Country 2 changes tariffs on the export of Country 0. Accordingly, in case of an FTA formation, one can denote,

$$T^1(II) = (T^1_1, T^1_2, \ldots, T^1_{m_0}; 0, 0, \ldots, 0; 0, 0, \ldots, 0), \tag{5}$$

$$T^2(II) = (T^2_1, T^2_2, \ldots, T^2_{m_0}; 0, 0, \ldots, 0; 0, 0, \ldots, 0), \tag{6}$$

---

[2] This assumption can be somewhat relaxed as long as the decision unit in a national economy is consistent, as in Shimomura and Wong (1998).

where

$$(T_1^K, T_2^K, \ldots, T_{m_0}^K) \equiv (T_1^K(I), T_2^K(I), \ldots, T_{m_0}^K(I))$$
$$= (T_1^K(II), T_2^K(II), \ldots, T_{m_0}^K(II)), \tag{7}$$

for $K = 1$ and 2.

On the other hand, *in the case of an interim PTA formation*, the tariffs between incumbent countries need not be abolished. Accordingly, the notations in Equations (2) and (3) remain valid instead of (5) and (6).

3. Main results

Let us consider the situation where the governments negotiate for reciprocal tariff eliminations (FTA) or reductions (interim PTA) in order to improve the welfare from consumption bundles for nations. After the formation of an FTA or an interim PTA by Country 1 and Country 2, the tariff rates between Countries 1 and 2 will be abolished or reduced. It would be natural to posit the following assumptions in accordance with the weak axiom of revealed preference because an FTA is mutually and voluntarily negotiated.

ASSUMPTION A1. Member countries do not grant any tariff concessions to the import from the non-member country.

ASSUMPTION A2. In State II, i.e., after the formation of an FTA or an interim PTA, both of Country 1 and Country 2 can command better consumption bundles than in State I.

ASSUMPTION A3. (Modified Weak Axiom of Revealed Preference): Suppose Assumption A2 is valid, then neither of the governments of Country 1 nor Country 2 in State I could have realized the consumption bundles C^1 (II) or C^2 (II). In other words, one has in terms of the inner product,

$$P^K(I)(C^K(I) - C^K(II)) < 0, \quad \text{for } K = 1, 2. \tag{8}$$

In passing one should note, by the efficiency of production under domestic prices,

$$P^K(I)(X^K(I) - X^K(II)) \geq 0, \quad \text{for } K = 0, 1, 2. \tag{9}$$

Define the following condition (10) that will be referred to later.

$$\sum_{K=0,1,2} T^K(I)(M^K(I) - M^K(II)) + \sum_{K=0,1,2} P^K(I)(X^K(I) - X^K(II)) \geq 0.$$
$$\tag{10}$$

The second term of the above inequality is always positive by Equation (9). The first term is *the sum across countries of the changes in hypothetical tariff revenues in the whole world calculated on the assumption that the tariff rates are maintained to those before the FTA or interim PTA agreement.* Then one can state

PROPOSITION 1. *Suppose that all Assumptions A1 through A3 hold. Then, the fulfillment of condition (10) implies that State I before negotiation of an FTA is revealed to be preferred by the rest of the world, Country 0, to State II after negotiation.*

PROOF. By hypothesis, we have

$$P^K(I)(C^K(I) - C^K(II)) < 0, \quad \text{for } K = 1, 2. \tag{11}$$

By the definition of net import in each good,

$$C^K(S) = M^K(S) + X^K(S), \quad \text{for } K = 1, 2; S = I, II, \tag{12}$$

one obtains,

$$P^K(I)(M^K(I) - M^K(II)) + P^K(I)(X^K(I) - X^K(II)) < 0 \quad \text{for } K = 1, 2. \tag{13}$$

Using the international price vector defined as $P^*(S)$ above, and its relationship to the domestic price vector $P^K(I)$, one can rewrite inequalities (13) as

$$P^*(I)(M^K(I) - M^K(II)) + T^K(I)(M^K(I) - M^K(II))$$
$$+ P^K(I)(X^K(I) - X^K(II)) < 0, \quad \text{for } K = 1, 2. \tag{14}$$

Summing the inequalities for two countries, one obtains

$$\sum_{K=1,2} P^*(I)(M^K(I) - M^K(II)) + \sum_{K=1,2} T^K(I)(M^K(I) - M^K(II))$$
$$+ \sum_{K=1,2} P^K(I)(X^K(I) - X^K(II)) < 0. \tag{15}$$

On the other hand, since the world markets are closed, we have

$$\sum_{K=0,1,2} M^K(I) = 0, \tag{16}$$

$$\sum_{K=0,1,2} M^K(II) = 0. \tag{17}$$

Therefore, Inequality (15) can be rewritten as,

$$- P^*(I)(M^0(I) - M^0(II)) + \sum_{K=1,2} T^K(I)(M^K(I) - M^K(II))$$
$$+ \sum_{K=1,2} P^K(I)(X^K(I) - X^K(II)) < 0, \tag{18}$$

or, by reversing the sign,

$$P^*(I)(M^0(I) - M^0(II)) - \sum_{K=1,2} T^K(I)(M^K(I) - M^K(II))$$

$$- \sum_{K=1,2} P^K(I)(X^K(I) - X^K(II)) > 0. \tag{19}$$

In terms of domestic price vector $P^0(I) = P^*(I) + T^0(I)$,

$$P^0(I)(M^0(I) - M^0(II)) - T^0(I)(M^0(I) - M^0(II))$$

$$> \sum_{K=1,2} T^K(I)(M^K(I) - M^K(II)) + \sum_{K=1,2} P^K(I)(X^K(I) - X^K(II)). \tag{20}$$

Since

$$P^0(I)(C^0(I) - C^0(II)) = P^0(I)(M^0(I) - M^0(II)) + P^0(I)(X^0(I) - X^0(II)), \tag{21}$$

we obtain from Equations (20),

$$P^0(I)(C^0(I) - C^0(II))$$

$$> \sum_{K=0,1,2} T^K(I)(M^K(I) - M^K(II)) + \sum_{K=0,1,2} P^K(I)(X^K(I) - X^K(II)). \tag{22}$$

The right-hand side (RHS) of the above inequality is assured to be positive if condition (10) in the premise is satisfied. Naturally, the left-hand side (LHS) of the same inequality is positive. That means that State I is revealed to be preferred by Country 0, the non-member country. That is,

$$P^0(I)(C^0(I) - C^0(II)) > 0. \tag{23}$$

This inequality implies that the first state $S = I$ is revealed to be preferred to the second state $S = II$ by Country 0, the rest of the world. (QED)

The proof has utilized only the initial values of specific tariffs, and not their values after the negotiation, so that this proposition holds for an FTA as well as an interim PTA.[3] Thus,

PROPOSITION 2. *Suppose that all Assumptions A1 through A3 hold. Then, the fulfillment of condition (10) implies that State I before negotiation of an interim PTA is revealed to be preferred to State II after negotiation of the interim PTA by the rest of the world, that is, Country 0.*

[3] Ohyama (2003) considered the welfare effect of forming interim PTA, and showed the possibility of achieving the state of the TTPS in the case of an interim PTA. This proposition, however, needs the adjustment of tariffs so as to keep its trades of all commodities with non-member countries at their previous levels, the same requirement applies in Ohyama (1972) and Kemp and Wan (1976).

The rest of the world will find its welfare deteriorated in State *II* as long as condition (10) is satisfied. In other words, as long as the condition (10) is satisfied, there will be no Pareto-improving FTA or interim PTA. Also the proof holds as long as both the government and the consumers in the member countries feel improved after the negotiation of an agreement, even if the changes of specific tariffs are in the direction of reduction.

Propositions 1 and 2 indicate that under condition (10), no Pareto-improving PTA will exist. We consider that condition (10) is a fairly reasonable restriction for a world economy. In the next section we will explain what the implication of condition (10) is.

4. Interpretation of the condition for the non-existence of Pareto-improving PTA

Since the condition expressed in Inequality (10) plays a crucial role in our derivations, it is worth considering the economic meaning of the condition. Inequality (10) is reproduced as

$$\sum_{K=0,1,2} T^K(I)(M^K(I) - M^K(II)) + \sum_{K=0,1,2} P^K(I)(X^K(I) - X^K(II)) \geq 0.$$

The second term is the world production gain under the domestic price vector $P^K(I)$ when production is corrected from $X^K(II)$ to $X^K(I)$. This term is always non-negative if production decisions are efficient. The first term is zero for the commodity that a country exports because of our assumption of no export taxes or subsidies. The first term for an importing country of a commodity means the following hypothetical loss (or gain) of tariff revenues. The discussion below will be conducted by an example of an interim PTA but the same applies for an FTA. Suppose the pre-PTA tariffs were applied to the post-PTA trade flows. Then the incumbent PTA countries might increase import inflows to levels higher than the pre-PTA situation and this term could be negative. For the outsider, imports may decrease or increase, one cannot decide the sign of change. If the first term is positive, condition (10) is naturally satisfied. If it is negative, its absolute value should not overwhelm the effect of the second term. Therefore, we will examine the case where first term is negative.

First of all, Inequality (10) will be satisfied if the initial tariff levels are small. That is, if the initial tariff levels $T^K(I)$ are small, the first term will not dominate the second.

Next, in order to understand this condition more clearly, consider a simple case where each country exports a single commodity. We maintain the Armington assumption. Country 1 exports Good 1, while Country 2 exports Good 2, and they negotiate the mutual elimination on Good 1 and Good 2. Country 0, the rest of the world, export Good 0, but the tariffs on

Good 0 all over the world will be unchanged after the formation of the interim PTA. In the previous notation $(m_0, m_1, m_2) = (0, 1, 2)$. Inequality (10) is sustained if

$$- \sum_{K=0,1,2} T^K(I)(M^K(I) - M^K(II)) \leq \sum_{K=0,1,2} P^K(I)(X^K(I) - X^K(II)),$$

(24)

which can be written as

$$- \sum_{K=0,1,2} \sum_{J=0,1,2} T_J^K(I)(M_J^K(I) - M_J^K(II))$$

$$\leq \sum_{K=0,1,2} \sum_{J=0,1,2} P_J^K(I)(X_J^K(I) - X_J^K(II)).$$

(25)

Though our condition refer to the comparison of the double sums of this inequality, it may be interesting to compare heuristically pair-wise the components of the inequality term by term in such a way that

$$-[T_J^K(I)(M_J^K(I) - M_J^K(II))] \text{ vs. } P_J^K(I)(X_J^K(I) - X_J^K(II)),$$

(26)

or, by decomposing to (arc) elasticity and other elements,

$$- \frac{T_J^K(I)(M_J^K(I) - M_J^K(II))}{(T_J^K(I) - T_J^K(II))M_J^K(I)} \text{ vs.}$$

$$\frac{P_J^K(I)(X_J^K(I) - X_J^K(II))}{(P_J^K(I) - P_J^K(II))X_J^K(I)} \frac{(P_J^K(I) - P_J^K(II))X_J^K(I)}{(T_J^K(I) - T_J^K(II))M_J^K(I)}.$$

(27)

The LHS of this contrast with the negative sign is an expression of the (arc) elasticity of import to tariff rate. The RHS is the product of the (arc) elasticity of production with respect to price changes, and the rate of response of a price to a change in tariffs[4] and the output and import ratio.

From this we can list the following factors that will contribute to securing Inequality (10) – we start the list from the factor that would reduce the absolute value of LHS like (a) below, to the factors that would increase the value of RHS like (b), (c), and (d).

(a) Trade flows in these countries are insensitive to tariff changes.
(b) Production decisions are sensitive to prices.
(c) Domestic prices are sensitive to tariff changes.

And most importantly,
(d) The ratios of import to production are small.

If those factors prevail on the average, then it will be harder to create a Pareto-improving FTA or interim PTA without concessions

---

[4] This ratio is positive in absence of the Metzler or the Lerner paradox. For a set of conditions to preclude those paradoxes, see Endoh and Hamada (2005).

of tariffs to outsiders. Incidentally, the factors (a), (b), and (d) are easily violated in the case of a PTA incorporating an entrepôt as a member. This corresponds to our results by a calculus (Endoh *et al.*, 2008) that a PTA involving an entrepôt is most likely to Pareto improving for the world.

5. Government interventions and the effect of a PTA

Finally, we will prove the following proposition in presence of Bhagwati–Ramaswami–Srinivasan (BRS) tax-subsidy scheme (Bhagwati and Ramaswami, 1963; Bhagwati *et al.*, 1969).

PROPOSITION 3. *In case the domestic economy is corrected by the Bhagwati–Ramaswami–Srinivasan (BRS) tax-subsidy scheme, then there exists no Pareto-improving PTA for any discrete reductions of tariffs in member countries.*

PROOF. Assume that both Country 1 and Country 2 prefer State *II*. Under the BRS tax-subsidy intervention scheme, the dominance relationship expressed in Inequalities (8) and (9) applies with respect to the international price vectors instead of with respect to domestic price vectors. Please be reminded that, with the scheme, production and consumption distortions are corrected, and the only remaining distortions are related to tariffs. Therefore, at each state, consumption bundles exploit all feasibility situations in terms of the international prices. Accordingly, under Assumptions A1–A3,

$$P^*(I)(C^K(I) - C^K(II)) < 0, \quad \text{for } K = 1, 2, \tag{28}$$

and, accordingly, from Inequality (13), one obtains

$$P^*(I)(M^K(I) - M^K(II)) + P^*(I)(X^K(I) - X^K(II)) < 0, \quad \text{for } K = 1, 2. \tag{29}$$

By adding up two equations and using the market balance equations, we obtain,

$$P^*(I)(M^0(I) - M^0(II)) - \sum_{K=1,2} P^*(I)(X^K(I) - X^K(II)) > 0. \tag{30}$$

Also, by the BRS scheme, we have

$$P^*(I)(X^K(I) - X^K(II)) > 0, \quad \text{for } K = 0, 1, 2. \tag{31}$$

Then, from Inequality (31) and utilizing the following relationship,

$$C^0(I) - C^0(II) = (M^0(I) - M^0(II)) + (X^0(I) - X^0(II)),$$

one obtains

$$P^*(I)(C^0(I) - C^0(II)) - \sum_{K=0,1,2} P^*(I)(X_K(I) - X_K(II)) > 0. \tag{32}$$

This proves that State I is revealed to be preferred by the rest of the world. (QED)

6. Concluding remarks

By appealing to the apparatus of revealed preference, we have shown that it is difficult to build a PTA without outside tariff concession that will be Pareto improving to the world. The GATT Article XXIV is often interpreted to allow a formation of an FTA, a CU, or an interim PTA as long as tariffs on the imports from the rest of the world are kept constant, and in practice countries build an FTA or a CU without making any tariff concessions to the outsiders. This chapter has shown that, under many circumstances, such a practice would deteriorate the welfare of the countries that are left behind. In terms of the well-known Kemp–Wan theorem, in order to attain the state of terms of trade preserving state to the rest of the world, reductions of tariffs on the imports from the rest of the world, or transfers to the rest of the world, are in many cases essential to realize the situation.

We do not claim, however, that Pareto-improving PTAs for the world are absolutely impossible in general without tariff concessions. Rather, according to our discussions in this chapter, as well as to those in our companion paper (Endoh *et al.*, 2008), a Pareto-improving PTA without outside tariff concessions can be formed, when the export of the rest of the world is a strong complement to the traded goods between member countries, and particularly when one of the countries participating in a PTA has the characteristic of "entrepôt" in terms of its trade flow network.

The strength of the revealed preference approach lies in the fact that we need not impose any restrictions on the preference or production patterns of national economies. In return, our results allow some room for indeterminate area as most of the conclusions of the revealed preference approach does. Thus in the revealed preference approach an additional condition like (10) on the levels of tariffs is needed to preclude the existence of Pareto-improving PTA's or interim PTA's, while in the analysis of incremental changes in tariffs the assumptions of normality of goods and (in three of more good case) the assumption of substitutes of goods are needed.

Finally, we would like the reader to note the substantial merits of this revealed preference approach. Above all, only by this global, revealed preference approach, can we properly analyze the mechanism of a

Free Trade Agreement where tariff rates between countries jump discretely to zero.

Acknowledgement

We thank Alan Deardorff and an anonymous referee for carefully reading the manuscript and giving valuable comments. Koji Shimomura, coauthor of the chapter, passed away on February 24, 2007, when the substance of this chapter had been almost completed.

References

Bernhofen, D.M., Brown, J.C. (2004), A direct test of the theory of comparative advantage: the case of Japan. *Journal of Political Economy* 112 (1), 48–67.

Bernhofen, D.M., Brown, J.C. (2005), An empirical assessment of the comparative advantage gains from trade: Evidence from Japan. *American Economic Review* 95 (1), 208–225.

Bhagwati, J., Ramaswami, V.K. (1963), Domestic distortions, tariffs, and the theory of optimum subsidy. *Journal of Political Economy* 71 (1), 44–50.

Bhagwati, J., Ramaswami, V.K., Srinivasan, T.N. (1969), Domestic distortions, tariffs, and the theory of optimum subsidy: some further results. *Journal of Political Economy* 77 (6), 1005–1010.

Deardorff, A.V. (1980), The general validity of the law of comparative advantage. *Journal of Political Economy* 88 (5), 941–957.

Endoh, M., Hamada, K. (2005), On the conditions that preclude the existence of the Lerner Paradox and the Metzler Paradox. *Keio Economic Studies* 42 (1–2), 39–50.

Endoh, M., Hamada, K., Shimomura, K. (2008), Can a preferential trade agreement benefit neighbor countries without compensating them? Center Discussion Paper No. 961, Economic Growth Center, Yale University.

Goto, J., Hamada, K. (1998), Economic integration and the welfare of those who are left behind: an incentive-theoretic approach. *Journal of the Japanese and International Economies* 12 (1), 25–48.

Goto, J., Hamada, K. (1999), Regional economic integration and Article XXIV of the GATT. *Review of International Economics* 7 (4), 555–570.

Iwasa, K., Riezman, R., Shimomura, K. (2008), Pareto-improving trading clubs without income transfers, to be presented at Chapter 10 of this volume.

Kemp, M.C., Wan, H.Y., Jr. (1976), An elementary proposition concerning the formation of customs unions. *Journal of International Economics* 6 (1), 95–97.

Ohyama, M. (1972), Trade and welfare in general equilibrium. *Keio Economic Studies* 9 (2), 37–73.

Ohyama, M. (2003), Free trade agreements and economic welfare: beyond the Kemp-Wan Theorem. Keio University, Market Quality Research Project, KUMQRP Discussion Paper Series DP2003-11.

Panagariya, A., Krishna, P. (2002), On necessarily welfare-enhancing free trade areas. *Journal of International Economics* 57 (2), 353–367.

Shimomura, K., Wong, K. (1998), The law of comparative advantage without social utility functions. *Review of International Economics* 6 (3), 401–406.

CHAPTER 8

Tariff Adjustments in Preferential Trade Agreements

Eric W. Bond[a] and Constantinos Syropoulos[b]

[a]Department of Economics, Vanderbilt University, VU Station B #351819, 2301 Vanderbilt Place, Nashville, TN 37235, USA
E-mail address: eric.bond@vanderbilt.edu
[b]Department of Economics and International Business, LeBow College of Business, Drexel University, 32nd and Market Streets, Philadelphia, PA 19104, USA
E-mail address: c.syropoulos@drexel.edu

Abstract

Purpose – This chapter examines how preferential liberalization between a pair of countries affects the terms of trade and welfare of the liberalizing countries and on the rest of the world (ROW). We adopt a model with symmetric countries that generalizes previous work by relaxing assumptions on functional forms, which allows for the possibility that exports of member countries are complements for exports of the ROW.

Methodology/approach – This chapter uses general equilibrium welfare analysis for a three-country trade model.

Findings – We show that Kemp–Wan tariff adjustments require a decrease (increase) in the external tariff of members in a preferential trade agreement to accompany internal liberalization in the neighborhood of internal free trade when member goods are substitutes (complements) for non-member goods. However, the adjustment path of the external tariff to reductions in the internal tariff could be non-monotonic when preferences are not of the CES type.

Practical implications – Our results are of interest for the design of rules for multilateral trade agreements with respect to preferential liberalization, since they indicate how tariffs must be adjusted to eliminate negative impacts on non-member countries.

Keywords: Preferential trade agreements, Kemp–Wan proposition

Paper type: Research paper

Frontiers of Economics and Globalization
Volume 5   ISSN: 1574-8715
DOI: 10.1016/S1574-8715(08)05008-2

1. Introduction

The question of how countries that have formed preferential trade agreements (i.e., customs unions (CUs) or free trade areas (FTAs)) adjust their external tariffs in response to the liberalization of intra-union trade is central in evaluating the desirability of dismantling trade barriers preferentially and in assessing their impact on the multilateral trading system. Arguably, if preferential trade agreements (PTAs) result in a more aggressive policy stance against non-member countries (or if they induce the excluded countries to respond more aggressively), PTAs may be a stumbling block to multilateral trade liberalization. On the other hand, if PTAs induce their constituent members to adopt less aggressive external trade policies, then their effects on the international trading system may be more benign.

In a series of papers (Bond and Syropoulos, 1996a, 1996b; Bond et al., 2001, 2004) we used a simple three-country endowment model of trade with CES preferences to address the above issues under alternative assumptions about the nature of strategic interactions between countries and the nature of PTAs.[1] By assuming that PTA members were symmetric in their preference and endowment structures, we were able to characterize the effects of PTAs using three tariffs: the external and internal tariffs of the representative PTA member and the tariff of the outside country. In that setting we were able to show how PTA members and the rest of the world (ROW) are affected by internal trade liberalization under alternative processes regarding the determination of the external tariff. An important benchmark in our analysis was a Kemp–Wan (1976) tariff adjustment; that is, an adjustment in the external tariff that is necessary to leave the non-member country's welfare unaffected by trade liberalization. By comparing the response of the external tariff to internal trade liberalization, we were able to identify how preferential liberalization affects the ROW and PTA members.

While the endowment model with CES preferences provides a simple environment within which to explore these issues, the adoption of specific

---

[1] The endowment/country structure in our model is an extension of Krugman (1991) that makes it possible to consider the role played by differences in country size and the degree of comparative advantage. In Bond and Syropoulos (1996a, 1996b) we examined how an increase in the size of trading blocs affects world welfare when each trading bloc takes the form of a customs union and sets its external tariff against the ROW optimally. In Bond et al. (BSW, 2001) we allowed the interaction between countries to be repeated over time so that multilateral trade negotiations may sustain cooperative tariff levels that represent a Pareto improvement over the one-shot Nash equilibrium. This framework enabled us to examine how preferential trade liberalization affects the sustainability of multilateral trade agreements. Lastly, in Bond et al. (BRS, 2004) we examined the case in which countries form FTAs, rather than CUs, under the assumption that individual countries set their external tariffs independently to maximize national welfare.

functional forms raises questions about the generality of the results obtained. In this chapter we explore the effects of preferential tariff reductions using more general production and preference structures. More specifically, we maintain the assumption that union members are symmetric in size and comparative advantage; however, we consider a general structure in which the restriction of symmetry is imposed on general expenditure and revenue functions. This approach has the advantage of allowing for a richer production structure while still permitting us to express trade policy in terms of the same tariffs: the internal tariff of the PTA, its external tariff and the tariff of the non-member. The resulting analysis, which can be carried out in terms of a representative PTA member and the outside country, is simplified because it retains many of the features of a two-country trade model.

Section 2 presents the key ingredients of the model and briefly summarizes the restrictions on excess demand functions that result from our symmetry assumptions. One generalization resulting from this production structure is that it admits the possibility that imports from union partner may be complementary to imports from the ROW.

Section 3 derives the effect of changes in tariffs on world prices and characterizes the nature of the Kemp–Wan tariff adjustment. It is shown that, in the neighborhood of internally free trade, a Kemp–Wan tariff adjustment calls for a reduction (increase) in the external tariff following the liberalization of internal trade when member and non-member imports are substitutes (complements) for member countries. When internal tariffs are positive, it is possible for internal trade liberalization to have positive spillovers to the ROW even in the absence of complementarity in import demand functions.

Focusing on the case of CUs, Section 4 examines the relationship between trade policy and welfare for member countries. We derive an optimal tariff formula for the external tariff as a function of the internal tariff that can be expressed as a simple extension of the two-good optimal tariff formula. We also derive an optimal formula for the internal tariff, given the level of the external tariff. The results of the general model are then compared with those obtained in the CES/endowment model utilized in our earlier work. Section 5 discusses some potential extensions of this work.

2. A symmetric three-country trade model

We consider a model in which three countries, labeled 1, 2 and 3, exchange three final goods, also labeled 1, 2 and 3, in perfectly competitive markets. To explore the implications of preferential trading arrangements we single out countries 1 and 2 as the potential members for a CU, and designate country 3 as the outside country, or the ROW. Each country i is an exporter of good i and an importer of the remaining products. Importantly, for tractability, we assume that potential union members are symmetric relative to each other and relative to ROW in the sense that we describe below.

Denote with p_j^i the price of good j in country i. We assume that consumer preferences are identical across countries and that they are described by the expenditure function $E(p_1, p_2, p_3, U)$. This function is increasing in its arguments, concave in prices and satisfies the symmetry condition

$$E(a, b, p_3, U) = E(b, a, p_3, U) \quad \text{for all} \quad a, b, p_3 > 0. \tag{1}$$

We also assume that all goods are normal in consumption. The production technology in each country i is described by the revenue function $R^i(p_1, p_2, p_3)$, which is increasing and convex in prices. The symmetry conditions imposed on the production side are

$$R^1(a, b, p_3) = R^2(b, a, p_3) \tag{2a}$$

$$R^3(a, b, p_3) = R^3(b, a, p_3) \tag{2b}$$

for goods 1 and 2 at all prices $a, b, p_3 > 0$. Countries 1 and 2 are assumed to differ symmetrically in their ability to produce goods 1 and 2. This could arise because of differences in endowments across countries that have identical technologies (e.g., different quantities of sector-specific factors in a specific factors model) or because of differences in technologies. Since the source of this difference is not essential to our analysis, we suppress factor endowments and simply characterize the revenue functions as being country-specific functions of prices.

Using the standard properties of expenditure and revenue functions, we can define the compensated excess demand function for good j in country i as

$$M_j^i(p, U) = \frac{\partial E^i(p, U)}{\partial p_j} - \frac{\partial R^i(p)}{\partial p_j},$$

where p is a vector of prices. The symmetry conditions on preferences and technologies (or on resource endowments) imply several restrictions on the excess demand functions. For the non-member country, we have

$$M_1^3(a, b, p_3, U) = M_2^3(b, a, p_3, U), \quad M_3^3(a, b, p_3, U) = M_3^3(b, a, p_3, U). \tag{3}$$

In addition to the usual symmetry conditions imposed by optimization, the second expression in (3) yields symmetry of substitution effects between the imports from the member countries, $M_{31}^3 = M_{32}^3$, where $M_{jk}^i = \partial M_j^i / \partial p_k$. When combined with the homogeneity of degree zero of excess demand functions, this ensures that goods 1 and 2 are necessarily net substitutes for good 3 in country 3 (i.e., $M_{31}^3 = M_{32}^3 > 0$).

For member countries the symmetry conditions in (1) and (2) imply

$$M_1^1(a,b,p_3,U) = M_2^2(b,a,p_3,U),$$

$$M_2^1(a,b,p_3,U) = M_1^2(b,a,p_3,U), \quad \text{and} \tag{4}$$

$$M_3^1(a,b,p_3,U) = M_3^2(b,a,p_3,U).$$

The conditions imposed on substitution effects by symmetry for the member countries will be somewhat weaker than for the non-member country because the prices of goods 1 and 2 do not enter symmetrically in the individual country revenue functions. In the case of an endowment model with preferences that are separable in member country goods (i.e., $E^i(\phi(p_1,p_2),p_3,U)$), we have $E_{31}^i = M_{31}^i = E_{32}^i = M_{32}^i > 0$, for $i = 1, 2$, as in our earlier work that utilized CES preferences. However, there exist production models that generate $R_{31}^i < 0$, in which case $M_{31}^i < 0$, if the substitution effects in demand are sufficiently small.[2] Thus, goods 1 and 2 can be either net substitutes or net complements for good 3 for PTA members.

Letting q_i denote the world price of good i and choosing good 3 as the numeraire, it is easy to show that the model will have a unique free trade equilibrium in which $q_1 = q_2$ and $U^1 = U^2$. The symmetry of demand and supply functions for goods 1 and 2 will ensure that their relative prices will be equal in equilibrium. Since $M_1^3 = M_2^3$, there will be two trade patterns that are potentially of interest. The first arises if country i exports good i and imports good $j \neq i$ from country j.[3] The second arises if country i imports good i from each of the other two countries. In this chapter we will focus on the former case, which is the trade pattern assumed in BSW (2001) and BRS (2004).

With the assumed trade pattern in which country i exports good i and imports good $j \neq i$, country i's trade policy can be summarized by the tariff

---

[2] An example of this is the model of Gruen and Corden (1970), in which sectors 1 and 2 employ labor and capital and good 3 employs labor and land. Since the returns to labor and capital are determined by the zero profit conditions for goods 1 and 2 (assuming both goods are produced), an increase in the price of the capital-intensive good will reduce the return to labor from the Stolper–Samuelson effect. The reduction in the cost of labor will expand production of good 3. A second example would be one in which each country consumes only its own output, but uses the outputs of each of the other two countries' goods as inputs to production of its output. In this case an increase in the price of country 2's output would reduce the total scale of country 1's output, leading to a reduction in the purchases of inputs from country 3. It should be emphasized that these cases of complementarity cannot be tied to the characteristics of goods 2 and 3 themselves, because the complementarity for country 2 must be between goods 1 and 3.

[3] There is also a case consistent with $M_1^3 = M_2^3 > 0$ in which $M_1^1 = M_2^2$, $M_1^2 = M_2^1 < 0$ at free trade. This is of less interest to the analysis of preferential liberalization agreements between countries 1 and 2 because there will be no need for these countries to trade with each other.

τ^i_j (which is the *ad valorem* tariff rate plus one) imposed by country i on its imports of good $j \neq i$. Domestic prices for good i will be $p^i_i = q_i$ and $p^i_j = \tau^i_j q_j$, for $j \neq i$. For brevity, we will refer to τ^i_j as "the tariff." Moreover, for simplicity we will occasionally identify ROW variables with an asterisk. In light of the aforementioned symmetry conditions, the following restrictions of symmetry in trade policy will also be imposed:

(C1) $t = \tau^1_2 = \tau^2_1$ common (internal) tariff on intra-union imports

(C2) $\tau = \tau^1_3 = \tau^2_3$ common external tariff on imports from ROW

(C3) $\tau^* = \tau^3_1 = \tau^3_2$ common tariff imposed by ROW.

While these conditions are treated here as assumptions about policy, they can in fact be derived as outcomes of tariff setting processes under a variety of different assumptions about government objectives.[4]

The symmetry conditions (1)–(3) and (C1)–(C3) will ensure that the pre-tariff prices of goods 1 and 2 will be equal, so that the terms of trade between the union members and ROW can be summarized by a single relative price. Choosing good 3 as numeraire, an equilibrium in product markets with $q = q_1 = q_2$ and $U^1 = U^2$ will hold if there exist $\{q, U^1, U^3\}$ satisfying

$$qM^1_1(q, tq, \tau, U^1) + qM^1_2(q, tq, \tau, U^1) + M^1_3(q, tq, \tau, U^1) = 0 \tag{5}$$

$$2qM^3_1(\tau^* q, \tau^* q, 1, U^3) + M^3_3(\tau^* q, \tau^* q, 1, U^3) = 0 \tag{6}$$

$$M^1_3(q, tq, \tau, U^1) = qM^3_1(\tau^* q, \tau^* q, 1, U^3). \tag{7}$$

Equation (5) describes the budget constraint of country 1 (the representative union member) and (6) captures country 3's budget constraint. Equation (7) is the condition for balanced trade with ROW and implicitly defines the world price q as a function of tariffs.

Before proceeding with the analysis, it will be useful to define three elasticities that appear frequently in the subsequent discussion. It will also be useful to identify the restrictions on these elasticities imposed by our symmetry assumptions.

Let

$$\eta \equiv \frac{\partial M^1_3(q, tq, \tau, U^1)}{\partial q} \frac{q}{M^1_3} = -\tau \frac{M^1_{33}}{M^1_3} > 0$$

denote the compensated elasticity of demand of country 1 imports from 3 with respect to q. The inequality in this expression follows from the

---

[4] If tariffs are set optimally, then (C3) will be a characteristic of ROW policy given (C1) and (C2). Similarly, (C2) would follow from optimal choice of member country policies given (C1) and (C3). If tariffs are the outcome of a bargaining process between countries, then it is natural to assume symmetry of bargaining power between symmetric member countries, which would also satisfy these conditions.

homogeneity of degree zero of import demands and the sign from the concavity of the expenditure function. Similarly, we define the compensated import demand elasticity for the non-member country as

$$\eta^* \equiv -\frac{\partial M_1^3(\tau^* q, \tau^* q, 1, U^3)}{\partial q} \frac{q}{M_1^3} = \frac{M_{13}^3}{M_1^3} > 0,$$

since $M_{13}^3 > 0$ as argued earlier. Lastly, we define the compensated cross-price elasticity of demand for a member country's imports from the non-member country as

$$\mu \equiv -\frac{\partial M_3^1(q, tq, \tau, U^1)}{\partial p_2^1} \frac{p_2^1}{M_3^1} = \frac{tq M_{32}^1}{M_3^1}.$$

This elasticity will be positive or negative depending on whether goods 2 and 3 are net substitutes or net complements. As noted in the discussion of (4), the separability assumptions we impose here allow for the possibility that goods 2 and 3 to be net either substitutes or net complements.

3. Tariffs and the terms of trade

Since terms of trade play a crucial role in determining the impact of a preferential trade agreement on ROW, we begin by deriving the relationship between the tariff rates noted above and the terms of trade. In models in which policymakers aim to maximize national, changes in domestic policy affect ROW through their impact on the terms of trade. Thus, in the Kemp and Wan (1976) proposition, the impact of the PTA on ROW is neutralized by adjusting external tariffs so that terms of trade remain unaffected. Bagwell and Staiger (2002) show that, for an important class of political economy models, the sole spillover of changes in domestic policy to ROW operates through the terms of trade.

The effect of policy changes on the terms of trade can be obtained by totally differentiating system (5)–(7) and solving. Totally differentiating the market-clearing condition (7) and using the homogeneity of degree zero property of import demand functions yields

$$(\eta + \eta^* - 1)\hat{q} = \eta\hat{t} - \mu\hat{i} - \eta^*\hat{\tau}^* - \frac{M_{3U}^1}{M_3^1} dU^1 + \frac{M_{1U}^3}{M_1^3} dU^3, \tag{8}$$

where a hat (" ˆ ") over a variable denotes a rate of change. The right-hand side indicates that an increase in a representative member country's external tariff (a decrease in the non-member country's tariff) will shift demand toward exports of the member countries at given q and real income levels. The impact of a change in t will be to lower (raise) the demand for member country goods if good 2 is a substitute (complement) for good 3.

Since the utility levels in (8) are endogenous, we must also differentiate the budget constraints to solve for the equilibrium impact. Differentiating the non-member country's budget constraint (6) and rearranging terms gives

$$A^* dU^3 = -2qM_1^3\{[1 + (\tau^* - 1)\eta^*]\hat{q} + (\tau^* - 1)\eta^* \hat{\tau}^*\}, \tag{9}$$

where $A^* \equiv 2qM_{1U}^3 + M_{3U}^3 > 0$ due to normality of goods in consumption. Note that in deriving (9) we have used the homogeneity (of degree zero) of the import demand functions in prices and the result that $M_{31}^3 = M_{32}^3 > 0$. At fixed terms of trade q, an increase in τ^* reduces welfare when $\tau^* > 1$ because it causes the volume of trade to contract. The reduction in the volume of trade is larger the larger the compensated price elasticity of demand for imports. Welfare is decreasing in q (the world price of country 3's imports) because such a price increase generates adverse terms of trade and volume of trade effects. Equation (9) is the standard result in the two-good case and arises here because goods 1 and 2 can be treated as a composite commodity from the point of view of country 3 (the country outside the PTA).

For the representative member country in the PTA, the welfare decomposition is more complicated for two reasons. First, the potential for differential treatment of imports from member and non-member countries generates an additional tariff term. Second, the symmetry conditions do not completely eliminate the possibility that two of the goods may be net complements. Totally differentiating (5) gives

$$AdU^1 = M_3^1\left(\left[1 + (\tau - 1)\eta - \frac{\tau(t - 1)}{t}\mu\right]\hat{q} - \left[(\tau - 1)\eta - \frac{\tau(t - 1)}{t}\mu\right]\hat{\tau}\right)$$
$$+ M_3^1\left[(\tau - 1)\mu + \frac{(t - 1)q^2 M_{22}^1}{M_3^1}\right]\hat{t} \tag{10}$$

where $A \equiv q(M_{1U}^1 + M_{2U}^1) + M_{3U}^1 > 0$. At constant terms of trade q, an increase in the external tariff τ affects welfare of PTA member 1 through its impact on the volume of distorted trade. When intra-union trade is free (i.e., when $t = 1$) and $\tau > 1$, an increase in τ will have a negative effect on welfare because it will reduce the volume of trade with the non-member. However, when $t > 1$, an increase in τ will increase (decrease) the volume of trade with the PTA partner when $\mu > 0$ (< 0) which is a favorable (unfavorable) trade volume effect. Combining these two effects, it is convenient to introduce the following definition which will play a significant role in the welfare expressions below:

DEFINITION 1. *An increase in the external tariff, τ, will have an unfavorable trade volume effect if*

$$\Gamma_\tau = \tau\left[\left(\frac{\tau - 1}{\tau}\right)\eta - \left(\frac{t - 1}{t}\right)\mu\right] > 0.$$

If $\mu < 0$, this condition will hold for all $t > 1$ and $\tau > 1$. If $\mu > 0$, $\Gamma_\tau > 0$ is more likely the greater are external barriers, $(\tau - 1)/\tau$, relative to internal barriers, $(t-1)/t$, and the greater is the own price compensated import demand elasticity, η, relative to the cross-price elasticity, μ. The fact that imports from non-members are imperfect substitutes means that it is illegitimate to automatically impose $\tau > t$ as a definition of preferential trade agreements. However, there is a presumption that the internal tariff barrier will be relatively lower in a preferential trade agreement. If $\tau > t$, then a sufficient condition for the trade volume changes due to a reduction in τ to increase welfare is $\eta \geq \mu$. Since we know from the homogeneity of degree zero of import demand functions in prices that $\eta = \mu + qM_{31}^1/M_3^1$, this condition will hold as long as goods 1 and 3 are not net complements.

A similar ambiguity arises in the effect of changes in internal tariffs on the terms of trade when $t > 1$. An increase in t reduces the volume of imports from country 2 (at fixed q and τ), and this has an adverse effect on welfare. However, an increase in t also leads to an increase (decrease) in the volume of trade with the outside country if $\mu > 0$ (< 0), which is a favorable (unfavorable) effect. The effect on trade in good 3 must dominate in the neighborhood of $t = 1$, but could be reversed if t is sufficiently large.

DEFINITION 2. *An increase in the internal tariff, t, will have a favorable trade volume effect if*

$$\Gamma_t = (\tau - 1)\mu + \frac{(t-1)tq^2 M_{22}^1}{M_3^1} > 0.$$

If goods 2 and 3 are net complements (i.e., $\mu < 0$), the trade volume effect of an increase in t must be unfavorable. If goods 2 and 3 are net substitutes, the following conditions are more likely to give rise to a favorable trade volume effect: (i) a τ large relative to t, (ii) a large value of μ relative to the compensated elasticity of demand for good 2, tqM_{22}^1/M_2^1 and (iii) a large volume of trade in good 2 relative to 3, qM_2^1/M_3^1. Note, in particular, that if $t = \tau$ and all goods are net substitutes, then $\Gamma_t < 0$. When all goods are net substitutes, own substitution effects dominate cross-effects and the adverse impact of an increase in t on its own trade volume must exceed that on the other market. Thus, it may well be the case that the sign of Γ_t will change over the process of internal tariff reduction when $\mu > 0$.

Finally, we note from (10) that an increase in q will have both a terms of trade and a trade volume effect on PTA member 1. The terms of trade effect of an increase in q will have a favorable impact on country 1's welfare because $M_1^1 + M_2^1 < 0$. The trade volume effect of an increase in q is equivalent to that for a decrease in τ, so the trade volume effect of an increase in q is favorable if $\Gamma_\tau > 0$.

The total impact of the trade policy instruments on the terms of trade can be found by substituting (9) and (10) into (8) and rearranging terms. Doing so yields

$$\frac{\hat{q}}{\hat{\tau}} = \frac{1}{\Delta}\left(\eta + \frac{M_{3U}^1}{A}\Gamma_\tau\right). \tag{11}$$

$$\frac{\hat{q}}{\hat{t}} = -\frac{1}{\Delta}\left(\mu + \frac{M_{3U}^1}{A}\Gamma_t\right). \tag{12}$$

$$\frac{\hat{q}}{\hat{\tau}^*} = -\frac{\eta^*}{\Delta}\left[1 + \frac{2qM_{1U}^3}{A^*}(\tau^* - 1)\right]. \tag{13}$$

Note that $\Delta \equiv \varepsilon + \varepsilon^* - 1 > 0$ is the familiar Marshall–Lerner condition for market stability, where ε and ε^* are the Marshallian price elasticities of import demand functions for extra-union trade and can be written as:

$$\varepsilon = \eta + \frac{M_{3U}^1}{A}(1 + \Gamma_\tau). \tag{14}$$

$$\varepsilon^* = \eta^* + \frac{2qM_{1U}^3}{A^*}\left[1 + (\tau^* - 1)\eta^*\right]. \tag{15}$$

These expressions decompose each of the elasticities into a pure substitution effect and an income effect. The first term in each expression is the net substitution elasticity of the imports between the union members and the non-member country's imports with respect to their relative price, and it is positive. The remaining term is the income effect, which is the product of the marginal propensity to consume the union export goods (evaluated at world prices) and the impact of a change in the terms of trade on the respective country income.

Equation (13) shows that an increase in the non-member's tariffs will worsen the terms of trade of the member countries as long as the market stability condition is satisfied. An increase in τ^* reduces the demand for member country exports at given prices, and this effect is reinforced by its negative trade volume effect on non-member country income when $\tau^* > 1$. The remaining expressions in (12)–(15) are complicated by the fact that there are trade volume effects on both extra-union and intra-union trade. To provide some intuition, it is useful to start by considering the comparative statics in the neighborhood of free internal trade between member countries; that is, when $t = 1$.

In the absence of internal trade barriers, goods 1 and 2 command the same relative price in all locations and

$$\Delta \equiv \eta\left[1 + \frac{M_{3U}^1}{A}(\tau - 1)\right] + \eta^*\left[1 + \frac{2qM_{1U}^3}{A^*}(\tau^* - 1)\right] + \left[\frac{M_{3U}^1}{A} - \frac{M_{3U}^3}{A^*}\right].$$

The expressions inside the brackets of the first two terms must be positive due to the compensated substitution effects when trade is not subsidized. The only potential source of instability arises from the last term, which is the difference in marginal propensities to consume good 3 (evaluated at world prices) between the member and non-member countries. An increase in q transfers purchasing power from non-member to member countries, which will be stabilizing (i.e., tending to raise the demand for the non-member's good) if the member countries have a higher marginal propensity to consume good 3. If preferences are homothetic as well as identical and there are no tariff distortions at all, then this term will be zero and the Marshall–Lerner stability condition will be satisfied. If marginal propensities to consume differ across countries, either because of non-homotheticity or differences in internal relative prices, then the stability condition will be satisfied as long as the substitution effects are sufficiently large.

Assuming that the stability condition is satisfied, in the case of $t = 1$ we have from (11)–(13) that

$$\hat{q} \equiv \frac{1}{\Delta} \left\{ \eta \left[1 + \frac{M_{3U}^1}{M_3^1} (\tau - 1) \right] \hat{\tau} - \eta^* \left[1 + \frac{2q M_{1U}^3}{A^*} (\tau^* - 1) \right] \hat{\tau}^* \right.$$
$$\left. - \mu \left[1 + \frac{M_{3U}^1}{M_3^1} (\tau - 1) \right] \hat{t} \right\}. \tag{16}$$

The direction of the change in prices due to tariffs is determined by the compensated substitution effects in this case, since the income effects arising from changes in trade volumes will operate in the same direction as the substitution effects when goods are normal and trade is not subsidized. An increase in τ will improve the terms of trade of union members, and this improvement must be less than the percentage increase in τ when the difference in marginal propensities to consume good 3 is sufficiently small. Similarly, an increase in τ^* must result in a deterioration of the member country's terms of trade. An increase in t will shift demand toward (away from) non-member goods and will thus worsen (improve) the member country's terms of trade if $\mu > 0$ (< 0).

In the case of $t > 1$, the potential for paradoxical results is primarily associated with the possibility of a reversal of trade volume effects from the case with $t = 1$. Referring to the definition of Δ it can be seen that the possibility that $\Gamma_\tau < 0$ is a potential source of market instability when $t > 1$. For the comparative statics results, $\Gamma_\tau > 0$ is a sufficient condition for an increase in τ to improve the terms of trade for a member country. However, if $\Gamma_\tau < 0$ an increase in τ could worsen the union's terms of trade if the terms of trade effect is sufficiently large and the marginal propensity to consume good 3 is also large. A similar result arises in the

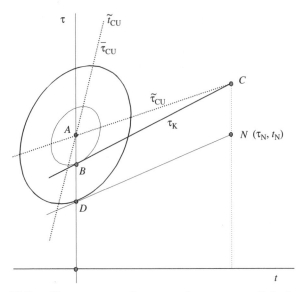

Fig. 1. ISO welfare contours for a member country: Substitutes case.

case of increases in t. At $t = 0$, sign $\hat{q}/\hat{t} = -\text{sign } \mu$. If $\mu > 0$, we could have $\hat{q}/\hat{t} > 0$ if $\Gamma_t < 0$ for t sufficiently large.

These results can be used to characterize the nature of the adjustment in external tariffs that must accompany a reduction in internal tariffs for the world price q to remain unaffected, which we refer to as Kemp–Wan adjustments. The Kemp–Wan adjustments can be characterized by $\tau_K \equiv \tau_K(t, q, \tau^*)$, which we christen Kemp–Wan tariff schedules.[5] From (16) this requires $(\hat{\tau}_K/\hat{t})|_{t=1} = \mu/\eta$ in the neighborhood of free internal trade.

We illustrate two Kemp–Wan schedules in the (t, τ) space of union tariffs in Figures 1 and 2 for given ROW tariffs. These schedules are positively or negatively sloped when they cross the τ-axis when the representative union member's imports from ROW and its union partner are net substitutes (i.e., $\mu > 0$) or net complements (i.e., $\mu < 0$), respectively. From (9) it can also be seen that, for given ROW tariffs, Kemp–Wan tariff adjustments by union members do not affect ROW welfare because they do not affect world prices. It follows that the τ_K tariff schedules in Figures 1 and 2 also capture the welfare contours of ROW.

---

[5] Srinivasan (1997) has addressed this question in the context of models with Cobb Douglas preferences and a variety of production models.

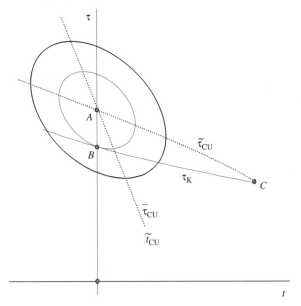

Fig. 2.   ISO welfare contours for a member country: Complements case.

For $t > 1$, the expression for Kemp–Wan tariff adjustments becomes more complicated. Utilizing (11) and (12) we find

$$\frac{\hat{\tau}_K}{\hat{t}} = \frac{\mu + (M^1_{3U}/A)\Gamma_t}{\eta + (M^1_{3U}/A)\Gamma_\tau}. \tag{17}$$

The elasticity of changes in τ_K with respect to changes in t could depart from its value in the neighborhood of $t = 1$ (i.e., μ/η) depending on how the trade volume effects change with t. For example, the above discussion suggested that if the initial point is one where $\tau = t$ and all goods are net substitutes, then $\Gamma_t < 0$, $\Gamma_\tau > 0$ and thus $\hat{\tau}_K/\hat{t} < \mu/\eta$. In addition, we have the possibility that the sign of (17) could be reversed for large values of t if one of the trade volume effects gets reversed and is sufficiently large so that the income effect of the trade volume change dominates the substitution elasticity.

In the CES/endowment model case, which necessarily implies $\mu > 0$, we showed in BSW (2001) that $\hat{\tau}_K/\hat{t} = (1 + t^\sigma)^{-1}$, where σ is the elasticity of substitution in consumption. In this case, Kemp–Wan tariff adjustments depend only on t and always require internal trade liberalization to be followed by a reduction in the external tariff. The result for the CES case indicates that, if internal trade liberalization is a gradual process, the Kemp–Wan external tariff reduction would call for smaller percentage reductions in τ in the early stages of trade liberalization than at the later stages.

4. Tariffs and member country welfare

The results linking terms of trade to trade policy instruments can now be used to derive the relationship between trade policy instruments and the welfare of member countries. Our main goal in this section is to study the union's optimal internal and external trade policies when ROW tariffs remain fixed at a pre-determined level. First, we examine the optimal external tariff policy of the union for given internal tariffs. Second, we derive the union's optimal internal trade policies when external tariffs are kept fixed at non-prohibitive levels. We then investigate the joint determination of optimal internal and external tariffs for the union (at constant ROW tariffs). The analysis enables us to describe the shape of the representative union member's (i.e., country 1's) welfare contours in (t, τ) space. It also enables us to link the analysis to Kemp–Wan tariff adjustments in external tariffs.

The effect of an increase in τ on U^1 is the sum of the direct (i.e., trade volume) effect and the effect operating through the induced change in the terms of trade. Substituting from (11) back into (9) we obtain

$$\tau \frac{\mathrm{d}U^1}{\mathrm{d}\tau} = \frac{M_3^1}{\Delta A}\left[\eta - \Gamma_\tau\left(\varepsilon^* - 1\right)\right]. \tag{18}$$

Substituting into (18) for the definition of Γ_τ gives the following expression for welfare in terms of τ and t:

$$\tau \frac{\mathrm{d}U^1}{\mathrm{d}\tau} = \frac{\varepsilon^* - 1}{\Delta A}\left[\eta - \left(\frac{t-1}{t}\right)\mu\right]M_3^1[\tilde{\tau}_{\mathrm{CU}} - \tau], \tag{19}$$

where

$$\tilde{\tau}_{\mathrm{CU}} \equiv \tilde{\tau}_{\mathrm{CU}}(t, \tau^*) = \lambda\frac{\varepsilon^*}{\varepsilon^* - 1} \quad \text{for } \lambda \equiv \lambda\left(\tau, t, \tau^*\right) = \frac{\eta}{\eta - ((t-1)/t)\mu}.$$

(Recall that ε^* is the Marshallian price elasticity of ROW's import demand function defined in (15).) If $\eta - ((t-1)/t)\mu > 0$ and $\varepsilon^* > 1$, country 1's welfare will be increasing (decreasing) in τ for $\tau < \tilde{\tau}_{\mathrm{CU}}$ ($\tau > \tilde{\tau}_{\mathrm{CU}}$). With these conditions being satisfied $\tilde{\tau}_{\mathrm{CU}}$ is the optimal external tariff of a CU.

Note that with $t = 1$ and $\lambda = 1$, Equation (19) reduces to the familiar elasticity formula for the optimal tariff (recall that τ is one plus the tariff rate). The condition for $\tilde{\tau}_{\mathrm{CU}}$ to be optimal in that case (i.e., $\varepsilon^* > 1$) reflects the fact that a country would want to raise its tariff without limit as long as it is operating in the inelastic section of the foreign country's offer curve. As can be seen from (18), the existence of internal trade barriers adds an additional requirement for $\tilde{\tau}_{\mathrm{CU}}$ to be optimal. For the expression in (18) to be zero, we must have $(\varepsilon^* - 1)\Gamma_\tau > 0$ to generate a trade-off between the trade volume and the terms of trade effect at the optimum. If $\varepsilon^* > 1$ and $\Gamma_\tau < 0$, it will be desirable to raise the tariff for any initial τ because of the magnitude of the internal tariff distortion. An increase in the external tariff

τ will generate a positive trade volume effect from intra-union trade as well as a favorable terms of trade effect on trade with ROW, which must raise welfare. The condition $\eta < ((t - 1)/t)\mu$ in (19) guarantees that $\Gamma_\tau > 0$ at the optimum.

Assuming the conditions for $\tilde{\tau}_{CU}$ to be optimal are satisfied with $t > 1$, we will have $\lambda > 1$ if $\mu > 0$. In this case the external tariff is set more aggressively than suggested by the usual elasticity formula because increases in this tariff have the additional benefit of generating a favorable expansion of distorted internal trade. If $\mu < 0$, this effect is reversed.

One interesting question is how a CU that sets its external tariff τ optimally might adjust this tariff as it reduces its internal tariff t. If the new external tariff exceeds the value associated with the requisite Kemp–Wan adjustment, ROW welfare will decrease along the path of optimal external tariff adjustments by the union. Since ε^* depends only on q and τ^*, it will be constant along the Kemp–Wan adjustment path. Thus, the question of how the optimal tariff will respond to internal tariff cuts depends on how λ varies along that path. Clearly this will depend on the specifics of the model chosen. In BSW (2001) we showed that $\lambda = (t^\sigma + t)/(t^\sigma + 1) \geqslant 1$, for $t \geqslant 1$ in the endowment model with CES consumer preferences. In this case, the $\tilde{\tau}_{CU}(t)$ locus will be flatter than the Kemp–Wan locus $\tau_K(t)$ (notice that we suppressed the τ^* argument, since τ^* is kept fixed in the background), indicating falling welfare for the non-member along the entire adjustment path, as long as $\lambda_t > 0$. This condition will hold for most parameter values, so that the loci will look as shown in Figure 1.

Figure 1 also illustrates two effects of CU formation on the optimal tariff. First, the coordination of external tariffs by union members will result in a jump in the external tariff from N to C even before any internal liberalization takes place. Union members internalize the effects of their tariff on the partner country, and thus choose a higher common external tariff against on imports from ROW. The second effect is that, even though the union reduces its external tariff along the path of internal liberalization to free trade, this reduction will be less than would be called for by the Kemp–Wan reduction. Thus, the outside country's welfare will fall monotonically along the adjustment path in this case. Note further that this path would be monotonic even if there were a restriction that prevented the union from increasing its external tariff as a result of the formation of the union (as required, e.g., by Article 24 of the GATT).

A similar question can be addressed for the case of FTAs if it is assumed that FTA members set their external tariff to maximize national (rather than FTA) welfare. In the case with $\mu > 0$, this will result in lower external tariffs because countries do not take into account the positive effect of their external tariff on the terms of trade of the partner country. In this case, the path of optimal tariffs will go through point N in Figure 1, which represents the initial Nash equilibrium. Unfortunately, the optimal tariff formulae for this case are quite complex and general results are not available. We showed in BRS (2004) that for the CES/endowment case, the change in the FTA's external tariff as a result of internal liberalization will be less than the Kemp–Wan adjustment. The favorable spillover of internal liberalization to ROW (as well as the fact that ROW will have an incentive to raise its external tariff) means that the member countries could actually lose from internal liberalization.

The possibility that $\mu < 0$ introduces a case that cannot arise with CES preferences. In this case a reduction in the internal tariff will shift demand toward the goods imported from ROW, so that an increase in the external tariff is required to keep the non-member country's welfare unaffected. If the PTA were constrained to follow the Article 24 requirement and maintain a constant external tariff, the welfare of the non-member would be improved. The welfare effect on the member countries would be ambiguous, since there is a worsening of the external terms of trade but an improvement in the internal trade volume.

Let us now suppose that the common external tariff remains fixed at a non-prohibitive level but the internal tariff is allowed to vary. To find the welfare effect of internal tariff changes, we note that $t(dU^1/dt) = q(\partial U^1/\partial q)(\hat{q}/\hat{t}) + t(\partial U^1/\partial t)$. Consider first the effect of an increase in t in the neighborhood of internal free trade. If $\mu > 0$, this will have an unfavorable terms of trade effect of reducing q from (16) but a favorable trade volume effect (for $\tau > 1$) of increasing trade with 3. If $\mu < 0$, an increase in t will shift demand toward union goods, which is a favorable terms of trade effect, but will have an unfavorable trade volume effect. In each case there is a trade-off between a trade volume effect and a terms of trade effect from an increase in t. Substituting from (10) and (16) into this expression at $t = 1$ gives

$$t\frac{dU^1}{dt} = \frac{\mu(\varepsilon^* - 1)M_3^1}{A\Delta}\left[\tau - \frac{\varepsilon^*}{\varepsilon^* - 1}\right] \tag{20}$$

If $\mu > 0$, the unfavorable terms of trade effect will dominate the trade volume effect as long as $\tau < \varepsilon^*/(\varepsilon^* - 1)$ and welfare will be reduced when t is increased. If $\mu < 0$, the favorable terms of trade effect dominates the unfavorable trade volume effect as long as $\tau < \varepsilon^*/(\varepsilon^* - 1)$ and welfare will be increased if t is raised instead. These features are illustrated in Figures 1 and 2. Note that, in either case, $\tau = \varepsilon^*/(\varepsilon^* - 1)(= \hat{\tau}_{CU}(t = 1))$ and $t = 1$ is the global optimum for the CU.[6]

A similar type of trade-off between terms of trade and trade volume effects can be conducted for the effects of tariff reductions for $t > 1$.

---

[6] We showed in BRS (2004) that this result will not hold in the case where the agreement takes the form of an FTA. In this case, FTA members reduce their external tariffs too much as the result of internal liberalization, so a positive internal tariff is desirable to encourage more aggressive setting of the external tariffs.

Substituting from (20) we obtain for the general case

$$t\frac{dU^1}{dt} = \frac{M_3^1}{A\Delta}\left[-\mu(1 + \Gamma_t) + \Gamma_t(\varepsilon^* + \eta - 1)\right]. \tag{21}$$

As long as *sign* $\Gamma_t = -sign \mu$, there will be a trade-off between terms of trade and trade volume effects. Since the signs of the terms in the welfare expression in (21) will remain unchanged in the neighborhood of $t = 1$, there will be an internal tariff $\tilde{t}_{CU} \equiv \tilde{t}_{CU}(\tau, \tau^*)$ that solves $dU^1/dt = 0$. However, care must be taken in deriving optimal tariff formulae because reversals are possible for large values of t.

Since the resulting expression is complicated we follow an indirect approach. Suppose there is an internal tariff $\tilde{t}_{CU}$ that solves $dU^1/dt = 0$ and assume that $\tilde{t}_{CU}$ monotonic in τ. Instead of working with τ as the independent variable, we may consider the inverse of $\tilde{t}_{CU}$ and focus on t as the independent variable instead. Specifically, define $\overline{\tau}_{CU}(t, \tau^*) = \tilde{t}_{CU}^{-1}(\tau, \tau^*)$. We may now establish that

$$t\frac{dU^1}{dt} = \frac{qM_{32}^1}{A\Delta}\left[\varepsilon^* - 1 - (t - 1)\frac{qM_{31}^1}{M_3^1}\right][\tau - \overline{\tau}_{CU}] \tag{22}$$

where

$$\overline{\tau}_{CU} = \frac{t\varepsilon^* M_{32}^1 + (t - 1)qM_{21}^1[\varepsilon^* - 1 + \eta]}{M_{32}^1[\varepsilon^* - 1 - (t - 1)(qM_{31}^1/M_3^1)]}.$$

Although this expression is cumbersome, it does reveal that country 1's welfare is increasing (decreasing) in the internal tariff t for $\tau > \overline{\tau}_{CU}(\tau < \overline{\tau}_{CU})$. Furthermore, if all goods are net substitutes we can show that country 1's welfare falls when we consider tariff adjustments along $\overline{\tau}_{CU}$ and away from the axis of external tariffs.

Lastly, let us form the ratio $\rho(t, \tau^*) \equiv \overline{\tau}_{CU}/\tilde{t}_{CU}$. Differentiating this ratio with respect to t and evaluating the resulting expression at $t = 1$ readily implies $\partial\rho(t = 1, \tau^*)/\partial t > 0$, when goods are net substitutes. This establishes the relative slopes of the loci illustrated in Figure 1.

It can also be shown that the welfare of PTA members must be increasing if the internal tariff is reduced and the external tariff is adjusted along the Kemp–Wan locus:

$$t\frac{dU^1}{dt}\bigg|_{\tau=\tau_K(t)} = -\frac{M_3^1(t - 1)/t}{A\left(\eta + (M_{3U}^1/A)\Gamma_\tau\right)}\left[\mu^2 - \frac{(tq)^2 M_{22}^1\eta}{M_3^1}\right]. \tag{23}$$

The bracketed expression must be positive because the compensated own substitution effect is negative. As long as the denominator of (23) is positive (which is a condition that requires an increase in τ to improve the member's terms of trade), this establishes that welfare of the representative CU member is decreasing in t along the Kemp–Wan tariff adjustment locus. Furthermore, (23) shows that at $t = 1$, member welfare will be maximized along the Kemp–Wan tariff adjustment locus. This is reflected by the tangency between iso-welfare contours of the member and the τ_K locus at $t = 1$ in Figures 1 and 2. Note also that, if country 1's importables are net substitutes, the schedule of the optimal internal tariff as a function of the external tariff (i.e., $\tilde{\tau}_{CU}$) will cross the τ-axis as indicated in Figure 1. In this case, for given external tariffs, the optimal internal intervention entails imports tariffs when $\tau > (\varepsilon^*/(\varepsilon^* - 1))$ and import subsidies when $\tau < (\varepsilon^*/(\varepsilon^* - 1))$. Exactly the opposite would be true if country 1's importables were net complements.

5. Conclusion

One of our objectives in this chapter has been to examine the impact of internal trade liberalization on tariffs and welfare of member countries in a PTA and the ROW in a general three-good environment where the member countries are symmetric. A related second objective has been to compare the results obtained to those that arise in the more restricted pure endowment model with CES preferences. We view these as worthwhile endeavors because they highlight the costs and benefits of using specific functional forms.

A key component of our analysis has been the description and characterization of Kemp–Wan tariff schedules (i.e., schedules that indicate how much the PTA's external tariff must be adjusted in response to internal trade liberalization in order to maintain the welfare of the ROW at its initial level). Our analysis revealed that, in the case where union and non-union exports are net substitutes, a Kemp–Wan adjustment to internal tariff cuts calls for a reduction of the external tariff in the neighborhood of internal free trade. A sufficient condition for this result to hold with positive internal barriers is that the sign of the trade volume effects not be reversed from their value at $t = 1$. We were also able to derive a simple formula characterizing the optimal tariff for the CU as a function of the internal tariff.

Our findings indicate that in the case where union and non-union goods are net substitutes, the characteristics of the welfare contours in the general case are similar to those for the CES case in the neighborhood of $t = 1$. Thus, qualitatively there is little loss of generality in considering models with specific functional forms in this region. However, for $t > 1$ the general model allows for paradoxes (e.g., reversals of the slope of the Kemp–Wan locus) that do not arise in the CES/endowment model. The CES/endowment model establishes that, as internal tariffs are reduced, welfare of the outside country will fall when a CU adjusts its external tariff optimally. Although this result is specific to this model, the optimal tariff formula indicates how this comparison can be made for the general case.

Specific functional forms are also needed to obtain results on the strategic analysis of FTAs, where the optimal tariff formulae are more complex. These results also suggest that strategic analysis that includes ROW tariffs requires either the adoption of specific functional forms or the imposition of plausible restrictions on how price elasticities vary with tariff levels in order to obtain more definitive results (as in Syropoulos, 2002).

In contrast to the CES/endowment model, the more general model allows for a case in which there is complementarity between the traded goods of PTA members and non-members. In this case, internal liberalization by the union will benefit the ROW at fixed external tariffs, so a Kemp–Wan adjustment calls for an increase in the external tariff of the union.

These results also suggest the desirability of extending the analysis to consider the other trade pattern consistent with this symmetric model, which is one in which each country imports a good from the other two countries. This introduces the possibility of explicit tariff discrimination.

Acknowledgement

We thank an anonymous referee for comments on an earlier draft.

References

Bagwell, K., Staiger, R.W. (2002), *The Economics of the World Trading System*. MIT Press, Cambridge, MA.

Bond, E.W., Syropoulos, C. (1996a), The size of trading blocs: market power and world welfare effects. *Journal of International Economics* 40 (3–4), 411–438.

Bond, E.W., Syropoulos, C. (1996b), Trading blocs and the sustainability of inter-regional cooperation. In: Canzoneri, M., Ethier, W.J., Grilli, V. (Eds.), *The New Transatlantic Economy*. Cambridge University Press, London, pp. 118–141.

Bond, E.W., Syropoulos, C., Winters, L.A. (2001), Deepening of regional integration and multilateral trade agreements. *Journal of International Economics* 53 (2), 335–361.

Bond, E.W., Syropoulos, C., Riezman, R.G. (2004), A strategic and welfare theoretic analysis of free trade areas. *Journal of International Economics* 64 (1), 1–27.

Gruen, F.H., Corden, W.M. (1970), A tariff that worsens the terms of trade. In: McDougall, I.A., Snape, R.H. (Eds.), *Studies in International Economics*. North Holland, Amsterdam, pp. 55–58.

Kemp, M.C., Wan, H. (1976), An elementary proposition concerning the formation of customs unions. *Journal of International Economics* 6 (1), 95–97.

Krugman, P. (1991), Is bilateralism bad? In: Helpman, E., Razin, A. (Eds.), *International Trade and Trade Policy*. MIT Press, Cambridge, MA, pp. 9–23.

Srinivasan, T.N. (1997), The common external tariff of a customs union: alternative approaches. *Japan and the World Economy* 9 (4), 447–465.

Syropoulos, C. (2002), Optimum tariffs and retaliation revisited: how country size matters. *Review of Economic Studies* 69 (3), 707–727.

CHAPTER 9

More (or Less) on Necessarily Welfare-Enhancing Free Trade Areas

Martin Richardson[a] and Niven Winchester[b]

[a]*School of Economics, Australian National University, Canberra ACT0200, Australia*
E-mail address: martin.richardson@anu.edu.au
[b]*Department of Economics, University of Otago, P.O. Box 56, Dunedin, New Zealand*
E-mail address: NWinchester@business.otago.ac.nz

Abstract

Purpose – This chapter suggests that the value of the extension to free trade areas (FTAs) of the Kemp–Wan (KW) theorem on necessarily welfare-improving customs unions is undermined by its very rationale – the greater popularity of FTAs over customs unions for 'political' reasons.
Methodology/approach – We discuss some intuition supported by partial equilibrium diagrammatic analysis and then present simulations of a global CGE model.
Findings – We argue that this sort of FTA will likely be unattractive to potential member countries. We then observe that the external tariffs here and in KW will be identical for many goods but illustrate, in a partial equilibrium setting, a context in which there might be some difference between them. Nevertheless, our analysis suggests that there are reasons to expect some harmonisation of tariffs between member countries in this sort of FTA.
Originality/value – We are the first to question the practical value of the extension of KW to FTAs. We also provide one of the few computable general equilibrium analyses of KW customs unions.

Keywords: Kemp–Wan, customs unions, free trade areas

Paper Type: Research paper

1. Introduction

In 1976 Kemp and Wan (KW henceforth) published a very significant contribution to the theory of preferential trading areas (PTAs) in "An elementary proposition concerning the formation of customs unions." They showed that, under certain weak conditions, any number of

Frontiers of Economics and Globalization
Volume 5   ISSN: 1574-8715
DOI: 10.1016/S1574-8715(08)05009-4

tariff-ridden countries could form a customs union (CU) with free trade amongst them and choose a common external tariff (CET) in a Pareto-improving fashion. Formally,

> Consider any competitive world trading equilibrium, with any number of countries and commodities and with no restrictions whatever on the tariffs and other commodity taxes of individual countries and with costs of transport fully recognized. Now let any subset of the countries form a customs union. Then there exists a common tariff vector and a system of lump-sum compensatory payments, involving only members of the union, such that each individual, whether a member of the union or not, is not worse off than before the formation of the union.
>
> (Kemp and Wan, 1976, p. 95)

The key to this result is that the CET is set at the so-called Vanek compensating tariff: the tariff that leaves all volumes of trade between the CU members and the rest of the world (ROW) unchanged from its pre-CU aggregate levels. Accordingly, ROW welfare is unaffected by the CU[1] and any gains from the internal trade liberalisation can be redistributed amongst the CU members in a Pareto-improving way through lump-sum redistribution instruments.

The importance of this result lies partly in its clarity – an unusual feature in this field of study in a second-best setting – but also in a number of further conclusions it implies. In particular, by repeated application of the theorem – suppose countries A and B form a KW CU then treat them as a single country and re-apply the theorem to show that they can form a KW CU with C and so on – KW have identified a path to global free trade through a series of PTAs. In the debate that has raged for some decades concerning the impact of PTAs on multilateralism, this has been a cornerstone of the case suggesting that PTAs can be beneficial and need not undermine the goals of multilateral liberalisation.

It is important to note that the KW result, as the authors themselves stress, is an existence result only. No claims are made concerning the optimality of the KW CU, merely that all members can be made better off than in the CU's absence in terms of economists' usual measure of economic welfare. Nevertheless, one could certainly envisage countries taking a KW path to multilateralism through bilateralism, precisely because of its neutrality properties for non-members.

In recent years, a number of authors have noted that free trade areas (FTAs) are a more popular form of PTA than are CUs and have

---

[1] In the context of the KW set-up, this conclusion requires either that the CU is infinitesimally small vis-à-vis the ROW or that the ROW is not behaving optimally – see Richardson (1995b). For a quite different setting in which this condition is not required, see Kemp and Shimomura (2001).

concluded that, therefore, it would be useful to have a result for FTAs that is analogous to KW's result for CUs. So Panagariya and Krishna (2002) write, for example, " ... we still lack a parallel result [to KW] on FTAs where members could use member-specific external tariff vectors ... The purpose of the present paper is to fill this gap in the literature – a major gap, in our judgment, given the relative popularity of FTAs over CUs in practice (p. 354). In endorsement of this chapter, Grinols and Silva (2003) suggest that, "Panagariya and Krishna (2002) have performed a great service to the economics profession, indeed to any country considering a FTA ... Their contribution does for FTAs what Kemp and Wan (1976) did for CUs twenty-six years earlier" (p. 1). The Panagariya and Krishna paper demonstrates that a result for FTAs that is similar to the KW result for CUs can be established: a number of countries can form an FTA, set their external tariffs so as to freeze trade with the ROW on a member country-by-member country basis and, with lump-sum transfers internal to the FTA and appropriate rules of origin, ensure a Pareto improvement.[2]

The purpose of this chapter is to consider this result – which we shall refer to as the Ohyama–Panagariya–Krishna or OPK result – in a little more detail. In particular, we argue that the very rationale for the relative popularity of FTAs vs. CUs undermines the usefulness of the OPK result. Furthermore, there are strong reasons to believe that the OPK tariff will be very similar to the corresponding KW tariff.

The remainder of the chapter is laid out as follows. In the next section we present a brief summary and proof of the OPK result before arguing that the OPK FTA will likely be unattractive to potential member countries. We then observe that in any PTA the OPK and KW external tariffs will be identical for many goods but illustrate, in a partial equilibrium setting, a context in which there might be some difference between them. Nevertheless, our analysis suggests that there are reasons to expect some harmonisation of tariffs between member countries in an OPK FTA. A further section then discusses a numerical simulation performed to illustrate the two forms of trade agreement in practice and a final section concludes.

2. The Ohyama–Panagariya–Krishna result

2.1. The OPK proposition

Following Grinols and Silva (2003), consider two countries $i = $ A,B forming an FTA in a world of n traded commodities. We can denote the

---

[2] Grinols and Silva (2003) provide a tidier proof of this result. It should also be noted that Ohyama (2002) independently notes the same result. We return to the rules of origin issue below.

change in welfare for country i by the compensating variation, where situation 0 is pre-FTA and situation 1 is post-FTA:

$$\Delta W^i = CV = e^i(p^1, u^{i1}) - e^i(p^1, u^{i0}) = \underbrace{p^1 y^{i1} + p^1 \omega^i + p^1 z^{i1}}_{e^i(p^1, u^{i1})} - e^i(p^1, u^{i0}),$$

(1)

where p^k is the $1 \times n$ vector of consumer prices in situation $k = 0,1$, y^{ik} is the $1 \times n$ vector of domestic production in country $i = A,B$ in situation $k = 0,1$ (treating inputs as negative outputs), ω^i is endowments and z^i denotes the vector of imports into country i (where exports are negative elements.) Thus we can write the change in welfare in country i as:

$$\Delta W^i = U^i_C + U^i_P + U^i_T$$

(2)

where

$$\begin{aligned}
U^i_C &= p^1 x^{i0} - e^i(p^1, u^{i0}) \\
&= p^1 y^{i0} + p^1 \omega^i + p^1 z^{i0} - e^i(p^1, u^{i0}) \\
U^i_P &= p^1(y^{i1} - y^{i0}) \\
U^i_T &= p^1(z^{i1} - z^{i0})
\end{aligned}$$

(3)

and x^{ik} denotes the vector of consumption in country $i = A,B$ in situation $k = 0,1$. In moving to the OPK FTA, utility maximisation by consumers implies that $U^i_C \geq 0$ so, if $U^i_P \geq 0$, then the change in the joint welfare of the FTA members is given by

$$\Delta W^A + \Delta W^B \geq U^A_T + U^B_T = p^1[(z^{A1} - z^{A0}) + (z^{B1} - z^{B0})] = 0$$

(4)

where the last equality follows from each country's trade with the ROW being unchanged and because any changes in A's trade with B are offset by changes in B's trade with A. Thus both countries gain jointly from this FTA if $U^i_P = p^1(y^{i1} - y^{i0}) \geq 0$.

Grinols and Silva (2003, p. 5) write this as $U^i_P = q^1(y^{i1} - y^{i0})$, where q^1 denotes the vector of producer prices within the FTA. In this case profit maximisation ensures that the expression is positive. Richardson (1995a) shows that, regardless of rules of origin, producer prices must be equated within an FTA but that consumers might face different prices for the same commodity. In particular, the producer price of some commodity initially imported from the ROW might exceed the consumer price if the country's FTA external tariff is less than that of its FTA partner, in which case it will export its entire production to its partner at the partner's internal price (the price received by its producers) and import its entire consumption from the ROW at, for consumers, the world price plus its tariff.[3] However, Grinols and Silva (2003) avoid this issue by differentiating goods by

---

[3] This is illustrated below.

location and so defining consumer and producer prices to be equal for all goods:[4] while the New Zealand (NZ) producer price of "NZ cheese in Australia" might be different to the NZ consumer price of "NZ cheese in NZ", for example, it can arbitrarily be set to equal the fictitious NZ consumer price of "NZ cheese in Australia" (fictitious, as none is consumed in NZ, by definition.)

2.2. An objection

The rationale for wishing to extend KW to FTAs is that the latter are far more popular, in practice, than are CUs. But why? The obvious attraction of an FTA over a CU is economic sovereignty: countries are unwilling to cede to others the power to set their external tariffs. A simple application of the KW theorem tells us that a CU weakly welfare dominates an FTA for member countries (as the latter is a set of tariff-ridden countries and so the KW theorem applies to it directly.) So if countries were willing to coordinate their tariff-setting we know that they should choose a CU *unless* they are motivated by an objective function other than our standard measure of economic welfare. "Free trade areas…are politically attractive compared to CUs which require members to agree to a CET" (Grinols and Silva, 2003, p. 1). But then what is the attraction of the OPK FTA? It leaves member countries with no more degrees of freedom in setting their external tariffs than does the KW CU – there is some tariff vector for each member country that yields the OPK FTA just as there is some (common) tariff vector that yields the KW CU – so its attraction cannot be that it leaves member countries less fettered in terms of external tariff policy. Nor does this literature tell us that there exists a path through PTAs to global free trade – we knew that already.

One case that might be made for the OPK FTA is that it yields a tariff vector that, while no less constrained than the Vanek compensating CET, is, nevertheless, different to the latter and perhaps more desirable given a country's trade policy preferences. That, of course, is quite possible but there are reasons to believe that, as a practical matter, the OPK tariff is unlikely to be very different to the KW CET and preserves less difference between members' external tariffs than prevailed before the FTA's formation.

To see this, consider a partial equilibrium analysis of two countries A and B contemplating a PTA excluding the ROW, country C. Initially, each country levies tariffs on an MFN basis.[5] For goods that are not traded at all by any of the countries before the PTA the external tariffs of

---

[4] This interpretation also validates Ohyama's (2002) proof of the same proposition.
[5] This is for simplicity of exposition only. It is not a part of the KW results which apply for *any* pattern of external tariffs and it is not necessary here either.

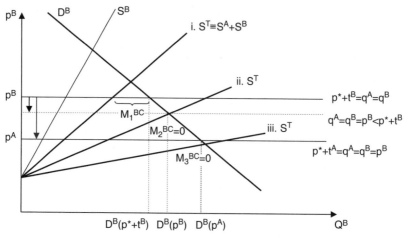

Fig. 1.   Demand in B and total PTA supply.

member countries are irrelevant in that they can be set at the highest of the
tariffs in A and B that preserve zero trade (i.e., the OPK FTA tariff) with
no consequence for the other partner (whose tariff might have water in it,
of course.) Similarly, for goods traded only between A and B the external
tariffs of the PTA are irrelevant and can be equalised upwards with no
effect. For any good traded only between C and a single PTA member the
same reasoning applies: preserving the PTA's trade (*à la* KW) is the same
as preserving the single trading country's trade and setting the other
country's tariff equal has no consequence at all.[6] This leaves the only
goods of interest (i.e., where the KW and OPK tariffs might differ to some
effect) as those which C trades with both A and B. Consider, without loss
of generality, some good exported by C to both A and B before the PTA is
formed. And suppose, also without loss of generality, that the pre-PTA
tariff in A, t^A, is less than that in B, t^B. We then have three generic cases to
consider as illustrated in Figure 1:

i. It could be that total supply in A and B at p^*+t^B (i.e., $S^T(p^*+t^B)\equiv$
   $S^A(p^*+t^B)+S^B(p^*+t^B)$, where S^i denotes supply of the good in country
   i = A,B and p^* denotes the world price) is less than consumer demand
   in B at $p^B = p^*+t^B$, $D^B(p^*+t^B)$, where D^i denotes demand for the good
   in country i = A,B.

---

[6] The exception to this is if the non-importing partner is only not importing because of a
prohibitive tariff that is greater than the partner's tariff. Such a case can then be considered as
one where C exports – in principle – to both partners and is the case we deal with next. We are
grateful to a referee for highlighting this case.

ii. Total PTA supply might exceed demand in B at the pre-PTA price – i.e. $S^{T}(p^{*}+t^{B}) > D^{B}(p^{*}+t^{B})$ – but is less than consumer demand in B at A's initial price, or $S^{T}(p^{*}+t^{A}) < D^{B}(p^{*}+t^{A})$.

iii. It could be that total PTA supply at A's initial price exceeds demand in B at that price: $S^{T}(p^{*}+t^{A}) > D^{B}(p^{*}+t^{A})$.

In the first case, following Richardson (1995a), the formation of an FTA will lead country A's producers to sell their entire output in B at price $p^{B} = p^{*}+t^{B} > p^{A} = p^{*}+t^{A}$ (which is fine, even if rules of origin require 100% local content, as it is all domestically produced) and all consumption in A will be imported from C and sold to consumers at price p^{A}. In country B, consumers still pay p^{B} as they did before the PTA, but some of the imports previously sourced from C are now displaced by (duty-free) imports from A' leaving imports from C of M_{1}^{BC}, as shown. All up, producers in A receive p^{B} for all their production of this good while consumers in A pay the lower price p^{A}. Producers and consumers in B both face the same price p^{B}.

In the second case this trade displacement from A to B suffices to squeeze out all imports from C (so $M_{2}^{BC} = 0$, as shown) and so reduces the price in B below the world price *cum* tariff.[7] Now producers in both A and B sell all their output in B at B's consumer price, p^{B}, which is something between $p^{*}+t^{A}$ and $p^{*}+t^{B}$. Consumers in A still import their entire consumption from C and pay the lower price $p^{A} = p^{*}+t^{A} < p^{B}$. Finally, in the third case, the volume of production from A is sufficient to equate both countries' prices at the lower $p^{A} = p^{*}+t^{A}$ in which case producers in A and B are indifferent about where they sell and all consumers and producers prices are equated within the FTA.

We now wish to consider each of these cases in turn and ask what will the tariffs in A and B have to be to preserve pre-PTA trade on a country-by-country basis in an OPK FTA and on aggregate in a KW CU.

In the first case, where induced trade from A does not displace all of B's imports from C, if an FTA were formed note that, at pre-PTA tariffs, B's trade with C is reduced by more (by $S^{B}(p^{*}+t^{B})$) than A's trade is increased (by $S^{A}(p^{*}+t^{B})$) so A and B's overall imports from C have risen. Figure 2, adapted from Panagariya and Krishna (2002), illustrates this case.

Here we start with t^{A} and t^{B} as the tariffs in A and B, respectively, and the formation of an FTA displaces A's production to be sold in B. Accordingly, imports from C rise in A (from M_{0}^{AC} to M^{AC}) and fall in B (from M_{0}^{BC} to M^{BC}) as shown. As all demand in A is met by imports from C, to find the tariff that restores imports from C to their previous level, we simply find the tariff $\underline{t}^{A}$ at which

---

[7] Note this qualification to the suggestion in Grinols and Silva (2003, p. 4) that the producer price of a good in an FTA will equal $p^{*}+\mathrm{Max}[t^{A}, t^{B}]$. In fact, producer prices are equated but the highest tariff may have water in it, as in this second case.

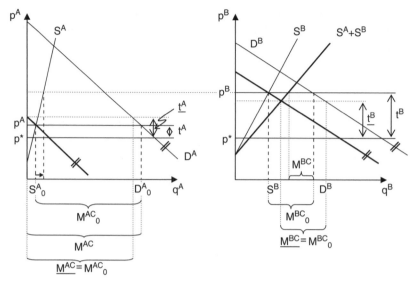

Fig. 2. *Total PTA supply less than demand in B.*

$D^A(p^* + \underline{t}^A) = D^A(p^* + t^A) - S^A(p^* + t^A) = M_0^{AC}$, as shown in Figure 2. Note that it must be true that $\underline{t}^A > t^A$. In country B, to find the tariff that restores imports from C to their pre-FTA levels we need to find the tariff $\underline{t}^B$ such that $D^B(p^* + \underline{t}^B) - S^A(p^* + \underline{t}^B) - S^B(p^* + \underline{t}^B) = D^B(p^* + t^B) - S^A(p^* + t^B) = M_0^{BC}$. Note that it must be true that $\underline{t}^B < t^B$.

So the OPK FTA ends with some tariff harmonisation here. If A and B formed a CU in this case then the KW CET will lie somewhere between t^A and t^B, clearly, at a level where the increase in B's imports from C exactly equal the decrease in A's imports from C, compared to the pre-PTA situation. Indeed, a little inspection reveals that it must lie between $\underline{t}^A$ and $\underline{t}^B$.[8]

Note that the adjustment of tariffs to the OPK levels offsets, at least in part, the incentive for trade displacement. It is quite possible, in fact, that even in this case we can get complete tariff harmonisation in the FTA (in which case the tariff is identical to the KW CET.) Consider the variant of Figure 2 shown in Figure 3.

---

[8] Consider going from the OPK FTA to the KW CU. If the CET in the latter were set at $\underline{t}^B$ exactly then total imports would be too low – A's production would be sold in A displacing a quantum of imports from C, compared to the FTA case, but would be exactly offset by increased imports from C into B. Thus the net impact on total imports is just the decline in demand in A and, as we started with total imports into A and B being at the desired pre-PTA level, so this means the CET is too high. A symmetric argument, *mutatis mutandis*, applies to $\underline{t}^A$.

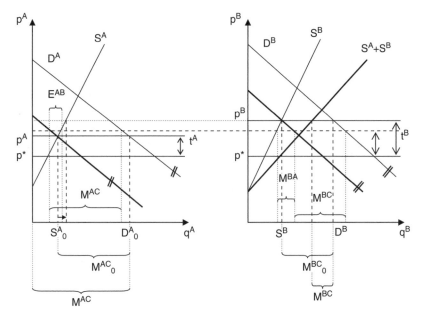

Fig. 3.   Total PTA supply less than demand in B (no trade displacement).

Here the tariff in A that would restore imports to their pre-FTA levels is so high that it leads to an internal price in excess of that in B: A's producers would not then wish to divert their sales to B. The equilibrium now involves a common tariff, no trade displacement and a common internal FTA price shown by the dotted line. This, of course, is fully equivalent to the Vanek compensating tariff in the KW CU although it is accompanied by some internal trade between A and B where none occurred before.

Similar analysis reveals that in the second of the cases discussed earlier we also get tariff convergence in the OPK FTA, in the sense just discussed and, again, it can be partial or complete. In the third case, however, it is always complete: the OPK tariff is the same as the KW CET. In the first two of these cases the existence of incomplete convergence is more likely the greater is the initial divergence between tariffs and the less significant is domestic production in the lower-tariff country relative to imports in its partner.

The conclusion we can draw from this discussion is that while the tariff vectors that support the OPK FTA will generally differ across member countries, they will not differ as much as the initial pre-FTA tariffs – there will be some convergence and they may, in many cases, converge to the KW CET. What does this do to the case for the OPK FTA in comparison to a KW CU? While it is quite possible that the OPK tariff is preferred to the KW CET by a particular country on political economy grounds, it seems to us that there is no presumption in favour of this over the alternative that a country is worse off under the OPK tariff. Furthermore, the leeway that the FTA allows for tariffs to differ across countries – the purported advantage of an FTA over a CU – is unlikely to be great.

However, this analysis is all partial equilibrium and general equilibrium considerations, affecting demands through income effects and supplies through factor prices, may upset these presumptions. A full analytical general equilibrium approach is unlikely to be very revealing so we turn to a numerical simulation of one popular global CGE model for illustrative purposes.

3. A numerical simulation

3.1. Background

Our simulation exercises employ version 6 the Global Trade Analysis Project (GTAP) database (Dimaranan, 2006), which is operationalised using the GTAP6inGAMS model (Rutherford, 2005). The model is a static, perfectly competitive general equilibrium representation of global trade and production in 2001.

Although our chosen model is discussed in detail elsewhere and is well known, we outline two features important for our analysis. First, unlike the standard GEMPACK version of the GTAP model, each region's trade balance is fixed in GTAP6inGAMS. Second, the treatment of imports in our general equilibrium model differs from that in the previous section. Specifically, imports are differentiated from domestic commodities and by region of origin according to the Armington assumption (Armington, 1969) in GTAP6inGAMS. That is, for each good, imports from different regions are gathered in a constant elasticity of substitution (CES) nest to create an import composite. The import composite is combined in a further CES nest with the domestically produced variety to generate a composite that is consumed in the domestic economy. We assign values of eight and four, respectively, as elasticity parameters governing substitution possibilities between imports from different regions, and the domestically produced variety and composite imports for all commodities. The structure of this model is highly unfavourable to our earlier arguments, in that each good here is differentiated by location so the possibility of a partner country's exports completely substituting for domestic production is removed.

We aggregate the GTAP database to fit our purpose. Our regional aggregation of the GTAP database identifies North America (the United States, Canada and Mexico), the EU (the EU 25) and ROW – all other regions. Our aggregation also identifies either three sectors (agriculture, manufacturing and services) or 22 (see Table 2) and two factors of production (capital and labour).

Before undertaking our FTA-CU simulations, we modify the base model to suit our needs. Specifically, we remove transport costs from the model, and eliminate tariffs and export taxes on intra-regional trade in North America and EU separately. We also calculate (regional) volume-weighted tariffs levied by North America on imports from the EU and ROW for each commodity, which we use to replace tariffs imposed by North America on imports from all regions. Similarly, we replace North American export taxes on goods shipped to other regions with volume-weighted average tax rates. Analogous changes are made to EU tariffs and export tariffs.[9] We create a database consistent with our modified model by introducing the above changes as shocks, solving the model and saving the updated data.

Turning to our simulations, both our FTA and CU simulations eliminate tariffs and export taxes on trade between North America and the EU but differ in their treatment of members' trade taxes on transactions with the ROW. In our FTA scenario, tariffs and exports taxes on North American and EU trade with the ROW are assigned so that, for each commodity, each member's exports to and imports from the ROW are unchanged. Our CU simulation stipulates common North American and EU import tariffs and export taxes on trade between member nations and the ROW, which are chosen so that, for each commodity, combined North America–EU exports to and imports from the ROW are constant.[10]

3.2. Simulation results

Table 1 shows our results in a highly aggregated case.

Note, first, that the welfare numbers indicate that North America loses from both an OPK FTA and a KW CU but that the EU gains in both and that, as expected, the CU leads to higher (aggregate) welfare than the FTA.

Looking at tariffs, we see that general equilibrium considerations can, indeed, offset the effects noted in the partial equilibrium analysis of the previous section. Note that the biggest change in tariff from the FTA to the CU – both absolutely and in relative terms – is the North American

---

[9] It is necessary to modify tariffs and export taxes is such a way as tariffs in the GTAP database are commodity-weighted averages, so recorded tariffs on, say, North American imports from nations facing the same MFN tariff can differ.

[10] We have conducted "sensitivity analysis" for these exercises, too, looking at how they respond to changes in assumed elasticities. However, as the point of this whole exercise is simply to illustrate our arguments numerically, the 'realism' of these numbers is not of great concern so we do not report these numbers here. These and more details from our simulations are available from the authors on request.

Table 1. Trade taxes imposed by North America and EU, 3 sectors

	North America	EU
	Import tariffs (%)	
	Base values	
Agriculture	0.541	1.850
Manufacturing	3.280	2.965
Services	0.000	0.012
	North America–EU FTA	
Agriculture	0.611	2.169
Manufacturing	2.806	3.159
Services	0.236	0.460
	North America–EU CU	
Agriculture	1.499	1.499
Manufacturing	2.902	2.902
Services	0.279	0.279
	Export taxes (%)	
	Base values	
Agriculture	0.000	−2.330
Manufacturing	−0.012	−0.425
Services	0.000	0.000
	North America–EU FTA	
Agriculture	0.019	−2.849
Manufacturing	−0.035	−0.880
Services	−0.109	−0.514
	North America–EU CU	
Agriculture	−0.814	−0.814
Manufacturing	−0.463	−0.463
Services	−0.266	−0.266

Changes in welfare (equivalent variation, 2001 US dollars, million)

	North America	EU	Total
FTA	−716.84	2439.81	1722.97
CU	−1328.50	3801.63	2473.13

tariff on agriculture which goes from around 0.6%–1.5%: an increase of over 145%. This is a massive percentage increase, of course, but represents an actual tariff increase of less than one percentage point. Perhaps a better measure can be gained by looking at a more disaggregated case in which we can consider trade-weighted tariffs. Tables 2 and 3 present results for import and export taxes, respectively, for a 22-sector disaggregation.

Again, there are some large relative changes here, most notably for the North American tariff on Forestry and Fishing which rises by some 180%

Table 2. Import tariffs imposed by North America and EU (%), 22 sectors

	Base values		FTA		CU
	North America	EU	North America	EU	North America and EU
Grains and plant-based fibres	2.474	8.164	2.437	7.861	6.188
Animal products	0.968	1.884	1.023	2.014	1.627
Forestry and fishing	0.431	1.308	0.493	1.659	1.385
Mining	0.062	0.027	0.121	0.411	0.376
Food	6.483	18.244	5.329	17.713	14.144
Textiles	10.590	4.485	8.617	4.954	6.784
Wearing apparel	12.393	5.561	10.686	5.874	8.504
Leather products	12.725	5.750	8.532	6.250	7.346
Wood products	1.192	0.697	1.111	1.042	1.185
Paper products and publishing	0.665	0.404	0.686	0.747	0.784
Petroleum and coal products	1.904	2.220	1.779	2.561	2.347
Chemical, rubber and plastic products	2.704	1.987	2.090	2.164	2.189
Mineral products nec	5.130	2.681	3.669	2.843	3.286
Ferrous metals	2.060	4.320	1.675	4.630	3.433
Metals nec	1.347	0.845	1.233	1.122	1.230
Metal products	3.475	2.055	3.066	2.329	2.803
Motor vehicles and parts	2.920	6.339	2.425	6.388	3.829
Transport equipment nec	0.779	1.591	0.666	1.360	1.146
Electronic equipment	0.576	0.864	0.617	1.048	0.920
Machinery and equipment nec	2.049	1.154	1.707	1.323	1.617
Manufactures nec	1.856	1.451	1.418	1.659	1.598
Services	0.000	0.012	0.169	0.351	0.328

from the OPK FTA to the KW CU but, once more, this masks a very small absolute change (from less than 0.5% in the FTA to around 1.3% in the CU.) Overall, if we weight all trade taxes by base-level trade with the ROW, the North American tariff in the base case is 2.8% (the EU tariff being 2.5%) and the North American tariff in the FTA is 2.3% (the EU tariff being 2.7%), which rises (falls, for the EU) to 2.6% in the CU: a 13% rise from the FTA for North America and a 3% fall for the EU.

To make some formal attempt at measuring these differences on a sectoral basis, we define the convergence ratio, ρ, as in (5):

$$\rho = \frac{\left|t_0^{US} - t_0^{EU}\right|/\overline{t}_0 - \left|t_1^{US} - t_1^{EU}\right|/\overline{t}_1}{\left|t_0^{US} - t_0^{EU}\right|/\overline{t}_0} \tag{5}$$

where $\overline{t}$ is the US–EU average tariff, and "0" and "1" identify, respectively, the initial and FTA states of affairs. So ρ varies from zero to one as tariffs converge, equalling unity if there is complete convergence, and is negative if there is divergence. Table 4 reports this metric for each of 22 sectors: in 13 of these we find $\rho > 0$.

Table 3. *Export taxes imposed by North America and EU (in %), 22 sectors*

	Base values		FTA		CU
	North America	EU	North America	EU	North America and EU
Grains and plant based fibres	–	−4.866	0.111	−6.034	−1.693
Animal products	–	−0.600	0.024	−0.881	−0.497
Forestry and fishing	–	–	−0.053	−0.381	−0.307
Mining	–	–	−0.060	−0.381	−0.322
Food	−0.161	−7.625	−0.171	−7.942	−4.246
Textiles	–	0.080	0.306	−0.307	−0.261
Wearing apparel	–	0.186	0.530	−0.215	−0.140
Leather products	–	–	0.838	−0.326	−0.227
Wood products	–	–	0.021	−0.368	−0.288
Paper products and publishing	–	–	−0.031	−0.384	−0.307
Petroleum and coal products	–	0.083	−0.047	−0.307	−0.275
Chemical, rubber and plastic products	–	–	0.041	−0.330	−0.252
Mineral products nec	–	–	0.041	−0.368	−0.280
Ferrous metals	–	–	0.026	−0.350	−0.245
Metals nec	–	–	0.004	−0.347	−0.271
Metal products	–	–	0.023	−0.367	−0.283
Motor vehicles and parts	−0.177	–	−0.078	−0.288	−0.227
Transport equipment nec	0.048	–	0.045	−0.285	−0.207
Electronic equipment	–	–	−0.028	−0.344	−0.281
Machinery and equipment nec	–	–	0.010	−0.342	−0.272
Manufactures nec	–	–	0.141	−0.348	−0.251
Services	–	–	−0.066	−0.403	−0.324

We also illustrate this convergence ratio on a sectoral basis in Figure 4.

Are these large differences between the OPK FTA and KW CU cases? This depends on the metric one uses to assess divergence, but it does not seem to us that these numbers provide much to support the notion that an OPK FTA will be attractive compared to a KW CU because of the resulting tariff levels: a 2.6% tariff (trade-weighted) does not seem like much vs. 2.3% or 2.7%.

Finally, Table 5 lists the welfare effects of the two schemes in this 22-sector disaggregation. Once more, the CU welfare dominates the FTA, as it must, from an aggregate welfare perspective. It is noteworthy again that one region actually loses from both the FTA and the CU which simply underscores the importance of transfers to make these trading areas mutually attractive.[11]

---

[11] Dixit and Norman (1980) have noted that the KW result can be implemented using only commodity taxes (although this scheme can only realize production gains from trade); it is not obvious that the logic would apply directly to the OPK result as well, however.

Table 4. Convergence metrics

	t_0^{Min}	t_0^{Max}	t_1^{Min}	t_1^{Max}	ρ
Grains and plant-based fibres	0.465	1.535	0.473	1.527	0.015
Animal products	0.679	1.321	0.674	1.326	−0.015
Forestry and fishing	0.496	1.504	0.458	1.542	−0.076
Mining	0.611	1.389	0.455	1.545	−0.402
Food	0.524	1.476	0.463	1.537	−0.130
Textiles	0.595	1.405	0.730	1.270	0.334
Wearing apparel	0.619	1.381	0.709	1.291	0.236
Leather products	0.622	1.378	0.846	1.154	0.591
Wood products	0.738	1.262	0.968	1.032	0.876
Paper products and publishing	0.756	1.244	0.957	1.043	0.824
Petroleum and coal products	0.923	1.077	0.820	1.180	−1.348
Chemical, rubber and plastic products	0.847	1.153	0.982	1.018	0.885
Mineral products nec	0.687	1.313	0.873	1.127	0.595
Ferrous metals	0.646	1.354	0.531	1.469	−0.323
Metals nec	0.771	1.229	0.953	1.047	0.793
Metal products	0.743	1.257	0.864	1.136	0.469
Motor vehicles and parts	0.631	1.369	0.550	1.450	−0.218
Transport equipment nec	0.657	1.343	0.657	1.343	0.000
Electronic equipment	0.800	1.200	0.741	1.259	−0.295
Machinery and equipment nec	0.720	1.280	0.873	1.127	0.547
Manufactures nec	0.878	1.122	0.922	1.078	0.361
Services	0.000	2.000	0.651	1.349	0.651

Note: t_0^{Min} is defined as $\min(t_0^{US}, t_0^{EU})/\bar{t}$ and t_0^{Max} as $\max(t_0^{US}, t_0^{EU})/\bar{t}$.

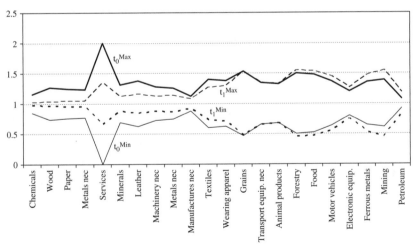

Note: Sectors are arranged in ascending order of convergence ratios.

Fig. 4. Initial and OPK tariffs.

Table 5.   Changes in welfare (equivalent variation, 2001 US dollars, million), 22 sectors

	North America	EU	Total
FTA	−955.21	3125.70	2170.49
CU	−2592.33	6958.31	4365.98

4. Conclusion

This chapter has looked at recent arguments extending Kemp and Wan's seminal theorem on necessarily welfare-improving customs unions to FTAs. We note that the very rationale for the relative popularity of FTAs vs. CUs – the degrees of freedom left to a policymaker in terms of setting external tariffs – undermines the usefulness of this extension. Furthermore, we suggest that the OPK tariff might be very similar to the corresponding KW tariff and provide a numerical CGE simulation to illustrate this.

We finish with an unproven conjecture. We have considered two pairs of tariff vectors that freeze the trade of FTA member countries with the ROW: the OPK tariffs that freeze such trade country by country and the KW tariffs that are identical for members and freeze the trade in aggregate (all on a good-by-good basis). We also know that aggregate welfare is higher in the KW case than in the OPK case, due simply to the fact that all prices are equalised within the member countries. Our conjecture is that there exists a continuum of tariff vectors between the OPK and KW levels that hold aggregate FTA trade with the ROW fixed (good-by-good) and that aggregate FTA welfare is increasing monotonically as the tariff is varied from the OPK value to that of KW.[12]

Acknowledgement

We acknowledge with gratitude the constructive comments from an anonymous referee.

Appendix

This appendix illustrates the chapter's closing conjecture in the context of our CGE simulations. We examine this by stipulating that European trade taxes are equal to weighted averages of KW and OPK trade taxes and adjusting North American trade taxes so that aggregate FTA trade with

---

[12] The Appendix provides a confirmation of this conjecture in the context of our CGE simulation.

ROW is held constant. So the European trade tax for a particular commodity, t^{EU}, is given by:

$$t^{EU} = \alpha t^{EU}_{KW} + (1 - \alpha)t^{EU}_{OPK},$$

where t^{EU}_{KW} and t^{EU}_{OPK} denote the appropriate European KW and OPK trade taxes, respectively (given the North American tariff), and α is a parameter bound between zero and one.

When α is equal to one this framework produces the KW tariffs in both regions, converging towards OPK tariffs as α approaches zero. We illustrate aggregate FTA welfare for alternative values of α in Figure A1; these results are consistent with our conjecture.

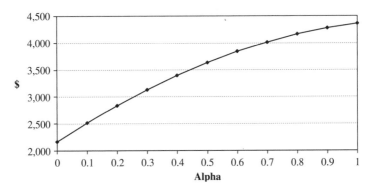

Fig. A1. Change in FTA welfare (equivalent variation, 2001 US dollars) for alternative tariff regimes.

References

Armington, P.S. (1969), A theory of demand for products distinguished by place of production. *IMF Staff Papers* 16, 159–176.

Dimaranan, B.V. (2006), *Global Trade, Assistance, and Production: The GTAP 6 Data Base.* Centre for Global Trade Analysis, Purdue University, Lafayette, IN.

Dixit, A., Norman, V. (1980), *Theory of International Trade.* Cambridge University Press, Cambridge, UK.

Grinols, E. L., Silva, P. (2003), An enhancement of modern free trade area theory. Office of Research Working Paper Series, 8. University of Illinois at Urbana-Champaign, Urbana-Champaign, IL.

Kemp, M.C., Shimomura, K. (2001), A second elementary proposition concerning the formation of customs unions. *Japanese Economic Review* 52 (1), 64–69.

Kemp, M.C., Wan, H.Y., Jr. (1976), An elementary proposition concerning the formation of customs unions. *Journal of International Economics* 6, 95–97.

Ohyama, M. (2002), The economic significance of the Gatt/WTO rules. In: Woodland, A.D. (Ed.), *Economic Theory and International Trade: Essays in Honour of Murray C.* Kemp, Edward Elgar, Cheltenham, UK, pp. 71–85.

Panagariya, A., Krishna, P. (2002), On necessarily welfare-enhancing free trade areas. *Journal of International Economics* 57, 353–367.

Richardson, M. (1995a), Tariff revenue competition in a free trade area. *European Economic Review* 39 (7), 1429–1437.

Richardson, M. (1995b), On the interpretation of the Kemp/Wan theorem. *Oxford Economic Papers* 47 (4), 696–703.

Rutherford, T.F. (2005), GTAP6inGAMS: The dataset and static model [online]. Ann Arbor, MI. Available at http://www.mpsge.org/gtap6/gtap6gams.pdf [Accessed on 29 May 2006].

CHAPTER 10

Pareto-Improving Trading Clubs without Income Transfers

Kazumichi Iwasa[a], Raymond Riezman[b] and Koji Shimomura[c]

[a]Graduate School of Economics, Kobe University, Kobe, Japan
E-mail address: kazumichi@hi-net.zaq.ne.jp
[b]Department of Economics, University of Iowa, Iowa City, IA 52242, USA
E-mail address: raymond-riezman@uiowa.edu
[c]Research Institute for Economics & Business Administration, Kobe University, Japan

Abstract

Purpose – We ask how far the Kemp–Wan Pareto-improving result can hold without inter-country transfers.

Methodology/approach – Assuming that the standard revenue and expenditure functions exist, we consider tariff adjustments for some group of countries such that they makes member countries better off without affecting non-member countries (*a la* Kemp–Wan).

Findings – Any group of countries can engage in a Pareto-improving non-discriminatory tariff reform *without income transfers,* if (i) there are more than two tradable goods and (ii) the initial tariff vectors of the member countries satisfy the non-proportionality condition. We then show that if these two conditions hold then countries can form a *Pareto-optimal* customs union. Depending on initial conditions, transfers may be necessary for the customs union to be *Pareto-improving*.

Originality/value of paper – The Pareto-improving result of this chapter is based on tariff reform only.

Keywords: Customs unions, Transfer payments

Paper type: Research paper

1. Introduction

Three decades have passed since Kemp and Wan (1976) published one of the most important papers on customs union theory. The Kemp–Wan theorem states that starting from any initial equilibrium, if inter-country transfers are allowed, there always exists a set of countries that can form a

Frontiers of Economics and Globalization
Volume 5   ISSN: 1574-8715
DOI: 10.1016/S1574-8715(08)05010-0

customs union that is Pareto-improving. Thus, starting from any initial equilibrium one can successively apply the Kemp–Wan theorem, enlarging the customs union, until free trade is reached.

The Kemp–Wan paper has spawned a large literature that has extended their result in many directions. Kowalczyk and Sjostrom (1994) show how inter-country transfer payments, calculated using the Shapley value, can be used to facilitate trade liberalization in a setting of multilateral trade negotiations. Konishi *et al.* (2003) prove an interesting result showing that starting from any initial equilibrium if customs unions are required to have no effects on non-member countries (be Kemp–Wan customs unions), then one can find a set of inter-country transfers that will lead all countries to choose free trade. That is, free trade is in the core of a Kemp–Wan customs union game.

Ohyama (2002) and Panagariya and Krishna (2002) get results for free trade areas rather than customs unions. Again, their results rely on the use of inter-country transfer payments.[1] Raimondos-Moller and Woodland (2004b) consider non-discriminatory tariff reforms in trading clubs and show that there exist such reforms which if accompanied by inter-country transfers within club members produce a Pareto improvement.

A series of papers Richardson (1995), Kemp and Shimomura (2001) and Raimondos-Moller and Woodland (2004a) explore the issue of what happens when some or all tariffs are set optimally in a Kemp–Wan framework.

All these contributions as well as the Kemp–Wan paper rely crucially on the existence of inter-country transfer payments within customs unions, free trade areas or trading clubs. Our paper takes a different approach. We ask how far the Kemp–Wan Pareto-improving result can hold *without* inter-country transfers. This chapter is not the first to discuss this possibility. Dixit and Norman (1980, pp. 191–194) demonstrate that, without inter-country transfers, Pareto-improving customs unions are possible by the use of commodity and factor taxes. In contrast with their paper, the Pareto-improving result of this chapter is based on *tariff reform only*, under the assumption that the standard revenue and expenditure functions exist.

Specifically, we show that for any trading club, if the initial tariff vectors of member countries satisfy a non-proportionality condition, then a Pareto-improving non-discriminatory tariff reform is possible. We also show that a Pareto-optimal customs union, which does not harm the rest of the world, is always possible with no inter-country transfers allowed.

---

[1] Their work requires that each member country keep its trade with the rest of the world fixed whereas Kemp–Wan requires only that the aggregate trade vector of all member countries is fixed with respect to the rest of the world. For a more complete discussion see Kemp (2007).

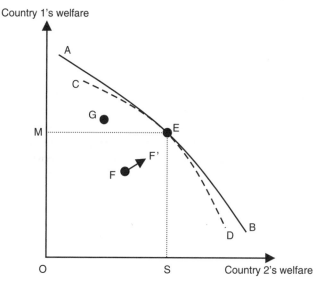

Fig. 1. *The utility possibility frontiers.*

However, this customs union need not be welfare improving for *all* member countries.

Before formally deriving the main results, let us outline what we do. In Figure 1 we consider a trading club formed by Country 1 and Country 2 which agree to implement non-discriminatory tariff reform. Point *F* is a pair of the initial utility levels of the two countries; the dashed line *CED* is the utility possibility frontier under the following constraints:

CONSTRAINT (I). Tariffs to outside countries are adjusted to keep the international price vector unchanged (*a la* Kemp–Wan) so that the welfare of non-member countries is unchanged.

CONSTRAINT (II). Income transfers are not allowed.

The solid line *AEB* is the utility possibility frontier when income transfers between the two countries are allowed and Constraint (i) holds. Thus, one could describe any point on the solid curve as Pareto-optimal.[2] Clearly, the initial utility pair is never above the dashed line *CED*, although it is not necessarily strictly below. Our first main result is to show that the initial utility pair is strictly below the dashed line if initial tariff vectors of Country 1 and Country 2 are not proportional to each other. Thus, as is depicted by the arrow *FF'* in Figure 1, there is a Pareto-improving non-discriminatory tariff reform possible between Country 1 and Country 2

---

[2] Strictly speaking, any point on *AEB* should be called *restricted* Pareto-optimal, since the frontier is derived subject to Constraint (i). For brevity, however, we omit the expression "restricted" in what follows.

without income transfers. Apparently, *the non-proportionality condition* is very mild. Hence, we can say that Pareto-improving non-discriminatory tariff reforms without inter-country transfers are generally possible.

Now, let us outline the second main result. Since the Pareto-optimal frontier AEB is derived under milder constraints than the dashed line CED, the former must lie above the latter. Our second main result is that there exists at least one point which is shared by the two curves, as is shown by point E. Since any point on AEB is Pareto-optimal, the marginal rates of substitution have to be the same between Country 1 and Country 2. Therefore, the two countries can get to point E by choosing a common tariff vector equal to the difference between the initial international price of each good in terms of the numeraire good and the marginal rate of substitution between them. One can think of point E as a pair of utilities that is established when the two countries form a customs union. Therefore, it follows that, under the non-proportionality condition, two countries can form a Pareto-optimal customs union without harming the rest of the world.

If the initial pair of utility levels is within the rectangular area $OMES$ in Figure 1, then even if inter-country transfers are unavailable, the two countries can set a common tariff vector which makes both countries better off without harming the rest of the world. This second result implies that for certain initial utility levels (i.e., within the rectangular area $OMES$ in Figure 1) a Kemp–Wan Pareto-improving customs union is possible without inter-member transfers.

We next explain the basic model.

2. The model and equilibrium conditions

In our model there are N countries and the rest of the world. We consider a non-discriminatory tariff reform by a trading club that consists of these N countries. The number of tradable goods is $M+1$, including the numeraire denoted as good 0. Let

$$\bar{p} \equiv \begin{pmatrix} \bar{p}_1 \\ \vdots \\ \bar{p}_M \end{pmatrix} \quad \text{and} \quad \bar{\tau}^n \equiv \begin{pmatrix} \bar{\tau}_1^n \\ \vdots \\ \bar{\tau}_M^n \end{pmatrix} \neq 0$$

be the initial international equilibrium price vector of the non-numeraire goods and the tariff vector of Country n, $n = 1, \ldots, N$, imposed by the government of Country n.[3]

---

[3] We assume here that specific tariffs are used and that no tariff is charged on the numeraire good. In the appendix, we show that there is no substantial difference if we consider the tariff imposed on the numeraire good or ad valorem tariffs.

Next, define $E^n(p_0, p, \bar{u}^n)$ as the aggregate expenditure function of Country n and $F^n(p_0, p)$ is the aggregate revenue function of Country n. We impose two equilibrium conditions. The first is a material balance condition.

$$S(\bar{p}) = \sum_{n=1}^{N} \{E_p^n(1, \bar{p} + \bar{\tau}^n, \bar{u}^n) - F_p^n(1, \bar{p} + \bar{\tau}^n)\}, \tag{1}$$

where $S(\bar{p})$, $E_p^n(1, \bar{p} + \bar{\tau}^n, \bar{u}^n)$, and $F_p^n(1, \bar{p} + \bar{\tau}^n)$ are the column vectors in R^M, whose mth entries are the excess supply of good m from the rest of the world, $\partial E^n(1, \bar{p} + \bar{\tau}^n, \bar{u}^n)/\partial p_m$ and $\partial F^n(1, \bar{p} + \bar{\tau}^n)/\partial p_m$, respectively. Material balance requires that net excess demand of the N countries must be equal to the excess supply from the rest of the world.

The second equilibrium condition is a balance of payments condition.

$$E^n(1, \bar{p} + \bar{\tau}^n, \bar{u}^n) - F^n(1, \bar{p} + \bar{\tau}^n)$$
$$= (\bar{\tau}^n)^T [E_p^n(1, \bar{p} + \bar{\tau}^n, \bar{u}^n) - F_p^n(1, \bar{p} + \bar{\tau}^n)], n = 1, ..., N, \tag{2}$$

where the superscript T denotes the transpose of a column vector to which it is attached. Equation (2) is a standard balance of payments condition. It requires that for all N countries expenditure equals revenue from production plus tariff revenue.

For convenience, in what follows, we write $E^n(1, \bar{p} + \bar{\tau}^n, \bar{u}^n)$ and $F^n(1, \bar{p} + \bar{\tau}^n)$ as $E^n(\bar{p} + \bar{\tau}^n, \bar{u}^n)$ and $F^n(\bar{p} + \bar{\tau}^n)$.

3. The first main result: Pareto-improving non-discriminatory reform

We now turn to establishing our first result, namely that under certain conditions one can achieve a Pareto-improving tariff reform without using international transfer payments. First, we totally differentiate (1) with respect to τ^n, $n = 1, ..., N$, and u^1 around the initial tariff-ridden equilibrium, we have

$$0 = \sum_{n=1}^{N} [E_{pp}^n(\bar{p} + \bar{\tau}^n, \bar{u}^n) - F_{pp}^n(\bar{p} + \bar{\tau}^n)]d\tau^n$$
$$+ E_{pu}^1(\bar{p} + \bar{\tau}^1, \bar{u}^1)du^1, \tag{3}$$

where $E_{pp}^n(\bar{p} + \bar{\tau}^n, \bar{u}^n)$ and $F_{pp}^n(\bar{p} + \bar{\tau}^n)$ are the $M \times M$ matrices whose mnth entries are $\partial E^n(1, \bar{p} + \bar{\tau}^n, \bar{u}^n)/\partial p_n \partial p_m$ and $\partial F^n(1, \bar{p} + \bar{\tau}^n)/\partial p_n \partial p_m$, respectively. Doing the same for (2) we get

$$[E_u^1(1, \bar{p} + \bar{\tau}^1, \bar{u}^1) - (\bar{\tau}^1)^T E_{pu}^1(1, \bar{p} + \bar{\tau}^1, \bar{u}^1)]du^1$$
$$= (\bar{\tau}^1)^T [E_{pp}^1(\bar{p} + \bar{\tau}^1, \bar{u}^1) - F_{pp}^1(\bar{p} + \bar{\tau}^1)]d\tau^1 \tag{4}$$

$$0 = (\bar{\tau}^n)^T [E_{pp}^n(\bar{p} + \bar{\tau}^n, \bar{u}^n) - F_{pp}^n(\bar{p} + \bar{\tau}^n)]d\tau^n, n = 2, ..., N. \tag{5}$$

Solving (4) for du^1 we get

$$du^1 = \frac{(\bar{\tau}^1)^T [E^1_{pp}(\bar{p} + \bar{\tau}^1, \bar{u}^1) - F^1_{pp}(\bar{p} + \bar{\tau}^1)]d\tau^1}{E^1_u(\bar{p} + \bar{\tau}^1, \bar{u}^1) - (\bar{\tau}^1)^T E^1_{pu}(\bar{p} + \bar{\tau}^1, \bar{u}^1)}. \tag{6}$$

We then substitute it into (3), to obtain

$$
\begin{aligned}
& -\sum_{n=2}^{N} [E^n_{pp}(\bar{p} + \bar{\tau}^n, \bar{u}^n) - F^n_{pp}(\bar{p} + \bar{\tau}^n)]d\tau^n \\
&= \left[I_M + \frac{E^1_{pu}(\bar{p} + \bar{\tau}^1, \bar{u}^1)(\bar{\tau}^1)^T}{E^1_u(\bar{p} + \bar{\tau}^1, \bar{u}^1) - (\bar{\tau}^1)^T E^1_{pu}(\bar{p} + \bar{\tau}^1, \bar{u}^1)} \right] \\
&\quad \times [E^1_{pp}(\bar{p} + \bar{\tau}^1, \bar{u}^1) - F^1_{pp}(\bar{p} + \bar{\tau}^1)]d\tau^1,
\end{aligned} \tag{7}
$$

where I_M is the $M \times M$ identity matrix. Pre-multiplying $(\bar{\tau}^1)^T$ to both sides of (7) we get,

$$
\begin{aligned}
& (\bar{\tau}^1)^T \left\{ -\sum_{n=2}^{N} [E^n_{pp}(\bar{p} + \bar{\tau}^n, \bar{u}^n) - F^n_{pp}(\bar{p} + \bar{\tau}^n)]d\tau^n \right\} \\
&= \left[(\bar{\tau}^1)^T + \frac{(\bar{\tau}^1)^T E^1_{pu}(\bar{p} + \bar{\tau}^1, \bar{u}^1)(\bar{\tau}^1)^T}{E^1_u(\bar{p} + \bar{\tau}^1, \bar{u}^1) - (\bar{\tau}^1)^T E^1_{pu}(\bar{p} + \bar{\tau}^1, \bar{u}^1)} \right] \\
&\quad \times [E^1_{pp}(\bar{p} + \bar{\tau}^1, \bar{u}^1) - F^1_{pp}(\bar{p} + \bar{\tau}^1)]d\tau^1 \\
&= \frac{(\bar{\tau}^1)^T [E^1_{pp}(\bar{p} + \bar{\tau}^1, \bar{u}^1) - F^1_{pp}(\bar{p} + \bar{\tau}^1)]d\tau^1}{E^1_u(\bar{p} + \bar{\tau}^1, \bar{u}^1) - (\bar{\tau}^1)^T E^1_{pu}(\bar{p} + \bar{\tau}^1, \bar{u}^1)} E^1_u(\bar{p} + \bar{\tau}^1, \bar{u}^1).
\end{aligned} \tag{8}
$$

Combining (6) and (8), we obtain

$$du^1 = \frac{(\bar{\tau}^1)^T \left\{ -\sum_{n=2}^{N} [E^n_{pp}(\bar{p} + \bar{\tau}^n, \bar{u}^n) - F^n_{pp}(\bar{p} + \bar{\tau}^n)]d\tau^n \right\}}{E^1_u(\bar{p} + \bar{\tau}^1, \bar{u}^1)}. \tag{9}$$

Note that this simply means if tariff adjustments for the N trading club countries, $d\tau^n$, $n = 1, ..., N$, satisfy the material balance condition (7), then the change in the trade vector of Country 1 which originates from $d\tau^1$ must be opposite to the sum of that of Country n, $n = 2, ..., N$, and du^1 is positive when the tariff adjustments yield an increase in the tariff revenue of Country 1.

The next step is to introduce the tariff-adjustment formulas for the N trading club countries which satisfies both the material balance condition and the budget constraint for Country n, $n = 2, ..., N$. Let

$$\tau^1(\varepsilon_2, ..., \varepsilon_N) \equiv \bar{\tau}^1 + \left\{ \chi_1 [E_{pp}^1(\bar{p} + \bar{\tau}^1, \bar{u}^1) - F_{pp}^1(\bar{p} + \bar{\tau}^1)] \right\}^{-1} \left(-\sum_{n=2}^{N} \Upsilon^n \varepsilon_n \right)$$

$$\tau^n(\varepsilon_n) \equiv \bar{\tau}^n + [E_{pp}^n(\bar{p} + \bar{\tau}^n, \bar{u}^n) - F_{pp}^n(\bar{p} + \bar{\tau}^n)]^{-1} \Upsilon^n \varepsilon_n, n = 2, ..., N,$$

where Υ^n is an orthogonal vector of $\bar{\tau}^n$, i.e., $(\bar{\tau}^n)^T \Upsilon^n = 0$, ε_n, $n = 1, ..., N$, are scalars, and

$$\chi_1 \equiv I_M + \frac{E_{pu}^1(\bar{p} + \bar{\tau}^1, \bar{u}^1)(\bar{\tau}^1)^T}{E_u^1(\bar{p} + \bar{\tau}^1, \bar{u}^1) - (\bar{\tau}^1)^T E_{pu}^1(\bar{p} + \bar{\tau}^1, \bar{u}^1)}.$$

These formulas describe how the tariffs of the member countries of the trading club are determined. The above tariff adjustments clearly satisfy the material balance condition (7), since totally differentiating $\tau^1(\varepsilon_2, ..., \varepsilon_N)$ and $\tau^n(\varepsilon_n)$ yields

$$d\tau^1 = \left\{ \chi_1 [E_{pp}^1(\bar{p} + \bar{\tau}^1, \bar{u}^1) - F_{pp}^1(\bar{p} + \bar{\tau}^1)] \right\}^{-1} \left(-\sum_{n=2}^{N} \Upsilon^n d\varepsilon_n \right) \tag{10}$$

$$d\tau^n = [E_{pp}^n(\bar{p} + \bar{\tau}^n, \bar{u}^n) - F_{pp}^n(\bar{p} + \bar{\tau}^n)]^{-1} \Upsilon^n d\varepsilon_n, n = 2, ..., N. \tag{11}$$

On the other hand, substituting (11) into (5), we see, for $n = 2, ..., N$

$$0 = (\bar{\tau}^n)^T [E_{pp}^n(\bar{p} + \bar{\tau}^n, \bar{u}^n) - F_{pp}^n(\bar{p} + \bar{\tau}^n)] d\tau^n$$
$$= (\bar{\tau}^n)^T \Upsilon^n d\varepsilon_n,$$

which holds, due to the definition of Υ^n, whatever value $d\varepsilon_n$, $n = 2, ..., N$, takes on. That is, the budget constraint always holds under the above tariff adjustments.

Next, we formulate the condition on initial tariffs we need to get our results.

NON-PROPORTIONALITY CONDITION. We say that tariff vector $\bar{\tau}^1$ satisfies the non-proportionality condition if the following holds:

Consider a linear subspace as follows

$$\Theta(s) \equiv \{ \theta \in R^M : \theta = \sum_{n=1, n \neq s}^{N} \Upsilon^n x_n, x_n \in R, n = 1, 2, ..., N, \text{ is a scalar} \}.$$

As long as there is a $\theta^* \in \Theta(1)$ such that $(\bar{\tau}^1)^T \theta^* \neq 0$ then $\bar{\tau}^1$ satisfies the non-proportionality condition.

Using (9) and (11), we obtain the following proposition.

PROPOSITION 1. *Assume that χ_1 and $[E_{pp}^n(\bar{p} + \bar{\tau}^n, \bar{u}^n) - F_{pp}^n(\bar{p} + \bar{\tau}^n)]$, $n = 1, ..., N$, are nonsingular and that for any $n = 1, ..., N$, the tariff vector $\bar{\tau}^n$ is non-zero. If $\bar{\tau}^1$ satisfies the non-proportionality condition then it is* *possible for the trading club countries to make a Pareto-improving tariff adjustment.*

PROOF. (9) and (11) together imply that

$$\text{sign}[du^1] = -\text{sign}\left[(\bar{\tau}^1)^T \sum_{n=2}^{N} \Upsilon^n d\varepsilon_n\right]$$
$$= -\text{sign}[(\bar{\tau}^1)^T \theta^*].$$

Since Θ is a linear subspace, $\theta^* \in \Theta$ means $-\theta^* \in \Theta$. It follows that as long as $(\bar{\tau}^1)^T \theta^* \neq 0$, we can make du^1 positive by choosing an appropriate $(d\varepsilon_2, ..., d\varepsilon_N)$. ∎

Proposition 1 says that if we consider a trading club in which the member countries' initial tariffs are not proportional to each other[4] then the trading club can implement a tariff reform that makes all trading club members better off without making the rest of the world worse off.[5] This result tells us that when initial tariffs are not proportional then there is room for tariff reform in the spirit of Kemp–Wan that does not require the use of transfer payments.

4. The second main result: Pareto-optimal customs unions without income transfers

We next turn to consideration of customs unions. We want to determine whether the use of transfer payments is necessary for the Kemp–Wan customs union result. We first formulate a constrained maximization problem in which the N countries jointly maximize a weighted sum of utilities by choosing an appropriate set of tariff vectors $(\tau^1, ..., \tau^N)$ subject to the condition that no country is hurt compared to their initial welfare levels. Formally, the constrained maximization problem is

$$\max_{u^n, \tau^n, n=1,...,N} U = \sum_{n=1}^{N} a_n u^n$$

subject to

$$u^i \geq \bar{u}^i, i = 1, ..., N \tag{12}$$

---

[4] Suppose $N-1$ countries have proportional tariffs. If the Nth country's tariff vector is not proportional to the $N-1$ countries' tariff vector then the non-proportionality condition is satisfied.

[5] If the member countries' initial tariffs are proportional to each other then the tariff adjustments (10) and (11) have no effect on the tariff revenue of Country 1, hence Country 1's welfare, as well as that of Country n, $n = 2, ..., N$.

$$S(\bar{p}) = \sum_{n=1}^{N} [E_p^n(\bar{p} + \tau^n, u^n) - F_p^n(\bar{p} + \tau^n)] \tag{13}$$

$$E^n(\bar{p} + \tau^n, u^n) - F^n(\bar{p} + \tau^n) = (\tau^n)^T [E_p^n(\bar{p} + \tau^n, u^n) - F_p^n(\bar{p} + \tau^n)],$$
$$n = 1, \ldots, N. \tag{14}$$

LEMMA. *Suppose that the numeraire good is indispensable in the sense that for any given q and u*

$$E_{p_0}^n(0, q, u) = \infty, n = 1, \ldots, N,$$

then the feasible set that satisfies the constraints (12)–(14) *is bounded and closed.*

PROOF. See Appendix.

This lemma allows us to apply the Weierstras theorem to the above constrained maximization problem. That is, the solution to this problem must exist. Moreover, Proposition 1 implies that if the initial tariff vectors, $\bar{\tau}^n$, $n = 1, \ldots, N$, are not proportional, then for small adjustments of tariffs (10) and (11) we have

$$\sum_{n=1}^{N} a_n u^n > \sum_{n=1}^{N} a_n \bar{u}^n,$$

which means that the solution is interior.

The problem we seek to solve does not require Pareto improvement for all countries but a much weaker condition, namely that the net external trade vector of the customs union is constant. This problem is solved with the following constrained optimization problem. Given these preliminary results, we now solve the main problem. We formulate the Lagrangian.

$$L = \sum_{n=1}^{N} a_n u^n + \Delta^T \{S(\bar{p}) - \sum_{n=1}^{N} [E_p^n(\bar{p} + \tau^n, u^n) - F_p^n(\bar{p} + \tau^n)]\}$$
$$+ \sum_{n=1}^{N} \lambda_n \{(\tau^n)^T [E_p^n(\bar{p} + \tau^n, u^n) - F_p^n(\bar{p} + \tau^n)]$$
$$+ F^n(\bar{p} + \tau^n) - E^n(\bar{p} + \tau^n, u^n)\}, \tag{15}$$

where $\Delta \equiv (\delta_1, \ldots, \delta_M)^T$. If there is an interior optimal solution, it has to satisfy the necessary conditions for optimality.

$$\frac{\partial L}{\partial u^n} = a_n - \Delta^T E_{up}^n(\bar{p} + \tau^n, u^n)$$
$$- \lambda_n \left[E_u^n(\bar{p} + \tau^n, u^n) - (\tau^n)^T E_{up}^n(\bar{p} + \tau^n, u^n) \right]$$
$$= 0, \quad n = 1, \ldots, N \tag{16}$$

$$\left[\frac{\partial L}{\partial \tau^n}\right]^T = -\Delta^T[E_{pp}^n(\bar{p}+\tau^n,u^n) - F_{pp}^n(\bar{p}+\tau^n)]$$

$$+ \lambda_n(\tau^n)^T[E_{pp}^n(\bar{p}+\tau^n,u^n) - F_{pp}^n(\bar{p}+\tau^n)]$$

$$= [\lambda_n(\tau^n)^T - \Delta^T][E_{pp}^n(\bar{p}+\tau^n,u^n) - F_{pp}^n(\bar{p}+\tau^n)]$$

$$= 0, \quad n = 1,\ldots,N \tag{17}$$

$$\frac{\partial L}{\partial \Delta} = S(\bar{p}) - \sum_{n=1}^{N}[E_p^n(\bar{p}+\tau^n,u^n) - F_p^n(\bar{p}+\tau^n)]$$

$$= 0 \tag{18}$$

$$\frac{\partial L}{\partial \lambda_n} = (\tau^n)^T[E_p^n(\bar{p}+\tau^n,u^n) - F_p^n(\bar{p}+\tau^n)]$$

$$+ F^n(\bar{p}+\tau^n) - E^n(\bar{p}+\tau^n,u^n)$$

$$= 0, \quad n = 1,\ldots,N. \tag{19}$$

First, from (17) and the nonsingularity of the substitution matrix for each $n = 1,\ldots,N$, we see that

$$\lambda_n(\tau^n)^T = \Delta^T, \quad n = 1,\ldots,N. \tag{20}$$

It follows from (16) that

$$a_n - \lambda_n E_u^n(\bar{p}+\tau^n,u^n) = 0, \quad n = 1,\ldots,N$$

or

$$\lambda_n = \frac{a_n}{E_u^n(\bar{p}+\tau^n,u^n)} > 0.$$

Thus, we have Proposition 2.

PROPOSITION 2. *If there is an interior solution for the above problem, it satisfies the proportionality condition*

$$\frac{a_1}{E_u^1(\bar{p}+\tau^1,u^1)}\tau^1 = \ldots = \frac{a_n}{E_u^n(\bar{p}+\tau^n,u^n)}\tau^n = \ldots = \frac{a_N}{E_u^N(\bar{p}+\tau^N,u^N)}\tau^N. \tag{21}$$

The existence of an interior solution is ensured if

for any $n = 1,\ldots,N$, there is $\theta^*(n) \in \Theta(n)$ such that $(\bar{\tau}^n)^T\theta^*(n) \neq 0$. $$\tag{22}$$

Now, consider the following mapping from $\Omega \equiv \{a \equiv (a_1,\ldots,a_N): \sum_n^N a_n = 1$ and $a_n \geq 0, \ n = 1,\ldots,N\}$ into itself

$$f^n(a) \equiv \frac{E_u^n(\bar{p}+\tau^n(a),u^n(a))}{\sum_j^N E_u^j(\bar{p}+\tau^j(a),u^j(a))}, \quad n = 1,\ldots,N, a \in \Omega.$$

Since Ω is a convex and compact set and $f^n(a)$, $n = 1, \ldots, N$, are continuous in a, we can apply the Brouwer Fixed Point theorem to assert the existence of the fixed point $a^* \equiv (a_1^*, \ldots, a_N^*) \in \Omega$ such that

$$a_n^* = \frac{E_u^n(\bar{p} + \tau^n(a^*), u^n(a^*))}{\sum_j^N E_u^j(\bar{p} + \tau^j(a^*), u^j(a^*))}, \quad n = 1, \ldots, N.$$

It then follows that

$$\frac{a_1^*}{E_u^1(\bar{p} + \tau^1(a^*), u^1(a^*))} = \ldots = \frac{a_n^*}{E_u^n(\bar{p} + \tau^n(a^*), u^n(a^*))} = \ldots$$
$$= \frac{a_N^*}{E_u^N(\bar{p} + \tau^N(a^*), u^N(a^*))}.$$

Using the proportionality condition (21) we conclude

$$\tau^1 = \ldots = \tau^n = \ldots = \tau^N. \tag{23}$$

Thus, N countries set a common tariff vector. We can now state the second main result of the chapter.

PROPOSITION 3. *Suppose that there exists an initial tariff-ridden equilibrium and that a subset of the countries forms a customs union. We show that, given the existence of the standard revenue and expenditure functions, the countries can form a Pareto-optimal customs union without income transfers, if (i) there are more than two tradable goods and (ii) the initial tariff vectors of the member countries satisfy the non-proportionality condition.*

REMARK 1. Proposition 3 just asserts that a *Pareto-optimal* customs union can be formed without income transfers among member countries. However, it does not ensure that the union is *Pareto-improving* (as a Kemp–Wan customs union is) compared with the initial tariff-ridden equilibrium. The proposition guarantees that there exists a customs union without income transfers that results in a Pareto-optimal pair of utilities like point E in Figure 1. However, the customs union will be *Pareto-improving* only if the initial utilities are within the rectangular area $OMES$ in Figure 1. If the initial equilibrium were instead a point like G in Figure 1 then transfer payments are *necessary* for a *Pareto-improving* customs union.

5. A diagrammatic exposition

In this section we provide a diagrammatic exposition of the main results to clarify them and to provide some intuition. For purposes of illustration, we consider a specific case, i.e., a pure exchange world economy with $N = 2$ and $M = 2$.

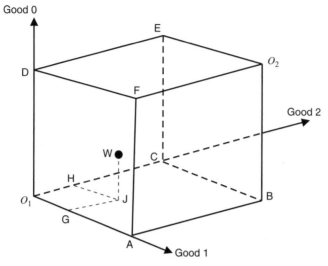

Fig. 2.   Edgeworth box.

Figure 2 is the three-dimensional Edgeworth box. O_1 and O_2 are the origins of Country 1 and Country 2, respectively. Point W which is located inside the box denotes the initial endowment point. For example, $(\bar{x}_1^1, \bar{x}_2^1, \bar{x}_0^1) = (O_1G, GJ, JW)$ is Country 1's initial endowments of Good 1, Good 2 and Good 0.

Next consider Figure 3. The surface SQR is the international price plane that contains the initial endowment point W. On this surface we have $p_1(x_1 - \bar{x}_1) + p_2(x_2 - \bar{x}_2) + (x_0 - \bar{x}_0) = 0$. The consumption points of both countries have to be on this plane.

Figure 4 depicts an indifference surface of Country 1. The intersection of the indifference surface and the international price plane is the closed curve $ACFBD$ on the plane.

Figure 5 is derived when we see the international price plane from above. Imagine a plane that is tangent to the indifference surface at point F. The segment lFl' is the intersection of the tangent plane and the international price plane. Point F, $(x_{F1}^1, x_{F2}^1, x_{F0}^1)$, is the consumption point of Country 1. Hence, the slope of the line lFl' gives us the relative domestic prices in Country 1. Denoting the direct utility function of Country 1 by $u^1 = U^1(x_1^1, x_2^1, x_0^1)$, we see that the tangent plane is

$$\frac{U_1^1}{U_0^1}(x_1 - x_{F1}^1) + \frac{U_2^1}{U_0^1}(x_2 - x_{F2}^1) + (x_0 - x_{F0}^1) = 0.$$

If point F is the consumption point, the marginal rates of substitution have to be equal to the domestic prices. That is,

$$\frac{U_1^1}{U_0^1} = p_1 + \bar{\tau}_1^1 \quad \text{and} \quad \frac{U_2^1}{U_0^1} = p_2 + \bar{\tau}_2^1.$$

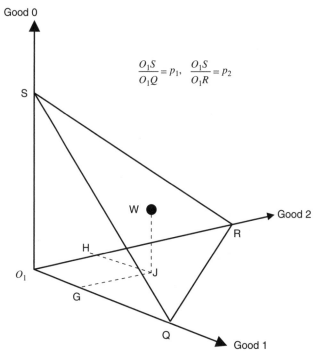

Good 0

$$\frac{O_1 S}{O_1 Q} = p_1, \quad \frac{O_1 S}{O_1 R} = p_2$$

Fig. 3.   The international price plane.

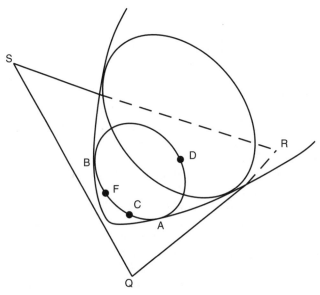

Fig. 4.   An indifference surface.

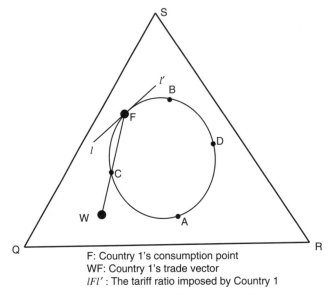

F: Country 1's consumption point
WF: Country 1's trade vector
lFl' : The tariff ratio imposed by Country 1

Fig. 5.   Country 1's initial consumption point.

Therefore, the equation for segment lFl' is

$$\bar{\tau}_1^1(x_1 - x_{F1}^1) = -\bar{\tau}_2^1(x_2 - x_{F2}^1) \left(= \frac{x_0 - x_{F0}^1}{p_2/\bar{\tau}_2^1 - p_1/\bar{\tau}_1^1} \right).$$

Clearly, the segment FW measures the net trade vector of Country 1.

A parallel argument can be made for Country 2. In Figure 6, the vectors WF_1 and WF_2 are the trade vectors of Country 1 and Country 2, respectively. So, the vector F_1F_2 denotes the net trade vector of countries 1 and 2, with the rest of the world. Figure 6 illustrates the pre-customs union world equilibrium.

Now, we illustrate how a customs union produces a Pareto improvement. First, solve the constrained maximization problem formulated in the previous section giving all the utility weight to Country 1, i.e., $a_1 = 1$ and $a_2 = 0$. Figure 7 illustrates the solution to this problem. The segment $\bar{l}_2 F_1 \bar{l}_2$ is parallel to $l_2 F_2 l_2'$ and the dashed indifference curve is just a parallel shift of the indifference curve $\bar{u}^2$. The smaller closed curve u^1 is depicted in such a way to be tangent to the dashed indifference curve at point $\bar{F}_1$. Notice that line $\bar{F}_1 \bar{F}_2$ is parallel and equal to $F_1 F_2$. This is because in the constrained optimization problem net trade of the customs unions countries to the rest of the world does not change. That is, if both countries adjust their tariff rates from $l_1' F_1 l_1$ and $l_2 F_2 l_2'$ to $l_1^{*} \bar{F}_1 l_1^{*\prime}$ and $l_2^{*} \bar{F}_2 l_2^{*\prime}$, the consumption points change from F_1 and F_2 to $\bar{F}_1$ and $\bar{F}_2$, respectively. Note that since the trade vector with the rest of the world is unchanged by the tariff adjustments, international prices do not change. Therefore, the rest of the world is not hurt by the tariff adjustment, and Country 1 is better off without hurting

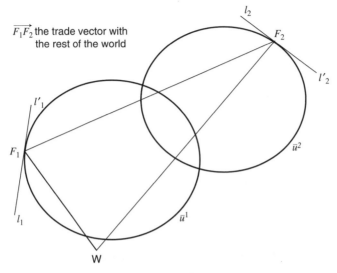

Fig. 6. The initial tariff-ridden equilibrium.

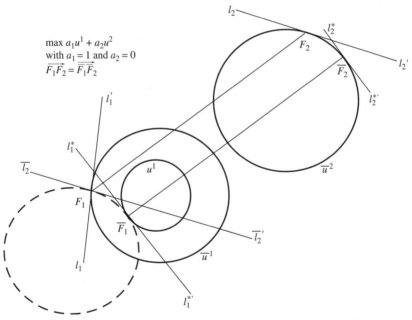

Fig. 7. The Pareto-optimal customs union with $u^2 = \bar{u}^2$.

Country 2. Also note that the new tariff lines, $l_1^* \bar{F}_1 l_1^{*\prime}$ and $l_2^* \bar{F}_2 l_2^{*\prime}$, are parallel with each other. That is the ratio τ_1^1/τ_2^1 at $\bar{F}_1$ is equal to τ_1^2/τ_2^2 at $\bar{F}_2$. Thus, what happens is that the customs union adjusts tariffs such that trade with the rest of the world is unchanged and within the customs union, agents in both countries face the same domestic prices. This is the same as in Kemp–Wan theorem, the difference being that we do not rely on transfer

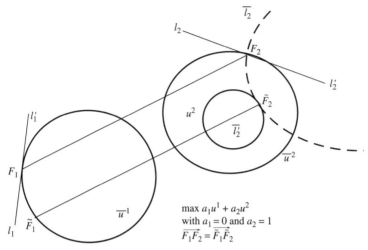

Fig. 8. *The Pareto-optimal customs union with $u^1 = \bar{u}^1$.*

payments to ensure that all customs union members do at least as well in the post-customs union equilibrium.

A similar argument can be made for the case in which all utility weight is place on Country 2, $a_1 = 0$ and $a_2 = 1$. This case is illustrated in Figure 8, where the consumption points move from (F_1, F_2) to $(\tilde{F}_1, \tilde{F}_2)$, which means that Country 2 is better off while Country 1 and the rest of the world have the same utility as before the tariff adjustment.

It is clear that by changing the (a_1, a_2) from $(0,1)$ to $(1,0)$ keeping $a_1 + a_2 = 1$, we derive a locus of the solutions of the constrained maximization problem for which both member countries have higher utility. Consumption points like (F_1^0, F_2^0) in Figure 9 have the property that both countries are better off without hurting the rest of the world.

Figure 10 illustrates the case in which customs unions cannot produce welfare improvement. Here domestic prices are the same ($l_1 F_1 l_1'$ and $l_2 F_2 l_2'$ are parallel) at the pre-union equilibrium. It is clear from the diagram, that it is impossible to make Pareto-improving tariff adjustments without using transfer payments. This case illustrates the relationship between our result and the Kemp–Wan theorem. Customs unions can improve welfare without using transfer payments, unless member countries have the same domestic prices. In this case transfer payments are required for a customs union to produce a Pareto improvement.

6. Concluding remarks

We have shown that a *Pareto-improving* non-discriminatory tariff reform is possible without income transfers if the number of goods is more than two and the pre-union tariff vectors of member countries satisfy the

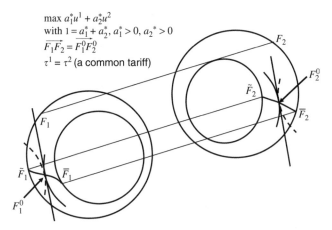

$\max a_1^* u^1 + a_2^* u^2$

with $1 = a_1^* + a_2^*, a_1^* > 0, a_2^{\,*} > 0$

$\overrightarrow{F_1 F_2} = \overrightarrow{F_1^0 F_2^0}$

$\tau^1 = \tau^2$ (a common tariff)

Fig. 9.   The loci of consumption points.

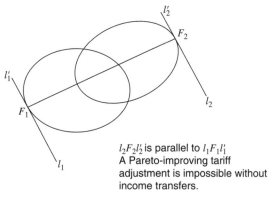

$l_2 F_2 l_2'$ is parallel to $l_1 F_1 l_1'$
A Pareto-improving tariff
adjustment is impossible without
income transfers.

Fig. 10.   The case of $\bar{\tau}_1^1 / \bar{\tau}_2^1 = \bar{\tau}_1^2 / \bar{\tau}_2^2$.

non-proportionality condition. In addition, under the same conditions a *Pareto-optimal* customs union always exists, however, transfers may be required for a *Pareto-improving* customs union.

Acknowledgments

Comments from Murray Kemp and Henry Wan greatly improved this chapter. We also received helpful comments from Koichi Hamada, Alan Woodland, and an anonymous referee. Professor Koji Shimomura passed away on February 24, 2007. This chapter was completed after his untimely death.

Appendix 1. Proof of Lemma 1

First of all, let us denote $q^n \equiv \bar{p} + \tau^n, n = 1, \ldots, N$, and define the set:

$$\Gamma \equiv \left\{ (q^1, \ldots, q^N) \geq 0 \;:\; {}^{\exists}(u^1, \ldots, u^N) \geq (\bar{u}^1, \ldots, \bar{u}^N) \text{ such that for} \right.$$

$$n = 1, \ldots, N,$$

$$0 \geq E^n(1, q^n, u^n) - F^n(1, q^n) - (q^n - \bar{p})^T [E_q^n(1, q^n, u^n) - F_q^n(1, q^n)], \text{ and}$$

$$\left. 0 = S(\bar{p}) - \sum_{s}^{N} [E_q^s(1, q^s, u^s) - F_q^s(1, q^s)] \right\}.$$

Let us prove that Γ is bounded. Suppose it is not. Then, there are $(q_*^1, \ldots, q_*^N)$ in Γ and $\{\varepsilon_i\}_{i=1}^{i=\infty}$, with $\varepsilon_1 < \varepsilon_2 < \ldots$, and $\lim_{i \to \infty} \varepsilon_i = \infty$, such that $(\varepsilon_i q_*^1, \ldots, \varepsilon_i q_*^N) \in \Gamma$ for ${}^{\forall}i$. Thus, there is $\{u_i^n\}_{i=1}^{i=\infty}$ such that for n $= 1, \ldots, N$, and $i = 1,2,3, \ldots$

$$0 \geq E^n(1, \varepsilon_i q_*^n, u_i^n) - F^n(1, \varepsilon_i q_*^n) - (\varepsilon_i q_*^n - \bar{p})^T [E_q^n(1, \varepsilon_i q_*^n, u_i^n) - F_q^n(1, \varepsilon_i q_*^n)]$$

$$0 = S(\bar{p}) - \sum_{s=1}^{N} [E_q^s(1, \varepsilon_i q_*^s, u_i^s) - F_q^s(1, \varepsilon_i q_*^s)].$$

Since both expenditure and revenue functions are homogeneous of degree one in all $m+1$ prices,

$$0 \geq \sum_{s}^{N} \{ E^s(1, \varepsilon_i q_*^s, u_i^s) - F^s(1, \varepsilon_i q_*^s) - (\varepsilon_i q_*^s - \bar{p})^T [E_q^s(1, \varepsilon_i q_*^s, u_i^s) - F_q^s(1, \varepsilon_i q_*^s)] \}$$

$$= \sum_{s}^{N} \{ E^s(1, \varepsilon_i q_*^s, u_i^s) - F^s(1, \varepsilon_i q_*^s) - (\varepsilon_i q_*^s)^T [E_q^s(1, \varepsilon_i q_*^s, u_i^s) - F_q^s(1, \varepsilon_i q_*^s)] \}$$

$$+ (\bar{p})^T \sum_{s}^{N} [E_q^s(1, \varepsilon_i q_*^s, u_i^s) - F_q^s(1, \varepsilon_i q_*^s)]$$

$$= \sum_{s}^{N} [E_{p_0}^s(1, \varepsilon_i q_*^s, u_i^s) - F_{p_0}^s(1, \varepsilon_i q_*^s)] + (\bar{p})^T S(\bar{p})$$

$$= \sum_{s}^{N} \left[E_{p_0}^s\left(\frac{1}{\varepsilon_i}, q_*^s, u_i^s\right) - F_{p_0}^s\left(\frac{1}{\varepsilon_i}, q_*^s\right) \right] + (\bar{p})^T S(\bar{p}),$$

where $[E_{p_0}^s - F_{p_0}^s]$ is the partial derivative of $[E^s - F^s]$ with respect to the price of Good 0, and therefore the net import of Good 0 of Country s. Since all goods are assumed to be normal, it follows from $u_i^n \geq \bar{u}^n$, for $n = 1, \ldots, N$, and $i = 1,2,3, \ldots$, that

$$0 \geq \sum_{s}^{N} \left[E_{p_0}^s\left(\frac{1}{\varepsilon_i}, q_*^s, u_i^s\right) - F_{p_0}^s\left(\frac{1}{\varepsilon_i}, q_*^s\right) \right] + (\bar{p})^T S(\bar{p})$$

$$\geq \sum_{s}^{N} \left[E_{p_0}^s\left(\frac{1}{\varepsilon_i}, q_*^s, \bar{u}^s\right) - F_{p_0}^s\left(\frac{1}{\varepsilon_i}, q_*^s\right) \right] + (\bar{p})^T S(\bar{p}).$$

Since Good 0 is assumed to be indispensable, $\lim_{i\to\infty} \varepsilon_i = \infty$ means that

$$\lim_{i\to\infty} \sum_{s}^{N} \left[E^s_{p_0} \left(\frac{1}{\varepsilon_i}, q^s_*, \bar{u}^s \right) - F^s_{p_0} \left(\frac{1}{\varepsilon_i}, q^s_* \right) \right]$$

$$= \lim_{i\to\infty} \sum_{s}^{N} E^s_{p_0} \left(\frac{1}{\varepsilon_i}, q^s_*, \bar{u}^s \right)$$

$$= \infty.$$

Therefore, for a sufficiently large i, we have

$$0 \geq \sum_{s=1}^{N} \left[E^s_{p_0} \left(\frac{1}{\varepsilon_i}, q^s_*, \bar{u}^s \right) - F^s_{p_0} \left(\frac{1}{\varepsilon_i}, q^s_* \right) \right] + (\bar{p})^T S(\bar{p}) \gg 0,$$

a contradiction. Therefore Γ is bounded.

By definition of Γ, for any $Q \equiv (q^1, \ldots, q^N) \in \Gamma$ there is at least one $(u^1(Q), \ldots, u^N(Q))$ such that for $n = 1, \ldots, N$, $u^n(Q) \geq \bar{u}^n$,

$$0 \geq E^n(1, q^n, u^n(Q)) - F^n(1, q^n) - (q^n - \bar{p})^T [E^n_q(1, q^n, u^n(Q)) - F^n_q(1, q^n)],$$

and $0 = S(\bar{p}) - \sum_{s}^{N} [E^s_q(1, q^s, u^s(Q)) - F^s_q(1, q^s)].$

Consider the set $\tilde{\Gamma} \equiv \{(Q, u^1(Q), \ldots, u^N(Q)) : Q \in \Gamma\}$. Since $\max u^n \geq u^n(Q) \geq \bar{u}^n$, $\tilde{\Gamma}$ is bounded. Since $\tilde{\Gamma}$ contains the feasible set and satisfies (12)–(14), the feasible set is bounded. That the feasible set is closed is obvious. ■

Appendix 2. Cases of specific tariffs and ad valorem tariffs imposed on all goods

We show that (i) if tariffs are imposed on not only non-numeraire goods but also the numeraire good, then the non-proportionality condition holds in a modified sense; (ii) whether specific or *ad valorem* tariffs do not make a substantial difference.

Specific tariffs

We consider the case where a tariff is possibly imposed on the numeraire good. Then, the material balance condition (1) becomes

$$S(\bar{p}) = \sum_{n=1}^{N} G^n_p(1 + \bar{\tau}^n_0, \bar{p} + \bar{\tau}^n, \bar{u}^n), \tag{24}$$

where $G^n_p(1 + \bar{\tau}^n_0, \bar{p} + \bar{\tau}^n, \bar{u}^n) \equiv E^n_p(1 + \bar{\tau}^n_0, \bar{p} + \bar{\tau}^n, \bar{u}^n) - F^n_p(1 + \bar{\tau}^n_0, \bar{p} + \bar{\tau}^n).$

On the other hand, the budget constraint of Country n becomes

$$G^n(1 + \bar{\tau}_0^n, \bar{p} + \bar{\tau}^n, \bar{u}^n) = \bar{\tau}_0^n G_{p_0}^n(1 + \bar{\tau}_0^n, \bar{p} + \bar{\tau}^n, \bar{u}^n)$$
$$+ (\bar{\tau}^n)^T G_p^n(1 + \bar{\tau}_0^n, \bar{p} + \bar{\tau}^n, \bar{u}^n). \tag{25}$$

Note that, due to the properties of the expenditure and the aggregate revenue functions, $G^n(1 + \bar{\tau}_0^n, \bar{p} + \bar{\tau}^n, \bar{u}^n)$ is linearly homogeneous in $1 + \bar{\tau}_0^n$ and $\bar{p} + \bar{\tau}^n$. Therefore, it follows that the identity

$$G^n(1 + \bar{\tau}_0^n, \bar{p} + \bar{\tau}^n, \bar{u}^n) = (1 + \bar{\tau}_0^n) G_{p_0}^n(1 + \bar{\tau}_0^n, \bar{p} + \bar{\tau}^n, \bar{u}^n)$$
$$+ (\bar{p} + \bar{\tau}^n)^T G_p^n(1 + \bar{\tau}_0^n, \bar{p} + \bar{\tau}^n, \bar{u}^n) \tag{26}$$

holds.[6] Combining (25) and (26) together, we obtain

$$G_{p_0}^n(1 + \bar{\tau}_0^n, \bar{p} + \bar{\tau}^n, \bar{u}^n) = -(\bar{p})^T G_p^n(1 + \bar{\tau}_0^n, \bar{p} + \bar{\tau}^n, \bar{u}^n). \tag{27}$$

The substitution of (27) into (25) yields

$$G^n(1 + \bar{\tau}_0^n, \bar{p} + \bar{\tau}^n, \bar{u}^n) = -\bar{\tau}_0^n(\bar{p})^T G_p^n(1 + \bar{\tau}_0^n, \bar{p} + \bar{\tau}^n, \bar{u}^n)$$
$$+ (\bar{\tau}^n)^T G_p^n(1 + \bar{\tau}_0^n, \bar{p} + \bar{\tau}^n, \bar{u}^n)$$
$$= [\bar{\tau}^n - \bar{\tau}_0^n \bar{p}]^T G_p^n(1 + \bar{\tau}_0^n, \bar{p} + \bar{\tau}^n, \bar{u}^n). \tag{28}$$

Since the function $G^n(1 + \bar{\tau}_0^n, \bar{p} + \bar{\tau}^n, \bar{u}^n)$ is linearly homogeneous in $1 + \bar{\tau}_0^n$ and $\bar{p} + \bar{\tau}^n$ (i.e., homogeneous of degree one in these price terms), the partial derivatives with respect to the price terms are homogeneous of degree zero. Therefore, (24) and (28) can be rewritten to

$$S(\bar{p}) = \sum_{n=1}^{N} G_p^n \left(1, \frac{\bar{p} + \bar{\tau}^n}{1 + \bar{\tau}_0^n}, \bar{u}^n \right) \tag{29}$$

$$G^n \left(1, \frac{\bar{p} + \bar{\tau}^n}{1 + \bar{\tau}_0^n}, \bar{u}^n \right) = \frac{[\bar{\tau}^n - \bar{\tau}_0^n \bar{p}]^T}{1 + \bar{\tau}_0^n} G_p^n \left(1, \frac{\bar{p} + \bar{\tau}^n}{1 + \bar{\tau}_0^n}, \bar{u}^n \right). \tag{30}$$

Finally, let

$$\Lambda^n \equiv \frac{\bar{\tau}^n - \bar{\tau}_0^n \bar{p}}{1 + \bar{\tau}_0^n}.$$

Then, since

$$\frac{\bar{p} + \bar{\tau}^n}{1 + \bar{\tau}_0^n} = \bar{p} + \Lambda^n,$$

---

[6] The identity is often called the Euler condition.

(29) and (30) become

$$S(\bar{p}) = \sum_{n=1}^{N} G_p^n(1, \bar{p} + \Lambda^n, \bar{u}^n) \tag{31}$$

$$G^n(1, \bar{p} + \Lambda^n, \bar{u}^n) = (\Lambda^n)^T G_p^n(1, \bar{p} + \Lambda^n, \bar{u}^n). \tag{32}$$

From the formal point of view, (31) and (32) are the same as (1) and (2), if Λ^n is replaced by $\bar{\tau}^n$. Therefore, we can make formally the same calculations as in the main text, considering the tariff change taking the specific form $d\Lambda^n$ instead of $d\tau_0^n$ and $d\tau^n$:

$$d\Lambda^1 = \left[\tilde{\chi}_1 G_{pp}^1(1, \bar{p} + \Lambda^1, \bar{u}^1) \right]^{-1} \left(-\sum_{n=2}^{N} \tilde{\Upsilon}^n d\varepsilon_n \right), \tag{33}$$

$$d\Lambda^n = \left[G_{pp}^n(1, \bar{p} + \Lambda^n, \bar{u}^n) \right]^{-1} \tilde{\Upsilon}^n d\varepsilon_n, \quad n = 2, \ldots, N, \tag{34}$$

yield

$$du^1 = \frac{(\Lambda^1)^T \left(-\sum_{n=2}^{N} \tilde{\Upsilon}^n d\varepsilon_n \right)}{E_u^1(\bar{p} + \Lambda^1, \bar{u}^1)}, \tag{35}$$

where $\tilde{\Upsilon}^n$ is an orthogonal vector of Λ^n, i.e., $(\Lambda^n)^T \tilde{\Upsilon}^n = 0$, and

$$\tilde{\chi}_1 \equiv I_M + \frac{E_{pu}^1(\bar{p} + \Lambda^1, \bar{u}^1)(\Lambda^1)^T}{E_u^1(\bar{p} + \Lambda^1, \bar{u}^1) - (\Lambda^1)^T E_{pu}^1(\bar{p} + \Lambda^1, \bar{u}^1)}. \tag{36}$$

Therefore, we can conclude that it is possible to form a Pareto-improving trading club, if the following *modified non-proportionality condition*.

There exists some n such that $\Lambda^1 \neq k\Lambda^n$ for $\forall k \in R$ or

$$\frac{\bar{\tau}^1 - \bar{\tau}_0^1 \bar{p}}{1 + \bar{\tau}_0^1} \neq k \frac{\bar{\tau}^n - \bar{\tau}_0^n \bar{p}}{1 + \bar{\tau}_0^n} \quad \text{for } \forall k \in R \tag{37}$$

holds in the pre-club tariff-ridden world equilibrium.[7]

Note that if the numeraire good is freely traded (i.e., $\bar{\tau}_0^1 = \bar{\tau}_0^n = 0$), then the modified non-proportionality condition is equivalent to the original

---

[7] It can be easily shown from (34) that $(\Lambda^n)^T \tilde{\Upsilon}^n d\varepsilon_n = 0$ yields $\bar{\tau}_0^n [G_{p_0p}^n(1, \bar{p} + \Lambda^n, \bar{u}^n)]^T d\Lambda^n + (\bar{\tau}^n)^T G_{pp}^n(1, \bar{p} + \Lambda^n, \bar{u}^n) d\Lambda^n = 0$. Clearly, the first term is the change in the tariff revenue of Country n originated from good 0 and the second term is the one originated from good $m \geq 1$, so this equation means that the tariff revenue of Country n is not affected by $d\Lambda^n$. Therefore, if the modified non-proportionality condition does not hold then the tariff adjustments (33) and (34) have no effect on the tariff revenue of Country 1, hence Country 1's welfare (see (35)). Thus, the modified non-proportionality condition has the same meaning of the original one.

non-proportionality condition. However, if the government of each country imposes a tariff on not only the non-numeraire good but also the numeraire good, the above modified non-proportionality condition is the one that makes possible the formation of a Pareto-improving trading club.

Ad valorem tariffs

Next, let us consider the case of *ad valorem* tariffs. To do so, we shall use the $M \times M$ diagonal matrix as follows

$$[\bar{t}^n] \equiv \begin{bmatrix} \bar{t}_1^n & \cdots & 0 \\ \vdots & \ddots & \vdots \\ 0 & \cdots & \bar{t}_M^n \end{bmatrix}. \tag{38}$$

Making use of this matrix as well as the $M \times M$ identity matrix I_M, we can describe the budget constraint of Country n as

$$G^n(1 + \bar{t}_0^n, (I_M + [\bar{t}^n])\bar{p}, \bar{u}^n) = \bar{t}_0^n G_{p_0}^n(1 + \bar{t}_0^n, (I_M + [\bar{t}^n])\bar{p}, \bar{u}^n)$$
$$+ (\bar{p})^T[\bar{t}^n]G_p^n(1 + \bar{t}_0^n, (I_M + [\bar{t}^n])\bar{p}, \bar{u}^n). \tag{39}$$

Note that $\bar{p}_0 = 1$. On the other hand, the Euler condition in the present case is

$$G^n(1 + \bar{t}_0^n, (I_M + [\bar{t}^n])\bar{p}, \bar{u}^n)$$
$$= (1 + \bar{t}_0^n)G_{p_0}^n(1 + \bar{t}_0^n, (I_M + [\bar{t}^n])\bar{p}, \bar{u}^n)$$
$$+ (\bar{p})^T(I_M + [\bar{t}^n])G_p^n(1 + \bar{t}_0^n, (I_M + [\bar{t}^n])\bar{p}, \bar{u}^n). \tag{40}$$

Combining (39) and (40), we have

$$G_{p_0}^n(1 + \bar{t}_0^n, (I_M + [\bar{t}^n])\bar{p}, \bar{u}^n) = -(\bar{p})^T G_p^n(1 + \bar{t}_0^n, (I_M + [\bar{t}^n])\bar{p}, \bar{u}^n). \tag{41}$$

The substitution of (41) into (39) yields

$$G^n(1 + \bar{t}_0^n, (I_M + [\bar{t}^n])\bar{p}, \bar{u}^n)$$
$$= (\bar{p})^T(-\bar{t}_0^n I_M + [\bar{t}^n])G_p^n(1 + \bar{t}_0^n, (I_M + [\bar{t}^n])\bar{p}, \bar{u}^n). \tag{42}$$

Due to the linear homogeneity of the function $G^n(\cdot)$ in price terms, we can rewrite (42) as

$$G^n\left(1, \left(\frac{I_M + [\bar{t}^n]}{1 + \bar{t}_0^n}\right)\bar{p}, \bar{u}^n\right)$$
$$= (\bar{p})^T\left(\frac{-\bar{t}_0^n I_M + [\bar{t}^n]}{1 + \bar{t}_0^n}\right)G_p^n\left(1, \left(\frac{I_M + [\bar{t}^n]}{1 + \bar{t}_0^n}\right)\bar{p}, \bar{u}^n\right). \tag{43}$$

Let

$$\Xi^n \equiv \left(\frac{-\bar{t}_0^n I_M + [\bar{t}^n]}{1 + \bar{t}_0^n}\right)\bar{p}.$$

Then, since

$$\left(\frac{I_M + [\bar{t}^n]}{1 + \bar{t}_0^n}\right)\bar{p} = \bar{p} + \Xi^n,$$

(43) becomes

$$G^n(1, \bar{p} + \Xi^n, \bar{u}^n) = (\Xi^n)^T G_p^n(1, \bar{p} + \Xi^n, \bar{u}^n),$$

which is formally the same as (32). The modified non-proportionality condition in the case of *ad valorem* tariffs is that there exists some n such that

$$\left(\frac{-\bar{t}_0^1 I_M + [\bar{t}^1]}{1 + \bar{t}_0^1}\right)\bar{p} \neq k\left(\frac{-\bar{t}_0^n I_M + [\bar{t}^n]}{1 + \bar{t}_0^n}\right)\bar{p} \text{ for } {}^\forall k \in R. \tag{44}$$

If the numeraire good is freely traded $\left(\bar{t}_0^1 = \bar{t}_0^n = 0\right)$, (44) can be rewritten as

$$[\bar{t}^1]\bar{p} \neq k[\bar{t}^n]\bar{p} \text{ for } {}^\forall k \in R.$$

Since $[\bar{t}^n]$ is the diagonal matrix, $[\bar{t}^1]\bar{p} \neq k[\bar{t}^n]\bar{p}$ is identical to $(\bar{t}_1^1, \ldots, \bar{t}_M^1) \neq k(\bar{t}_1^n, \ldots, \bar{t}_M^n)$, which looks close to the original non-proportionality condition.

References

Dixit, A.K., Norman, V. (1980), *Theory of International Trade*. Cambridge University Press, Cambridge, UK.

Kemp, M.C. (2007), Normative comparisons of customs unions and other types of free trade association. *European Journal of Political Economy* 23 (2), 416–422.

Kemp, M.C., Shimomura, K. (2001), A second elementary proposition concerning the formation of customs unions. *Japanese Economic Review* 52 (1), 64–69.

Kemp, M.C., Wan, H.Y., Jr. (1976), An elementary proposition concerning the formation of customs unions. *Journal of International Economics* 6 (1), 95–98.

Konishi, H., Kowalczyk, C., Sjostrom, T. (2003). Free Trade, Customs Unions, and Transfers. Boston College Working Paper #568.

Kowalczyk, C., Sjostrom, T. (1994), Bringing GATT into the core. *Economica* 61 (243), 301–317.

Ohyama, M. (2002), The economic significance of the GATT/WTO rules. In: Woodland, A.D. (Ed.), *Economic Theory and International Trade.* Edward Elgar, Cheltenham, UK, pp. 71–85.

Panagariya, A., Krishna, P. (2002), On necessarily welfare-enhancing free trade areas. *Journal of International Economics* 57 (2), 353–367.

Raimondos-Moller, P., Woodland, A.D. (2004a), On two elementary propositions on customs unions. In: Heiduk, G., Wong, K.-Y. (Eds.), *WTO and World Trade: Challenges in a New Era.* Springer-Verlag Company, Heidelberg.

Raimondos-Moller, P., Woodland, A.D. (2004b), *Non-Preferential Trading Clubs.* mimeo.

Richardson, M. (1995), On the interpretation of the Kemp-Wan theorem. *Oxford Economic Papers* 33, 135–153.

PART III

Trade and Welfare

CHAPTER 11

The Contribution of Murray Kemp to the Discipline of International Trade and Welfare Economics

Binh Tran-Nam

Atax, University of New South Wales, Sydney, NSW 2052, Australia
E-mail address: b.tran-nam@unsw.edu.au

Abstract

Purpose − The principal aim of this chapter is to present a comprehensive and critical review of Murray Kemp's contributions to the discipline of international trade and welfare economics.

Methodology/Approach − This chapter employs the critical literature review approach, including archival analysis and face-to-face interviews.

Findings − It is shown that Kemp has been a key player in the modernization of trade theory. In particular, he has extended the theorems of gains from trade in many different directions and under the most general conditions.

Practical implications − In surveying Kemp's research contributions this chapter provides a useful overview of the development of the normative theory of trade. It also examines a number of methodological issues that may prove to be useful to economic theorists.

Keywords: Murray Kemp, International trade, Gains from trade, Welfare economics

Paper type: Research paper

1. Introduction

It is indeed a daunting task to write about Murray Kemp's achievements in economic theory. This is so for two main reasons. First and foremost, Kemp has consistently made fundamental contributions to the discipline of economics over the past five or six decades. In fact, at the advanced age of 82, he is still actively writing and publishing academic papers. To summarize his lifetime's work is a touch premature and to do so within the constraint of a single chapter is definitely a very challenging assignment.

Frontiers of Economics and Globalization
Volume 5   ISSN: 1574-8715
DOI: 10.1016/S1574-8715(08)05011-2

Second, Kemp has been portrayed as an economic theorist on various occasions (Leonard, 1991; Wan and Long, 1998; Kakkar, 2004; Coleman, 2005). These articles have been written by colleagues who know him and economic theory extremely well, and by those who know less about him or theoretical economics. Correspondingly, they took polar forms: a technical review (Wan and Long, 1998) or an interview (Coleman, 2005). Between them, these articles provide a wealth of information about Kemp and his many achievements in economics. It would therefore be not easy to find new information or perspectives that may interest general readers.

Nevertheless, the recent occasion of Kemp's 80th birthday seems to be a perfect opportunity to take stock of his remarkable contributions to economic theory in a coherent fashion. This task is also necessary partly because the various papers written about him are now somewhat dated. Clearly, it would be impractical to examine in depth Kemp's accomplishment in all aspects of broadly defined economic theory. To make this task more manageable, this chapter will focus on his contribution to international trade and welfare economics, simply because these are the areas where Kemp's remarkable achievements have had a long lasting and most profound influence.

The content of this chapter is derived from three separate sources of information. First, and most importantly, the chapter is based on the many conversations and correspondence between Kemp and the author. These conversations have taken place in different contexts over many years.[1] Second, this chapter makes selective use of the information and discussions obtained from previous articles about Kemp. Third, there are of course Kemp's many articles and books which are publicly available to readers. To cater for the general reader, who may not be completely familiar with the complexity of trade theory, the exposition of this chapter will be as non-technical as possible.

The remainder of this chapter is organized as follows. Section 2 sketches out some of Kemp's biographic details. This section concentrates on events that have led Kemp to an illustrious career in economic theory. Section 3 systematically examines his contributions to economic theory. This section covers three broad areas, welfare economics, exhaustible resources and international trade, with special focus on the gains from trade. In so doing, some of his most cherished papers will also be identified and briefly discussed. Section 4 considers Kemp as a discipline builder and his contributions to economic methodology. It emphasizes his rigorous and uncompromising approach to research and the various academic controversies in which he has been involved. It also provides Murray Kemp's personal views on the future directions of research in trade theory and welfare economics. The final section summarizes the key points of this chapter.

---

[1] The conversations mainly took place in the last few years although they had started in 1978 when the author first became Kemp's doctoral student at the University of New South Wales (UNSW).

2. How Murray Kemp came to economic theory

So how did a person who was raised in rural Victoria become Australia's pre-eminent economic theorist since the mid-1960s?

The story began with Captain Anthony Fenn Kemp (Murray's grandfather's grandfather) who first came to Australia five years after the First Fleet in 1793 and returned much later, after an eventful intervention, to settle in Tasmania.[2] Murray Chilvers Kemp was born in Melbourne in 1926 but, due to a clerical error, he did not officially exist until two months after his actual birthday.[3] His father was a manager of the State Savings Bank of Victoria (later taken over by the Commonwealth Bank), an army boxing champion and an elite footballer. Because of his father's profession, Kemp's family used to move from country town to country town as he grew up. Eventually he was sent to Wesley College, a reputed Methodist high school in Melbourne, and won the Draper Scholarship in Year 12. The Kemp family left some kind of a record at Wesley as Murray became a dux of the college and his younger brother achieved the same feat about a decade later.

There were two events in high school that might have guided Murray Kemp to a successful career in economic theory. First, there was an introduction to the wonderful world of calculus in a very informal setting. Murray did only elementary maths at junior high school and did not take any formal maths course at senior high school. In fact, he only received intensive lessons in calculus from Major Potts (a maths teacher) at a wood chopping camp. He found a natural liking for calculus but did not appreciate at this time how significant the tool was going to be in his later career. Second, Murray Kemp was himself an excellent sportsman. At Wesley, he chose his subjects to fit in with his football and cricket training schedules. Thus he did not do any Latin or science. As a result, he could not enrol in law or medicine, despite coming top at Wesley. One day, Mr P.L. Williams (a well-known cricket coach at Wesley who trained several Australian national cricket players) casually suggested that Murray should study economics at the 'shop'.[4] Mr Williams' suggestion was entirely based on the profession of Kemp Sr, but agreeable to Murray since he did do some economics in high school.

---

[2] Captain Anthony Fenn Kemp is popularly known as the Father of Tasmania for having produced 18 children, mostly from the same wife. His son, George Kemp, was very active in local politics and the town of Kempton in Tasmania was named after George. The colourful life of Captain Anthony Fenn Kemp (mutiny leader, church elder, republican, monopolist) has been documented in Kemp and Kemp (1965) and more recently and less favourably by Nicholas Shakespeare (2004), a joint descendant of the Kemp and Shakespeare clans.

[3] It used to be a well-known joke in the School of Economics at the UNSW that Kemp shares with the Queen the privilege of having an official birthday different from the true one.

[4] Then a slang term for University of Melbourne.

At the University of Melbourne, Kemp took five years to complete a double major: an honours degree in economics (first class) and an arts degree. The curriculum was particularly severe, requiring undergraduate students to read the original writings of Smith, Ricardo, Mill, Wicksell, Marshall, Keynes, Chamberlin, Robinson and Schumpeter. Although there was no formal course in trade, it is useful to remember that at that time Australian economics courses were all taught from an open economy perspective.[5] To supplement his mathematics, Kemp also took a first year maths course at the university.

Kemp graduated top in both economics and philosophy, and there was a suggestion that he should have considered specializing in philosophy, regarded as the queen of all disciplines in those days. However, he decided to stay with economics and wrote a Master thesis under the supervision of Ben Higgins, who had just arrived from McGill to take up the Ritchie Chair. Toward the end of his Master degree, Kemp was almost lost to the public sector. One day, Kemp told Higgins that he had gone to Canberra for an interview and accepted a job with the Australian Treasury. Ben Higgins exploded and insisted that Kemp should instead complete a doctoral degree in North America, which, in Higgins' view, had replaced the United Kingdom as the leading centre of economic excellence. Higgins wrote to several universities in the United States and at least two of them (Johns Hopkins and Minnesota) offered Murray doctoral scholarships in economics. Upon Higgins' advice, Kemp decided to accept the Johns Hopkins offer.

After several weeks of sailing from Sydney, Kemp arrived at Johns Hopkins (Baltimore) in 1949. At that time, the Department of Economics at Johns Hopkins was dominated by Fritz Machlup. Murray Kemp soon joined an outstanding cohort, which included Merton Miller (Nobel prize winner in 1990), Edith Penrose (of Penrose effect fame), Robert Eisner (famous macroeconomic policy economist and former president of AEA) and John Chipman (AEA Distinguished Fellow 2000). This group used to come to the trade classes conducted by Jean–Jacques Polak (a former student of Jan Tinbergen and Head of the Research Department of the IMF in Washington DC) and mathematical economics classes by T.C. Liu.[6] The group of Kemp, Chipman, Carl Christ and Arnold Harberger also took a course in linear algebra in order to read Samuelson's (1947) *Foundations* which had come out a few years earlier.

After completing two years of coursework at Johns Hopkins, Kemp took up an offer of employment from his former mentor, Higgins, who was by then Chairman of the Department of Economics at McGill.

---

[5] Australian economists were very interested in the effects of tariff on trade and posed the right question but could not provide a proof for the Stolper–Samuelson theorem.

[6] After moving to Cornell, Liu related that going to each lecture with Kemp and Chipman in the audience was an intellectual challenge (Wan and Long, 1998, p. 698).

Soon after joining McGill, Murray attended a mathematical logic course in order to understand Arrow's path breaking book on social choice (Arrow, 1951). Murray began writing his PhD from McGill and was initially supervised by Christ (then a very young academic), who eventually moved on to another institution. Murray's attempt to present several papers in welfare economics as a thesis was resisted by the Chairman of the Department at Johns Hopkins. He was then assigned a new supervisor, Evsey Domar, a more experienced professor, and chose a new topic, trade theory. His PhD thesis was completed in 1955.

In 1956–1957, Murray spent a year as Nuffield postdoctoral fellow at Cambridge. While in London he met Thérèse Belleau, a French Canadian, who had recently written her thesis for a very famous French anthropologist, the Abbé Henri Breuil, in Paris. At the time, Thérèse was teaching part-time at the Sorbonne and working with Sir Max Mallowan[7] in London. Fate reunited them later when Thérèse took up a teaching position at the University of Montreal. They got married in 1959, the year in which everything seemed to happen to Murray. Soon after his marriage, he was head hunted by David Rowan, then Head of the School of Economics at UNSW, for the second chair in the school. But by that time, Murray had already agreed with Domar, now at MIT, to teach there for at least two years. Kemp accepted the UNSW offer on condition that he would fulfil his commitments at MIT.

Kemp's stay at MIT was a turning point in his academic career. This was where he "grew up and became a man, as an economist" (Coleman, 2005, p. 8). Not surprisingly, the decisive influence was his exposure to Paul Samuelson's work.[8] MIT was also where Murray further developed his interest in micro-based trade models. This was partly because of Samuelson's pioneering work in the gains from trade, which inspired Kemp to write at MIT the first of his many papers on the gains from trade (Kemp, 1962a). The other reason was that Murray was asked by Charles Kindleberger to take over his graduate course in international trade. Kemp's own notes for this course later became his famous 1964 textbook, a point which will be elaborated in Section 3 of this chapter.

Murray returned to Australia in 1961 and immediately became Head of the School of Economics at UNSW. He was at times Chairman of the Faculty of Commerce, Chairman of the Faculty of Arts and acting Dean of Commerce. Unhappy with his administrative burden, Murray contemplated taking a position in the Research School at ANU. To prevent Murray from leaving UNSW, the then Vice Chancellor, Philip Baxter (later Sir Philip), made him a Research Professor, a unique position

---

[7] Professor Sir Max Mallowan was a renowned archeologist and the second husband of the internationally famous crime novelist Agatha Christie.

[8] A secretary at MIT gave Murray a collection of Samuelson's published papers and Murray read every paper that Samuelson had published (Coleman, 2005, p. 8).

in the history of UNSW until the early 2000s. Although he was once seriously tempted by an offer from University of California at Berkeley, Murray stayed as a research professor at UNSW until 2004.

Murray Kemp's decision to become an economic theorist has been vindicated by his rich and rewarding academic career. Over the years he has held many distinguished visiting positions, including Hill Foundation Professor at University of Minnesota, Keynes Professor of Economics at University of Essex, Ford Foundation Professor at the University of California at Berkeley, Wesley C. Mitchell Visiting Professor at Columbia and Winsemius Visiting Professor at Nanyang Technological University, as well as positions at LSE, Southampton, Stockholm, Paris–Dauphine, Mannheim, Western Ontario, Hebrew University of Jerusalem, Kobe, Shanghai University of Finance and Economics, Kiel, Munich, Nagoya City, Copenhagen Business School, Chukyo, Ritsumeikan, and City University of Hong Kong. He is one of the few Australian Fellows of the Econometric Society (since 1971), a former member of the Council of the Econometric Society (1964–1967 and 1995–1998) and a past President of the International Economic and Finance Society (1997–1998). Kemp has also received many prestigious awards, including the Alexander von Humboldt Foundation Prize (1987) and the Distinguished Fellow of the Economic Society of Australia (1989) as well as honorary doctorates from universities around the globe.

3. Murray Kemp's major contributions to trade and welfare economics

Due to his education at Melbourne and the influence of Higgins, Kemp began his academic career as a Keynesian economist. In fact, a close examination of his Keynesian papers reveals that his work in this area would be most appropriately classified as post-Keynesian, a school of thought that formally emerged many years later. But Kemp would soon become dissatisfied with the special assumption of fixed price in Keynesian economics. Thanks to inspiration from Samuelson and Arrow, Kemp became preoccupied with welfare economics soon after arriving at McGill. By the mid-1950s, his central research interest shifted to micro-based trade models. In the late 1970s and during the 1980s, Kemp turned his attention to the economics of exhaustible and renewable resources. This section will examine Kemp's contributions to these three areas although the focus will be his impact on trade theory.

3.1. Kemp and welfare economics

In a chronological sense, it seems plausible to start with Kemp's endeavours in welfare economics. But it is obviously not easy to separate his contributions to welfare economics from those in international trade.

This is so because a major part of his work has been concerned with the gains from trade, which represents the intersection of trade theory and welfare economics. This subsection will attempt to sketch out Kemp's major contributions to the general theory of welfare economics, which are not directly connected to international trade.

Perhaps Kemp's most significant contribution to welfare economics is his clarification of the relationship between individual and social welfare functions. In a series of joint papers, Kemp and Ng (Kemp and Ng, 1976, 1977) successfully took on the formidable Samuelson who had previously claimed that the construction of a Bergson–Samuelson social welfare function only requires ordinal individual utility functions. This claim had been generally accepted by economic theorists prior to 1976. Kemp and Ng were able to demonstrate that cardinal individual utilities are needed in order to construct an internally consistent social welfare function of the Bergson–Samuelson type.

Another important contribution to welfare economics is his work on Arrow's social choice theory. In fact, his second publication in welfare economics provided a critical interdisciplinary review of Arrow's Impossibility Theorem (Kemp, 1953–1954). In this paper, Kemp argued that the Impossibility Theorem is no surprise to political philosophers. The philosophers have known for hundreds of years, ever since Hobbes and Locke, that it is not possible to find a constitution that satisfies the axioms postulated by Arrow. What is new in Arrow's book is the mathematics. Kemp also showed that the Impossibility Theorem would be annihilated if one were willing to assume that utilities are comparable across people.

In a joint paper decades later, Kemp and Ng (1987, p. 325) clarified the relationship between Arrow's social choice theory and the Bergson–Samuelson tradition. They argued that Arrow's definition of independence of irrelevant alternatives (IIA) implies three elements: (i) social ordering depends only on individual preferences, (ii) ordinalism (ordinal preferences are to count) and (iii) independence (the social ordering of any two alternatives depends on only individual preferences concerning those alternatives and not on the preferences concerning irrelevant alternatives. Kemp and Ng suggested that the problem with the Arrovian framework arises because IIA implies ordinalism and that any reasonable constitutional rule requires interpersonal cardinal utilities.

Kemp also made a considerable contribution to welfare economics through his joint work with Long on the evaluation of social income in a dynamic economy. Under the assumption that the social utility function and the technology are stationary (i.e., independent of time), Kemp and Long (1982) demonstrated that it is possible in a changing world to define the net national product of a closed economy in such a way that it is both welfare-relevant and ideally computable. In a sequel paper, Kemp and Long (1998) extended this conclusion to less strict assumptions: (i) the social rate of time discount is not a given constant but depends on both the paths of consumption flows or the paths of capital stocks and (ii) economies may be open to trade with each other.

As a welfare economist, Kemp does not have sympathy with people who argue for interpersonal comparison of utility or even intertemporal comparison of the same person's utility (Kakkar, 2004, p. 2). He believes in the Paretian approach to welfare comparison of different economic situations. Thus it seems fitting that Kemp has lately refocused his attention on Pareto's compensation principle (Kemp and Pezanis–Christou, 1999). In a very recent paper, Kemp (2008b) confirmed his own interpretation of Pareto's principle of compensation, which is at variance with a popular strand of welfare economics. This school of thought, based on the work of Kaldor (1939) and Hicks (1939), has argued that compensation need only be hypothetical (feasible but not necessarily carried out). This line of thinking has been enthusiastically expounded by authors such as Schumpeter (1949, p. 163) and Chipman (1976, pp. 92–93). Relying on Pareto's original writing (Pareto, 1894), Kemp was able to reaffirm that Pareto had in mind actual, rather than hypothetical, compensation.

3.2. Kemp and exhaustible and renewable resources

Kemp has made an invaluable contribution to the economic theory of exhaustible and renewable resources in the 1970s and 1980s. Together with George Hadley, a mathematician, Kemp published a textbook in control theory (Hadley and Kemp, 1971), which served as a standard reference for optimal economic growth for decades. More importantly, he published extensively and significantly in the field of exhaustible resources, often jointly with N.V. Long. Their joint work, selectively summarized in Kemp and Long (1980a, 1984a), covers a wide variety of themes in the economics of exhaustible and renewable resources. In view of the volume of their joint output,[9] it is not possible to conduct a comprehensive survey in the present chapter. Nevertheless some key themes and publications deserve special mention:

- uncertainty about the size of the resource stock ("how to eat a cake of unknown size") (Kemp, 1976, 1977; Kemp and Long, 1980b, 1985, 2008);
- optimal search, extraction and consumption of resources (Kemp and Long, 1978, 1980c, 1980d, 2008);
- international trade with exhaustible resources (Kemp and Long, 1979a, 1979b, 1984c);

---

[9] The collaboration between Kemp and Long in exhaustible resources generated two edited books and approximately 30 journal articles and book chapters.

- sustainability (Hung *et al.*, 1984) and survival (Kemp, 1976; Kemp and Long, 1984b; Kemp *et al.*, 1984);
- optimal harvesting of renewable resources such as trees and fisheries (Kemp and Moore, 1979; Kemp and Long, 1983; Chiarella *et al.*, 1984).

In is worthwhile to note that Kemp's work in resource economics often gave rise to a stream of literature. A good example is his joint work on the economics of forestry, which was later generalized by Mitra and Wan (1985, 1986).

3.3. Kemp and international trade

Building on the earlier work of Heckscher, Ohlin, Harberler, Viner, Lerner and Samuelson, a small group of post-war economists, including Harry Johnson, Kemp, Chipman and Ronald Jones, strove to modernize trade theory. Together, they provided trade theory with a firm and wide theoretical foundation. As a member of this group, Kemp has left his intellectual imprint on virtually all parts of the vast trade literature. It seems plausible to classify his contributions to trade theory under three broad categories:

- the formalization of the trade curriculum;
- positive trade theory, in particular the extension of the Heckscher–Ohlin–Samuelson (HOS) model;
- normative trade theory, particularly the gains from trade.

Kemp is often credited with being responsible for the mathematization[10] of the trade curriculum. This claim is primarily based on the publication of his trade book in 1964 (Kemp, 1964), which grew out of his own notes for the graduate trade course that he taught at MIT several years earlier. Unlike any authors before him, Kemp freely used the language of calculus to express and convey trade ideas. His book employed a uniform set of notations and formulas in developing theoretic trade models. The impact of Kemp's book was immediate, profound and lasting. It was quickly adopted in the United States, and was used around the world in advanced undergraduate and graduate classes for over two decades. It has also become an indispensable reference in all subsequent textbooks in trade theory. The 1964 text was revised in 1969 (Kemp, 1969) and later translated into Japanese with an added chapter on exhaustible resources (Kemp, 1981).

Kemp's book has over the years provided graduate students and academics with ideas and tools to pursue their study and research in trade

---

[10] Broadly interpreted as the use of mathematical techniques (geometry, algebra, calculus, topology, etc.) in conveying, explaining, formulating, arguing, deriving and stating propositions.

theory. It is a tough book to follow, even for graduates, and, despite its age, still full of ideas to be exploited as PhD thesis topics. Not surprisingly, his book has been criticized as being too brief or too terse (Coleman, 2005, p. 15). That is perhaps a small price to pay for clarity, concision, elegance and generality. In some sense, what Kemp's 1964 trade book has done to international trade can be compared with what Samuelson's *Foundations* has achieved for economic theory. It is thus most appropriate to sum up by citing Samuelson's (1993, p. vii) authoritative assessment of Kemp's book:

> The great Maxwell spoke of thermodynamics as "a science with secure foundations, clear definitions, and distinct boundaries". Willard Gibbs asserted that all this could be said to be true only after the 1850 synthesis by Clausius of the heuristics of Carnot, Thomson, and Joule. When I pick up the first edition of Kemp's *The Pure Theory of International Trade* and compare it with the fine prewar texts of Marshall, Haberler, and Ohlin, I can only use the words like those of Gibbs. At last, coherence and closure was achieved. Originality is not a hallmark of us textbook writers, but *early* authors who set a standard of coverage and rigor do get seated by Saint Peter in the very front pews of the cathedral of science.

Kemp's contribution to the positive theory of trade was discussed in detail by Wan and Long (1998). These authors demonstrated how Kemp has over the years extended the HOS model by relaxing assumptions concerning the production technology, the nature of products and productive factors (Wan and Long, 1998, pp. 700–702). A sample of Kemp's pioneering work in this field includes:

- Kemp–Jones model of variable labour supply (Kemp and Jones, 1962);
- Kemp–MacDougall model of international capital flow (Kemp, 1962b, 1962c, 1966);
- Herberg–Kemp model of variable return to scale (Herberg and Kemp, 1969);
- Generalizations of the Stolper–Samuelson and Samuelson–Rybczynski theorems (Kemp *et al.*, 1973);
- Kemp–Wan model of trade with adjustment costs (Kemp and Wan, 1973);
- Kemp–Long–Shimomura model of trade in the presence of labour union (Kemp *et al.*, 1991).

In addition, Wan and Long also provided examples of Kemp's contributions to trade under uncertainty, general equilibrium model with transport costs and international finance.

Although the appraisal by Wan and Long of Kemp's accomplishments in positive trade theory was very comprehensive, it has somewhat become dated. Subsequent to this review, Kemp has continued to produce significant papers under the HOS paradigm. A selective sample of his important papers on positive trade theory in the past 10 years includes:

- a second correspondence principle (Kemp *et al.*, 2002);
- trade patterns in the presence of voluntary and involuntary international transfers (Kemp and Shimomura, 2002, 2003a);
- a dynamic HOS model in the case of costly factor reallocation (Kemp and Shimomura, 2003b).

Kemp's contributions to normative trade theory are both diverse and significant. They include, for example,

- infant industry protection (Kemp, 1960, 1974);
- optimal tariff (Kemp, 1967);
- second best tax policies (Kemp and Negishi, 1969; Bhagwati and Kemp, 1969);
- the gains from international migration (Kemp, 1993);
- the welfare impact of voluntary and involuntary international transfers (Kemp and Shimomura, 2002, 2003a);
- the gains from trade.

This subsection will concentrate on Kemp's life-long devotion to the perennial issue of gains from trade.

The normative theory of the gains from international trade has a long and somewhat obscure beginning. It is well known that the benefits of free trade were expounded by Adam Smith in his response to the English Mercantilists. However, Kemp (2001a, p. 1)[11] reminded us that it was the French social philosopher Montesquieu (1749) who had posed the right sort of questions well before the first appearance of the *Wealth of Nations*. The defining novelty in Montesquieu's approach is that he considered the benefits of international trade from the perspective of individual citizens, rather from that of the king. His question can be interpreted in modern terminology as having two separate components: (i) what is the basis for beneficial trade? and (ii) in what sense can trade be said to be gainful/harmful to individual economic agents?

David Ricardo, the best known and most influential trade theorist, provided the answer to (i) through the celebrated principle of comparative advantage. He, however, avoided question (ii) by concentrating on economic models with representative agents. This kind of model is not helpful in analyzing the welfare impact of trade on a heterogeneous population. Pareto (1894) offered the answer to question (ii) through the now well-known concepts of Paretian welfare improvement and the

---

[11] Kemp took this clue from Nguyen Manh Hung at Université Laval during Kemp's short trip to Laval to receive an honorary doctorate of economics in 1995.

compensation principle.[12] However, his insight was misunderstood and ignored by generations of English-speaking economists until it was exploited, in an implicit manner, by Samuelson (1939). In this brilliant paper, Samuelson proved, under a number of standard assumptions, that free trade is gainful to a small open economy as follows. When such an economy moves from autarky to free trade (due to a difference in autarkic price ratio and the terms of trade), there exist balanced schemes of lump-sum transfers for each country, such that no individual is worse off post-transfer and at least one person is better off than under autarky. Samuelson's special small-country result was later generalized by Kemp (1962a) for open economies of any size.[13]

Soon after the proof of the existence of a perfectly competitive equilibrium, the Walras–Arrow–Debreu–McKenzie (WADM) model was applied to problems relating to the gains from trade, and Montesquieu's agenda can be considered to have been satisfactorily settled. However, general propositions concerning the gains from trade only appeared just over 35 years ago (Grandmont and McFadden, 1972; Kemp and Wan, 1972). In a period that spans over 50 years, Kemp has demonstrated the gains from trade in many possible situations and under the most relaxed assumptions. In particular, he has shown that trade is potentially gainful in the presence of

- small or large countries (Kemp, 1962a);
- free or restricted trade (Kemp and Wan, 1972; Kemp and Wan, 1976; Kemp and Wan, 1986a; Kemp and Shimomura, 2001a; Kemp, 2007b);
- perfect or imperfect competition (Kemp and Wan, 1972; Kemp and Negishi, 1970; Kemp and Shimomura, 2001b);
- uncertainty or chaos (Kemp and Ohyama, 1978; Kemp and Shimomura, 1999);
- exhaustible resources (Kemp and Long, 1979a);
- monetary economies (Kemp, 1990; Kemp and Wong, 1995b);
- command economies (Kemp, 2001b);
- overlapping generations and infinite economies (Kemp, 1973; Kemp and Wong, 1995c; Kemp and Wolik, 1995);
- incomplete markets (Kemp and Wong, 1995a);[14]
- trade-dependent technology and preferences (Kemp et al., 2001);
- Gossen time constraints (Kemp, 2008c).

---

[12] Kemp and Pezanis–Christou (1999, p. 443) suggested that the idea of compensation should at least go back to Mill (1825, pp. 52–53).

[13] Strictly speaking, Kemp showed that for a single country, large or small, it is impossible by means of compensating lump-sum transfers to make everyone better off in autarky than in a given free trade equilibrium. His demonstration was thus incomplete.

[14] With missing markets and without compensation, everyone might still be better off as a result of trade.

Kemp has insisted that any rigorous proposition concerning the gains from trade requires three components:

(i) the existence of the world's autarkic equilibrium;
(ii) the specification of trading nations (preferences, endowments, technology and market structure) including a suitable scheme of transfers;
(iii) the existence of the world's post-trade equilibrium under compensation.

It seems worthwhile to make some remarks concerning the first two components of the normative theory of the gains from trade. It is customary to assume that all trading nations possess autarkic equilibria. Kemp (2003) argued plausibly that many countries have grown to be trade-dependent to the extent that they could not possibly survive in autarky. He went on to demonstrate that the absence of autarkic equilibrium, even for one trading nation, can give rise to the absence of the world trading equilibrium.

Kemp has, more than anyone else, been responsible for discharging Samuelson's agenda on compensation in the context of international trade. First, Kemp forcefully argues that, in the absence of actual compensation, the theorems on the gains from trade are "true but irrelevant" (Kemp, 1962a). This appears to be consistent with his interpretation of Pareto's principle of compensation, as discussed above. Second, he carefully points out that, in a general case, a scheme of transfers may change the terms of trade and, as a result, winners and losers before compensation may not be winners or losers, respectively, after a partial compensation not involving them.

Third, and most significantly, he has led many pioneering studies on the nature of compensation schemes. Until 1980, compensation was typically understood to be in the form of lump-sum transfers. Dixit and Norman (1980) claimed that lump-sum transfers are not necessary and that carefully chosen taxes on goods and services can always make free trade Pareto superior to autarky. However, Kemp and Wan (1986b) showed that Dixit and Normans' non-lump sum claim only holds true in some cases.[15] In particular, Kemp and Wan constructed examples of WADM economies to show that there are cases in which free trade is superior to autarky if and only if the compensation of losers is effected by lump-sum transfer and that there are cases in which free trade is Pareto superior to autarky if and only if compensation is not lump sum. More recently, Kemp and Shimomura (2001b) demonstrated that in a very general economy (including perfect and imperfect competition, increasing returns

---

[15] Their initial example contained an inconsequential numerical error, which was later corrected and reprinted in Kemp (1995).

to scale and strategic behaviour), trade is, subject to the existence of equilibrium, still potentially better than autarky but compensation may require both (*ex ante*) lump-sum and (*ex post*) non-lump-sum transfers.

Fourth and finally, although he strongly believes in the potential gains from trade, Kemp has been very alert of the possibilities of Pareto inferior trade. It is well known that, in a WADM economy, uncompensated free trade is generally Pareto incomparable with autarky. Kemp and Long (1979a) provided one of earliest (if not the earliest) examples of Pareto inferior uncompensated trade, using a model which incorporates over-lapping generations and exhaustible resources. They also showed how this suboptimality can be removed by the creation of a sufficiently large stock of bonds. Taking the money-in-the-utility-function approach, Kemp (1990) was able to show that free trade might be harmful to a monetary economy.[16] Under certain conditions, the traditional production and consumption gains may be swamped by a loss of satisfaction from holding cash when relative prices change.

To sum up this section it is perhaps appropriate to remark briefly on the publications that Kemp himself considers his finest and most important contributions to trade theory and welfare economics. These papers will be grouped in terms of the core propositions in the normative theory of international trade:

- *For any economy, large or small, free trade in better than no trade* (Kemp, 1962a; Kemp and Wan, 1972; Kemp and Shimomura, 2001a).

Kemp (1962a) offers the first demonstration that, for a country of any size, there exists a suitable lump-sum compensation scheme such that no individual is worse off under free trade than in autarky. This slightly incomplete demonstration was later rectified in Kemp and Wan (1972), which, together with Grandmont and McFadden (1972), provided the first rigorous proof of the gains from free trade using the WADM framework. Kemp and Shimomura (2001b) demonstrated the potential gainfulness of free trade in a Cournot–Nash general equilibrium in which neither increasing returns nor trade-induced changes in the strategy sets of individual agents are ruled out. There appears to be no other gains-from-trade proposition under assumptions of imperfect competition of comparable generality.

- For a small open economy, an improvement in the terms of trade is beneficial (Kemp, 1962a).
- Any subset of trading countries can form a mutually advantageous customs union or free trade area (Kemp and Wan, 1976, 1986a; Kemp and Shimomura, 2001a; Kemp, 2007b).

---

[16] Money in the production function would have generated the same possibility.

Kemp and Wan (1976) proved the famous Kemp–Wan proposition which states that a group of two or more trading nations can form a customs union and choose a common tariff vector and a system of intra-union lump-sum compensatory payments such that all individuals within the union are better off and no individual outside the union is made worse off. The beauty of this remarkable proposition is that it includes the gains from free trade as a limiting case when membership of the customs unions is extended to all trading countries. However, a complete proof of the Kemp–Wan proposition only appeared a decade later in Kemp and Wan (1986a). Kemp and Shimomura (2001b) subsequently extended the Kemp–Wan proposition to the situation where, after the formation of the union, each excluded country responds by choosing an optimal tariff vector. The extended Kemp–Wan proposition remains valid in the mixed case in which some excluded countries always choose the same tariff vector and others always choose an optimal tariff structure. Finally, Kemp (2007b) demonstrated that the Kemp–Wan proposition continues to hold true for any form of free trade association. It was also shown that sense can be made of the common conjecture that a customs union is more beneficial to the world economy than a comparable but distinct free trade association.

In addition to the above seven papers, Kemp has also included Kemp and Ng (1976, 1987) on social welfare and Kemp and Wan (2005) on economic methodology in the group of papers that gave him the greatest pleasure. Kemp and Ng (1976) was briefly discussed previously, whereas Kemp and Wan (2005) will be considered in the next section.

4. Kemp as a discipline builder and his contributions to economic methodology

In assessing the role of Kemp as a discipline builder, we need to examine his contributions both as a scholar and a teacher. Kemp is a prolific scholar by any standard. He has published over 250 journal articles and book chapters, and 19 books. His publications have penetrated all leading international economics journals, including *Econometrica*, *American Economic Review*, *Journal of Political Economy*, *Quarterly Journal of Economics*, *Review of Economic Studies*, *International Economic Review* and *Journal of International Economics*. He has been the most cited economist in Australasia. According to the second edition of Wheatsheaf Books' *Who's Who in Economics* (1986), Kemp was one of the 11 Australian economists who were included in the 1000 most frequently cited living economists in the world between 1972 and 1983. By the ISI Web of Science measure of citations, he has been cited more in the post-1980 literature than any other Australian economist (Coleman, 2005, p. 1).

As a teacher, through his 1964 textbook, Kemp has influenced the teaching of trade theory amongst developed countries, especially English-speaking countries. After more than four decades, his textbook continues to exert a certain degree of authority over the teaching of modern trade theory. In addition, he also assisted China to reformulate its undergraduate international trade curriculum through a series of invited lectures in Shanghai in the late 1980s. Many leading economic theorists attribute their interests and achievements in international trade to Kemp's influence or their associations with him. As a doctoral supervisor, he enjoyed a 100% success rate and produced more PhD graduates in economics than anyone else at UNSW. Kemp has also rendered his valuable services to the profession. He has held many editorial positions including associate editor of the *International Economic Review* (1960–1996), *Journal of International Economics* (1971–1991) and *Bulletin of Economic Research* (1989–2006), as well as editorial board member of *Review of International Economics* (1993–2005).

Kemp's success as a scholar is a result of a host of factors. First, there is his passion for economic theory, which does not seem to diminish with the passage of time, coupled with the ambition to fulfil his potential. He is never satisfied with a particular finding, but constantly strives to improve or refine it. The evolution of the Kemp–Wan proposition serves as a good example. Second, Kemp has adopted a highly selective and disciplined approach to research. He selects every single research topic carefully, reads every relevant paper on the chosen topic and becomes totally immersed in it until some results are derived. Third, Kemp has been blessed with excellent health, both physically and mentally. At the advanced age of 82, he remains intellectually as alert as ever and, until a few years ago, was still a highly competent player on the tennis court. Fourth, and most importantly, Kemp's main strengths as a researcher lie in his ability to philosophize, and the breadth and depth of his analytical knowledge. This final aspect will be further elaborated below.

Kemp's ability to philosophize became apparent very early on, dating at least to his undergraduate days at Melbourne University. Gradually cultivated and matured over the years, this ability has helped him to pose the right sort of questions, to make the appropriate assumptions and to choose the suitable approach for solution. Kemp also possesses a wide array of powerful analytical knowledge and skills, ranging from history of economic thought to mathematics. He has never avoided any research work because the required mathematics is too demanding (Wan and Long, 1998, p. 699). Instead, in the early stage of his career, Kemp was willing to spend the time and effort to master whatever novel mathematical tools are needed in his research. This sometimes resulted in an excellent textbook such as Hadley and Kemp (1971). His mastery over tools is perhaps best illustrated by the statement and proof of the original Kemp–Wan proposition. Arguably his most discussed and republished paper, Kemp and Wan (1976) contains not a single mathematical symbol.

Kemp has always been practising what he has been preaching. He specializes and collaborates. He has had a tremendous number of coauthors over the years. Kemp modestly suggested that he could write better papers if he at least sometimes shared them with other people who had skills that he did not have or did not have in sufficient quantity (Kakkar, 2004, p. 3). Samuelson (1939, p. viii) attributed Kemp's propensity to do original works with new collaborators everywhere he goes to Kemp's exceptional qualities of being friendly, generous, humanitarian and likeable. The collaboration of Kemp and Jones (1962) serves to support Samuelson's observation. Kemp wrote the original paper and Jones refereed it. Since Jones wrote such a long and helpful report, Kemp suggested to the editor of *Journal of Political Economy* that the referee be made a coauthor. The result was the now famous Kemp–Jones model of variable labour supply, a classic extension of the standard HOS model.

Kemp's scholarship epitomizes the purest tradition of mathematical economics. To support such a claim we need to identify fundamental features of the discipline of mathematical economics. Perhaps no one does it better than Debreu (1991, p. 4) who, in his presidential address to the *American Economic Association*, stated:

[Mathematics] ceaselessly asks for weaker assumptions, for stronger conclusions, for greater generality. In taking a mathematical form, economic theory is driven to submit to those demands ... Mathematics also dictates the imperative of simplicity.

Debreu's words beautifully summarize Kemp's contributions to economic theory: stronger and simpler conclusions under weaker assumptions and more general framework.

Perhaps a defining characteristic of Kemp as an economic theorist is his unconditional insistence on internal consistency of the economic modelling process. He does not take any theoretical model, however well established or widely accepted, for granted. He always goes back to basic and, if necessary, challenges the model's validity and, if possible, proposes an alternative approach. Because of his uncompromising and rigorous approach to economic theorizing, Kemp has been involved in many debates and controversies. An example is the lump-sum versus non-lump-sum compensation controversy mentioned earlier. It is interesting to note that his approach to academic debates does not discriminate between friends or rivals. He is not the type who would politely avoid disagreements for the sake of friendship or harmony. Thus, we often find his friends, many of whom have known him for a long time, end up on the other side of the debate.

It now seems worthwhile to briefly discuss some of Kemp's relatively recent contributions to economic methodology via his critics of the current theories or approaches. These include:

- generality versus tractability;
- modelling integrity;
- dynamic Walrasian adjustment process;
- representative agent;
- price-taking general equilibrium in the WADM context.

Each of the above will be briefly elaborated in turn.

Kemp does not like special or hidden assumptions. In fact, it was his dissatisfaction with the Keynesian special assumption of fixed price that converted him to a neoclassical economist. Later in his career, he was not impressed with the partial equilibrium approach adopted by strategic trade theorists (Coleman, 2005, p. 13). He saw that partial equilibrium can only be the beginning of any serious study and that there is eventually a need to tackle strategic behaviour in a general equilibrium context. Most recently, Kemp (2008a, pp. 202–203) took up issue with trade theorists who want to answer real world problems by trading off generality for tractability. He proposed that reliance should not be placed on a single restricted model where restrictions may apply to the dimension of the model or to the mathematical form of the model relationships or both. He argued that when special restrictions are imposed on a model, the researcher should at least resolve the model under a substantial variety of restrictions.[17] Until this responsibility has been discharged, no real world questions can be considered as having been satisfactorily addressed.

Many results in trade theory were initially established in the two countries, two commodities, two factors context. Not all propositions proved for the $2 \times 2 \times 2$ case admit of straightforward generalization. Quite often, generalization to higher dimensions can only be achieved at the cost of special, restrictive assumptions. Kemp and Wan (2005) have illustrated this point using the example of equivalent tariffs. It has long been known that in the simple case of two countries trading two commodities, international transfers can be replaced by equivalent tariffs (Mayer, 1981). There have been several attempts in the literature to generalize Mayer's proposition in terms of commodities and countries. Kemp and Wan (2005) have shown that, with conditions imposed on exogenous variables only, Mayer's proposition cannot be extended to accommodate more than two countries. In addition, the sufficient conditions so far provided for the existence of generalized equivalent tariff factors relate to equilibrium values of the endogenous variables,

---

[17] After all, several competing models can be observationally equivalent, so that if a particular model with special assumptions describes economic reality well, it may not necessarily provide the best possible theoretical explanation.

which are difficult to empirically justify. Finally, for modelling integrity, such special assumptions or restrictions on endogenous variables must be fully and explicitly stated at the model formulation stage so that readers can fully appreciate the role played by these assumptions.

Turning now to Walrasian general equilibrium, it was taken for granted that the dynamic *tâtonnement* process described by Walras is a consistent mechanism. However it is now well known that dynamic Walrasian models are internally inconsistent. In such models, costless adjustment is assumed to take place at a finite pace. But if adjustment is costless then, given any finite speed of adjustment, there is a profit or utility incentive to increase the speed of adjustment. To derive from stability analysis an acceptable constraint on the sign of the matrix of coefficients, one must develop a model in which market adjustments are costly and chosen optimally over time by producers and consumers. So far, there are available only the small-country models developed by Kemp *et al.* (2002) and Kemp and Shimomura (2003b).

The assumption of representative agents, implicit in the discussions of trade gains of Smith and Ricardo, became widespread and systematic in economic theory after the First World War. It is now a fairly common assumption in theoretical public economics, international trade and labour economics. But if representative agents possess perfect knowledge (another common assumption in economic models) that they are identical, then no agent will choose his/her strategy on the assumption that the strategies of all other agents in the same class are given, i.e., the Nash equilibrium concept must be abandoned. Any equilibrium must reflect the cooperative behaviour of members of the class (Kemp and Long, 1992; Kemp and Shimomura, 1995). In the conventional literature, this problem is often avoided by assuming that representative agents are unaware that they are identical, i.e., they are not completely informed. However, alert and intelligent agents in repeated games will soon discover that they are identical so that they will choose the same strategy. The modern theory of endogenous growth and general equilibrium theory of tax incidence appear to be particularly vulnerable to the representative agent problem (Hu *et al.*, 2006; Kemp, 2007a).

The WADM models are based on several assumptions, which include: (i) households and commodities are finite in number and constant over time, both in number and identity and (ii) the endowment point of each household is in the interior of its consumption set. Kemp (2005) and Kemp and Shimomura (2005) have argued that any completely informed and rational agent can appreciate that under the above assumptions it possesses market power. Thus, price-taking behaviour in the WADM model cannot be taken for granted. In fact, the WADM model can only be restored to internal consistency by the imposition of one or both of the additional (and quite severe) assumptions that households are (a) unaware that they are finite in number or/and (b) incompletely rational in the sense that they cannot appreciate the fact that (i) and (ii) imply market power. On the constructive side, Kemp and Shimomura (2001b) have developed a model which rules out both (a) and (b), and therefore admits market power on the part of individual households.

To conclude this section, it seems appropriate to briefly examine various normative trade issues that Kemp considers to deserve the further attention of economic theorists. Kemp (2005) listed three serious gaps in the extension of the gains from trade. First, it is difficult to accommodate internally increasing returns to scale and household strategic behaviour. Kemp and Shimomura (2001b) have shown that trade remains potentially gainful in such a general economy, but their result assumes the existence of equilibrium.[18] Although Nishimura and Friedman (1981) did provide a set of sufficient conditions for a static, finite economy in which households possess market power and behave strategically, there is still a need to prove the existence of equilibrium in the Kemp–Shimomura type of model, and, if possible, extend it to economies with overlapping generations and infinite horizons.

Second, it is also very difficult to accommodate both overlapping generations and intergenerational caring (of parents for their children or children for their parents). Although Kemp and Wolik (1995) have shown that the standard theorem of gains from trade carries over to an economy with overlapping generations, an infinite horizon and price-taking behaviour by households and firms, their finding assumes that there are no intergenerational bequests and no gifts *inter vivos*. The strategic relationships of two pairs of parents in law, each pair aware of the relationship, will generate two complications: (i) the uncertainty about equilibrium and (ii) the extent of resource misallocation caused by these strategic relationships may be exacerbated by the introduction of free trade. Third, the gains from trade have not yet been formally established in sequential economies where there are false expectations associated with them.

To this list of three major gaps in the normative theory of trade, we can now add the issue of time constraints on consumption introduced by Hermann Heinrich Gossen (1854). Although Kemp (2008c) has shown that both the standard theorem of gains from trade and the Kemp–Wan proposition (and subsequent generalizations) survive the incorporation of Gossenian time constraints, richer normative results can still be obtained in a more general (i.e., non-price-taking) model where consumption takes time.

---

[18] As Kemp (2005, p. 362) explained, the stumbling block is the inability to establish the existence of equilibrium when the quantities produced are strategic variables drawn from non-convex sets.

5. Conclusion

Almost six decades ago, a young Murray Kemp left the shore of Australia in search of a doctoral degree in economics and a career in the academia. A dozen years later, he left MIT, one of the world's leading centres of excellence in economic research, to return to his country of birth. His settlement in Sydney has brought substantial benefits to the economics profession in Australia, as many economists and university students have been able to share his insights and knowledge through their professional and personal contacts with him. In fact, Murray is always more than willing to share and collaborate with friends, colleagues and students wherever he visits. In that sense, Murray can be regarded as a public good for the economics discipline.

Murray Kemp is one of the world's best known and leading economic theorists, with a distinguished career spanning almost six decades. His published works in welfare economics, exhaustible resources and, in particular, trade theory are both familiar to and greatly valued by economists and generations of graduate students. His classic 1964 text *The Pure Theory of International Trade* has revolutionized the teaching of international trade all over the developed world. Although he has left his intellectual footprints on virtually all aspects of the trade literature, Kemp will perhaps be best remembered for his outstanding contribution to the normative theory of trade where he has extended the potential gainfulness of trade to many different situations and under the most relaxed assumptions. His pioneering and persistent efforts in normative trade theory have provided strong theoretical justifications for free trade as well as any form of restricted or preferential trade. The policy implications of his research will assume an even greater degree of importance in view of the current trends of globalization and regionalization.

To sum up this tribute paper, the author invites readers to join him in acknowledging and celebrating the achievements of Murray Kemp, economic theorist, a gentleman and a scholar of the finest tradition.

Acknowledgement

The author has benefited from many conversations with Murray Kemp and comments from a referee. All remaining errors are his alone.

References

Arrow, K.J. (1951), *Social Choice and Individual Values*. Wiley, New York.
Bhagwati, J., Kemp, M. (1969), Ranking of tariffs under monopoly power in trade. *Quarterly Journal of Economics* 83 (2), 330–335.

Chiarella, C., Kemp, M., Long, N.V., Okuguchi, K. (1984), On the economics of international fisheries. *International Economic Review* 25 (1), 85–92.

Chipman, J.S. (1976), The Paretian heritage. *Revue Européenne des Sciences Sociales et Cahiers Vilfredo Pareto* 14 (37), 65–171.

Coleman, W. (2005), A conversation with Murray Kemp. *History of Economic Review* 41 (Winter), 1–18.

Debreu, G. (1991), The mathematization of economic theory. *American Economic Review* 81 (1), 1–7.

Dixit, A., Norman, V. (1980), *Theory of International Trade*. Cambridge University Press, Cambridge.

Grandmont, J.M., McFadden, D. (1972), A technical note on classical gains from trade. *Journal of International Economics* 2 (2), 109–125.

Gossen, H.H. (1854), *The Law of Human Relations and the Rules of Human Action Derived Therefrom*. Translated by Blitz, R.C., 1983, MIT Press, Cambridge, MA.

Hadley, G., Kemp, M. (1971), *Variational Methods in Economics*. North–Holland, Amsterdam.

Herberg, H., Kemp, M. (1969), Some implications of variable returns to scale. *Canadian Journal of Economics* 2 (3), 403–415.

Hicks, J.R. (1939), The foundations of welfare economics. *Economic Journal* 49 (196), 696–712.

Hu, Y.F., Kemp, M.C., Shimomura, K. (2006), Endogenous growth: Fragile foundations? *Review of Development Economics* 10 (1), 113–115.

Hung, N.M., Kemp, M.C., Long, N.V. (1984), On the transition from an exhaustible resource-stock to an inexhaustible substitute. In: Ingham, A., Ulph, A.M. (Eds.), *Demand, Equilibrium and Trade: Essays in Honour of Professor Ivor Pearce*. Macmillan, London, pp. 105–121.

Kaldor, N. (1939), Welfare propositions of economics and inter-personal comparisons of utility. *Economic Journal* 49 (195), 549–552.

Kakkar, V. (2004), Interview with Professor Murray Kemp. *City Economist* 14 (1), 1–3.

Kemp, M.C. (1953–1954), Arrow's general possibility theorem. *Review of Economic Studies* 21 (3), 240–243.

Kemp, M.C. (1960), The Mill–Bastable infant industry dogma. *Journal of Political Economy* 68 (1), 65–67.

Kemp, M.C. (1962a), The gain from international trade. *Economic Journal* 87 (288), 803–819.

Kemp, M.C. (1962b), Foreign investment and the national advantage. *Economic Record* 38 (81), 56–62.

Kemp, M.C. (1962c), The benefits and costs of private investment from abroad: comment. *Economic Record* 38 (81), 108–110.

Kemp, M.C. (1964), *The pure theory of International Trade*. Prentice-Hall, Englewood Cliffs, NJ.

Kemp, M.C. (1966), The gain from international trade and investment: A neo-Heckscher−Ohlin approach. *American Economic Review* 66 (4), 788–809.

Kemp, M.C. (1967), Notes on the theory of optimal tariffs. *Economic Record* 63 (103), 395–404.

Kemp, M.C. (1969), *The pure theory of International Trade and Investment.* Prentice-Hall, Englewood Cliffs, NJ.

Kemp, M.C. (1973), Trade gains in a pure consumption-loan model. *Australian Economic Papers* 12 (1), 124–126.

Kemp, M.C. (1974), Learning-by-doing: Formal tests of intervention in an open economy. *Keio Economic Studies* 11 (1), 1–7.

Kemp, M.C. (1976), How to eat a cake of unknown size. In: Kemp, M.C. (Ed.), *Three Topics in the Theory of International Trade.* North–Holland, Amsterdam.

Kemp, M.C. (1977), Further generalizations of the cake-eating problem under uncertainty. *Theory and Decision* 8 (4), 363–367.

Kemp, M.C. (1981), *The Pure Theory of International Trade and Investment,* revised Japanese edition, Nihon Hyoron Sha, Tokyo.

Kemp, M.C. (1990), The gains from free trade for a monetary economy. *Kobe Economic and Business Review* 35, 27–30.

Kemp, M.C. (1993), The welfare gains from international migration. *Keio Economic Studies* 30 (1), 1–5.

Kemp, M.C. (1995), *The gains from trade and the gains from aid.* Routledge, London.

Kemp, M.C. (2001a), *International trade and national welfare.* Routledge, London.

Kemp, M.C. (2001b), The gains from trade for a socialist economy. In: Kemp, M.C. (Ed.), *International Trade and National Welfare.* Routledge, London, pp. 171–174.

Kemp, M.C. (2003), International trade without autarkic equilibria. *Japanese Economic Review* 54 (4), 353–360.

Kemp, M.C. (2005), Trade gains: The end of the road. *Singapore Economic Review* 50 (Special Issue), 361–368.

Kemp, M.C. (2007a), Optimal commodity taxation with a representative agent. *Review of Development Economics* 11 (2), 385–389.

Kemp, M.C. (2007b), Normative comparisons of customs unions and other types of free trade association. *European Journal of Political Economy* 23 (2), 416–422.

Kemp, M.C. (2008a), *International trade theory: A critical review.* Routledge, London.

Kemp, M.C. (2008b), Vilfredo Pareto's principle of compensation. In: Kamihigashi, T., Zhao, L. (Eds.), *International Trade and Economic Dynamics: Essays in Memory of Koji Shimomura.* Springer, New York, forthcoming.

Kemp, M.C. (2008c), Normative trade theory under Gossenian assumptions. In: Samuelson, P.A. (Ed.), *Essays in Honour of Ian Steedman*. Routledge, London, forthcoming.

Kemp, M.C., Jones, R. (1962), Variable labor supply and the theory of international trade. *Journal of Political Economy* 70 (1), 30–36.

Kemp, T.B., Kemp, M.C. (1965), Captain Anthony Fenn Kemp. *Journal and Proceedings of the Royal Australian Historical Society* 51 (1), 10–22.

Kemp, M.C., Long, N.V. (1978), Optimal consumption of depletable natural resources: Comment. *Quarterly Journal of Economics* 92 (2), 345–353.

Kemp, M.C., Long, N.V. (1979a), The under-exploitation of natural resources: A model with overlapping generations. *Economic Record* 55 (150), 214–221.

Kemp, M.C., Long, N.V. (1979b), International trade with an exhaustible resource: A theorem of Rybczynski type. *International Economic Review* 20 (3), 671–677.

Kemp, M.C., Long, N.V. (Eds.) (1980a), *Exhaustible Resources, Optimality, and Trade*, North–Holland, Amsterdam.

Kemp, M.C., Long, N.V. (1980b), Eating a cake of unknown size: pure competition versus social planning. In: Kemp, M.C., Long, N.V. (Eds.), *Exhaustible Resources, Optimality, and Trade*, North–Holland, Amsterdam, pp. 55–70.

Kemp, M.C., Long, N.V. (1980c), Optimal search and extraction: a general-equilibrium formulation". In: Kemp, M.C., Long, N.V. (Eds.), *Exhaustible Resources, Optimality, and Trade*, North–Holland, Amsterdam, pp. 157–163.

Kemp, M.C., Long, N.V. (1980d), On two folk theorems concerning the extraction of exhaustible resources. *Econometrica* 18 (3), 663–673.

Kemp, M.C., Long, N.V. (1982), On the evaluation of social income in a dynamic economy: Variations on a Samuelsonian theme. In: Feiwel, G.R. (Ed.), *Samuelson and Neoclassical Economics*. Kluwer–Nijhoff Publishing, Boston, MA, pp. 185–189.

Kemp, M.C., Long, N.V. (1983), On the economics of forests. *International Economic Review* 24 (1), 113–131.

Kemp, M.C., Long, N.V. (Eds.) (1984a), *Essays in the Economics of Exhaustible Resources*, North–Holland, Amsterdam.

Kemp, M.C., Long, N.V. (1984b), The problem of survival: a closed economy. In: Kemp, M.C., Long, N.V. (Eds.), *Essays in the Economics of Exhaustible Resources*, North–Holland, Amsterdam, pp. 13–26.

Kemp, M.C., Long, N.V. (1984c), The role of natural resources in trade models. In: Jones, R.W., Kenen, P.B. (Eds.), *Handbook of International Economics*, vol. I, North–Holland, Amsterdam, pp. 367–417.

Kemp, M.C., Long, N.V. (1985), How to eat a cake of unknown size: The case of a growing cake. *Economics Letters* 17 (11985), 67–69.

Kemp, M.C., Long, N.V. (1992), Some properties of egalitarian economies. *Journal of Public Economics* 49 (3), 383–387.

Kemp, M.C., Long, N.V. (1998), On the evaluation of social income in a dynamic economy: Generalizations. In: Koch, K–J., Jaeger, K. (Eds.), *Trade, Growth, and Economic Policy in Open Economies, Essays in Honour of Hans-Jürgen Vosgerau*. Springer, Berlin, pp. 101–110.

Kemp, M.C., Long, N.V. (2008), Extracting several resource deposits of unknown size: optimal order. Special issue of *German Economic Review in Honour of Robert Solow*, forthcoming.

Kemp, M.C., Moore, E.J. (1979), Biological capital theory: A question and a conjecture. *Economics Letters* 4 (2), 141–144.

Kemp, M.C., Negishi, T. (1969), Domestic distortions, tariffs and the theory of optimum subsidy. *Journal of Political Economy* 77 (6), 1011–1013.

Kemp, M.C., Negishi, T. (1970), Variable returns to scale, commodity taxes, factor market distortions and their implications for trade gains. *Swedish Journal of Economics* 72 (1), 1–13.

Kemp, M.C., Ng, Y.–K. (1976), On the existence of social welfare functions, social orderings, and social decision functions. *Economica* 43 (169), 59–66.

Kemp, M.C., Ng, Y.–K. (1977), More on social welfare functions: The incompatibility of individualism and ordinalism. *Economica* 44 (1), 89–90.

Kemp, M.C., Ng, Y.–K. (1987), Arrow's independence condition and the Bergson–Samuelson tradition. In: Feiwel, G.R. (Ed.), *Arrow and the Foundations of the Theory of Economic Policy*. Macmillan, London, pp. 223–241.

Kemp, M.C., Ohyama, M. (1978), The gain from free trade under conditions of uncertainty. *Journal of International Economics* 8 (1), 139–141.

Kemp, M.C., Pezanis–Christou, P. (1999), Pareto's compensation principle. *Social Choice and Welfare* 16 (3), 441–444.

Kemp, M.C., Shimomura, K. (1995), The apparently innocuous representative agent. *Japanese Economic Review* 46 (3), 247–256.

Kemp, M.C., Shimomura, K. (1999), Trade gains in chaotic equilibria. *Review of International Economics* 7 (3), 403–409.

Kemp, M.C., Shimomura, K. (2001a), A second elementary proposition concerning the formation of customs unions. *Japanese Economic Review* 52 (1), 64–69.

Kemp, M.C., Shimomura, K. (2001b), Gains from trade in a Cournot–Nash general equilibrium. *Japanese Economic Review* 52 (3), 284–301.

Kemp, M.C., Shimomura, K. (2002), A theory of voluntary unrequited international transfers. *Japanese Economic Review* 53 (3), 290–300.

Kemp, M.C., Shimomura, K. (2003a), A theory of involuntary unrequited international transfers. *Journal of Political Economy* 111 (3), 686–692.

Kemp, M.C., Shimomura, K. (2003b), A dynamic Heckscher-Ohlin model: The case of costly factor reallocation. *Japanese Economic Review* 54 (3), 237–252.

Kemp, M.C., Shimomura, K. (2005), Price taking in general equilibrium. *American Journal of Applied Sciences* (Special Issue), 78–80.

Kemp, M.C., Wan, H.Y., Jr. (1972), The gains from free trade. *International Economic Review* 13 (3), 509–522.

Kemp, M.C., Wan, H.Y., Jr. (1973), Hysteresis of long-run equilibrium from realistic adjustment costs. In: Horwich, G., Samuelson, P.A. (Eds.), *Trade, Stability and Macroeconomics. Essays in Honor of Lloyd A. Metzler*. Academic Press, New York, pp. 221–242.

Kemp, M.C., Wan, H.Y., Jr. (1976), An elementary proposition concerning the formation of customs unions. *Journal of International Economics* 6 (1), 95–97.

Kemp, M.C., Wan, H.Y., Jr. (1986a), The comparison of second-best equilibria: the case of customs unions. In: Bos, D., Seidl, C. (Eds.), *Welfare Economics of the Second Best, Supplementum 5 to the Zeifschrift für Nationalökonomie*. Springer–Verlag, Vienna, pp. 161–167.

Kemp, M.C., Wan, H.Y., Jr. (1986b), Gains from trade without lump-sum compensation. *Journal of International Economics* 21 (1/2), 99–110.

Kemp, M.C., Wan, H.Y., Jr. (2005), On the existence of equivalent tariff vectors – when the status quo matters. *Singapore Economic Review* 50 (Special Issue), 345–360.

Kemp, M.C., Wolik, N. (1995), The gains from trade in the context of overlapping generations. In: Kemp, M.C. (Ed.), *The Gains from Trade and The Gains from Aid*. Routledge, London, pp. 129–146.

Kemp, M.C., Wong, K.-Y. (1995a), The gains from trade when markets are possibly incomplete. In: Kemp, M.C. (Ed.), *The Gains from Trade and The Gains from Aid*. Routledge, London, pp. 47–72.

Kemp, M.C., Wong, K.-Y. (1995b), The gains from trade for a monetary economy when markets are possibly incomplete. In: Kemp, M.C. (Ed.), *The Gains from Trade and The Gains from Aid*. Routledge, London, pp. 78–100.

Kemp, M.C., Wong, K.-Y. (1995c), Gains from trade with overlapping generations. *Economic Theory* 6 (2), 283–303.

Kemp, M.C., Kimura, Y., Shimomura, K. (2002), A second correspondence principle. In: Woodland, A.D. (Ed.), *Economic Theory and International Trade. Essays in Honour of Murray C. Kemp*. Edward Elgar, Aldershot, Hants, pp. 37–56.

Kemp, M.C., Long, N.V., Shimomura, K. (1984), The problem of survival: an open economy. In: Kemp, M.C., Long, N.V. (Eds.), *Essays in the Economics of Exhaustible Resources*, North–Holland, Amsterdam, pp. 27–35.

Kemp, M.C., Long, N.V., Shimomura, K. (1991), *Labour Unions and the Theory of International Trade*, North–Holland, Amsterdam.

Kemp, M.C., Shimomura, K., Wan, H.Y., Jr. (2001), Trade gains when the opportunity to trade changes the state of information. *Review of International Economics* 9 (1), 24–28.

Kemp, M.C., Uekawa, Y., Wegge, L.L. (1973), P- and PN-matrices, Minkowski- and Metzler-matrices, and generalization of the Stolper–Samuelson and Samuelson-Rybczynski theorems. *Journal of International Economics* 3 (1), 53–76.

Leonard, D. (1991), The enigmatic Professor Kemp: The early years. *Reconaissance* 1 (2), 1–5.

Mayer, W. (1981), Theoretical considerations on negotiated tariff adjustments. *Oxford Economic Paper* 33 (1), 135–153.

Mill, J.S. (1825), The Corn Laws. *Westminster Review* 3 (4), 394–420.

Mitra, T., Wan, H.Y., Jr. (1985), Some theoretical results on the economics of forestry. *Review of Economic Studies* 52 (2), 263–282.

Mitra, T., Wan, H.Y., Jr. (1986), On the faustmann solution to the forest management problem. *Journal of Economic Theory* 40 (2), 229–249.

Montesquieu, (C.-L. de Secondat, baron de la Bredè et de Montesquieu) (1749), Une letter à William Domville, reproduced in Masson, A. (Ed.) (1950–55), *Oeuvres Complètes de Montesquieu*, vol. II, Nagel, Paris, pp. 593–595.

Nishimura, K., Friedman, J.W. (1981), Existence of Nash equilibrium in n person games without quasi-concavity. *International Economic Review* 22 (3), 637–648.

Pareto, V. (1894), Il massimo di utilità dato dalla libera concorenza. Giornaledegli Economisti, 9(2), 48–66. Translated In: Chipman, J.S. (Ed.), *Collected Papers of Vilfredo Pareto in Mathematical and Quantitative Economics*, vol. II, Academic Press, New York. Forthcoming.

Samuelson, P.A. (1939), The gains from international trade. *Canadian Journal of Economic and Political Science* 5 (2), 195–205.

Samuelson, P.A. (1947), *Foundations of Economic Analysis*. Harvard University Press, Cambridge, MA.

Samuelson, P.A. (1993), Foreword. In: Herberg, H., Long, N.V. (Eds.), *Trade, Welfare, and Economic Policies*. Michigan University Press, Ann Arbor, MI, pp. vii–viii.

Schumpeter, J.A. (1949), Vilfredo Pareto (1848–1923). *Quarterly Journal of Economics* 63 (2), 147–173.

Shakespeare, N. (2004), *In Tasmania*. Random House Australia, Sydney.

Wan, H.Y., Jr., Long, N.V. (1998), Profile of Murray Kemp. *Review of International Economics* 6 (4), 698–705.

CHAPTER 12

The Gains from Trade and Refusal to Trade

Arye L. Hillman

Department of Economics, Bar-Ilan University, Israel
E-mail address: hillman@mail.biu.ac.il

Abstract

Purpose — Instances of refusal to trade stand in contrast to the theorems on the gains from trade. Two paradigms, second-best and political economy, have been used to explain refusal to trade. Murray Kemp (1962) provided a foundation for the political economy paradigm when he noted that, in the absence of lump-sum redistribution, the theorems on the gains from trade are "true but irrelevant". This chapter takes Murray Kemp's observation as a point of departure for a consideration of the relation between individual and group gains from trade. Paradigms in explaining refusal to trade are distinguished.

Methodology/Approach — This chapter examines ideas underlying explanations for refusal to participate in international trade.

Findings — Two different approaches are identified in modeling and explaining why the gains from trade are compromised by refusal of governments to allow free trade. The second-best approach suggests a justification for refusal to trade while the political economy approach with public-choice foundations proposes an explanation.

Practical implications — Ideology expressed in how governments are viewed can influence economic analysis.

Keywords: Gains from trade, political economy, second-best, Murray Kemp

Paper type: Research paper

Frontiers of Economics and Globalization
Volume 5 ISSN: 1574-8715
DOI: 10.1016/S1574-8715(08)05012-4

1. Introduction

In the classical liberal paradigm, no individual can gain by arbitrarily refusing to trade.[1] In international trade theory, the issue is however not whether an individual chooses to live a Robinson Crusoe type existence and refuses to trade with others. The issue is rather *with whom* trade takes place. Trade might be limited to domestic markets. Preferential trading agreements might permit trade in selected foreign markets. Or trade might be allowed with anyone anywhere willing to trade. The trade that is permitted may also be restricted.

Two paradigms, second-best and political economy, have explained refusal to allow free trade in face of the gains from trade. The second-best paradigm demonstrates societal or collective gains from refusal to trade. Policies are at the same time suggested whereby market intervention can improve social welfare.[2] The political economy paradigm acknowledges societal or collective gains from free trade and bases refusal to allow free trade on inability to transform the collective or aggregate gains from trade into the individual gains that would ensure a free-trade consensus.

To accept the second-best paradigm, one has to believe that closing of economies to trade or trade intervention can increase aggregate or societal welfare. We additionally have to believe that socially benevolent governments choose policies of refusal to allow free trade with the objective of achieving second-best efficiency gains. To accept the political economy paradigm, one has to believe that the realization of societal gains from trade can be compromised by majority voting or through political influence of self-interested groups on trade policies.

A point of beginning for the political economy paradigm is the observation by Murray Kemp (1962) that, in the absence of lump-sum taxes and transfers, the theorems on the gains from trade are "true but irrelevant". In the absence of lump-sum taxes and transfers, the efficiency losses from domestic redistribution aimed at providing all individuals in a population with personal gains from trade could in principle outweigh the societal efficiency gains from trade. Without lump-sum redistribution, there need then not be consensus support among voters for free trade. Insurance and asset markets are possible alternatives to compensating payments for achieving a free-trade consensus. When achieving consensus on free trade is not feasible, we are in the domain of the political economy

---

[1] The rule of law and the private property rights that facilitate trade are in the background of the liberal paradigm, since people cannot sell what they do not own and will not be prepared to receive in exchange that which they cannot be assured will after payment belong to them. The paradigm also includes the role of the state, as intervening or assisting where necessary when public goods, externalities, natural monopoly, and social justice require. See Mueller (2003), Hillman (2003).

[2] The second-best encompasses the classical exceptions of optimum tariffs and infant industries.

paradigm and refusal to allow free trade can follow from majority voting under direct democracy (Mayer, 1984) or from the more common political decisions of representative democracy (Hillman, 1982, 1989b; Grossman and Helpman, 1994, 2002).

2. The individual and gains from trade

An individual gains from trade compared to personal autarky.[3] We summarize this in a proposition that underlies the benefits from market exchange. In a population of n individuals, denote by U_i^a individual i's utility in personal autarky and by U_i^e individual i's utility from any set of opportunities to engage in personal exchange (reflected in offer curves that confront the individual or market-determined prices). Then

PROPOSITION 1A. *For any individual i, $U_i^e > U_i^a, i = 1, ..., n$; that is, all individuals gain from accepting trade offers (or cannot lose) relative to circumstances of personal autarky.*

Proposition 1A excludes presence of externalities: for example, Proposition 1A may be compromised if a ship that brings or takes goods also brings risk of disease or if we object to child labor used in production abroad. Proposition 1A assumes that transactions costs of exchange are not excessive; transportation costs could exceed the personal benefits from exchange. We can associate Proposition 1A with classical liberal thought, including Adam Smith who viewed scale economies or division of labor as a benefit of market organization and exchange, in recognition that goods may be less costly to produce when individuals produce for many others. An implication of Proposition 1A is:

PROPOSITION 1B. *If individuals vote between remaining in personal isolation and being presented with opportunities of exchange with others, they by consensus vote for opportunities for exchange.*

The consensus reflects the personal Pareto-improvement of Proposition 1A.

For convenience, we use a Benthamite social welfare function to aggregate personal utilities. Then:

PROPOSITION 1C. *For a population of n individuals, trade results in* $\sum_i U_i^e > \sum_i U_i^a.$

This proposition describes aggregate gains from trade. All n individuals are first placed in isolation where each has utility U_i^a, $i = 1, ..., n$. Then they are allowed to trade with one another in a competitive market where

---

[3] I shall omit reference to cases where individuals are indifferent between trading and not trading.

they achieve utilities U_i^e $i = 1, \ldots, n$. Proposition 1C follows by aggregation from Proposition 1A.

3. Domestic and foreign trade

To introduce foreign or international trade, we note the complexity that is hidden in proposition 1C that the choice may not be between free trade *with everybody* and no personal trade at all. We subdivide the population of n individuals into h "fellow citizens" and z "foreigners". Restrictions on trade with the h fellow citizens are not allowed. In a closed economy, the domestic population of h individuals initially engages in "domestic" exchange among themselves, with the consequence of Proposition 1A. Individuals achieve levels of utility U_i^d, $i = 1, \ldots, h$ from domestic exchange. Utility from exchange that includes free trade with the z foreigners is U_i^f, $i = 1, \ldots, h$.

There can be further partitions of the population z through preferential trading. Free trade or less restrictive trade with some sub-segment of the foreign population may be allowed. Analogs can now be stated to Propositions 1A, 1B, and 1C. We shall presently consider if the analog propositions hold.

PROPOSITION 2A. *For any individual i, $U_i^f > U_i^d$; that is, all individuals gain from foreign trade relative to only domestic trade amongst themselves.*

PROPOSITION 2B. *A vote to allow international trade has consensus support.*

PROPOSITION 2C. *For the entire population of n individuals, $\sum U_i^e > \sum U_i^a$; that is, the population collectively gains from international trade relative to domestic trade.*

4. A Ricardian economy

We consider these propositions first in a Ricardian economy. Suppose that workers in a Ricardian economy have the same productive capabilities and the same consumption preferences, and that workers abroad have different production capabilities. There are aggregate and personal gains from foreign trade compared to domestic trade (2A and 2C) and all workers in the Ricardian model would vote to allow international trade (2B). Individuals have a comparative advantage in international trade but their homogeneity provides them with no source of comparative advantage in domestic exchange. For domestic trade, Proposition 1A does not hold. The only source of gains from trade is therefore foreign trade.

5. A more general model with asymmetric income sources

In a more general model, individuals have asymmetric income sources through differing productivities or personal skill endowments (or human-capital investments). Proposition 1A then holds for domestic trade.

Paul Samuelson (1939) showed that Proposition 2C is true.[4] Samuelson (1939) compared the binary choice of free trade at given terms of trade with domestic trade (or national autarky). Murray Kemp (1962) showed that collective or aggregate gains from international trade in Proposition 2C apply when choice is not restricted to being binary between free trade and no trade, but includes any restricted trading opportunity relative to no trade, and when terms of trade are not necessarily fixed but depend upon trading offers.[5] Kemp thus showed that any opportunity to engage in international trade, even subject to artificial and arbitrary restrictions, is *collectively* preferable to the outcome achievable through domestic trade alone. However, this does not imply Proposition 2A, which requires a distribution of the collective benefit to allow all individuals to personally benefit.

Samuelson (1939) had stated the gains from trade in terms of potential compensation: "if an unanimous decision were required in order for trade to be permitted, it would always be possible for those who desired trade to buy off those who opposed trade, with the result that all could be made better off" (p. 204). Murray Kemp observed that lump-sum taxes and transfers were required if the redistribution were to be consistent with retaining the gains from trade. The efficiency losses from non-lump-sum compensation could in principle outweigh the gains from trade. Without lump-sum compensation, Propositions 2A and 2B could therefore not be assured. Kemp pointed out that: "If the only types of taxes or subsidies that are available are those that carry with them a deadweight loss of allocative inefficiency, then *the theorems are true but irrelevant*" (p. 819).

This was a prescient observation at a time when the political economy paradigm was far from mainstream thought in the study of international trade. Kemp was stating that it was true that replacing domestic trade with free trade or any restricted form of foreign trade could increase aggregate welfare or national income. However, we should not necessarily expect to see foreign trade realized if income-distribution impediments to foreign trade could not be overcome and actual compensation could not take place.

The impediments to free trade are the efficiency losses when redistribution occurs. If redistribution cannot take place to ensure Propositions 2A

---

[4] That is, for any group of individuals taken together, the consumption opportunities for the group available through foreign trade dominate the consumption opportunities available through domestic trade.

[5] On the foreign offer curve and aggregate domestic consumption possibilities, see also Samuelson (1962), which accompanies Murray Kemp's paper, and previously Baldwin (1948). On further extension of the proofs of the gains from trade, see Ohyama (1972).

and 2B, we may observe a collective decision of refusal to trade, notwithstanding the aggregate gains from trade (Proposition 2C).[6]

6. The feasibility of free-trade consensus

Traditional models of international trade describe economies where tax bases allow lump-sum taxes. The tax bases are assured by an assumption that factors of production are inelastically supplied.[7] Factor rewards however in general influence factor supply.[8] Still, even if in practice feasible, lump-sum taxation and income transfers are not policy instruments that governments use. Lump-sum taxes if uniform are regressive. If not uniform, lump-sum taxes become arbitrary and may be intentionally or inadvertently discriminatory.

Lump-sum taxation is therefore *politically not feasible*. In the absence of lump-sum taxation, there is no assurance that a tax base will exist to allow the gains from international trade to increase utility for all individuals in a population.[9] We can envisage a case where trade liberalization occurs and the gainers from trade who are to be taxed to finance compensating transfers to losers have preferences such that utility from income and leisure are almost perfect substitutes over the range of market factor prices where taxes are levied. The tax base can then sufficiently contract when taxes are levied so that tax revenue required to make any required compensating transfers cannot be collected. That is, income redistribution is constrained by the Laffer curve. The tax base may also contract because the factor of production that is to be taxed is internationally mobile.[10]

---

[6] In the companion piece to Murray Kemp's paper, Paul Samuelson writes: "Practical men and economic theorists have always known that trade may help some people and hurt others. Our problem is to show that trade lovers are theoretically able to compensate trade haters for the harm done to them, thereby making everyone better off" (1962, p.823). Samuelson drew a distinction between economic enquiry concerned only with achieving efficiency and political economy. As Murray Kemp inferred, however, compensation in principle is not sufficient to move self-interested voters to support free trade.

[7] This is quite as Marx and Engels would have had it: in these models people contribute according to ability and not according to reward.

[8] On variable factor supply in models of international trade, see Kemp and Jones (1962).

[9] Regressive income taxes can decrease the magnitudes of the substitution responses that contract tax bases but are not in general politically feasible. See Hillman (2003, chapter 7).

[10] Dixit and Norman (1980, 1986) proposed a means of compensatory transfers whereby the production gains from trade could be assured and then the surplus consumption over autarky consumption or part thereof could be provided to consumers through market prices that were distorted by commodity taxes and subsidies. The production gains from trade are achieved and the taxes and subsidies distribute the increased output. The problem is to find the market means of redistribution that result in the required compensation. See also Kemp and Wan (1986) for exposition of some special cases comparing lump-sum and non-lum- sum distribution of the gains from trade.

With the tax base present, the efficiency losses from non-lump-sum redistribution can in principle exceed the societal gains from trade.

There are other practical impediments to redistribution. Moral hazard may be encountered if the intention is that compensating payments persist as long as individuals have not adjusted to new employment (although unemployment is not present in the usual trade models).[11] If the compensation is the present value of individual losses incurred, capital markets are required to allow the compensatory transfers to be financed from the future income of the gainers from trade liberalization. Again there is a prospective moral hazard problem. Borrowing against future income requires collateral other than human capital.

7. The evolutionary case for free trade

If gains from trade cannot be assured for all individuals through compensating transfers, can other means ensure consensus support for free trade? Following on from and adapting the propositions of Friedrich von Hayek and others, an evolutionary case can be made in the face of uncertainty about future comparative advantage and the terms of trade. Let

$$x_{1t}, x_{2t}, \ldots, x_{mt}, \quad t = 0, 1, \ldots, T$$

denote the goods available at time t from present time 0 up to a time horizon T and let relative prices determined through a suitable numéraire be

$$p_{1t}, p_{2t}, \ldots, p_{mt}, \quad t = 0, 1, \ldots, T.$$

The attributes and identity of the goods and relative prices in the future are subject to uncertainty at time 0. Future comparative advantage therefore is not known with certainty. Nor are the goods that will be traded known, nor substitutability with other goods. The uncertainty affects individuals' expected utilities and leads risk-adverse individuals to seek insurance. For well-known reasons relating to asymmetric information, the sought insurance may not be offered in private markets.[12]

An alternative to insurance markets for personal incomes is self-insurance through income diversification in asset markets. In a limiting case under appropriate conditions, Propositions 2A and 2B can hold in the presence of non-diversifiable human capital. Inability to diversify human

---

[11] In experience with "structural adjustment programs", a finding is that the programs often subsidize firms that release and then re-hire the same labor.

[12] In principle, people with incomes tied to traded goods' prices could enter into contract whereby protection would serve as the instrument of income insurance contingent on realization of comparative advantage and terms of trade. On the feasibility of such insurance in a specific-factors model, see Cassing *et al.* (1986).

capital because of moral hazard can however impede achievement of a free trade consensus through asset markets.[13]

Personal gains from free trade cannot be assured because of limitations on compensatory payments through government. If neither insurance nor asset markets allow individuals to resolve personal income uncertainty, we are left with the evolutionary case for free trade. That is, over the course of human history, only free markets have persistently sustained benefits for the broad population.[14]

8. Political economy and refusal to allow free trade

The evolutionary case for the market is based on societal benefits with personal gains and losses averaging out over time. A shorter time horizon is involved when collective decisions and political influence lead to refusal to allow free trade. The political economy paradigm then predicts refusal to trade because neither *ex post* lump-sum or other compensating transfers nor *ex ante* means of resolving income uncertainty through insurance are available to establish consensus for free trade.

For each individual, there exists a subset of a population with whom trade maximizes personal utility in competitive markets. Individuals with common interests cannot however use the political process to implement refusal to trade with any arbitrarily sought group. Institutions and transactions costs favor collective and political decisions to exclude or restrict trade with foreigners. The political economy paradigm thereby in particular applies to foreign trade.[15]

---

[13] Whether a free trade consensus is feasible depends on whether individuals with personal endowments of physical and human capital can restructure sources of personal income through asset markets to end personal interest in protectionist policies (Feeney and Hillman, 2004).

[14] A related case, also associated with Hayek, is that free markets and the accompanying rule of law that protect private property rights preserve individual freedom. For a summary of Hayek's case for the market, see Hillman (2003, Chapter 1, Section 3).

[15] A related question is why refusal to trade with foreigners is used when more efficient production subsidies can be expected to be available. Behavioral economics and issues of framing appear to have a role: people may believe that their government should not stand idly by as their fellow citizens or they themselves lose their jobs because foreigners are selling in their domestic markets Wolfgang Mayer and Raymond Riezman (1990) summarize various reasons why informed voters might prefer use of trade policy instruments. Voters may not be informed; "rational ignorance" or transparency is often proposed as the reason for using foreign trade policy to preserve or redistribute income domestically. Steven Magee (1988) used the term "obfuscation". See also Hillman (1989b) on the Brigden case for the Australian tariff. Tullock (1989) has pointed to the related puzzle of the non-transparent means that are sometimes used to redistribute income or to provide rents to rent seekers. With regard to whether voters are informed, the evidence is anecdotal but we can all be the source of anecdotes if our students have been surprised to learn that tariffs are not merely taxes on foreign goods but are equivalent to domestic production subsidies for protected import-competing producers in conjunction with equivalent domestic consumption taxes, and that through general equilibrium effects tariffs affect incomes throughout the economy.

9. The second-best view

An economist may believe that the theory of international trade is (or should be) exclusively normative and may have been trained to maximize social welfare or else the utility of a representative individual. Aspects of collective action and political calculation are then missing from the model that is used. The model without collective action and political calculation is consistent with a benevolent government that maximizes social welfare. The economist may then observe a government that does not allow free trade. The model in use only allows a second-best explanation for the policies of intervention of government. Minimum wages can be proposed to make a labor-abundant country look like and trade like a country where labor is a relatively scarce factor, in which case autarky is shown to be preferable to free trade. Society at large then gains from the intervention of benevolent government, which closes off trading opportunities. An efficiency justification is thus provided for refusal to trade.[16] A reversal of comparative advantage can in principle similarly occur because of externalities. The externalities are now the reason for refusal to trade. Although the case has been made in principle, no empirical evidence ever seems to have been offered that second-best circumstances have justified refusal to trade. The proposed second-best gains from refusal to trade protected the vision of benevolent government. The political economy perspective in contrast viewed government as the means for political decisions made by people who had political and self-interested objectives.

10. Strategic trade policy and rent seeking

Rent seeking remains outside of the description of government policy decisions so long as government is described as maximizing social welfare or the utility of a representative consumer. The second-best defends the government paradigm as benevolent when rents are being created and being assigned through political decisions. A government may for example be observed to be giving subsidies to a domestic industry or firm whose owners or shareholders are resident principally within its jurisdiction. Pigovian solutions to externality problems under designated legal rights could justify such subsidies. The firms receiving the subsidies compete against foreign firms in various markets. A public-choice or political economy explanation suggests that successful rent seeking has taken place to influence rent

---

[16] Because of the minimum wage "distorting" the true cost of labor, the country is trading contrary to comparative advantage and is exporting in terms of factor content its relatively scarce factor capital. Eliminating the trade that is contrary to comparative advantage increases national income.

assignment. The second-best strategic trade policy explanation proposes *social benefits* from subsidies provided by governments.

11. Trade liberalization

The second-best defense of benevolent government also makes an appearance in views of trade liberalization. Through a series of multilateral negotiations, the high-income countries of the world liberalized trade among themselves. The MFN (most favoured nation) clause ensured that the liberalizations were multilateral. The multilateralism avoided opportunism in making "concessions" when granting "market access" (Ethier, 2001, 2002). Protectionist possibilities nonetheless remained because of the incomplete-contract nature of the liberalization agreements (Ethier, 2005). The economic interest of exporting industries favored trade liberalization as the exchange of market access. The conceptions there were applied were mercantilist, with presumptions of national rights to markets and exchange of rights through compromises that allowed foreigners market access. The mercantilist ideology was consistent with the interests of exporters who were the beneficiaries of the "exchange of market access" (Hillman and Moser, 1996). The conception of "exchange of market access" is outside of the paradigm of the social-welfare maximizing government. Consistent with the latter paradigm is an explanation that governments had previously imposed optimum tariffs and had now found a way to escape the Nash equilibrium, and were able to negotiate their way back to the contract curve through the liberalization agreements.

The empirical evidence and declarations of intent by governments do not support the second-best descriptions. No government ever seems to have declared that the reason for not refusing to allow free trade was the intention to benefit from an optimum tariff. Indeed, governments have often appeared to fear a decline in the world price of import-competing goods. Murray Kemp, through his observations on lump-sum taxes and transfers and the gains from trade, can have the final word. The gains from the optimum tariff to the population at large require means of distributing the tariff revenue for Pareto-improvement for the population.

12. Trade diversion: The second-best within political economy

The political economy view can accommodate the second-best. Murray Kemp has written about preferential trading and has made influential contributions to our understanding of this topic.[17] In particular, together

---

[17] See Kemp (1969).

Table 1.   The prisoners' dilemma of trade diversion

	Person 2 ignores the new duty-free source	Person 2 buys from new duty-free source
Person 1 ignores the new duty-free source	3,3	1,4
Person 1 buys from new duty-free source	4,1	2,2

with Henry Wan, he has shown that in principle it is always possible to avoid welfare-reducing preferential trade.[18]

We might also ask why welfare reduction at all occurs since relaxing a constraint should not result in welfare loss. That is, allowing free trade where restricted trade previously was permitted should not reduce welfare, since the opportunities thereby provided, if disadvantageous, can be ignored. Yet, in the circumstances where trade diversion occurs, changed opportunities to buy from a new source reduce individuals' utility.

I have previously shown that the circumstances here are those of a multi-person prisoners' dilemma.[19] The dilemma hinges on a common pool problem for revenue from a tariff. Table 1 shows the two-person case. Each of two persons can ignore the new duty-free source for imports and thereby achieve the symmetric efficient outcome (3, 3). The personally best outcome for one person and the personally worst outcome for the other person occur at (4, 1) and (1, 4). At (4, 1), person 2 buys from the source with the lower world price and pays the tariff, so providing revenue for the government, from which person 1 benefits. Person 1 contributes no tariff revenue in having purchased from the duty-free source. The Nash equilibrium is at (2, 2) where there is no tariff revenue and trade diversion has taken place.

An enforceable contract to ignore the duty-free import source would increase utility for both persons. Mutual gain at (3, 3) relative to the Nash equilibrium (2, 2) would be ensured if each consumer were to receive back from the government the precise sum that the consumer paid in tariff revenue. However, governments do not return individually paid tariff revenue.

13. International externalities and refusal to trade

A second-best political economy can be based on Ostrogorski's paradox.[20] In Table 2, there are 4 groups of voters. Groups A, B, and C each consist of 20% of voters. Voters in these groups benefit from the protection of

---

[18] Kemp and Wan (1976).

[19] See Hillman (1989a).

[20] On the Ostrogorski paradox, see Nurmi (1999) or Hillman (2003).

Table 2.   Free trade wins with either direct voting or representative democracy

	Protection for A	Protection for B	Protection for C
Group A (20%)	Yes (*F* candidate)	No (*F* candidate)	No (*P* candidate)
Group B (20%)	No (*F* candidate)	Yes (*P* candidate)	No (*F* candidate)
Group C (20%)	No (*P* candidate)	No (*F* candidate)	Yes (*F* candidate)
Group D (40%)	No (*F* candidate)	No (*F* candidate)	No (*F* candidate)

Table 3.   Free trade wins with representative democracy, protection wins with a direct vote on policy for each industry

	Protection for A	Protection for B	Protection for C
Group A (20%)	Yes (*F* candidate)	No (*F* candidate)	No (*P* candidate)
Group B (20%)	No (*F* candidate)	Yes (candidate 2)	No (*F* candidate)
Group C (20%)	No (candidate 2)	No (*F* candidate)	No (*F* candidate)
Group D (40%)	Yes (*P* candidate)	Yes (*P* candidate)	Yes (*P* candidate)

their own industry (they have industry-specific incomes) and lose from the protection of any other industry. Group D consisting of the remaining 40% of the population loses from protection provided to any industry. Under majority voting on the single issue of protection for each industry, the majority favors free trade for each industry by 80–20%. Under representative democracy, voters vote once and support the candidate closest to their own preferred position. The voters in groups A, B, and C prefer free trade to protection for all three industries. In a choice between the protectionist candidate *P* and the free-trade candidate *F*, they support the latter. The *F* candidate thus wins.

In Table 3 group D might support protection because foreign production takes place with child labor or with lower environmental standards than domestic production. Ideally the voters want foreign governments to change their policies and they view the second-best response as refusal to trade. Direct voting on the issue of protection for each individual industry now results in a majority favoring protection in each case, since group D forms a winning coalition with the group that benefits from protection for the industry on which the vote is taken. Under representative democracy where there is a single vote on the choice between the *F* and *P* candidates, all industry groups vote for free trade (they do not care about the foreign externality and lose from protection of all industries but one gain from free trade). The outcome is electoral success for the *P* candidate. Ostrogorski's paradox is present because the choice of the collective decision making mechanism determines the outcome. In this example, group D wants foreign societies to adhere to the group's desired norms.[21] The collective action of refusal to trade internalizes externalities that members of this group perceive from imports purchased by anybody, and not just themselves. Individual action cannot achieve the sought objective. Left to their individual decisions, without group discipline, the persons in group D may confront a prisoners' dilemma and in the Nash equilibrium perhaps purchase the socially unacceptable good.

14. Other explanations for refusal to trade

For completeness, we should add other explanations for refusal to trade. Mercantilist ideology results in refusal to trade since the object of the ruler is to accumulate gold and silver through a trade surplus: if everybody wants only to sell and not to buy, there is no trade. Refusal to trade can also occur because of trade embargoes.[22] A country confronting an embargo threat can also refuse to trade, for reasons of national defense.[23] Refusal to trade is also a consequence of the ideology of communism, which is inconsistent with market exchange with foreigners since decentralized decisions through foreign markets can contradict the intentions of central planning. Of course, absence of private property rights altogether contradicts personal exchange in markets.

15. Conclusions

The primary policy question in international trade is why refusal to trade occurs given the theorems on the gains from trade. The political economy

---

[21] In the public debate and subsequent voting on NAFTA in the U.S., for example, there was a public perception that free trade with Mexico might be disadvantageous because of differing environmental standards and prospective "loss of jobs" as U.S. industry relocated or invested in Mexico. U.S. industry perceived the benefits of access to the Mexican market, but more so the advantage of free re-entry of goods produced at Mexican wages into the U.S., although as in case 2 above each industry would have, we can believe, preferred protection as an exception for itself.

[22] For example, some Arab and also other Muslim countries have maintained an embargo on trade with the state of Israel to express their opposition to the existence of Israel. There has also been a secondary boycott whereby non-Israeli firms doing business with Israel were placed on a boycott list. Often, as we would expect, self-interest results in governments ignoring ideologically based boycotts. Agence France Presse (AFP) reported on July 5, 2006 that the Damascus-based Arab League Central Boycott Office (CBO) had informed the Swiss food company Nestlé that it had been placed on the boycott list. Nestlé was given a one-year respite to cease operations in Israel. Nestlé did not comply and consumers in most Arab countries continue to buy Nestlé products. Danish products were boycotted in Muslim countries to protest cartoons in the Danish press that depicted the prophet Muhammad. The U.S. maintained an embargo against Cuba during the period of the Castro regime.

[23] See for example Mayer (1977) and Arad and Hillman (1979).

view of trade policy allows for general self-interested behavior, including political decision makers who are viewed as having political objectives. Second-best theory responds to refusal of governments to allow free trade by adopting the perspective of Dr Pangloss, who declared that any observed outcome must necessarily be the best of all possibilities chosen by a benevolent decision maker. I have presented an overview of refusal to trade. Refusal to trade is a particularly appropriate topic for this volume because of the observation by Murray Kemp (1962) without lump-sum taxes and transfers, the theorems on societal gains from trade are "true but irrelevant". In making this observation, Murray Kemp can be regarded as having laid the foundations for the modern political economy explanation that places income distribution and political or collective decisions at the core of the explanation for refusal to trade.

Acknowledgement

I acknowledge with gratitude the constructive comments of an anonymous referee.

References

Arad, R.W., Hillman, A.L. (1979), Embargo threat, learning and departure from comparative advantage. *Journal of International Economics* 9 (2), 265–275.

Baldwin, R.E. (1948), Equilibrium in international trade: A diagrammatic analysis. *Quarterly Journal of Economics* 62 (5), 748–762.

Cassing, J.H., Hillman, A.L., Long, N.V. (1986), Risk aversion, terms of trade variability, and social consensus trade policy. *Oxford Economic Papers* 38 (2), 234–242.

Dixit, A., Norman, V. (1980), *The Theory of International Trade*. James Nisbet, Welwyn, UK.

Dixit, A., Norman, V. (1986). Gains from trade without lump-sum compensation. *Journal of International Economics* 21 (1/2), 111–122. Reprinted in Neary, J.P. (Ed.) (1995), *International Trade*, Edward Elgar, Cheltenham, UK.

Ethier, W.J. (2001), Theoretical problems in negotiating trade liberalization. *European Journal of Political Economy* 17 (2), 209–232.

Ethier, W.J. (2002), Unilateralism in a multilateral world. *Economic Journal* 112 (479), 266–292. Reprinted in Ethier, W.J., Hillman, A.L. (Eds.) (2008), *The WTO and the Political Economy of Trade Policy*, Edward Elgar, Cheltenham, UK, pp. 567–593.

Ethier, W.J. (2005), Punishments and dispute settlement agreements: the equivalent withdrawal of concessions. *Keio Economic Studies* 42 (1–2), 1–23.

Feeney, J., Hillman, A.L. (2004), Trade liberalization through asset markets. *Journal of International Economics* 64 (1), 151–167. Reprinted in Ethier, W.J., Hillman, A.L. (Eds.) (2008), *The WTO and the Political Economy of Trade Policy*, Edward Elgar, Cheltenham, UK, pp. 173–189.

Grossman, G.M., Helpman, E. (1994), Protection for sale. *American Economic Review* 94 (5), 833–850. Reprinted in Neary, J.P. (Ed.) (1995), *International Trade*. Edward Elgar, Cheltenham, UK.

Grossman, G.M., Helpman, E. (2002), *Interest Groups and Trade Policy*. Princeton University Press, Princeton, NJ.

Hillman, A.L. (1982), Declining industries and political-support protectionist motives. *American Economic Review* 72 (5), 1180–1187. Reprinted in Brown, C. (Ed.) (2006), *The WTO, Safeguards, and Temporary Protection from Imports*, Edward Elgar, Cheltenham, UK.

Hillman, A.L. (1989a), Resolving the puzzle of welfare-reducing trade diversion: A prisoners' dilemma interpretation. *Oxford Economic Papers* 41 (2), 452–455.

Hillman, A.L. (1989b), *The Political Economy of Protection*. Harwood Academic Publishers, Chur. Reprinted (2001) Routledge, London.

Hillman, A.L. (2003), *Public Finance and Public Policy: Responsibilities and Limitations of Government*. Cambridge University Press, New York.

Hillman, A.L., Moser, P. (1996), Trade liberalization as politically optimal exchange of market access. In: Canzoneri, M., Ethier, W.J., Grilli, V. (Eds.), *The New Transatlantic Economy*. Cambridge University Press, Cambridge, UK, pp. 295–312. Reprinted in Anderson, K., Hoekman, B. (2002), (Eds.), The Global Trading System, Vol. 2 Core Rules and Procedures, I.B. Tauris and Co Ltd, London and New York.

Kemp, M.C. (1962), The gains from international trade. *Economic Journal* 72 (288), 803–819.

Kemp, M.C. (1969), *A Contribution to the General Equilibrium Theory of Preferential Trading*. North Holland, Amsterdam.

Kemp, M.C., Jones, R.W. (1962), Variable labor supply and the theory of international trade. *Journal of Political Economy* 70 (1), 30–36.

Kemp, M.C., Wan, H.Y. (1976), An elementary proposition concerning the formation of customs unions. *Journal of International Economics* 6 (1), 95–97. Reprinted with an addendum in Kemp, M.C. (2001), *The Gains From Trade and the Gains From Aid*. Routledge, London, pp. 37–46.

Kemp, M.C., Wan, H.Y. (1986), Gains from trade with and without lump-sum compensation. *Journal of International Economics* 21 (1/2), 99–110.

Magee, S.P. (1988), Optimal obfuscation and the theory of the second-worst: a theory of public choice. In: Magee, S.P., Brock, W.A., Young, L. (Eds.), *Endogenous Policy Theory*. Cambridge University Press, Cambridge, UK.

Mayer, W. (1977), The national defense tariff argument reconsidered. *Journal of International Economics* 7 (4), 363–377.

Mayer, W. (1984), Endogenous tariff formation. *American Economic Review* 74(5), 970–985. Reprinted in Neary, J.P. (Ed.) (1995), *International Trade*. Edward Elgar, Cheltenham, UK.

Mayer, W., Riezman, R. (1990), Voter preferences for trade policy instruments. *Economics and Politics* 2 (3), 259–273.

Mueller, D. (2003), *Public Choice III*. Cambridge University Press, New York.

Nurmi, H. (1999), *Voting Paradoxes and How to Deal with Them*. Springer, Berlin.

Ohyama, M. (1972), Trade and welfare in general equilibrium. *Keio Economic Studies* 9 (1), 37–73. Reprinted in Neary, J.P. (Ed.) (1995), *International Trade*. Edward Elgar, Cheltenham, UK.

Samuelson, P.A. (1939), The gains from international trade. *Canadian Journal of Economics and Political Science* 5 (2), 195–205.

Samuelson, P.A. (1962), The gains from international trade once again. *Economic Journal* 72 (288), 820–829.

Tullock, G. (1989), *The Economics of Special Privilege and Rent Seeking*. Kluwer Academic Publishers, Boston and Dordrecht.

CHAPTER 13

A Two-Country Model of International Trade with Increasing Returns and Oligopoly

Kenji Fujiwara[a], Nobuhito Suga[b] and Makoto Tawada[c]

[a]School of Economics, Kwansei Gakuin University, Uegahara 1-1-155, Nishinomiya, Hyogo, 662-8501, Japan
E-mail address: kenjifujiwara@kwansei.ac.jp
[b]Graduate School of Economics and Business Administration, Hokkaido University, Kita-9, Nishi-7, Kita-ku, Sapporo, 060-0809, Japan, and
E-mail address: suga@econ.hokudai.ac.jp
[c]Graduate School of Economics, Nagoya University, Furo-cho, Chikusa-ku, Nagoya 464-8601, Japan
E-mail address: mtawada@soec.nagoya-u.ac.jp

Abstract

Purpose – This chapter aims to examine trade patterns and gains from trade in a two-country general equilibrium model of increasing returns and oligopoly.

Approach – A general equilibrium model of increasing returns and oligopoly.

Findings – The determination of patterns of specialization and trade and gains from trade highly depends on the interaction between the degree of increasing returns and market power as well as the cross-country difference in factor endowments.

Originality – Unlike the existing literature, we endogenize the determination of specialization by using an allocation curve approach by Ethier (1982). To our knowledge, there is no comparable study that incorporates Ethier's (1982) approach to oligopolistic models of international trade.

Keywords: Oligopoly, increasing returns, trade patterns, gains from trade

Paper type: Research paper

1. Introduction

The past 25 years have generated a significant body of literature on trade under increasing returns and/or imperfect competition. The first research conducted, such as that by Kemp and Negishi (1970), focuses on Marshallian externalities that are compatible with perfect competition. Among others, Ethier (1982) constructs a two-country model in which

Frontiers of Economics and Globalization
Volume 5   ISSN: 1574-8715
DOI: 10.1016/S1574-8715(08)05013-6

increasing returns are external to firms and countries differ only in terms of factor endowment. This led to the conclusion that the large country exports the increasing returns good, which results in it making gains, whereas the small country may lose from trade.

However, there are two strands of literature that deal with *internal* economies of scale: monopolistically competitive and oligopolistic approaches. Neglecting strategic interdependences among firms and assuming free entry, monopolistically competitive approaches become tractable as well as having a good fit with a general equilibrium model.[1]

However, no parallel applies to oligopolistic approaches *without* free entry.[2] This difficulty has prevented oligopolistic general equilibrium trade theory from making significant progress. For instance, while Markusen (1981) and Ruffin (2003a, 2003b) have both made representative contributions to this field, their core results on trade patterns and gains from trade rest on the assumption of constant returns.

Relaxing the constant returns assumption, Fujiwara and Shimomura (2005) prove the Heckscher–Ohlin trade pattern under international duopoly and increasing returns. However, they *a priori* assume that both countries incompletely specialize in free trade. Invoking that increasing returns can make a country specialize in the production of a non-increasing good, the above presumption is inevitably vulnerable. Furthermore, the Cournot–Nash equilibrium outputs cannot be explicitly solved in the existing models except by assuming linear demand and costs, which constitutes another difficulty in oligopolistic trade theory.

The purpose of this chapter is to present a two-country general equilibrium model of oligopoly and increasing returns to overcome the above difficulties and provide new insights on international trade. Three comments on what is new in our approach are in order. First, we explicitly treat decreasing marginal costs as well as strategic interdependences among firms. Second, all of the general equilibrium solutions are solvable by our choice of functional forms. We expect that this solvability will enhance the tractability of the model and have many potential applications. Third, unlike predecessors that *a priori* assume multilateral diversification, we allow for the possibility of complete specialization in a country.[3] In doing this, Ethier's (1982) *allocation curve* technique is made use of.

---

[1] See, for example, Krugman (1979, 1980), Dixit and Norman (1980), and Helpman (1981). Recent contributions made by Ottaviano *et al.* (2002) are based on a monopolistically competitive model with strategic interdependences among firms.

[2] When free entry is allowed in an oligopolistic general equilibrium model, the tractability, as in a monopolistically competitive model, is maintained as Lahiri and Ono (1995) and Shimomura (1998) show.

[3] Some may criticize that incomplete specialization is justified in a Heckscher–Ohlin setting like Markusen (1981). However, under strong economies of scale such that the convex segment of the production possibility frontier dominates, specialization may be inevitable.

These features will be utilized to reconsider trade patterns and gains from trade. As a by-product, the results on trade patterns and gains from trade in Ethier's (1982) externality model are shown to emerge under strong scale economies. In contrast, Markusen's (1981) conclusion follows when the number of oligopolistic firms is so small that each oligopolistic firm's market power is dominant. That is, the two seminal contributions by Ethier (1982) and Markusen (1981) reemerge as two polar cases.

The chapter proceeds as follows. Section 2 lays out a basic model and describes the autarkic equilibrium. Extending it to a two-country world, Section 3 characterizes a trading equilibrium and Section 4 derives the propositions concerning trade patterns. Section 5 turns to the No of gains from trade. Section 6 sums up the conclusion of the chapter. Two appendices deal with technical notes in the main text.

2. An autarkic equilibrium

A two-country (Home and Foreign), two-good (Goods 1 and 2), one-primary-factor (labor) model is developed. An asterisk (*) is attached to all the Foreign variables to distinguish them from the Home variables. This section describes the autarkic equilibrium of Home. Exactly the same argument applies to Foreign. Both countries share identical technology and preference, and labor is fully employed and inelastically supplied.

Let us begin by specifying the production technology. One unit of labor produces one unit of Good 2 (numeraire), which, together with the competitive condition, makes the wage rate equal to unity as long as Good 2 is positively supplied. Sector 1 is oligopolized by $n \geq 2$ identical firms and their technology is characterized by a strict convexity:

$$x_i = l_i^\alpha, \quad \alpha > 1, \quad i = 1, \ldots, n,$$

where x_i and l_i are respectively a representative firm's output and labor input in sector 1. Thus, recalling the unitary wage rate, the corresponding cost function is given by $x_i^{1/\alpha}$.

The demand side is now introduced. Assume a community utility function, which takes a Cobb–Douglas form:

$$u = C_1^\gamma C_2^{1-\gamma}, \quad \gamma \in (0, 1),$$

where u is the utility level and C_1 and C_2 are the consumption of each good. The demand function of Good 1 associated with this preference is

$$C_1 = \frac{\gamma I}{p},$$

where p and I are the price of Good 1 and the national income, respectively.

Based on these set-ups, the autarkic equilibrium is now described. First of all, note that the autarkic equilibrium, if it exists, must involve a positive supply of Good 2 due to the Cobb–Douglas preference. A representative oligopolistic firm, say, firm i's profit is then defined as $px_i - x_i^{1/\alpha}$.

Following most of the existing literature, each oligopolistic firm is supposed to maximize profit by assuming that any oligopolist consumes only Good 2.[4] Assuming that the oligopolistic firms play a Cournot–Nash game and that they take the national income as given, a firm's first-order condition for profit maximization is given by[5]

$$p\left(1 - \frac{1}{n}\right) - \frac{1}{\alpha}x^{(1/\alpha)-1} = 0. \tag{1}$$

In the present general equilibrium model, p and I are determined through the following system of equations:

$$\frac{\gamma I}{p} = nx \tag{2}$$

$$I = pnx + L - nx^{1/\alpha}, \tag{3}$$

where (2) represents the autarkic market-clearing condition of Good 1 and (3) the definition of the national income. Hence, solving for p gives

$$p = \frac{\gamma}{1 - \gamma}\frac{L - nx^{1/\alpha}}{nx}.$$

Substituting this equilibrium price into (1), the first-order condition for an *interior* autarkic equilibrium becomes

$$\frac{\gamma}{1 - \gamma}\frac{L - nx^{1/\alpha}}{nx}\left(1 - \frac{1}{n}\right) - \frac{1}{\alpha}x^{(1/\alpha)-1} = 0, \tag{4}$$

whose solution is obtained by[6]

$$x^A = \left\{\frac{\alpha\gamma(n - 1)L}{n[\alpha\gamma(n - 1) + (1 - \gamma)n]}\right\}^\alpha \equiv \left(l^A\right)^\alpha, \tag{5}$$

---

[4] When oligopolists consume both goods, the assumption of profit maximization is vulnerable as Kemp and Okawa (1995) and Kemp and Shimomura (1995, 2002) have argued. However, this problem can be overcome by assuming that oligopolists consume only the numeraire good.

[5] Taking account of the effect of each oligopolistic firm's output on the national income, Tawada and Okawa (1995) prove that the marginal revenue is smaller if monopolistic firms maximize profits by allowing for the effect of their output on the national income than taking it as given. Hence, the profit-maximizing solution with this income effect taken into account is less than that when the national income is given to each monopolistic firm.

[6] Some may wonder if there is an asymmetric equilibrium where $x_i \neq x_j$, $i \neq j$. However, we can prove that only the symmetric equilibrium such that $x_i = x_j$ is economically meaningful due to the identical technology. The proof is available from the authors upon request.

where the superscript A indicates the autarkic equilibrium. Thus, we can immediately state:

LEMMA 1. *There uniquely exists an autarkic equilibrium in each country if and only if*

$$\frac{\alpha}{\alpha - 1} \geq n \geq 2.$$

PROOF. As mentioned, any autarkic equilibrium, if exists, must involve $x^A > 0$ but this is not always the case since increasing returns can make oligopolistic firms' profit negative. In order to ensure the positivity of profits, substitute x^A into the definition of profits to get the per-firm maximized profit:

$$\pi^A \equiv \frac{[n - \alpha(n - 1)]\gamma L}{n[\alpha\gamma(n - 1) + (1 - \gamma)n]}.$$

Hence, we easily see that $\pi^A \geq 0$ if and only if

$$n \leq \frac{\alpha}{\alpha - 1}.$$

When the parameter set satisfies this inequality, $x^A > 0$ is safely guaranteed. Moreover, since $n \geq 2$, the lemma is now proved. Q. E. D.

Having proved the unique existence of autarkic equilibrium, let us briefly address the No of stability. The output per firm is assumed to be adjusted according to the difference between marginal revenue and marginal cost. Letting respectively the first and second terms in the left-hand side in (4) be denoted by $MR(x, L)$ and $MC(x)$ respectively, the stability condition is

$$MR_x(x^A, L) - MC'(x^A) < 0,$$

where $MR_x(\cdot)$ is the partial derivative of $MR(\cdot)$ with respect to x. Utilizing the fact that x^A is the solution to (4), the above stability condition is equivalent to

$$-\frac{MR_x(x^A, L)x^A}{MR(x^A, L)} > -\frac{MC'(x^A)x^A}{MC(x^A)},$$

or equivalently,

$$\frac{n(x^A)^{1/\alpha}}{L - n(x^A)^{1/\alpha}} > -1.$$

This condition is necessarily satisfied since the left-hand side is positive, while the right-hand side is negative. Note that this condition constitutes not only the stability condition but the second-order condition which has to be met as another regularity condition. Hence, we have established:

LEMMA 2. *The stability and the second-order conditions of autarkic equilibrium are satisfied for any set of parameters, α and n.*

We conclude this section by giving the utility level in the autarkic equilibrium. Since we have assumed a representative consumer, a country's welfare can be measured by its indirect utility function:

$$V(p, I) \equiv \gamma^{\gamma}(1 - \gamma)^{1-\gamma}\frac{I}{p^{\gamma}},$$

from the Cobb–Douglas preference. Substitution of (5) into the solutions of p and I in (2) and (3) and further substitution of them into $V(p,I)$, we have

$$V(p^A, I^A) = \gamma^{\gamma}(1 - \gamma)^{1-\gamma}\left\{\frac{\gamma L}{[\alpha\gamma(n - 1) + (1 - \gamma)n]\left\{\frac{\alpha\gamma(n-1)L^*}{n[\alpha\gamma(n-1)+(1-\gamma)n]}\right\}^{\alpha}}\right\}^{\gamma}$$
$$\times \frac{nL}{\alpha\gamma(n - 1) + (1 - \gamma)n}.$$

$$(6)$$

This completes the analysis of a closed economy. We will make extensive use of the above results when trade patterns and gains from trade are addressed.

3. Free trade equilibria

This and the subsequent sections extend the above model to a two-country world consisting of Home and Foreign whose labor endowment is possibly different and Foreign is larger than Home, namely, $L < L^*$.[7] In the rest of the chapter, we focus on equilibria in which Good 2 is positively supplied in both countries, which implies that both countries' wage rate is fixed to unity.[8] Due to the identical preference, technology, and number of oligopolistic firms between the countries, and symmetries among oligopolistic firms, the first-order condition for profit maximization of a representative firm in each country is

---

[7] Throughout the chapter, the number of firms in each country is supposed to be equal, as we want to focus on the interaction between the market power and degree of scale economies for trade patterns and trade gains. The same assumption is also made by Markusen (1981) and Ruffin (2003b).

[8] Appendix 2 derives the condition for the positive production of Good 2 in both countries.

respectively given by[9]

$$p\left[1 - \frac{x}{n(x + x^*)}\right] - \frac{1}{\alpha}x^{(1/\alpha)-1} = 0 \qquad (7)$$

$$p\left[1 - \frac{x^*}{n(x + x^*)}\right] - \frac{1}{\alpha}x^{(1/\alpha)-1} = 0. \qquad (8)$$

As in the previous section, the market-clearing price and national income in the countries are determined through the system of equations:

$$\frac{\gamma(I + I^*)}{p} = n(x + x^*), \qquad (9)$$

$$I = pnx + L - nx^{1/\alpha}, \qquad (10)$$

$$I^* = pnx^* + L^* - nx^{*1/\alpha}, \qquad (11)$$

which yields

$$p = \frac{\gamma}{1 - \gamma}\frac{L + L^* - n(x^{1/\alpha} + x^{*1/\alpha})}{n(x + x^*)}.$$

Thus, substituting this market-clearing price into (7) and (8) yields

$$\frac{\gamma}{1 - \gamma}\frac{L + L^* - n(x^{1/\alpha} + x^{*1/\alpha})}{n(x + x^*)}\left[1 - \frac{x}{n(x + x^*)}\right] - \frac{1}{\alpha}x^{(1/\alpha)-1} = 0 \qquad (12)$$

$$\frac{\gamma}{1 - \gamma}\frac{L + L^* - n(x^{1/\alpha} + x^{*1/\alpha})}{n(x + x^*)}\left[1 - \frac{x^*}{n(x + x^*)}\right] - \frac{1}{\alpha}x^{*(1/\alpha)-1} = 0. \qquad (13)$$

In the subsequent arguments, we use an alternative expression of the above system to apply Ethier's (1982) *allocation curve* technique. Using a labor term, (12) and (13) are rewritten as

$$\frac{\gamma}{1 - \gamma}\frac{L + L^* - n(l + l^*)}{n(l^\alpha + l^{*\alpha})}\left[1 - \frac{l^\alpha}{n(l^\alpha + l^{*\alpha})}\right] - \frac{1}{\alpha}l^{1-\alpha} = 0 \qquad (14)$$

$$\frac{\gamma}{1 - \gamma}\frac{L + L^* - n(l + l^*)}{n(l^\alpha + l^{*\alpha})}\left[1 - \frac{l^{*\alpha}}{n(l^\alpha + l^{*\alpha})}\right] - \frac{1}{\alpha}l^{*1-\alpha} = 0. \qquad (15)$$

Figures 1–3 show three candidates for the trading equilibrium. In the figures, the mountain-shaped locus *ONB* is the Home firm's allocation

---

[9] As in the foregoing argument, we suppose that all firms in a country choose the same output level, which is verifiable as long as the symmetric autarkic equilibrium is considered as an initial state of the dynamic adjustment process introduced below.

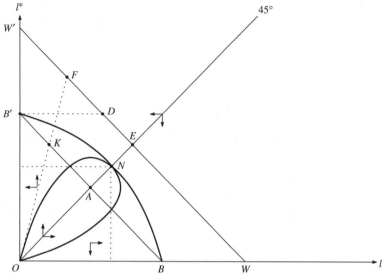

Fig. 1.   The case with $n > \frac{2\alpha - 1}{2(\alpha - 1)}$.

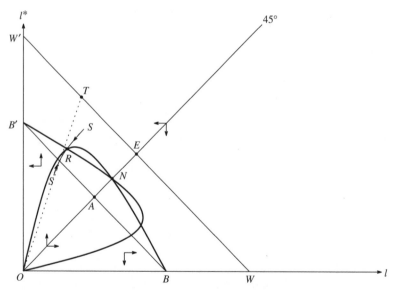

Fig. 2.   The case with $\frac{2\alpha - 1}{2(\alpha - 1)} > n > \frac{\alpha}{2(\alpha - 1)}$.

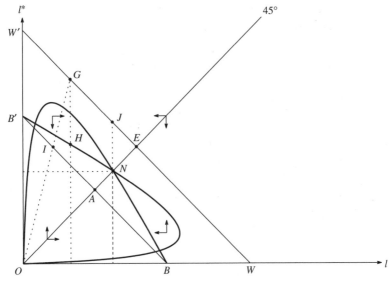

Fig. 3. *The case with* $n < \frac{\alpha}{2(\alpha-1)}$.

curve, i.e., the pair of (l, l^*) that satisfies (14). Similarly, the locus ONB' is the Foreign firm's allocation curve such that (15) is met.[10]

We see, from (14) and (15), at least one Cournot–Nash equilibrium involves a symmetry, i.e., $l = l^* = l^N$ where the superscript N stands for the interior Cournot–Nash equilibrium. In such a symmetric Nash equilibrium given by N in the figures, each firm's optimal input becomes

$$l^N = \frac{\alpha\gamma(2n - 1)\left(L + L^*\right)}{2n[\alpha\gamma(2n - 1) + 2(1 - \gamma)n]}. \tag{16}$$

However, this is not the only equilibrium, i.e., multiple equilibria are possible depending on the parameters. In what follows, how the three possibilities arise is analyzed.

First, let us derive three figures. The Home firm's allocation curve is flatter than the Foreign firm's at N in Figure 1, while the opposite holds in Figures 2 and 3. As shown in Appendix 1, Figure 1 emerges if and only if

$$n > \frac{2\alpha - 1}{2(\alpha - 1)}, \tag{17}$$

which requires the Home firm's allocation curve to be flatter than the Foreign firm's at N. However, the condition under which the other

---

[10] Appendix 1 examines a few properties of the allocation curve.

two are obtained is given by

$$n < \frac{2\alpha - 1}{2(\alpha - 1)}. \tag{18}$$

Conditions (17) and (18) have a clear interpretation. Figure 1 is basically the same as that in Ethier's (1982) externality model, while Figures 2 and 3 correspond to those in Markusen's (1981) oligopolistic model. Equation (17) states that the equilibrium in our model tends to resemble Ethier's (1982) as the degree of increasing returns (α) is sufficiently large.[11] In contrast, when the number of firms (n) is so small that (18) holds, i.e., each firm's market power is dominant, the model behavior is likely to approach Markusen's (1981).

In the figures, the arrows indicate the dynamic process of the world economy. They are based on the following adjustment process:

$$\dot{l} = \widetilde{MR}(l, l^*, L + L^*) - MC(l) \tag{19}$$

$$\dot{l}^* = \widetilde{MR}(l^*, l, L + L^*) - MC(l^*), \tag{20}$$

where $\widetilde{MR}(\cdot)$ denotes the first term and $MC(\cdot)$ the second term in the left-hand side in (14) and (15).

We are now ready to consider how Figures 2 and 3 are sub-divided. Both figures are similar in the sense that the Home firm's allocation curve is steeper than the Foreign firm's at N.[12] The difference lies in that each firm's maximized profit obtained at N is negative in Figure 2, while it is positive in Figure 3. In other words, point N is meaningful only in Figure 3 from an economic viewpoint and hence N in Figure 2 cannot constitute the free trade equilibrium.[13]

To verify the above, let us substitute l^N into the definition of each firm's profit. Then, the maximized profit at N is obtained as

$$\pi^N = \frac{\gamma[2(1 - \alpha)n + \alpha](L + L^*)}{2n[\alpha\gamma(2n - 1) + 2(1 - \gamma)n]},$$

which turns out to be non-negative if and only if

$$n \leq \frac{\alpha}{2(\alpha - 1)}. \tag{21}$$

---

[11] Note that the right-hand side in (17) and (18) is decreasing in α.

[12] In Figures 2 and 3, there are three intersections of the allocation curves. However, N is the only interior equilibrium because the others are on the upward-sloping segment of the firm's allocation curve, which violates the second-order condition for profit maximization. Moreover, even if both allocation curves are downward sloping on these points, such points constitute a saddle point. Hence, any path except for the saddle path will diverge and approach one of B', N, and B, which enables us to take the side intersections out of consideration.

[13] Note that the same is true of Figure 1 in which Ethier's type equilibrium is described.

That is, in order to assure the interior Cournot–Nash equilibrium such that $l = l^* = l^N$, an additional condition given by (21) must be imposed. Note that (21) implies (18). In summary, we can conclude that Figure 1 is drawn under (17), that Figure 2 is drawn under $(2\alpha - 1)/[2(\alpha - 1)] > n > \alpha/2[(\alpha - 1)]$, and that Figure 3 is drawn under (21).

4. Trade patterns

From Figures 1–3, we can derive the propositions on patterns of specialization and trade. See Figure 2 in which the locus SS gives a saddle path associated with the steady state R and the line OT goes through the intersection of BB' and SS. Letting ψ be the slope of OT in the figure, we can derive the following results regarding patterns of specialization and trade that depend on the parameters:

PROPOSITION 1. *Suppose $L^* > L$ and that the dynamic behavior of the world economy follows the adjustment process defined in (19) and (20). Then, the following trade patterns are observed.*

(i) The case under (17) in Figure 1: Foreign diversifies and exports Good 1, while Home specializes in Good 2 and imports Good 1;

(ii) The case under (18) in Figures 2 and 3: if the relative size of the two countries satisfies $L^*/L > \psi$, Foreign diversifies and exports Good 1, while Home specializes in Good 2 and imports Good 1. On the other hand, if (21) and $L^*/L > \psi$ hold, both countries diversify and produce the same amount of Good 1. Then, Home exports Good 1.

PROOF. Two points must be noted. First, any autarkic equilibrium is captured by the intersection of BB' and the straight line connecting the origin and the endowment point on WW'.[14] Second, the allocation curve outside the rectangle shaped by the origin and the endowment point on WW' need not be considered.[15] Bearing this in mind, let us prove each case separately.

Part (i) is associated with Figure 1. Suppose that the distribution of each country's labor endowment is given by F. Then, one can see that each country's autarkic labor per firm is given by K. Therefore, moving from autarky to free trade entails the movement of equilibrium from K to B' at which Foreign diversifies and Home specializes in Good 2. In the figure, N

---

[14] WW' gives the per-firm labor endowment pair and formally given by $nl + nl^* = \overline{L}$, where $\overline{L}$ denotes the world labor endowment.

[15] For the details, see Ethier (1982) and Suga (2005).

proves to be a saddle point and the 45° line gives the corresponding saddle path. Consequently, the above-mentioned specialization emerges for any $L^* > L$. The trade pattern is trivially obtained from the specialization pattern.

The former half of part (ii) is proved by making use of Figure 2. Under $L^*/L > \psi$, where ψ is the slope of OT, the distribution of the world labor endowment is on $W'T$ in which case the autarkic equilibrium is on the portion of BB' contained in the upper region of OT. It follows from this observation that the post-trade economy goes to B'. The rest of the argument follows that in part (i).[16]

However, in the latter half of part (ii) such that $L^*/L > \psi$ holds, the world converges to N. At N, $l^N > 0$ follows due to the positivity of the equilibrium profits and Home exports Good 1 since its demand for Good 1 is lower than Foreign's demand.   Q. E. D.

Proposition 1 asserts that the patterns of specialization and trade obtained in Ethier's (1982) externality model and Markusen's (1981) oligopolistic model arise as a special case in our model. According to part (i) in the proposition where the number of oligopolistic firms is sufficiently large, the free trade equilibrium becomes similar to Ethier's (1982) in which the large country exports the increasing returns good. In contrast, Markusen's (1981) trade pattern proposition, i.e., the small country exports the non-competitive good, is observed if the number of oligopolistic firms is small enough to satisfy (21).[17]

The intermediate case given in the former half of part (ii) and Figure 2 is new. In this case, one may guess that the trade pattern resembles Markusen's (1981) diversified pattern of specialization since Figures 2 and 3 are the same in the sense that the Home firm's allocation curve is steeper than the Foreign firm's at N. However, Proposition 1 clarifies that such a guess is incorrect and that the pattern of specialization and trade becomes similar to that by Ethier (1982). That is, the equilibrium involves complete specialization to the numeraire good by the small country.

5. Gains from trade

It is well-known that trade patterns do not affect gains from trade in the Arrow–Debreu framework. However, in imperfectly competitive models, particularly under oligopoly without free entry, the direction of trade crucially affects the gains from trade.[18] The same is true of our model as

---

[16] Note that any path converging to N is not realized since each firm's profit evaluated there is negative.

[17] Strictly speaking, $L^* = L < \psi$ must also be met.

[18] See Markusen and Melvin (1984) and Schweinberger (1996).

well. The following lemma is a helpful preliminary in discussing gains from trade:

LEMMA 3. *Suppose that any active oligopolistic firm's equilibrium profit is non-negative. Then, free trade is beneficial to the country whose production of Good* 1 *expands after the opening of trade.*

PROOF. Attaching a subscript T to denote the variable at the trading equilibrium and letting $E(p, u)$ be the expenditure function, we have the following inequalities.

$$
\begin{aligned}
E(p^T, u^T) &= p^T C_1^T + C_2^T \\
&= p^T X_1^T + X_2^T \\
&= n\left[p^T(l^T)^{\alpha-1} - 1\right] l^T + L \\
&> n\left[p^T(l^A)^{\alpha-1} - 1\right] l^A + L \qquad\qquad (22) \\
&= np^T(l^A)^{\alpha} + L - nl^A \\
&= p^T X_1^A + X_2^A \\
&= p^T C_1^A + C_2^A
\end{aligned}
$$

$$
> E(p^T, u^A), \qquad\qquad (23)
$$

where $X = nx$, (22) follows from the fact that $(pl^{\alpha-1}-1)l$ is increasing in l given p, and (23) is implied by expenditure minimization. Therefore, $l^T > l^A$ or $x^T > x^A$ is sufficient for $u^T > u^A$. Q. E. D.

The above lemma immediately convinces us that both countries gain from trade in a special case where $L = L^*$, which can be confirmed in Figure 3. Where $L = L^*$, each country's autarkic equilibrium becomes A, from which the trading countries move to N along the 45° line. This entails an expansion in both countries' production of Good 1 so that bilateral gains from trade arise. This finding is alternatively described in Figure 4, wherein the bold locus which is strictly convex is a country's production possibility frontier.

The equilibrium moves from A to F, which results in the country's gains from trade. The intuition behind it is basically the same as Markusen's (1981) case; the opportunity to trade makes each oligopolistic firm behave more competitively than under autarky, thereby enhancing the country's welfare. Moreover, the presence of increasing returns, together with expansion in output, lowers each firm's average costs and increases its profit, which is another force for positive gains from trade.

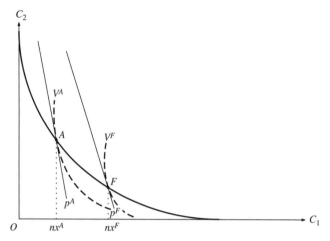

Fig. 4. Gains from trade in a symmetric equilibrium.

Combining Lemma 3 with Proposition 1, we can say that the exporter of Good 1 necessarily gains from trade stated in:

PROPOSITION 2. *Regarding the gains from trade for the exporter of Good 1, we have:*

(i) *the case under* (17) *in Figure 1: Foreign gains from trade;*

(ii) *the case under* (18) *in Figures 2 and 3: if the relative size between the countries satisfies* $L^*/L > \psi$, *Foreign gains from trade. On the other hand, Home gains under* (21) *and* $L^*/L < \psi$.

In view of Proposition 2, the remainder of our main task is to examine whether the importer of Good 1 gains from trade. Of course, the answer is conditional. The following proposition summarizes the results based on the possibility of gainful trade for the importer of Good 1:

PROPOSITION 3. *Regarding the gains from trade for the importer of Good 1, we have:*

(i) *the case under* (17) *with Figure 1: the necessary and sufficient condition for gainful trade for Home is*

$$\frac{L^*}{L} > \left[\frac{n}{\alpha\gamma(n-1)+(1-\gamma)n}\right]^{1/\gamma(\alpha-1)} - 1; \tag{24}$$

(ii) *the case under* (18) *with Figures 2 and 3: if the relative size between the countries satisfies* $L^*/L > \psi$, (24) *constitutes the equivalent condition for gainful trade for the Home country. On the other hand,* *under* (21) *and* $L^*/L < \psi$, *the necessary and sufficient condition for Foreign to gain is*

$$\left\{ \left[\frac{\alpha\gamma(n-1)+(1-\gamma)n}{\alpha\gamma(2n-1)+2(1-\gamma)n} \right]^{\alpha-1} \left[\frac{2n-1}{2(n-1)} \right]^{\alpha} \left(\frac{L+L^*}{L^*} \right)^{\alpha-1} \right\}^{\gamma}$$

$$\times \frac{[\alpha\gamma(n-1)+(1-\gamma)n]\{2[\alpha\gamma(2n-1)+2(1-\gamma)n]+\gamma[2(1-\alpha)n+\alpha]\frac{L+L^*}{L^*}\}}{2n[\alpha\gamma(2n-1)+2(1-\gamma)n]}$$

$$> 1.$$

$$(25)$$

PROOF. Since the proofs are nothing but tedious calculation exercises, only an outline of the proof is sketched. Let p^T and I^T be the world price and national income of the importer of Good 1 in the trading equilibrium. Then, substituting them into the indirect utility function $V(p, I) \equiv \gamma^{\gamma}(1-\gamma)^{1-\gamma}I/p^{\gamma}$ and taking its ratio to $V(p^A, I^A)$ yield[19]

$$\frac{V(p^T, I^T)}{V(p^A, I^A)} = \left(\frac{p^A}{p^T} \right)^{\gamma} \frac{I^T}{I^A}.$$

All we have to do is substitute l and l^* in each trading equilibrium into the above index of welfare comparison and derive the condition for $V(p^T, I^T)/V(p^A, I^A) > 1$. In Figures 1 and 2, $l^T = 0$ and

$$l^{*T} = \frac{\alpha\gamma(n-1)(L+L^*)}{n[\alpha\gamma(n-1)+(1-\gamma)n]},$$

are obtained.

However, Figure 3 gives

$$l^T = l^{*T} = \frac{\alpha\gamma(2n-1)(L+L^*)}{2n[\alpha\gamma(2n-1)+2(1-\gamma)n]}.$$

Substitution of these into p and I or I^* and further substitution into the above index give us $V(p^T, I^T)/V(p^A, I^A)$ of the importing country. After that, some calculations and rearrangements yield the necessary and sufficient conditions for the importer to gain from trade given by (24) and (25). Q. E. D.

While Proposition 3 gives the necessary and sufficient conditions for the importer to gain from trade, it is of some use to consider the possibility of losses from trade. In Figures 1 and 2, Foreign diversifies, which requires the per-firm Foreign labor endowment, i.e., L^*/n, to be larger than the vertical interception of the Foreign firm's allocation curve given by

$$\frac{\alpha\gamma(L+L^*)}{n[\alpha\gamma(n-1)+(1-\gamma)n]}.$$

---

[19] Recall that $V(p^A, I^A)$ is given in (6).

This condition is explicitly given by

$$\frac{L^*}{L} > \frac{\alpha\gamma(n-1)}{(1-\gamma)n}.$$

Pulling (24) together with the above 'diversification' condition, Home loses if and only if

$$\left[\frac{n}{\alpha\gamma(n-1)+(1-\gamma)n}\right]^{1/\gamma(\alpha-1)} - 1 > \frac{L^*}{L} > \max\left\{1, \frac{\alpha\gamma(n-1)}{(1-\gamma)n}\right\}. \qquad (26)$$

Equation (26) asserts that when both countries are sufficiently close to each other in terms of labor endowments, the tendency for the small country to lose from trade is strengthened. However, condition (25) requires the opposite in the case where the large country becomes the importer of Good 1. Since the left-hand side in (25) is monotonically decreasing in L^*/L, (25) becomes more likely to be violated as L^* deviates from L, that is, the two countries become more asymmetric. If L^*-L is quite large, Foreign loses from trade.

6. Concluding remarks

It has been thought difficult to deal with both increasing returns and imperfect competition in a single framework of general equilibrium. Of course, there are two exceptions in the literature. The first assumes monopolistic competition like Dixit and Norman (1980) and Helpman and Krugman (1985), while the second allows for free entry in an oligopolistic model, e.g., Lahiri and Ono (1995) and Shimomura (1998). Owing to the assumption of free entry and zero profit, the structure in these models turns to be similar to that in the neoclassical model, which makes the analysis simple and tractable.

However, there are few studies that formulate international oligopoly with restricted entry and increasing returns in a general equilibrium setting. As a recent contribution, Fujiwara and Shimomura (2005) construct an extended Markusen (1981) model to show the validity of the factor proportions theory by allowing for arbitrary differences in the factor endowment ratio.

This chapter has provided an alternative theory of international trade under increasing returns and international oligopoly. We believe that our model has two virtues. First, we have endogenized the determination of specialization patterns by using Ethier's (1982) allocation curve method. Depending on the relative country size and the interaction between the degree of scale economies and market power, a country can specialize in the production of a numeraire good. In this case, such a country tends to lose from trade. This is in sharp contrast to the existing literature on the procompetitive gains from trade in which all countries are *a priori* assumed to incompletely specialize.

Second, the solvability of the general equilibrium solutions is fully utilized to argue trade patterns and gains from trade. We believe that it can be applied in many ways, such as the welfare effect of various trade policies.

Finally, we would like to comment on the direction of future research. While we have treated *national* economies of scale, it is also important to consider *international* economies of scale. Looking at the modern world, international returns to scale have been increasingly observed. Extending the present analysis to international economies of scale would be a fruitful future endeavor.

Acknowledgements

Earlier versions of this chapter were presented at Kobe University, Ritsumeikan University and University of New South Wales. Helpful comments from Partha Gangopadhyay, Jota Ishikawa, Hiroshi Izawa, Ronald W. Jones, Edwin Lai, Murray C. Kemp, Hiroshi Kurata, Kaz Miyagiwa, Noritsugu Nakanishi, Yew Kwang Ng, Takao Ohkawa, Makoto Okamura, Masayuki Okawa, Albert G. Schweinberger, Koji Shimomura, Frank Staehler, Binh Tran-Nam, Chisato Yoshida, Kar-yiu Wong, Ian Wooton, Laixun Zhao and an anonymous referee are gratefully acknowledged. Of course, all the remaining errors are our own responsibility.

Appendix 1. Some properties of the allocation curve

This appendix examines some properties of the Home firm's allocation curve. Invoke (14):

$$\frac{\gamma}{1-\gamma}\frac{L+L^*-n(l+l^*)}{n(l^\alpha+l^{*\alpha})}\left[1-\frac{l^\alpha}{n(l^\alpha+l^{*\alpha})}\right]-\frac{1}{\alpha}l^{1-\alpha}$$
$$\equiv \widetilde{MR}(l,l^*,L+L^*)-MC(l)=0.$$

Let us begin with setting $l^*=0$ and computing the best response to it. Substituting $l^*=0$ and solving for l, we have

$$l=\frac{\alpha\gamma(n-1)(L+L^*)}{n[\alpha\gamma(n-1)+(1-\gamma)n]}>0.$$

However, we see that the other interception is given by $l^*=0$ by setting $l=0$, i.e., the Home firm's allocation curve goes through the origin.

We next look at the slope of the allocation curve. Differentiating the above first-order condition with respect to l and l^* and rearranging, the absolute value of the slope of the allocation curve takes the form of

$$-\frac{dl^*}{dl} = \frac{\Gamma(l, l^*)}{\Delta(l, l^*)}, \tag{27}$$

where

$$\Gamma(l, l^*) \equiv \widetilde{MR}_l(l, l^*, L + L^*) - MC'(l)$$

$$= \frac{\gamma}{1-\gamma} \frac{1}{[n(l^\alpha + l^{*\alpha})]^3} \left\{ -n^2 (l^\alpha + l^{*\alpha}) [(n-1)l^\alpha + nl^{*\alpha}] \right.$$

$$\left. - n\alpha l^{\alpha-1} [L + L^* - n(l + l^*)] [(n-1)l^\alpha + (n+1)l^{*\alpha}] - \frac{1-\alpha}{\alpha} l^{-\alpha} \right\}$$

$$\Delta(l, l^*) \equiv \widetilde{MR}_{l^*}(l, l^*, L + L^*)$$

$$= \frac{\gamma}{1-\gamma} \frac{1}{[n(l^\alpha + l^{*\alpha})]^3} \left\{ -n^2 (l^\alpha + l^{*\alpha}) [(n-1)l^\alpha + nl^{*\alpha}] \right.$$

$$\left. - n\alpha l^{*\alpha-1} [L + L^* - n(l + l^*)] [(n-2)l^\alpha + nl^{*\alpha}] \right\},$$

where the subscripts denote the partial derivative of $\widetilde{MR}(\cdot)$ with respect to l and l^*. Note that $\Delta(\cdot)$ is negative for any l or l^*, and parameters.

Considering the system of (14) and (15), the two allocation curves intersect on the 45° line. And there are two candidates for how they intersect. One possibility is that the Home firm's curve cuts the Foreign firm's from above, i.e., the Home firm's allocation curve is steeper than the Foreign firm's. The other is opposite to the first case, that is, the Home firm's allocation curve is not as steep as the Foreign firm's. Of course, this difference comes from the interaction of parameters. In particular, the relative magnitude of n and α plays a significant role, which we will show. This difference will also have a significant influence on patterns of specialization and hence gains from trade.

Evaluating (27) at $l = l^*$, it is simplified to

$$-\frac{dl^*}{dl}\bigg|_{l=l^*} = \frac{\dfrac{-\gamma}{1-\gamma} \dfrac{(2n-1)l + \alpha(L + L^* - 2nl)}{4nl^{\alpha+1}} + \dfrac{\alpha-1}{\alpha} \dfrac{1}{l^\alpha}}{\dfrac{-\gamma}{1-\gamma} \dfrac{n(2n-1)l + (n-1)\alpha(L + L^* - 2nl)}{4n^2 l^{\alpha+1}}}. \tag{28}$$

In the first case where the Home firm's curve is steeper, (29) must exceed unity, which leads to

$$\frac{L + L^* - 2nl}{2nl} \frac{\alpha\gamma}{2n(1-\gamma)} > \frac{\alpha-1}{\alpha}. \tag{29}$$

At the interior Cournot–Nash equilibrium, each firm's input is determined as

$$l = l^* = \frac{\alpha\gamma(2n - 1)(L + L^*)}{2n[\alpha\gamma(2n - 1) + 2(1 - \gamma)n]}.$$

Substituting this into (29), the Home firm's allocation curve cuts the Foreign firm's from above if and only if

$$n < \frac{2\alpha - 1}{2(\alpha - 1)}. \tag{30}$$

Analogously, the condition where the Home firm's allocation curve is not so steep as the Foreign firm's is

$$n > \frac{2\alpha - 1}{2(\alpha - 1)}. \tag{31}$$

Appendix 2. The factor price equalization condition

Throughout the chapter, we have assumed that Good 2 is always positively produced to ensure unitary wage rates between the countries. This is a convenient assumption but a sufficient condition is needed to justify such factor price equalization. This appendix is devoted to giving such a condition.

See Figure 1 in which Ethier's (1982) type specialization takes place. In the figure, the Foreign country specializes in Good 1 if the labor endowment point is given between DE on WW'. Thus, to exclude this, we need

$$\frac{\alpha\gamma(n - 1)(L + L^*)}{n[\alpha\gamma(n - 1) + (1 - \gamma)n]} < \frac{L^*}{n},$$

where the left-hand side represents the Foreign firm's optimal labor input corresponding to $l = 0$. This condition is equivalent to

$$\frac{L^*}{L} > \frac{\alpha\gamma(n - 1)}{(1 - \gamma)n}. \tag{32}$$

Next, see Figure 3. In the figure, if the endowment is distributed at G, the resulting trading equilibrium will be H, which involves the Home country's specialization in Good 1. Thus, the endowment must be between J and E to exclude such a specialization possibility. This condition is given by

$$\frac{\alpha\gamma(2n - 1)(L + L^*)}{2n[\alpha\gamma(2n - 1) + 2(1 - \gamma)n]} < \frac{L}{n},$$

which is equivalent to

$$\frac{L^*}{L} < \frac{\alpha\gamma(2n-1) + 4(1-\gamma)n}{\alpha\gamma(2n-1)}. \tag{33}$$

In sum, the condition for excluding complete specialization in Good 1 requires

$$\frac{\alpha\gamma(2n-1) + 4(1-\gamma)n}{\alpha\gamma(2n-1)} > \frac{L^*}{L} > \frac{\alpha\gamma(n-1)}{(1-\gamma)n}. \tag{34}$$

If (34) is satisfied, both countries positively produce Good 2 in any trading equilibrium.

References

Dixit, A.K., Norman, V. (1980), *Theory of International Trade*. Cambridge University Press, Cambridge.

Ethier, W.J. (1982), Decreasing costs in international trade and Frank Graham's argument for protection. *Econometrica* 50 (5), 1243–1268.

Fujiwara, K., Shimomura, K. (2005), A factor endowment theory of international trade under imperfect competition and increasing returns. *Canadian Journal of Economics* 38 (1), 273–289.

Helpman, E. (1981), International trade in the presence of product differentiation, economies of scale and monopolistic competition. *Journal of International Economics* 11 (3), 305–340.

Helpman, E., Krugman, P.R. (1985), *Market Structure and Foreign Trade*. MIT Press, Cambridge, MA.

Kemp, M.C., Negishi, T. (1970), Variable returns to scale, commodity taxes, factor market distortions, and their implications for trade gains. *Swedish Journal of Economics* 72 (2), 1–11.

Kemp, M.C., Okawa, M. (1995), The gains from free trade under imperfect competition. In: Chang, W.W., Katayama, S. (Eds.), *Imperfect Competition in International Trade*. Kluwer Academic Publishers, Boston, pp. 53–62.

Kemp, M.C., Shimomura, K. (1995), The apparently innocuous representative agent. *Japanese Economic Review* 46 (3), 247–256.

Kemp, M.C., Shimomura, K. (2002), A new approach to the theory of international trade under increasing returns: the two-commodities case. In: Woodland, A.D. (Ed.), *Economic Theory and International Trade: Essays in Honor of Murray C.* Kemp, Edward Elgar, Cheltenham, UK, pp. 3–21.

Krugman, P.R. (1979), Increasing returns, monopolistic competition, and international trade. *Journal of International Economics* 9 (4), 469–479.

Krugman, P.R. (1980), Scale economies, product differentiation, and the pattern of trade. *American Economic Review* 70 (5), 950–959.

Lahiri, S., Ono, Y. (1995), The role of free entry in an oligopolistic Heckscher-Ohlin model. *International Economic Review* 36 (3), 609–624.

Markusen, J.R. (1981), Trade and the gains from trade with imperfect competition. *Journal of International Economics* 11 (4), 531–551.

Markusen, J.R., Melvin, J.R. (1984), The gains-from-trade theorem with increasing returns to scale. In: Kierzkowski, H. (Ed.), *Monopolistic Competition and International Trade*. Clarendon Press, Oxford, UK, pp. 10–33.

Ottaviano, G.I.P., Tabuchi, T., Thisse, J. (2002), Agglomeration and trade revisited. *International Economic Review* 43 (2), 409–436.

Ruffin, R. (2003a), Oligopoly and trade: what, how much, and for whom? *Journal of International Economics* 60 (2), 315–335.

Ruffin, R. (2003b), International trade under oligopoly conditions. *Review of International Economics* 11 (4), 577–587.

Schweinberger, A.G. (1996), Procompetitive gains from trade and comparative advantage. *International Economic Review* 37 (2), 361–375.

Shimomura, K. (1998), Factor income function and an oligopolistic Heckscher-Ohlin model of international trade. *Economics Letters* 61 (1), 91–100.

Suga, N. (2005), International economies of scale and the gains from trade. *Journal of Economics* 85 (1), 73–97.

Tawada, M., Okawa, M. (1995), On the behavior of monopoly in general equilibrium trade models. In: Chang, W.W., Katayama, S. (Eds.), *Imperfect Competition in International Trade*. Kluwer Academic Publishers, Norwell, MA, pp. 63–78.

CHAPTER 14

Tariff Policy and Foreign Economic Aid for the Economy with a Monopolistically Competitive Nontraded Industry and Capital Inflow

Masayuki Okawa

Department of Economics, Ritsumeikan University, Biwako-Kusatsu Campus, 1-1-1 Noji-Higashi, Kusatsu, Shiga 525-8577, Japan
E-mail address: mokawa@ec.ritsumei.ac.jp

Abstract

Purpose – This chapter examines whether a small open economy in the presence of a nontraded good produced under a monopolistically competitive market and foreign capital inflow can raise its national welfare by adopting trade liberalization coupled with foreign economic aid.

Methodology/approach – The chapter employs a general equilibrium, comparative static analysis of a small open economy involving two factors and two industries.

Findings – It is shown that an import tariff can raise the welfare of a country or impoverish it, depending on the production and trade structures and preferences of the country, but foreign economic aid is always welfare enhancing. Thus, even when a tariff reduction reduces national welfare, the government still has an incentive to adopt the policy combination of trade liberalization and foreign economic aid.

Originality/value of paper – The results obtained explain a widely recognized fact that economic aid by developed donor countries, trade liberalization and capital market liberalization typically take place simultaneously in developing recipient countries.

Keywords: Foreign economic aid, foreign capital inflow, monopolistic competition, tariff policy, trade liberalization

Paper Type: Research paper

Frontiers of Economics and Globalization
Volume 5 ISSN: 1574-8715
DOI: 10.1016/S1574-8715(08)05014-8

1. Introduction

Since the 1990s many developing countries and transitional economies have liberalized their goods and service markets and opened their capital markets to the developed countries. Many of the developing countries are also receiving economic aid from developed countries. It is widely observed that the economic aids by donor countries and trade liberalization and capital market liberalization policies by recipient countries precede simultaneously.[1]

Focusing upon the tariff policy of a small country in monopolistically competitive frameworks, various researchers have examined the welfare effects of an import tariff and have derived the conditions under which an import tariff raises the welfare of the country (see, e.g., Venables, 1982, 1987; Gros, 1987; Flam and Helpman, 1987; Hertel, 1994; Sen, 2005). These models seem to reflect some properties of production and trade structures of developing countries.[2] In these analyses, however, foreign capital inflows are not considered. Sen *et al.* (1997) have examined the welfare effects of capital inflows in the tariff-imposing small open economy with monopolistically competitive nontraded industry.

The international income transfer or foreign economic aid has attracted much attention in the literature in the theory of international trade.[3] It has been shown that paradoxical welfare outcomes of income transfers are possible in stable settings and that if there exist exogenously given distortions, a transfer paradox can occur (see among others, Gale, 1974; Ohyama, 1974; Guesnerie and Laffont, 1978; Chichilnisky, 1980; Brecher and Bhagwati, 1982; Bhagwati *et al.*, 1983; Yano, 1983; Hazari and Sgro, 1992; Kemp and Shimomura, 2002, 2003). Also the effects of economic aid tied to the trade policy of the recipient country are analyzed by, for example, Kemp and Kojima (1985), Schweinberger (1990), Lahiri and Raimondos-Møller (1995, 1997), Lahiri *et al.* (2001) and Kemp (2005). One common assumption in the studies cited above is that all markets are perfectly competitive. Recently some papers examined the welfare effects of the international income transfer and the tied economic assistance in

---

[1] For example, according to OECD (2007), Mexico, a member of NAFTA formed in 1994, received 128.6 millions of dollars and 5.8 millions of dollars as Official Development Assistance (ODA) from the United States and Canada, respectively, in 2005. Also, Indonesia received 1223.1 millions of dollars as ODA from Japan in 2005. Indonesia and Japan agreed to form a FTA in 2006.

[2] Venables (1982, p. 226) also writes, "The economy may perhaps be identified with a less-developed economy which exports primary commodities and imports manufactures which replace the output of the traditional manufacturing industry."

[3] We use the terms "international income transfer" and "foreign economic aid" interchangeably throughout this chapter.

imperfectly competitive settings (see, Brakman and Marrewijk, 1995; Okawa, 2007).[4]

This chapter sets up a small country trading model with a monopolistically competitive nontraded industry and foreign capital inflow and studies the effects of both an import tariff and foreign economic aid from abroad. Thus in our setting, there exist two distortions in the economy: a tariff distortion and monopolistic competition. Although the country is a small country and the "terms of trade effects" cannot appear, it might be worthwhile examining the welfare effects of a foreign economic aid on the small country with two distortions cited above and with capital owned by foreigners.[5] We thus examine whether a small developing country with characteristics described above can raise its national welfare by adopting trade liberalization policy that is connected with foreign economic aid. Section 2 sets up our model and Section 3 examines the effects of an import tariff and an income transfer from abroad on the national welfare of the country. Section 4 offers some concluding remarks.

2. The model

Consider a small open economy which consists of two industries: one industry is perfectly competitive and the other industry is monopolistically competitive. The country exports a homogenous good produced with constant returns to scale (CRS) technology in a perfectly competitive market and imports a variety of goods from the world market. The country also produces nontraded variety of goods with increasing returns to scale (IRS) technologies in a monopolistically competitive market. The country imposes *ad valorem* import tariff on the imports of variety of goods and introduces constant amount of capital from abroad. This assumption reflects the fact that many developing countries have now opened their capital market and set some regulations on the inflow of the capital. We assume that the country is the recipient of an international income transfer as economic aid from abroad.

We first look at the consumers in the economy. The consumers provide labor and capital to the firms, obtain factor rewards and choose products

---

[4] For a review of literature on the theory of international income transfer and tied aid, see for example Brakman and Marrewijk (1998).

[5] Bhagwati and Tironi (1980) set up a two factor (labor and capital), two goods small country model and showed that a reduction of a tariff reduces the welfare of the country when all capital is owned by foreigners and the imports are labor-intensive. The Stolper–Samuelson effect and the assumption that all capital is owned by foreigners play crucial role in deriving the result. Yano and Nugent (1999) showed that, even in a small country setting, a transfer paradox that the welfare of the recipient decreases as the result of foreign economic aid can occur when foreign aid is provided in terms of capital goods and there exist nontraded industries in the recipient.

to maximize their utilities. We assume all consumers are identical in all respects and thus focus on a representative consumer; the number of consumers is normalized to one. The utility function of the consumer is of a Cobb–Douglas type:

$$u = X^\alpha y^{1-\alpha}, \quad 0 < \alpha < 1, \tag{1}$$

where y is the homogenous good and is taken as the numeraire and X is the aggregate of the differentiated good. The subutility function X is assumed to be of the Dixit–Stiglitz type:

$$X = \left(\sum_{i=1}^{n} x_i^{(\sigma-1/\sigma)} + \sum_{j=1}^{n*} x_j^{*(\sigma-1/\sigma)} \right)^{(\sigma/\sigma-1)}, \quad \sigma > 1, \tag{2}$$

where x_i is the domestic output of variety (brand) i of the differentiated good, n the number of varieties produced in the country, $\sigma > 1$ the constant elasticity of substitution between varieties and n^* the number of brands imported from abroad. The price index of X, P is written as

$$P = \left(\sum_{i=1}^{n} p_i^{1-\sigma} + \sum_{j=1}^{n*} p_j^{*(1-\sigma)} \right)^{(1/1-\sigma)}, \tag{3}$$

where p_i is the price of domestic variety i and p_j^* is the domestic price of foreign variety j. We assume that the government imposes *ad valorem* tariffs on the foreign varieties:

$$p_j^* = (1 + t)p_j^f, \tag{4}$$

where $t > 0$ is the *ad valorem* tariff rate and p_j^f is the constant world price of foreign variety j. The budget constraint of the consumer is:

$$y + PX = m, \tag{5}$$

where m is the national income. Solving the utility maximizing problem of consumers from (1) and (5), we obtain:

$$y = (1 - \alpha)m, \quad 0 < \alpha < 1, \tag{6a}$$

$$PX = \alpha m. \tag{6b}$$

We obtain from (1), (6a) and (6b) the indirect utility function of the consumer:

$$V(p,m) = (1 - \alpha)^{1-\alpha} \left(\frac{\alpha}{P} \right)^\alpha m. \tag{7}$$

The demands for individual varieties are:

$$x_i = p_i^{-\sigma} P^{\sigma-1} \alpha m, \tag{8a}$$

$$x_j^* = p_j^{*-\sigma} P^{\sigma-1} \alpha m. \tag{8b}$$

Let us now turn to the behavior of the producers. This country produces two goods (good x_i and good y) by employing two factors: labor and capital. Good y is produced under conditions of free entry and perfect competition and the technology of the good is subject to constant returns to scale. The zero-profit condition for the good is:

$$a_{LY}w + a_{KY}r = 1, \tag{9}$$

where a_{hk} is the amount of variable input h ($h = L, K$) used to produce one unit of good k ($k = x, y$), w the wage rate and r the rental rate of capital. The differentiated goods are produced in a monopolistically competitive market by using labor and capital as variable inputs, while only capital is used as a fixed input. The variable input component is homogeneous of degree one. The first-order condition for the profit maximization for a variety may be written as:

$$a_{LX}w + a_{KX}r = p\left(1 - \frac{1}{\sigma}\right). \tag{10}$$

Free entry to the market drives the profits of the firms to zero. Thus, the fixed cost must be equal to the total revenue minus variable cost:

$$a_{KF}r = \left(\frac{1}{\sigma}\right)px, \tag{11}$$

where a_{KF} is the amount of capital used as fixed input and assumed to be constant.

We here assume that the homogeneous good y is more labor-intensive than the variable cost component of the import-competing good x:

$$\frac{a_{KY}}{a_{LY}} < \frac{a_{KX}}{a_{LX}}. \tag{12}$$

The factor-intensity condition will play a crucial role in deriving our results.

We assume that the government introduces foreign capital and regulates the quantity of inflow at a constant level. Thus the rental rate of capital is endogenously determined and full rental rate is assumed to be repatriated to the foreign owners of the capital. Thus the factor market-clearing conditions are:

$$a_{LY}Y + a_{LX}nx = \overline{L}, \quad \text{and} \tag{13}$$

$$a_{KY}Y + a_{KX}nx + a_{KF}n = K^d + K^f, \tag{14}$$

where Y is the output of the homogeneous good, $\overline{L}$ the given endowment of labor, K^d the constant amount of capital owned by domestic residents and K^f the capital owned by foreigners which is also exogenously given constant. The balance of trade is written as:

$$Y - y = p^f n^* x^*, \tag{15}$$

where $(Y-y)$ is the exports of the homogeneous good. The national income is given by:

$$m = Y + npx + tn^*p^fx^* - rK^f + T = w\overline{L} + rK^d + tp^fn^*x^* + T, \qquad (16)$$

where T is the foreign aid this country receives from abroad in terms of homogeneous good. The national income is the sum of factor income of domestic residents, tariff revenue and the income transferred as economic aid from abroad.

3. The effects of import tariffs and foreign economic aid

3.1. Comparative static analysis of the effects of import tariffs and foreign economic aid

We now examine the effects of import tariffs and of an income transfer as a foreign economic aid to this small open economy. In the following comparative static analysis, we use variables in terms of proportionate changes: $\hat{a} = \mathrm{d}\log a = \mathrm{d}a/a$.

From (6a) and (6b), we have:

$$\hat{y} = \hat{m}, \qquad (17a)$$

$$\hat{P} + \hat{X} = \hat{m}. \qquad (17b)$$

From (8a) and (8b),

$$\hat{x} = -\hat{p}\sigma + (\sigma - 1)\hat{P} + \hat{m}, \qquad (18a)$$

$$\hat{x}^* = -\sigma(1 + t)^{-1}\mathrm{d}t + (\sigma - 1)\hat{P} + \hat{m}. \qquad (18b)$$

From (3),

$$\hat{P} = \beta(1 - \sigma)^{-1}\hat{n} + \beta\hat{p} + (1 - \beta)(1 + t)^{-1}\mathrm{d}t. \qquad (19)$$

where $\beta \equiv (np^{1-\sigma}/P^{1-\sigma})$ and $0 < \beta < 1$. From (15), we have:

$$\hat{m} = s_L\hat{w} + s_K\hat{r} + s_M\mathrm{d}t + ts_M\hat{x}^* + s_T\hat{T}, \qquad (20)$$

where $s_L \equiv w\overline{L}/m$, $s_K \equiv rK^d/m$, $s_M \equiv p^fn^*x^*/m$ and $s_T \equiv T/m$.

Let us now turn to the production side of the economy. From (9)–(11),

$$\theta_{LY}\hat{w} + \theta_{KY}\hat{r} = 0, \qquad (9')$$

$$\theta_{LX}\hat{w} + \theta_{KX}\hat{r} = \hat{p}, \qquad (10')$$

$$\hat{r} = \hat{p} + \hat{x}, \qquad (11')$$

where θ_{ij} $(i = L, K; j = X, Y)$ is the distributive share of the ith factor in the unit variable cost of good j. We see from (9') and (10') that the

Stolper–Samuelson relationship between the price of the differentiated good and factor prices hold, and from (12) that an increase in p raises r and reduces w. From the market-clearing conditions for factor markets, we obtain:

$$\lambda_{LY}\hat{Y} + \lambda_{LX}\hat{n} + \lambda_{LX}\hat{x} = (\lambda_{LY}\theta_{KY}\varepsilon_Y + \lambda_{LX}\theta_{KX}\theta_{FX}^{-1}\varepsilon_X)(\hat{w} - \hat{r}) \tag{21}$$

$$\lambda_{KY}\hat{Y} + (1 - \lambda_{KY})\hat{n} + \lambda_{KX}\hat{x} = -(\lambda_{KY}\theta_{LY}\varepsilon_Y + \lambda_{KX}\theta_{LX}\theta_{FX}^{-1}\varepsilon_X)(\hat{w} - \hat{r}), \tag{22}$$

where $\lambda_{LY} \equiv a_{LY}Y/\overline{L}$, $\lambda_{KY} \equiv a_{KY}Y/(K^d + K^f)$, $\theta_{FX} \equiv a_{KF}r/px \in (0,1)$, $\varepsilon_j \equiv -(\hat{a}_{Lj} - \hat{a}_{Kj})/(\hat{w} - \hat{r})$, $(j = X, Y)$ and so forth. From (9')–(11'),

$$\hat{w} = -(\theta_{KY}/\theta_{LX})\hat{x}, \tag{23a}$$

$$\hat{r} = (\theta_{LY}/\theta_{LX})\hat{x}, \tag{23b}$$

$$\hat{p} = [(\theta_{LY} - \theta_{LX})/\theta_{LX}]\hat{x}. \tag{23c}$$

From (18a) and (18b):

$$\hat{x}^* = -\sigma(1 + t)^{-1}dt + \hat{x} + \hat{p}\sigma. \tag{24}$$

Substituting (23c) in (24), we obtain

$$\hat{x}^* = -\sigma(1 + t)^{-1}dt + [1 + \sigma(\theta_{LY} - \theta_{LX})/\theta_{LX}]\hat{x}. \tag{25'}$$

Thus the proportionate change in national income can be rewritten as

$$\hat{m} = \frac{s_M}{(1+t)}dt + \left\{-s_L\frac{\theta_{KY}}{\theta_{LX}} + s_K\frac{\theta_{LY}}{\theta_{LX}} + ts_M\left[1 + \frac{\sigma(\theta_{LY} - \theta_{LX})}{\theta_{LY}}\right]\right\}\hat{x} + s_T\hat{T}. \tag{26}$$

On the other hand, from (18a) and (19), we obtain:

$$\left\{1 - [-\sigma + (\sigma - 1)\beta]\left(\frac{\theta_{LY} - \theta_{LX}}{\theta_{LX}}\right)\right\}\hat{x}$$
$$= (\sigma - 1)(1 - \beta)(1 + t)^{-1}dt - \beta\hat{n} + \hat{m}. \tag{27}$$

From (26) and (27),

$$H\hat{x} + \beta\hat{n} = Gdt + s_T\hat{T}, \tag{28}$$

where

$$H \equiv 1 + [\sigma - (\sigma - 1)\beta]\left(\frac{\theta_{LY} - \theta_{LX}}{\theta_{LX}}\right) + \left(s_L\frac{\theta_{KY}}{\theta_{LX}} - s_K\frac{\theta_{LY}}{\theta_{LX}}\right)$$
$$- ts_M\left[1 + \frac{\sigma(\theta_{LY} - \theta_{LX})}{\theta_{LY}}\right],$$

and $G \equiv (1 + t)^{-1}[(\sigma - 1)(1 - \beta) + s_M] > 0$.

We now look at the sign of H. Recall that $\theta_{LY} - \theta_{LX} > 0$ from factor-intensity condition in (12). We here assume that (i) $(\theta_{LY}/\theta_{LX})[1 - (\sigma - 1)\sigma^{-1}\beta] \geq ts_M$ and (ii) $s_L \geq (\theta_{LY}/\theta_{KY})s_K$. If all capital is owned by foreigners ($s_K = 0$) then (ii) is always satisfied. Thus we assume $H > 0$.

Substituting (23a) and (23b) in (21) and (22) and deleting $\hat{Y}$, we find that

$$J\hat{n} + F\hat{x} = 0, \tag{29}$$

where $\delta_L \equiv \lambda_{LX} + (\lambda_{LY}\theta_{KY}\varepsilon_Y + \lambda_{LX}\theta_{KX}\theta_{FX}^{-1}\varepsilon_X)/\theta_{LX}$, $\delta_K \equiv \lambda_{KX} - (\lambda_{KY}\theta_{LY}\varepsilon_Y + \lambda_{KX}\theta_{LX}\theta_{FX}^{-1}\varepsilon_X)/\theta_{LX}$, $J \equiv \lambda_{KY}\lambda_{LX} - \lambda_{LY}(1 - \lambda_{KY})$ and $F \equiv \lambda_{KY}\delta_L - \lambda_{LY}\delta_K$. We see from the factor-intensity assumption that $J \equiv \lambda_{KY}\lambda_{LX} - \lambda_{LY}(1 - \lambda_{KY}) < 0$. Recalling the definitions of δ_L and δ_K, we also find that $F \equiv \lambda_{KY}[\lambda_{LX} + \lambda_{LY}\theta_{LX}^{-1}\varepsilon_Y + \lambda_{LX}\theta_{KX}\theta_{FX}^{-1}\theta_{LX}^{-1}\varepsilon_X] + \lambda_{LY}\lambda_{KX}(\theta_{FX}^{-1}\varepsilon_X - 1) > 0$ if $\varepsilon_X \geq \theta_{FX}$. Thus we hereafter assume that $F > 0$.

The Equations (28) and (29) may be rewritten in a matrix form:

$$\begin{bmatrix} \beta & H \\ J & F \end{bmatrix} \begin{bmatrix} \hat{n} \\ \hat{x} \end{bmatrix} = \begin{bmatrix} Gdt + \lambda_T\hat{T} \\ 0 \end{bmatrix}. \tag{30}$$

Solving the system, we have:

$$\hat{n}/dt = (G/\Delta)F > 0 \tag{31}$$

$$\hat{x}/dt = -(G/\Delta)J > 0 \tag{32}$$

$$\hat{n}/\hat{T} = (s_T/\Delta)F > 0 \tag{33}$$

$$\hat{x}/\hat{T} = -(s_T/\Delta)J > 0, \tag{34}$$

where

$$\Delta \equiv \beta F - JH > 0. \tag{35}$$

We first see that an increase in the tariff rate raises the domestic price of imported varieties and causes substitution of domestic demand from imported to the domestic ones. Since domestic differentiated goods are more substitutable for the imports than the homogenous good, an increase in the tariff rate raises the price and output of each nontraded variety and causes new entry to the monopolistically competitive industry raising the number of domestic varieties. Also an increase in the income transfer from abroad raises both the number of domestic varieties and the output and price of each variety through the direct income effect. The increase in the number of varieties and the output of each variety implies the reduction of a distortion caused by monopolistic competition and we will shortly see that the reduction of the distortion will raise the national welfare of the country.[6]

---

[6] See Bhagwati (1975).

3.2. The welfare effects of import tariff and foreign economic aid

We now turn to the welfare effects of an import tariff and a foreign economic aid from abroad. We obtain from (7) the change in the welfare of this country:

$$\hat{V} = -\alpha\hat{P} + \hat{m}. \tag{36}$$

We see from (19) and (36) that an increase in n reduces P and raises the welfare, while an increase in the tariff rate raises the price of each domestic variety and P and works to reduce national welfare.

Substituting from (19), (23c) and (26) in (36), we find

$$\hat{V} = (1+t)^{-1}[s_M - \alpha(1-\beta)]dt - \alpha\beta(1-\sigma)\hat{n}$$
$$+ \{-s_L(\theta_{KY}/\theta_{LX}) + s_K(\theta_{LY}/\theta_{LX}) + ts_M[1 + \sigma(\theta_{LY} - \theta_{LX})/\theta_{LX}]$$
$$- \alpha\beta(\theta_{LY} - \theta_{LX})/\theta_{LX}\}\hat{x} + s_T\hat{T}. \tag{36'}$$

Let us first turn our attention to the effects of an import tariff. Solving for $\hat{V}/dt$, we find after some calculations that

$$\hat{V}/dt = \frac{1}{(1+t)\Delta}(A_1 + A_2 + A_3 + A_4), \tag{37}$$

where

$$A_1 \equiv s_M\beta\left(1 - \frac{\alpha}{1-\sigma}\right)F > 0, \tag{38a}$$

$$A_2 \equiv -s_M J\left(1 + \frac{\theta_{LY} - \theta_{LX}}{\theta_{LX}}(\alpha + \beta)\right) > 0, \tag{38b}$$

$$A_3 \equiv \alpha(1-\beta)J\left\{1 + \frac{\theta_{LY} - \theta_{LX}}{\theta_{LX}}[\alpha(1-\beta) + \beta\sigma]\right\} < 0, \tag{38c}$$

$$A_4 \equiv -(1-\beta)(\alpha + \sigma - 1)J\theta_{LX}^{-1}\{ts_M[\theta_{LX} + \sigma(\theta_{LY} - \theta_{LX})]$$
$$+ s_K - \theta_{KY}(1 - ts_M)\} \gtrless 0. \tag{38d}$$

We see that the sign of $\hat{V}/dt$ is in general ambiguous. We first study the possibility that $\hat{V}/dt > 0$. Since $A_1 > 0$, we look at $A_1 + A_2$:

$$A_2 + A_3 = J\{-s_M + \alpha(1-\beta) + \frac{\theta_{LY} - \theta_{LX}}{\theta_{LX}(\alpha + \beta)}(-s_M + \omega)\}, \tag{39}$$

where $\omega \equiv \alpha(1-\beta)(\alpha+\beta)^{-1}[\alpha(1-\beta) + \beta\sigma] > 0$.

Therefore if s_M is larger than both ω and $\alpha(1-\beta)$ then $A_2 + A_3 > 0$. We see that if $\sigma \in (1, 1+\alpha)$ then $0 < \omega < \alpha(1-\beta) < 1$. Also if $\sigma \in (\alpha + 1, (\alpha + 1)[\alpha(1-\beta)]^{-1} + 1)$ then $\alpha(1-\beta) < \omega < 1$. In both cases s_M can be larger than both ω and $\alpha(1-\beta)$. Turning to A_4, we find that if $s_K \geq \theta_{KY}(1 - ts_M)$ then $A_4 > 0$. Thus if the share of the import sector in national income (s_M) is larger than the critical value, σ is small enough and the income share of capital owned by domestic residents in national income (s_K) is larger than $\theta_{KY}(1 - ts_M)$ then an increase in the tariff rate on the imports of foreign varieties raises national welfare: $\hat{V}/dt > 0$.

The economic intuition is as follows. We have seen in (31) and (32) that an imposition of a tariff on the imports of foreign varieties shifts demand from imported to domestic ones, raises the number of domestic varieties and the output of each variety. Thus the total output of the differentiated goods increases and the production distortion that the outputs of differentiated goods are under-produced under monopolistic competition will be reduced. Also the increase in the number of varieties will raise national welfare. We see that this is a straightforward application of Bhagwati theorem which states that "a reduction (increase) in a single distortion is welfare increasing (lowering)" (see Bhagwati, 1975).

On the other hand turning to the income effects of the tariff, we see that an increase in the tariff rate raises the tariff revenue. We recall that σ is the elasticity of substitution between varieties and also the price elasticity of demand for each variety. Thus, as σ is smaller, the tariff revenue raised by a small increase in the tariff rate becomes larger. It also raises capital income but reduces labor income through the Stolper–Samuelson effect.[7] Therefore if both the shares of trading sector and capital income of domestic residents are large enough, the import tariff will raise the national welfare.

We next turn to the immiserization possibility of the import tariff that $\hat{V}/dt < 0$. Consider a special case where the monopolistically competitive industry is foreign capital-dependent and all capital is owned by foreigners ($s_K = 0$), then $A_4 \leq 0$. We also see that if the share of tariff revenue in national income is small enough and σ is large enough then $\sum_{j=1}^{3} A_j < 0$. Thus we will find that $\hat{V}/dt < 0$. The economic intuition may be as follows: If all capital is owned by foreigners (or the ownership-share of capital by domestic residents is very small) and if there is no economic aid then the national income is only the sum of the tariff revenue and labor income. Though an increase in the tariff rate raises the tariff revenue, it reduces labor income by lowering wage rate through the Stolper–Samuelson effect. Thus if the share of tariff revenue is small enough then national income must decrease. If this negative income effect of the import tariff outweighs the positive effects on the welfare such as the increase in the number of domestic varieties and reduction of production distortion, the national welfare of the country must decrease. Thus the subsidy policy for imports will raise the national welfare. This result contrasts with those obtained by

---

[7] This negative effect of the import tariff on labor income through the Stolper–Samuelson effect cannot appear in a Ricardian model.

preceding papers (see, e.g., Flam and Helpman, 1987; Venables, 1987) which showed that import tariffs are welfare improving for the country.

Let us finally look at the welfare effect of foreign economic aid. Keeping the tariff rate constant and substituting (19), (23c), (26), (33) and (34) in (36), we find that

$$\hat{V}/\hat{T} = (s_T/\Delta)\left\{\beta F\left(1 + \frac{\alpha\beta}{\sigma - 1}\right) - \left[1 + \frac{\theta_{LY} - \theta_{LX}}{\theta_{LX}}(\alpha + \beta)\right]J\right\} > 0. \quad (40)$$

Thus an international income transfer raises the national welfare of the recipient country. We have seen that the imposition of import tariff can be welfare improving. In the case, the trade liberalization policy or tariff reduction policy to open the import markets reduces the national welfare of the country and thus the government of the country would be reluctant to agree to liberalize its import markets. However if the trade liberalization policy by the country is accompanied by the foreign economic aid provided by the trading partners to compensate the loss caused by the policy changes, then the combination of the policies will raise the national welfare of the country and the government would reach agreement with the trade liberalization.

4. Concluding remarks

This chapter sets up a simple two factor, two sector small open economy model in which the country introduces capital from abroad and produces two goods: homogeneous exports and differentiated varieties in a monopolistically competitive nontraded industry. We have examined the effects of import tariffs and an international income transfer on national welfare of the country. It is first shown that both the import tariff and income transfer raise the number of nontraded varieties and the output of each variety. As for the welfare effects of the import tariff, the results in general depend on the production structure and preferences of the country. We however have seen that the assumptions that domestic monopolistically competitive industry is more capital intensive than the homogeneous good industry and that all or a large share of the capital is owned by foreigners will play an important role. Thus, if the share of the trading sector in national income and the share of the tariff revenue are relatively small and if a large share of the capital is owned by foreigners, the import tariff would reduce the national welfare of the country. In this case, the policy implications of the import tariffs derived from our analysis is the opposite of those obtained by earlier papers, in which the import tariffs are welfare improving. We have also shown that an income transfer to this economy from abroad will be welfare improving. Therefore, even when a tariff reduction policy reduces national welfare, if the trade liberalization policy is accompanied by foreign economic aid from abroad then the government would have an incentive to accept such policy combination. In our small country setting, the income transferred to the country is exogenously given and the effects on the donor country are left outside of the analysis. The analysis based on a two-country setting would be more interesting. However, that work will be left for our future work.

Acknowledgements

I gratefully acknowledge Arghya Ghosh, Murray C. Kemp, Binh Tran Nam and an anonymous referee for their helpful comments on the earlier version of this paper. However any remaining errors are mine. Financial support from Japan Society for Promotion of Science (JSPS) through a Grant in-Aid for Science Research (No. 20330052) is gratefully acknowledged.

References

Bhagwati, J.N. (1975), The general theory of distortions and welfare. In: Bhagwati, J., Jones, R., Mundell, R., Vanek, J. (Eds.), *Trade, Balance of Payments and Growth*. Amsterdam, North-Holland.

Bhagwati, J.N., Tironi, E. (1980), Tariff change, foreign capital and immiserization: a theoretical analysis. *Journal of International Economics* 7 (1), 71–83.

Bhagwati, J.N., Brecher, R.A., Hatta, T. (1983), The generalized theory of transfers and welfare: bilateral transfers in a multilateral world. *American Economic Review* 73 (4), 606–618.

Brakman, S., Marrewijk, C. (1995), Transfers, returns to scale, tied aid and monopolistic competition. *Journal of Development Economics* 47 (2), 333–354.

Brakman, S., Marrewijk, C. (1998), *The Economics of International Transfer*. Cambridge University Press, Cambridge.

Brecher, A.R., Bhagwati, J. (1982), Immiserizing transfers from abroad. *Journal of International Economics* 13 (3–4), 353–364.

Chichilnisky, G. (1980), Basic goods, the effects of commodity transfers and the international economic order. *Journal of Development Economics* 7 (4), 505–519.

Flam, H., Helpman, E. (1987), Industrial policy under monopolistic competition. *Journal of International Economics* 22 (1/2), 79–102.

Gale, D. (1974), Exchange equilibrium and coalitions: an example. *Journal of Mathematical Economics* 1 (1), 63–66.

Gros, D. (1987), A note on the optimal tariff, retaliation and the welfare loss from tariff wars in a framework with intra-industry trade. *Journal of International Economics* 23 (3/4), 357–367.

Guesnerie, R., Laffont, J. (1978), Advantageous reallocation of initial endowments. *Econometrica* 46 (4), 835–842.

Hazari, B.R., Sgro, P. (1992), Transfers, structural change, welfare, and unemployment in a north-south framework. *International Review of Economics & Finance* 1 (1), 15–32.

Hertel, T. (1994), The 'Procompetitive' effects of trade policy reform. *Journal of International Economics* 36 (3–4), 391–411.

Kemp, M.C. (2005), Aid tied to the Donor's exports. *Pacific Economic Review* 10 (3), 317–322.

Kemp, M., Kojima, S. (1985), Tied aid and paradoxes of donor-enrichment and paradoxes and recipient-improvement. *International Economic Review* 26 (3), 721–729.

Kemp, M., Shimomura, K. (2002), A theory of voluntary unrequited international transfers. *Japanese Economic Review* 53 (3), 290–300.

Kemp, M., Shimomura, K. (2003), A theory of involuntary unrequited international transfers. *Journal of Political Economy* 111 (3), 682–692.

Lahiri, S., Raimondos-Møller, P. (1995), Welfare effects of aid under quantitative trade restriction. *Journal of International Economics* 39 (3–4), 297–315.

Lahiri, S., Raimondos-Møller, P. (1997), On the tying of aid to tariff reform. *Journal of Development Economics* 54 (2), 479–491.

Lahiri, S., Raimondos-Møller, P., Wong, K., Woodland, A.D. (2001), Optimal foreign aid and tariffs. *Journal of Development Economics* 67 (1), 79–99.

Ohyama, M. (1974), Tariffs and the transfer problem. *Keio Economic Studies* 11 (1), 29–45.

Okawa, M. (2007), International income transfer under imperfect competition. *Review of Development Economics* 11 (2), 242–257.

Schweinberger, A. (1990), On the welfare effects of tied aid. *International Economic Review* 31 (2), 457–462.

Sen, P. (2005), Tariffs in a Ricardian model with a monopolistically competitive sector: the role of nontradables. *Review of International Economics* 13 (4), 676–681.

Sen, P., Ghosh, A., Barman, A. (1997), The possibility of welfare gains with capital inflows in a small tariff-distorted economy. *Economica* 64 (254), 345–352.

Venables, A. (1982), Optimal tariffs for trade in monopolistically competitive commodities. *Journal of International Economics* 12 (3–4), 224–241.

Venables, A. (1987), Trade and trade policy with differentiated products: a Chamberlinian–Ricardian Model. *Economic Journal* 97 (387), 700–717.

Yano, M. (1983), The welfare aspects of the transfer problem. *Journal of International Economics* 15 (3–4), 277–289.

Yano, M., Nugent, J.B. (1999), Aid, nontraded goods, and the transfer paradox in small countries. *American Economic Review* 89 (3), 431–449.

CHAPTER 15

Infrastructure Aid and Deindustrialization in Developing Countries

E. Kwan Choi[a] and Jai-Young Choi[b]

[a]Department of Economics, Iowa State University, Ames, IA 50011 USA; Department of
Economics and Finance, City University of Hong Kong, Tat Chee Avenue, Kowloon, Hong Kong
E-mail address: kchoi@iastate.edu
[b]Department of Economics and Finance, Lamar University, Beaumont, TX 77710, USA
E-mail address: Jai-Young.Choi@lamar.edu

Abstract

Purpose – This chapter investigates the role of infrastructure aid to
developing countries for determining the effect on national income and
consumer welfare. The chapter further demonstrates the conditions for the
Dutch disease effect by decomposing the output effects of infrastructure
aid into the initial factor-saving effect, factor-substitution effect and
nontraded good effect.

Methodology/approach – This chapter extends the Heckscher–Ohlin
model to a 3×2 case with two traded goods and a nontraded good, and
derives comparative static results on factor prices, the price of nontraded
goods, foreign exchange rate, sectoral outputs, and national income and
consumer welfare.

Findings – It is shown that for a recipient country, infrastructure aid to either
the export or import sector necessarily raises national income and consumer
welfare, whereas the same aid to the nontraded good sector does not affect
national income but raises consumer welfare. Infrastructure aid may lead to
a Dutch disease effect via its three effects on industrial outputs: the initial
factor-saving effect, factor-substitution effect and nontraded good effect.

Research limitations/implications – This chapter considers infrastructure
capital as a public input, but it is devoid of analysis of inter-industrial
spillover effects that the infrastructure capital generates to other sectors.

Practical implications – This chapter reveals several aspects of infrastructure aid that the practitioners of aids must consider.

Keywords: Infrastructure aid, deindustrialization, Dutch disease,
nontraded good, Heckscher–Ohlin

Paper type: Research paper

Frontiers of Economics and Globalization
Volume 5   ISSN: 1574-8715
DOI: 10.1016/S1574-8715(08)05015-X

1. Introduction

Despite continued growth in income, official development assistance (ODA) has steadily declined throughout the 1990s. For the few low-income countries that have received funds, it has been argued that the aid may undermine their growth through a Dutch disease-like effect, i.e., currency appreciation and the subsequent decline of the export sector.[1] These studies are of concern to policy makers of donor countries as well as to the recipient countries that constantly clamor for increased aid. Possible deindustrialization and adverse welfare impacts on the recipient countries may justify reluctance or caution on the part of donor countries.

There is now a substantial body of literature that explores the impacts of aid in developing countries. Based on his analysis of 62 developing countries, Elbadawi (1999) reported currency overvaluation in aid recipients and the failure of low-income countries in sub-Saharan Africa to attract private capital flows. Younger (1992) noted that an increase in aid resulted in currency appreciation and Dutch disease in Ghana.[2]

Bandara (1995) showed that despite currency appreciation, foreign capital inflows to Sri Lanka caused some industries to contract while inducing others to expand. Using a computable general equilibrium (CGE) model, Vos (1998) stated that aid produced a strong Dutch disease effect in Pakistan. However, Nyoni (1998) reported that aid inflows together with increased openness resulted in currency depreciation, and this refutes the proposition that foreign aid caused the Dutch disease in Tanzania. Meanwhile, Torvik (2001) demonstrated that learning by doing can have different effects on the productivity growth in the traded and nontraded goods sector, and a foreign exchange gift can cause currency appreciation. Adam and Bevan (2003) cited the presence of the Dutch disease effect of aid in their simulation study of Uganda.

Using the Salter (1959) model of two goods, Nkusu (2004) showed that currency appreciation may not occur in the presence of unemployment. Subsequently, Choi and Choi (2007) considered infrastructure aid under urban unemployment, and delineated sufficient conditions under which infrastructure aid may lead to a Dutch disease effect. It is noteworthy that these empirical and simulation studies suggest that (i) development aid may not necessarily cause currency appreciation, and (ii) aid may not

---

[1] There are now some empirical studies of the Dutch disease. Spatafora and Warner (1999) show the presence of a weak Dutch disease from a resource boom, while Stijns (2003) demonstrates a strong Dutch disease effect. Specifically, Stijns shows that a 1% increase in energy exports results in an 8% decline in manufacturing exports. Benjamin et al. (1989) constructed a CGE model of Cameroon and reported that a boom in the oil sector is likely to hurt the agricultural sector but benefit the manufacturing sector.

[2] The sub-Saharan countries in which aid programs were not successful include Cameroon, Ethiopia, Ghana, Mozambique, Nigeria, and Zaire, among others.

necessarily cause deindustrialization of the export sector. Moreover, aid-induced Dutch disease does not imply that aid hurts the recipients.

The objective of this chapter is to investigate the effects of infrastructure aid upon a developing country by extending the Heckscher–Ohlin model to a 3×2 case with two traded goods and a nontraded good.[3] Several significant results emerged from the analysis. In particular, for a recipient country, infrastructure aid to either the export or import sector necessarily raises national income and consumer welfare, whereas the same aid to the nontraded good sector does not affect national income but raises consumer welfare. Infrastructure aid may lead to a Dutch disease effect for the recipient country via its three effects on industrial outputs: the initial factor-saving effect, factor-substitution effect and nontraded good effect. In addition, the effects of infrastructure aid on factor prices, the price of the nontraded good, and the foreign exchange rate are systematically analyzed.

2. Assumptions and the basic properties of the model

To investigate the effects of foreign infrastructure aid for a recipient country, we extend the Heckscher–Ohlin (HO, henceforth) model to a 3×2 case with a nontraded good, and employy the following assumptions.

ASSUMPTIONS.

(1) The aid recipient is a small developing country, abundant in labor.
(2) Two primary factors, capital (K) and labor (L), are used to produce two traded goods, an exportable good (Y_1) and an importable good (Y_2), and a nontraded good (Y_N). The developing country exports the labor-intensive good and imports the capital-intensive good, and the factor intensity ranking, $k_2 > k_N > k_1$, is not altered by infrastructure aid, where $k_i = K_i/L_i$ is the capital–labor ratio in sector $i = 1, 2, N$.
(3) Factors are fully employed and mobile among sectors.
(4) Perfect competition prevails in both the product and factor markets.
(5) Infrastructure capital S_j is a sector-specific public good and cannot be appropriated by individual firms.

---

[3] The HO model assumes perfect competition and no currency manipulation. Many LDCs often are "large" exporters of a few products and aid may affect their terms of trade. Ebrahim-zadeh (2003) noted that a coffee boom in Columbia caused currency appreciation and deindustrialization of the traditional export sectors. Also, the domestic price of the nontraded good may rise or fall, depending on its factor intensity and the response of factor prices. Prati *et al.* (2003) analyzed the effect of sterilization in offsetting the adverse effect of currency appreciation and the ensuing deindustrialization.

2.1. Short-term effect of infrastructure investment on production costs

Developing countries lack infrastructure such as highways and clean water. The absence of modern infrastructure renders existing capital equipment inefficient or expedites its wear and tear. Good infrastructure also can make it possible for workers to maintain their health, and work more efficiently.

Let the input–output coefficient be

$$a_{ij} = a_{ij}(w, r, S_j), \quad i = L, K, \quad j = 1, 2, N,$$

where w, r, and S_j, respectively denote the real wage rate, the real rental rate, and the infrastructure capital in the jth sector. The unit cost of the jth good is denoted by

$$a_{Lj}(w, r, S_j)w + a_{Kj}(w, r, S_j)r = g_j(w, r, S_j), \quad j = 1, 2, N.$$

The unit-profit of the jth good is

$$\pi_j = p_j - g_j(w, r, S_j), \quad j = 1, 2, N.$$

In the short run, factor prices are fixed and do not respond to infrastructure investment. However, the infrastructure investment, whether it saves labor or capital, lowers unit cost in the targeted sector,

$$\frac{\partial g_j}{\partial S_j} = \frac{\partial a_{Lj}}{\partial S_j} w + \frac{\partial a_{Kj}}{\partial S_j} r < 0,$$

and increases the unit-profit (π_i) of the sector,

$$\frac{\partial \pi_j}{\partial S_j} = -\frac{\partial g_j(w, r, S_j)}{\partial S_j} > 0, \quad j = 1, 2, N.$$

Thus, infrastructure aid invested in a sector makes it more competitive, causing the sector to expand in the short run.

2.2. Factor prices, price of the nontraded good, and the exchange rate

In some developing countries, lack of infrastructure makes it difficult for capital and labor inputs to realize their productivity potentials. Consequently, their export and import sectors have absolute disadvantages over their counterparts in developed economies. Whereas they grudgingly export primary products, their wage–rent ratio is lower than that in developed economies. In this situation, infrastructure aid initially will improve the productivity and lower the production cost of the targeted sector. Infrastructure aid to the export or the import sector eventually will cause a realignment of factor prices, which in turn will have a secondary impact on outputs in all three sectors.

We first consider how targeted infrastructure aid affects factor prices and the price of the nontraded good. Since product and factor markets are competitive, in the long run average cost pricing prevails

$$a_{Lj}w + a_{Kj}r = p_j, \quad j = 1, 2, N. \tag{1}$$

Totally differentiating (1), we obtain

$$\theta_{Lj}\hat{w} + \theta_{Kj}\hat{r} = \hat{p}_j - (\theta_{Lj}\hat{a}_{Lj} + \theta_{Kj}\hat{a}_{Kj}), \quad j = 1, 2, N, \tag{2}$$

where a circumflex (^) denotes the rate of change.

Recall that the input–output coefficients are functions of the wage–rental ratio ($\omega = w/r$) and the infrastructure investment, and hence can be written as $a_{ij} = a_{ij}(\omega, S_j)$. Totally differentiating $a_{ij} = a_{ij}(\omega, S_j)$, we get

$$\hat{a}_{ij} = b_{ij}^* - \delta_{ij}^* = \varepsilon_{ij\omega}\hat{\omega} - \varepsilon_{ijs}\hat{S}_j, \quad j = 1, 2, N, \tag{3}$$

where $b_{ij}^* = (1/a_{ij})(\partial a_{ij}/\partial\omega)\mathrm{d}\omega$ is the change in input–output coefficient due to a change in wage–rental ratio, $\delta_{ij}^* = -(1/a_{ij})(\partial a_{ij}/\partial S_j)\mathrm{d}S_j$ is the change in a_{ij} due to infrastructure aid into the jth sector, and ε_{ijk} the elasticity of a_{ij} with respect to variable k ($i = L, K; j = 1, 2, N; k = \omega, S_j$).[4]

Define the elasticity of factor substitution of the jth sector as

$$\sigma_j = \frac{\hat{a}_{Kj} - \hat{a}_{Lj}}{\hat{w} - \hat{r}}, \quad j = 1, 2, N, \tag{4}$$

where each σ_j is positive.

Cost minimization implies

$$wa_{Lj}b_{Lj}^* + ra_{Kj}b_{Kj}^* = 0. \tag{5}$$

Dividing (5) by p_j, we obtain

$$\theta_{Lj}b_{Lj}^* + \theta_{Kj}b_{Kj}^* = 0, \quad j = 1, 2, N. \tag{6}$$

Utilizing (3)–(6), we get

$$\hat{a}_{Lj} = -\theta_{Kj}\sigma_j(\hat{w} - \hat{r}) - \delta_{Lj}^*, \quad \hat{a}_{Kj} = \theta_{Lj}\sigma_j(\hat{w} - \hat{r}) - \delta_{Kj}^*, \tag{7}$$

where θ_{ij} is the share of the ith factor in the total value of the jth good ($i = L, K$ and $j = 1, 2, N$). Note that $\theta_{Lj} + \theta_{Kj} = 1$ ($j = 1, 2, N$). Let $t_j = \theta_{Lj}\varepsilon_{LjS} + \theta_{Kj}\varepsilon_{KjS}$. Then using (7), (2) can be reexpressed as

$$\theta_{Lj}\hat{w}_j + \theta_{Kj}\hat{r} = \hat{p}_j + (\theta_{Lj}\delta_{Lj}^* + \theta_{Kj}\delta_{Kj}^*) = \hat{p}_j + T_j^*, \tag{8}$$

where $T_j^* = t_j\hat{S}_j = \theta_{Lj}\delta_{Lj}^* + \theta_{Kj}\delta_{Kj}^* = (\theta_{Lj}\varepsilon_{LjS} + \theta_{Kj}\varepsilon_{KjS})\hat{S}_j$ represents the decline in unit cost of good j directly resulting from the increase in infrastructure aid to that sector, but not through the induced change in the wage–rent ratio.

---

[4] A similar mathematical procedure has been used by Batra (1973) and Choi and Yu (1987) in their analysis of the effects of technical progress.

The developing country is a price taker of traded goods in the world market. Thus, $\hat{p}_1 = \hat{p}_2 = 0$. Then, (8) can be rewritten as

$$\theta_{L1}\hat{w} + \theta_{K1}\hat{r} = T_1^*, \quad \theta_{L2}\hat{w} + \theta_{K2}\hat{r} = T_2^*, \quad \text{and}$$
$$\theta_{LN}\hat{w} + \theta_{KN}\hat{r} = \hat{p}_N + T_N^*. \tag{9}$$

In the three equations in (9), there are three unknowns ($\hat{w}, \hat{r}$, and $\hat{p}_N$) and three parameters ($T_j^*, \; j = 1, 2, N$). The first two equations of (9) completely determine the rates of changes in factor prices, $\hat{w}$ and $\hat{r}$, which in turn determine the change in the price of the nontraded good, $\hat{p}_N$, in the third equation.

$$\hat{w} = \frac{\theta_{K2}T_1^* - \theta_{K1}T_2^*}{|\theta|}, \quad \hat{r} = \frac{-\theta_{L2}T_1^* + \theta_{L1}T_2^*}{|\theta|}, \quad \text{and}$$
$$\hat{p}_N = \frac{-(\theta_{L2}\theta_{KN} - \theta_{LN}\theta_{K2})T_1^* + (\theta_{L1}\theta_{KN} - \theta_{LN}\theta_{K1})T_2^* - |\theta|T_N^*}{|\theta|}, \tag{10}$$

where $|\theta| = \theta_{L1}\theta_{K2} - \theta_{L2}\theta_{K1} = wrL_1L_2(k_2 - k_1)/p_1p_2Y_1Y_2$ is the determinant of θ_{ij} matrix, and it is positive since $k_2 > k_1$ by Assumption 2.[5]

2.3. Infrastructure aid to the export sector

When infrastructure aid is invested in the export sector, $T_1^* > T_2^* = T_N^* = 0$. Thus, from (10), we obtain

$$\frac{\hat{w}}{T_1^*} = \frac{\theta_{K2}}{|\theta|} > 0, \quad \frac{\hat{r}}{T_1^*} = -\frac{\theta_{L2}}{|\theta|} < 0, \quad \frac{\hat{p}_N}{T_1^*} = \frac{\theta_{L2}\theta_{LN}(r/w)(k_2 - k_N)}{|\theta|} > 0. \tag{11}$$

That is, infrastructure aid invested in the export sector (which is the most labor-intensive sector) raises the economy's wage rate and the price of the nontraded good, but decreases the rental rate. Even though world prices of traded goods are held constant, infrastructure aid to the export sector decreases its unit production cost, causing a Stolper–Samuelson-like effect, similar to that of an increase in the price of the exportable good, thereby raising the return to labor and lowering the rental rate. Whereas the terms of trade between the two traded goods are fixed at the world prices, the Corden and Neary (1982) real exchange rate p_N/p_2 necessarily appreciates since $(\hat{p}_N/T_1^*) - (\hat{p}_2/T_1^*) = (\hat{p}_N/T_1^*) > 0$.

---

[5] Note that in the presence of a nontraded good, $|\theta| \neq \theta_{L1} - \theta_{L2} \neq \theta_{K2} - \theta_{K1}$.

2.4. Infrastructure aid to the import sector

With infrastructure investment in the import sector, $T_2^* > T_1^* = T_N^* = 0$. From (10), we get

$$\frac{\hat{w}}{T_2^*} = -\frac{\theta_{K1}}{|\theta|} < 0, \qquad \frac{\hat{r}}{T_2^*} = \frac{\theta_{L1}}{|\theta|} > 0, \qquad \frac{\hat{p}_N}{T_2^*} = \frac{\theta_{L1}\theta_{LN}(r/w)(k_N - k_1)}{|\theta|} > 0.$$

$$(12)$$

Any infrastructure aid to the import sector decreases the unit cost of the capital-intensive good, and again gives rise to a Stolper–Samuelson-like effect, lowering the wage rate, and raising the rental rate. Moreover, it increases the price of the nontraded good (since $k_N > k_1$ by Assumption 2), and causes an appreciation of the Corden and Neary (1982) real exchange rate (p_N/p_2) because $(\hat{p}_N/T_2^*) - (\hat{p}_2/T_2^*) = (\hat{p}_N/T_2^*) > 0$.

2.5. Infrastructure aid to the nontraded good sector

When infrastructure aid is invested in the nontraded good sector, $T_N^* > T_1^* = T_2^* = 0$, and in this case, it only improves productivity of that sector without causing a realignment of factor prices. From (10), we obtain:

$$\frac{\hat{w}}{T_N^*} = \frac{\hat{r}}{T_N^*} = 0, \qquad \frac{\hat{p}_N^*}{T_N^*} = -1 < 0.$$

$$(13)$$

That is, infrastructure aid to the nontraded good sector, while not affecting the domestic factor prices, lowers the price of the nontraded good and causes a depreciation of the Corden and Neary (1982) real exchange rate.

We now summarize the *factor price effects* of infrastructure aid.

PROPOSITION 1. *(1) Infrastructure aid to the export sector raises the economy's wage rate and the price of the nontraded good, lowers the rental rate, and causes an appreciation of the Corden and Neary (1982) real exchange rate.*

(2) Any infrastructure aid to the import sector lowers the economy's wage rate, raises the economy's rental rate and the price of the nontraded good, and causes an appreciation of the Corden and Neary real exchange rate.

(3) Any infrastructure aid to the nontraded good sector does not affect the factor prices of the economy, while it lowers the price of the nontraded good and decreases the Corden and Neary real exchange rate.

3. Infrastructure aid, welfare, and deindustrialization

3.1. Infrastructure aid and national income

In the previous section, we investigated how infrastructure aid affects the relative prices in both the product and factor markets. We now consider how these relative price changes affect national income and consumer welfare. In competitive markets, producer revenue $R = p_1 Y_1 + p_2 Y_2 + p_N Y_N$ is distributed to factor owners, either as labor or rental income. Thus, national income is $I = wL + rK$, which yields

$$\hat{I} = \frac{\hat{w}wL + \hat{r}rK}{I}. \tag{14}$$

Substituting the expressions for the effects of the infrastructure aid on factor prices in (11)–(13), we derive

$$\frac{\hat{I}}{T_1^*} = \frac{\hat{w}wL + \hat{r}rK}{T_1^* I} = \frac{wrLL_2(k_2 - k)}{I|\theta|p_2 Y_2} > 0,$$

$$\frac{\hat{I}}{T_2^*} = \frac{\hat{w}wL + \hat{r}rK}{T_2^* I} = \frac{wrLL_1(k - k_1)}{I|\theta|p_1 Y_1} > 0, \quad \text{and}$$

$$\frac{\hat{I}}{T_N^*} = \frac{\hat{w}wL + \hat{r}rK}{T_N^* I} = 0, \tag{15}$$

where $k = K/L$ is the overall capital–labor ratio of the economy. Since the exportable (importable) good is most (least) capital-intensive, it follows that $k_1 < k < k_2$,[6] and hence $\hat{I}/T_1^* > 0$ and $\hat{I}/T_2^* > 0$. Thus, infrastructure aid to either of the two traded good sectors increases national income. However, infrastructure aid to the nontraded good sector does not change the factor prices, and hence it has no effect on national income.[7] Thus, consumers would be better off as the price of the nontraded good declines without affecting the prices of traded goods and real national income.

To investigate the welfare effects of infrastructure aid, consider the indirect utility:

$$V(p_1, p_2, p_N, I) = U\big(X_1(p_1, p_2, p_N, I), X_2(p_1, p_2, p_N, I), X_2(p_1, p_2, p_N, I)\big). \tag{16}$$

Recall that the aid recipient is a small country. Accordingly, infrastructure aid does not affect the world prices, p_1 and p_2, but the

---

[6] Using the full-employment conditions $L_1 + L_2 + L_N = L$ and $K_1 + K_2 + K_N = K$, we obtain $L_1(k_1 - k_2) + L_N(k_N - k_2) = L(k - k_2)$. Since $k_1 < k_2$ and $k_N < k_2$, it follows that $k < k_2$. Using the same procedure, it can be easily shown that $k_1 < k$.

[7] The total value of outputs is $R = p_1 y_1 + p_2 y_2 + p_N y_N = wL + rK$, which is distributed to factor owners. Since the infrastructure aid to the nontraded goods sector does not affect factor prices or endowments, national income remains unchanged.

price of the nontraded good p_N may be altered. Moreover, infrastructure aid will affect national income. Consumer welfare will be affected by changes in both prices and income. Let $s_i = p_i Y_i / I$ be the share of industry i or the fraction of national income produced by that sector, $s_1 + s_2 + s_N = 1$. When the prices of traded goods are held constant, we have

$$\hat{I} = s_1 \hat{Y}_1 + s_2 \hat{Y}_2 + s_N (\hat{p}_N + \hat{Y}_N). \tag{17}$$

Infrastructure aid may have direct and indirect effects on outputs. In the short run when the factor prices are held constant, infrastructure aid to a sector makes the industry more efficient and uses less resources. Thus, the saved resources then must be reallocated between the two traded sectors, which will affect them differentially. These may be called the *initial output effects*. Since world prices are held constant, the increased productivity in one sector results in positive profits immediately. These must necessarily disappear in the long run through a realignment of factor prices, which in turn changes the output in each sector. These may be called the *factor-substitution effects*. Finally, infrastructure aid also affects the cost of the nontraded good and income, which in turn affects the demand and hence production of the nontraded good. Thus, the output effects of the traded goods are further contingent on how much of each input they have to release to accommodate the expansion (or contraction) of the nontraded good sector.

The welfare effects of infrastructure aid to either the export or import sector on consumer welfare can be obtained by differentiating (16) with respect to S_j and holding the prices of traded goods constant. Using Roy's identity, $\partial V / \partial p_j = -(\partial V / \partial I) X_j$ and (17) we get

$$\frac{dV}{dS_j} = \left(\frac{\partial V}{\partial p_N} \frac{\partial p_N}{\partial S_j} + \frac{\partial V}{\partial I} \frac{\partial I}{\partial S_j} \right) = V_I \left(-X_N \frac{\partial p_N}{\partial S_j} + \frac{\partial I}{\partial S_j} \right)$$

$$= \frac{IV_I}{S_j \hat{S}_j} \left(-s_N \hat{p}_N + \hat{I} \right) = \frac{IV_I}{S_j \hat{S}_j} \left(s_1 \hat{Y}_1 + s_2 \hat{Y}_2 + s_N \hat{Y}_N \right) > 0, \tag{18}$$

where

$$\hat{I}^o = s_1 \hat{Y}_1 + s_2 \hat{Y}_2 + s_N \hat{Y}_N > 0 \tag{19}$$

is the percentage change in income evaluated at pre-aid prices. Compared to $\hat{I}$ in (17), $\hat{I}^o$ ignores the effect of change in the price of the nontraded good on income.[8] Of course, outputs of all industries, and hence income, will be affected as factor prices are realigned. A small amount of infrastructure aid which does not affect domestic factor prices necessarily increases national income by improving the productivity of other inputs.

---

[8] Note that $\hat{I}^o$ is not the level of national income when factor prices are held constant. If factor prices were held constant, infrastructure aid to the export sector will only raise Y_1, without affecting the outputs in other industries.

When outputs are evaluated at pre-aid prices, foreign aid necessarily raises national income, at first by enhancing productivity of the sector in which the aid is invested even if resources are not reallocated among sectors.[9] Subsequent reallocation of capital and labor inputs among the three sectors will further increase national income.[10] Thus, infrastructure aid necessarily raises national income evaluated at pre-aid prices. No developing country would consider accepting foreign aid if it would lower national income at pre-aid prices.

There will be a secondary effect induced by a change in the price of the nontraded good, which will partly offset or reinforce the positive income effect. Thus, the percentage change in national income in (17) overstates (understates) the change in real income, due to the subsequent rise (fall) in the price of the nontraded good. Equation (18) indicates that consumer welfare and national income evaluated at pre-aid prices move in the same direction when foreign aid is invested in either of the two traded sectors.

Next, consider the percentage change in national income resulting from infrastructure aid to the nontraded goods sector. Recall that aid to the nontraded good sector merely lowers the price of the nontraded good without affecting consumer income, $dI = Ldw_1 + Kdr = 0$. Differentiating (16) with respect to S_N and using Roy's identity, $\partial V/\partial p_N = -(\partial V/\partial I)X_N$, we get

$$\frac{\partial V}{\partial p_N}\frac{\partial p_N}{\partial S_N} + \frac{\partial V}{\partial I}\frac{\partial I}{\partial S_N} = V_I\left(-X_N\frac{\partial p_N}{\partial S_N} + \frac{\partial I}{\partial S_N}\right) = V_I\left(-X_N\frac{\partial p_N}{\partial S_N}\right) > 0.$$

(20)

Thus, infrastructure aid to the nontraded good sector unambiguously raises consumer welfare. Thus, we can state the following proposition:

PROPOSITION 2. *(i) Infrastructure aid to the export or import sector necessarily raises national income, $I = p_1 Y_1 + p_2 Y_2 + p_N Y_N$, whereas infrastructure aid to the nontraded good sector has no effect on national income. (ii) Despite their differential impacts on the nontraded goods price, infrastructure aid to the export or import sector raises national income at pre-aid prices, $\hat{I}^o = s_1 \hat{Y}_1 + s_2 \hat{Y}_2 + s_N \hat{Y}_N > 0$, and increases consumer welfare. (iii) Infrastructure aid to the nontraded sector lowers its price without affecting national income, and hence raises consumer welfare.*

Noteworthy is that the price of the nontraded good rises (remains unaffected) when the infrastructure aid is invested in the export or import (the nontraded good) sector, but regardless of the change in the nontraded

---

[9] Otherwise, no firms would be interested in attracting the infrastructure aid to that sector.

[10] Otherwise, national income could be maintained by not allowing resource reallocation among industries. However, reallocating resources among the three sectors in response to the induced change in factor prices further raises income.

goods price, *infrastructure aid necessarily raises consumer welfare of the recipient country.*

4. Sectoral outputs and deindustrialization

Having examined the relative price and welfare effects, we now are in a position to analyze the output effect of infrastructure aid. The output effect has three components. First, infrastructure aid to any sector results in factor savings. The targeted industry uses fewer resources as $a_{ij}(\omega, S_j)$ declines, and releases resources to be used in all three industries. Such factor savings will have the usual Rybczynski-type effect on the three industries, and the resulting output effects are to be termed the *initial factor-saving effects.*

In the short run, each industry necessarily earns positive profit, which must disappear in the long run through a change in factor prices and substitution between competing factors. The resulting changes in outputs are called the *secondary factor-substitution effects.* Infrastructure aid necessarily causes changes in the price of the nontraded good as well as national income, and hence affects the consumption of the nontraded good. The output effects on traded goods through the change in the demand for the nontraded good are called the *tertiary nontraded good effects*, which are no longer present in the absence of the nontraded good.

Bearing these three effects in mind, we now consider the output effects of infrastructure aid. Optimal output of the ith sector can be written as $Y_j(p_1, p_2, L, K, w, r, S_j)$ for $j = 1, 2, N$. The employment conditions of labor and capital markets, $L_1 + L_2 + L_N = L$ and $K_1 + K_2 + K_N = K$, can be rewritten respectively as

$$a_{L1} Y_1 + a_{L2} Y_2 + a_{LN} Y_N = L \quad \text{and}$$
$$a_{K1} Y_1 + a_{K2} Y_2 + a_{KN} Y_N = K. \tag{21}$$

Differentiating (21), we obtain

$$\lambda_{L1} \hat{Y}_1 + \lambda_{L2} \hat{Y}_2 = \hat{L} - \left(\lambda_{L1}\hat{a}_{L1} + \lambda_{L2}\hat{a}_{L2} + \lambda_{LN}\hat{a}_{LN} + \lambda_{LN}\hat{Y}_N\right) \quad \text{and}$$
$$\lambda_{K1} \hat{Y}_1 + \lambda_{K2} \hat{Y}_2 = \hat{K} - \left(\lambda_{K1}\hat{a}_{K1} + \lambda_{K2}\hat{a}_{K2} + \lambda_{KN}\hat{a}_{KN} + \lambda_{KN}\hat{Y}_N\right),$$

$$\tag{22}$$

where λ_{ij} ($i = L, K; j = 1, 2, N$) is the proportion of the ith factor employed in the jth sector. Setting $\hat{L} = \hat{K} = 0$, and substituting (7) into (22), we obtain

$$\lambda_{L1} \hat{Y}_1 + \lambda_{L2} \hat{Y}_2 = \beta_L(\hat{w} - \hat{r}) + T_L^* - \lambda_{LN}\hat{Y}_N \quad \text{and}$$
$$\lambda_{K1} \hat{Y}_1 + \lambda_{K2} \hat{Y}_2 = -\beta_K(\hat{w} - \hat{r}) + T_K^* - \lambda_{KN}\hat{Y}_N, \tag{23}$$

where

$$\beta_L = \lambda_{L1}\theta_{K1}\sigma_1 + \lambda_{L2}\theta_{K2}\sigma_2 + \lambda_{LN}\theta_{KN}\sigma_N,$$
$$\beta_K = \lambda_{K1}\theta_{L1}\sigma_1 + \lambda_{K2}\theta_{L2}\sigma_2 + \lambda_{KN}\theta_{LN}\sigma_N,$$
$$T_L^* = \lambda_{L1}\delta_{L1}^* + \lambda_{L2}\delta_{L2}^* + \lambda_{LN}\delta_{LN}^*, \quad \text{and}$$
$$T_K^* = \lambda_{K1}\delta_{K1}^* + \lambda_{K2}\delta_{K2}^* + \lambda_{KN}\delta_{KN}^*.$$

Note that β_i $(i = L, K)$ represents the change in the amount of the ith factor per unit of output that occurs in the three sectors due to the change in wage–rental ratio (w/r) and T_i^* $(i = L, K)$ reduction in the requirement of the ith factor as the result of the infrastructure investment in the three sectors.

From (9), we obtain $\hat{w} - \hat{r} = (T_1^* - T_2^*)/|\theta|$, and substituting this into (23) we get

$$\lambda_{L1}\hat{Y}_1 + \lambda_{L2}\hat{Y}_2 = \frac{\beta_L(T_1^* - T_2^*)}{|\theta|} + T_L^* - \lambda_{LN}\hat{Y}_N \quad \text{and}$$

$$\lambda_{K1}\hat{Y}_1 + \lambda_{K2}\hat{Y}_2 = -\frac{\beta_K(T_1^* - T_2^*)}{|\theta|} + T_K^* - \lambda_{KN}\hat{Y}_N. \tag{24}$$

Solving (24) for $\hat{Y}_1$ and $\hat{Y}_2$, we get

$$\hat{Y}_1 = \frac{(\lambda_{K2}T_L^* - \lambda_{L2}T_K^*)}{|\lambda|} + \frac{(\lambda_{K2}\beta_L + \lambda_{L2}\beta_K)T_1^* - (\lambda_{K2}\beta_L + \lambda_{L2}\beta_K)T_2^*}{|\lambda||\theta|}$$
$$- \frac{(\lambda_{K2}\lambda_{LN} - \lambda_{L2}\lambda_{KN})\hat{Y}_N}{|\lambda|} \quad \text{and}$$

$$\hat{Y}_2 = \frac{(\lambda_{L1}T_K^* - \lambda_{K1}T_L^*)}{|\lambda|} - \frac{(\lambda_{L1}\beta_K + \lambda_{K1}\beta_L)T_1^* + (\lambda_{L1}\beta_K + \lambda_{K1}\beta_L)T_2^*}{|\lambda||\theta|}$$
$$- \frac{(\lambda_{L1}\lambda_{KN} - \lambda_{K1}\lambda_{LN})\hat{Y}_N}{|\lambda|}, \tag{25}$$

where $|\lambda| = \lambda_{L1}\lambda_{K2} - \lambda_{K1}\lambda_{L2} = (L_1L_2/LK)(k_2 - k_1)$ is the determinant of λ_{ij} matrix and it is positive since $k_2 > k_1$ by Assumption 2.

In the two equations in (25), the first terms reflect the *initial factor-saving effects* resulting from the foreign aid. The sign of these terms depends on the nature of the relative factor-saving effects of foreign aid, i.e., whether they are neutral, labor-saving, or capital-saving.

The second terms represent the *secondary factor-substitution effects* caused by the induced changes in factor prices on outputs. Finally, as shown in Proposition 2, foreign aid in either of the traded sectors necessarily affects the price of the nontraded good and/or national income, which in turn affects consumption and production of the nontraded good. These *tertiary nontraded good effects* operate differentially on three industries. The induced change in the nontraded good either takes resources from or releases to the traded sectors, and has a Rybczynki-type effect, which is measured by the third terms.

4.1. Infrastructure aid to the export sector and deindustrialization

In the presence of infrastructure aid to the exportable sector, $\delta_{i1}^* > \delta_{i2}^* = \delta_{iN}^* = 0$ $(i = L,\ K)$ and $T_1^* = \theta_{L1}\delta_{L1}^* + \theta_{K1}\delta_{K1}^* > T_2^* = T_N^* = 0$. Further, $T_L^* = \lambda_{L1}\delta_{L1}^*$ and $T_K^* = \lambda_{K1}\delta_{K1}^*$. Thus, the two equations in (24) become

$$\hat{Y}_1 = \frac{\lambda_{L1}\lambda_{L2}\delta_{L1}^*(L/K)\big(k_2 - k_1(\delta_{K1}^*/\delta_{L1}^*)\big)}{|\lambda|}$$
$$+ \frac{(\lambda_{K2}\beta_L + \lambda_{L2}\beta_K)(\theta_{L1}\delta_{L1}^* + \theta_{K1}\delta_{K1}^*)}{|\lambda||\theta|}$$
$$- \frac{(\lambda_{L2}\lambda_{LN})(L/K)(k_2 - k_N)\hat{Y}_N}{|\lambda|} \quad \text{and} \tag{26}$$

$$\hat{Y}_2 = \frac{\lambda_{L1}\lambda_{K1}\big((\delta_{K1}^*/\delta_{L1}^*) - 1\big)}{|\lambda|} - \frac{(\lambda_{L1}\beta_K + \lambda_{K1}\beta_L)(\theta_{L1}\delta_{L1}^* + \theta_{K1}\delta_{K1}^*)}{|\lambda||\theta|}$$
$$- \frac{\lambda_{L1}\lambda_{LN}(k_N - k_1)\hat{Y}_N}{|\lambda|}. \tag{27}$$

Equations in (26) and (27) show that the effects of infrastructure aid to the export sector on the outputs of the two traded goods include three components. In view of (23) and (24), it is not difficult to discern that the first, second, and third terms in the right-hand side of equations in (26) and (27) represent the initial factor-saving effects, the secondary factor-substitution effects, and the tertiary nontraded good effects of the infrastructure aid.

The first terms in the right-hand side of equations in (26) and (27) represent the effects of the infrastructure aid to the export sector on the outputs of the traded goods via the reduction in labor and capital requirement per unit of the exportable good.

To be specific, (a) in the first component in (26), $(1/|\lambda|)\lambda_{L1}\lambda_{L2}\delta_{L1}^*(L/K)$ $\big(k_2 - k_1(\delta_{K1}^*/\delta_{L1}^*)\big)$, the bracketed term, $k_2 - k_1(\delta_{K1}^*/\delta_{L1}^*)$, indicates the difference in factor intensities of the two traded goods after the infrastructure aid to the export sector. Obviously, this resource saving effect is positive if the importable good remains capital-intensive relative to the exportable good after the infrastructure aid (i.e., $k_2 > k_1(\delta_{K1}^*/\delta_{L1}^*)$).

At this juncture, three types of factor-saving infrastructure aid need to be differentiated: (i) If the infrastructure aid is neutral in factor-saving $\big(\delta_{K1}^* = \delta_{L1}^*\big)$, the first term, $(1/|\lambda|)\lambda_{L1}\lambda_{L2}\delta_{L1}^*(L/K)\big(k_2 - k_1(\delta_{K1}^*/\delta_{L1}^*)\big)$, is reduced to δ_{L1}^*; (ii) If the infrastructure aid is the labor-saving type $\big(\delta_{K1}^* < \delta_{L1}^*\big)$, the first term is greater than δ_{L1}^* and hence the secondary effect is strengthened vis-à-vis the neutral case; (iii) If the infrastructure aid is capital-saving type $\big(\delta_{K1}^* > \delta_{L1}^*\big)$, the first term is less than δ_{L1}^* and hence the initial factor-saving effect is weakened vis-à-vis the neutral case.

Next, in the first term of (27), $(1/|\lambda|)\lambda_{L1}\lambda_{K1}((\delta_{K1}^*/\delta_{L1}^*)-1)$, $(\delta_{K1}^*/\delta_{L1}^*)$ determines the sign of the initial factor-saving effect on the output of the importable: (i) In the case of neutral factor-saving infrastructure aid $(\delta_{K1}^* = \delta_{L1}^*)$, this initial factor-saving effect on the output of the importable good vanishes; (ii) If the infrastructure aid is the labor-saving type $(\delta_{K1}^* < \delta_{L1}^*)$, the first term is negative, and the initial factor-saving effect tends to lower the output of the importable; (iii) If the infrastructure aid is the capital-saving type $(\delta_{K1}^* > \delta_{L1}^*)$, the first term is positive, and the secondary factor-saving effect tends to raise the output.

Meanwhile, (a) the second term, $(1/|\lambda||\theta|)(\lambda_{K2}\beta_L + \lambda_{L2}\beta_K)(\theta_{L1}\delta_{L1}^* + \theta_{K1}\delta_{K1}^*)$, in (26) represents the output effect on the exportable good via the factor-substitution, and it is positive since $|\lambda|$ and $|\theta|$ are both positive. (b) Similarly, the second term in (27), $-(1/|\lambda||\theta|)(\lambda_{L1}\beta_K + \lambda_{K1}\beta_L)(\theta_{L1}\delta_{L1}^* + \theta_{K1}\delta_{K1}^*)$ denotes the output effect on the importable good via the factor-substitution, and it is negative since $|\lambda|$ and $|\theta|$ are both positive.

Infrastructure aid changes the output of the nontraded good, and hence draws (releases) resources from (to) the export and import sectors. This tertiary nontraded good effects are captured in the third terms in the right of (26) and (27). Let $I = p_1 Y_1 + p_2 Y_2 + p_N Y_N$ denote national income, and $X_N(p_1, p_2, p_N, I) = X_N(p_1, p_2, p_N, p_1 Y_1 + p_2 Y_2 + p_N Y_N)$ the demand for the nontraded good. For the nontraded good, $X_N = Y_N$. As in Komiya (1967), the output of the nontraded good is determined by its demand,

$$\hat{Y}_N = \hat{X}_N = (\hat{X}_N/\hat{p}_N)\hat{p}_N + (\hat{X}_N/\hat{I})\hat{I}. \tag{28}$$

If the nontraded good is a normal good, then $\hat{X}_N/\hat{I} > 0$ and $\hat{X}_N/\hat{p}_N < 0$. It has been shown in (11) that the infrastructure aid to the export sector changes factor prices and raises the unit cost of the nontraded good, i.e., $\hat{p}_N/T_1^* = \theta_{L2}\theta_{LN}(r/w)(k_2 - k_N)/|\theta| > 0$. Thus, the price effect of infrastructure aid on the output of the nontraded good is negative, $(\hat{X}_N/\hat{p}_N)\hat{p}_N < 0$. Further, in (15), it has been shown that $\hat{I}/\hat{T}_1^* > 0$. Therefore, the income effect of infrastructure aid to the output of the nontraded good is positive, $(\hat{X}_N/\hat{I})\hat{I} > 0$. The net effect of the infrastructure aid to the export sector on the demand and output of the nontraded good depends on the relative magnitudes of the price and income effects.

Specifically, $\hat{Y}_N = \hat{X}_N \gtrless 0$ if $(\hat{X}_N/\hat{I})\hat{I} \gtrless |(\hat{X}_N/\hat{p}_N)\hat{p}_N|$. Therefore, given $k_2 - k_N > 0$, the third term in (26), $-(1/|\lambda|)(\lambda_{L2}\lambda_{LN})(L/K)(k_2 - k_N)\hat{Y}_N\theta$, is negative (positive) if $\hat{Y}_N > (<)0$. That is, infrastructure aid to the export sector tends to lower (raise) the output of the exportable via the expansion (contraction) of the nontraded good sector.

Similarly, given $k_N > k_1$, the third term in (27), $-(1/|\lambda|)\lambda_{L1}\lambda_{LN}(k_N - k_1)\hat{Y}_N$, is negative (positive) if $\hat{Y}_N > (<)0$. That is, infrastructure aid to the export sector tends to lower (raise) the output of the importable if it results in an expansion (a contraction) of the nontraded good sector.

Noting that the Findlay-Grubert (1959) type of normal (ultra-biased) growth-output effect (derived from the 2×2 Heckscher–Ohlin model) stipulates that growth in one sector increases the output of the own sector and decreases that of the other sector, we expect that in the present model, the normal growth-output effect occurs if the infrastructure investment in the export sector increases the output of the exportable good and decreases that of the importable good. However, the previous analyses show that in the present 3×2 model, the net effects of infrastructure aid to the export sector on the outputs of the traded goods depend on the signs and the relative magnitudes of the three component effects.

To be specific, if $\hat{Y}_N \leq 0$, the sum of the three component effects in (26) is clearly positive, and the infrastructure aid to the export sector necessarily increases the output of the sector – thus, the normal result holds. However, if $\hat{Y}_N > 0$ and hence the tertiary nontraded good effect is negative, the infrastructure aid to the export sector can increase or decrease the output of the sector. The Dutch disease or deindustrialization in the export sector occurs ($\hat{Y}_1 < 0$),[11] if

$$\hat{Y}_N > 0 \text{ and}$$
$$(1/|\theta|)(\lambda_{K2}\beta_L + \lambda_{L2}\beta_K)(\theta_{L1}\delta^*_{L1} + \theta_{K1}\delta^*_{K1})$$
$$+ \lambda_{L1}\lambda_{L2}\delta^*_{L1}(L/K)\big(k_2 - k_1(\delta^*_{K1}/\delta^*_{L1})\big) < \big|\lambda_{L2}\lambda_{LN}(L/K)(k_2 - k_N)\hat{Y}_N\big|.$$

As for the output effect on the importable, the secondary factor-substitution effect in (27) is negative, while the initial factor-saving effect and the tertiary nontrade good effects can have any sign. The factor-saving effect is zero if the infrastructure aid is neutral in factor saving $\big(\delta^*_{K1} = \delta^*_{L1}\big)$. However, the factor-saving effect is negative if the infrastructure aid is the labor-saving type $\big(\delta^*_{K1} < \delta^*_{L1}\big)$, and it is positive if infrastructure aid is the capital-saving type $\big(\delta^*_{K1} > \delta^*_{L1}\big)$. Since $k_N > k_1$, the tertiary nontraded good effect is negative (positive) if $\hat{Y}_N > (<)0$. Thus, the sum of the three component effects can have any sign. Sufficient conditions for the Dutch disease (or deindustrialization) to occur in the import sector are:

(i) infrastructure aid to the export sector is neutral in factor saving $\big(\delta^*_{K1} = \delta^*_{L1}\big)$ or the labor-saving type $\big(\delta^*_{K1} < \delta^*_{L1}\big)$, and the nontraded good sector expands ($\hat{Y}_N > 0$), or

(ii) infrastructure aid is the capital-saving type $\big(\delta^*_{K1} > \delta^*_{L1}\big)$, $\hat{Y}_N > 0$, and

$$(1/|\theta|)(\lambda_{L1}\beta_K + \lambda_{K1}\beta_L)(\theta_{L1}\delta^*_{L1} + \theta_{K1}\delta^*_{K1})$$
$$+ \lambda_{L1}\lambda_{LN}(k_N - k_1)\hat{Y}_N > \big|\lambda_{L1}\lambda_{K1}\big((\delta^*_{K1}/\delta^*_{L1}) - 1\big)\big| \text{ or}$$

---

[11] Here, the term "deindustrialization" is used to denote a contraction of any industry.

(iii) infrastructure aid is the labor-saving type $(\delta^*_{K1} < \delta^*_{L1})$, $\hat{Y}_N < 0$, and

$$(1/|\theta|)(\lambda_{L1}\beta_K + \lambda_{K1}\beta_L)(\theta_{L1}\delta^*_{L1} + \theta_{K1}\delta^*_{K1})$$
$$+ |\lambda_{L1}\lambda_{K1}((\delta^*_{K1}/\delta^*_{L1}) - 1)| > \lambda_{L1}\lambda_{LN}(k_N - k_1)\hat{Y}_N.$$

4.2. Infrastructure aid to the import sector and deindustrialization

In the presence of infrastructure investment in the import sector, $\delta^*_{i2} > \delta^*_{i1} = \delta^*_{iN} = 0\,(i = L, K)$ and $T^*_2 > T^*_1 = T^*_N = 0$. Furthermore, $T^*_L = \lambda_{L2}\delta^*_{L2}$ and $T^*_K = \lambda_{K2}\delta^*_{K2}$. Thus, the two equations in (25) can be written as

$$\hat{Y}_1 = \frac{(\lambda_{K2}\lambda_{L2}\delta^*_{L2} - \lambda_{L2}\lambda_{K2}\delta^*_{K2})}{|\lambda|} - \frac{(\lambda_{K2}\beta_L + \lambda_{L2}\beta_K)(\theta_{L2}\delta^*_{L2} + \theta_{K2}\delta^*_{K2})}{|\lambda||\theta|}$$
$$- \frac{(\lambda_{K2}\lambda_{LN} - \lambda_{L2}\lambda_{KN})\hat{Y}_N}{|\lambda|}$$
$$= \frac{\lambda_{K2}\lambda_{L2}\delta^*_{L2}(1 - (\delta^*_{K2}/\delta^*_{L2}))}{|\lambda|} - \frac{(\lambda_{K2}\beta_L + \lambda_{L2}\beta_K)(\theta_{L2}\delta^*_{L2} + \theta_{K2}\delta^*_{K2})}{|\lambda||\theta|}$$
$$- \frac{\lambda_{L2}\lambda_{LN}(k_2 - k_N)\hat{Y}_N}{|\lambda|} \quad \text{and} \tag{29}$$

$$\hat{Y}_2 = \frac{(\lambda_{L1}\lambda_{K2}\delta^*_{K2} - \lambda_{K1}\lambda_{L2}\delta^*_{L2})}{|\lambda|} + \frac{(\lambda_{L1}\beta_K + \lambda_{K1}\beta_L)(\theta_{L2}\delta^*_{L2} + \theta_{K2}\delta^*_{K2})}{|\lambda||\theta|}$$
$$- \frac{(\lambda_{L1}\lambda_{KN} - \lambda_{K1}\lambda_{LN})\hat{Y}_N}{|\lambda|}$$
$$= \frac{\lambda_{L1}\lambda_{L2}\delta^*_{L2}(L/K)(k_2(\delta^*_{K2}/\delta^*_{L2}) - k_1)}{|\lambda|}$$
$$+ \frac{(\lambda_{L1}\beta_K + \lambda_{K1}\beta_L)(\theta_{L2}\delta^*_{L2} + \theta_{K2}\delta^*_{K2})}{|\lambda||\theta|}$$
$$- \frac{\lambda_{L1}\lambda_{LN}(L/K)(k_N - k_1)\hat{Y}_N}{|\lambda|}. \tag{30}$$

As in the case of infrastructure aid to the export sector, the effect of infrastructure aid to the import sector on the output of each traded good has three components: the initial factor-saving effects, the secondary factor-substitution effects, and the tertiary nontraded good effects.

(a) The first term in (29), $(1/|\lambda|)\lambda_{K2}\lambda_{L2}\delta^*_{L2}(1 - (\delta^*_{K2}/\delta^*_{L2}))$, represents the factor-saving effect on the output of the exportable, and the sign of the term is determined by $\delta^*_{K2}/\delta^*_{L2}$. To be specific, (i) in the case of neutral factor-saving infrastructure aid $(\delta^*_{K2} = \delta^*_{L2})$, the factor-saving effect on the output of the exportable vanishes; (ii) if the infrastructure aid is the labor-saving type $(\delta_{K2}^* < \delta_{L2}^*)$, the first term is positive and the secondary effect tends to increase the output of the exportable; and (iii) if the infrastructure aid is the capital-saving type $(\delta_{K2}^* > \delta_{L2}^*)$, the first term is negative, which tends to decrease the output of the exportable.

(b) Similarly, the first term of (30), $(1/|\lambda|)\lambda_{L1}\lambda_{L2}\delta_{L2}^*(L/K)$ $(k_2(\delta_{K2}^*/\delta_{L2}^*) - k_1)$, represents the factor-saving effect on the output of the importable. Note that the term, $k_2(\delta_{K2}^*/\delta_{L2}^*) - k_1$, is positive for the importable good to remain capital-intensive relative to the exportable good after the infrastructure aid. Here again, three types of factor-saving infrastructure aid need to be differentiated: (i) If infrastructure aid is neutral in factor-saving $(\delta_{K2}^* = \delta_{L2}^*)$, the first term is reduced to $\delta_{L2}^* > 0$; (ii) If infrastructure aid is the labor-saving type $(\delta_{K2}^* < \delta_{L2}^*)$, the first term is less than δ_{L2}^* and hence, the initial factor-saving effect is weakened vis-à-vis the neutral case; (iii) If infrastructure aid is the capital-saving type $(\delta_{K2}^* > \delta_{L2}^*)$, the first term is greater than δ_{L2}^*, and the factor-saving effect is strengthened vis-à-vis the neutral case.

In view of (23) and (24), the second terms in the right-hand side of equations in (29) and (30) contain the secondary factor-substitution effects via the changes in the factor prices.

To be specific, (a) the second term in (29), $-(1/|\lambda||\theta|)(\lambda_{K2}\beta_L + \lambda_{L2}\beta_K)$ $(\theta_{L2}\delta_{L2}^* + \theta_{K2}\delta_{K2}^*)$, represents the secondary factor-substitution effect on the output of the exportable via the changes in factor prices, and it is negative. (b) Similarly, the second term in (30), $(1/|\lambda||\theta|)(\lambda_{L1}\beta_K + \lambda_{K1}\beta_L)$ $(\theta_{L2}\delta_{L2}^* + \theta_{K2}\delta_{K2}^*)$, denotes the secondary factor-substitution effect on the output of the importable via the changes in factor prices, and it is positive.

The third terms in the right-hand side of equations in (28) and (29) represent the effects of the infrastructure aid to the import sector on the outputs of the traded goods via the tertiary nontraded good effects. For a nontraded good, $Y_N = X_N$. Recall that the output of the nontraded good is determined by its demand and that $\hat{Y}_N = \hat{X}_N = (\hat{X}_N/\hat{p}_N)\hat{p}_N + (\hat{X}_N/\hat{I})\hat{I}$. In the absence of an inferior good, $\hat{X}_N/\hat{p}_N < 0$ and $\hat{X}_N/\hat{I} > 0$. It has been shown in (12) that the infrastructure aid to the import sector raises the supply price of the nontraded good by raising the unit cost of the nontraded good, $\hat{p}_N/T_2^* = \theta_{L1}\theta_{LN}(r/w)(k_N - k_1)/|\theta| > 0$ and hence $(\hat{X}_N/\hat{p}_N)\hat{p}_N < 0$. Further in (15), it has been demonstrated that $\hat{I}/\hat{T}_2^* > 0$. Thus, $(\hat{X}_N/\hat{I})\hat{I} > 0$. The net effect of the infrastructure aid to the import sector on the demand and output of the nontraded good depends on the relative magnitudes of the price and income effects. To be specific,

$$\hat{Y}_N = \hat{X}_N \underset{<}{\overset{>}{=}} 0 \quad \text{if } (\hat{X}_N/\hat{I})\hat{I} \underset{<}{\overset{>}{=}} |(\hat{X}_N/\hat{p}_N)\hat{p}_N|.$$

Then, (a) given $k_2 > k_N$, the third term in (29), $-(1/|\lambda|)\lambda_{L2}\lambda_{LN}$ $(k_2 - k_N)\hat{Y}_N$, is negative (positive) if $\hat{Y}_N > (<)0$. That is, infrastructure

aid to the import sector tends to lower (raise) the output of the exportable
if it results in an expansion (a contraction) of the nontraded good sector.
(b) Meanwhile, given $k_N > k_1$, the third term in (30), $-(1/|\lambda|)\lambda_{L1}\lambda_{LN}$
$(L/K)(k_N - k_1)\hat{Y}_N$, is clearly negative (positive) if $\hat{Y}_N > (<)0$. That is,
infrastructure aid to the import sector tends to lower (raise) the output
of the sector via an expansion (a contraction) of the nontraded good
sector.

The foregoing analysis shows that in the present 3×2 HO model, the
net effects of infrastructure aid to the import sector on the outputs of the
traded goods depend on the signs and the relative magnitudes of the three
component effects, and the Findlay-Grubert (1959) type of ultra-biased
growth-output effect does not necessarily hold. As for the effect on the
export sector, the secondary factor-substitution effect in (29) is always
negative, while the initial factor-saving and the tertiary nontraded
good effect can have any sign. If the factor-saving effect is zero or
negative because the infrastructure aid is neutral ($\delta^*_{K2} = \delta^*_{L2}$) or capital-
saving ($\delta^*_{K2} > \delta^*_{L2}$), and the nontraded good effect is negative, the sum of
the three component effects is unambiguously negative. Thus, the export
sector contracts and the Dutch disease or deindustrialization occurs in the
sector. However, if the factor-saving and/or nontraded good effects
are positive because the infrastructure aid is the labor-saving type
($\delta^*_{K2} < \delta^*_{L2}$) and/or $\hat{Y}_N < 0$, the effect on the agricultural output is
indeterminate. Sufficient conditions for the Dutch disease in the exportable
sector ($\hat{Y}_1 < 0$) are

(i) $\delta^*_{K2} \geq \delta^*_{L2}$ and $\hat{Y}_N > 0$ or

(ii) $\delta^*_{K2} \geq \delta^*_{L2}$, $\hat{Y}_N < 0$, and

$$\left|(1/|\theta|)(\lambda_{K2}\beta_L + \lambda_{L2}\beta_K)(\theta_{L2}\delta^*_{L2} + \theta_{K2}\delta^*_{K2}) + \lambda_{K2}\lambda_{L2}\delta^*_{L2}\left(1 - (\delta^*_{K2}/\delta^*_{L2})\right)\right|$$
$$> \lambda_{L2}\lambda_{LN}(k_2 - k_N)\hat{Y}_N \text{ or}$$

(iii) $\delta^*_{K2} < \delta^*_{L2}$, $\hat{Y}_N > 0$, and

$$\left|(1/|\theta|)(\lambda_{K2}\beta_L + \lambda_{L2}\beta_K)(\theta_{L2}\delta^*_{L2} + \theta_{K2}\delta^*_{K2}) + \lambda_{L2}\lambda_{LN}(k_2 - k_N)\hat{Y}_N\right|$$
$$> \lambda_{K2}\lambda_{L2}\delta^*_{L2}[1 - (\delta^*_{K2}/\delta^*_{L2})] \text{ or}$$

(iv) $\delta^*_{K2} < \delta^*_{L2}$, $\hat{Y}_N < 0$, and

$$\left|(1/|\theta|)(\lambda_{K2}\beta_L + \lambda_{L2}\beta_K)(\theta_{L2}\delta^*_{L2} + \theta_{K2}\delta^*_{K2})\right|$$
$$> \lambda_{K2}\lambda_{L2}\delta^*_{L2}\left(1 - (\delta^*_{K2}/\delta^*_{L2})\right) + \lambda_{L2}\lambda_{LN}(k_2 - k_N)\hat{Y}_N$$

As for the output effect on the importable, the factor-saving and factor-substitution effects in (30) are positive, but the nontraded good effect is positive (negative) if $\hat{Y}_N$ is negative (positive). Thus, the Dutch disease in the import sector occurs if $\hat{Y}_N > 0$ and the negative nontraded good effect outweighs the sum of the positive factor-saving and factor-substitution effects. This case may arise when the infrastructure aid to the import sector leads to a strong expansion of the nontraded good sector, and a sufficient condition for this phenomenon to occur is:

$$\hat{Y}_N > 0, \quad \text{and}$$
$$(1/|\lambda|)(\lambda_{L1}\beta_K + \lambda_{K1}\beta_L)(\theta_{L2}\delta_{L2}^* + \theta_{K2}\delta_{K2}^*)$$
$$+ \lambda_{L1}\lambda_{L2}\delta_{L2}^*\big(k_2(\delta_{K2}^*/\delta_{L2}^*) - k_1\big) < \lambda_{L1}\lambda_{LN}(L/K)(k_N - k_1)\hat{Y}_N.$$

4.3. Infrastructure aid to the nontraded good sector and deindustrialization

In the presence of infrastructure investment to the nontraded good sector, $\delta_{iN}^* > \delta_{i1}^* = \delta_{i2}^* = 0$ ($i = L, \ K$) and $T_N^* > T_1^* = T_2^* = 0$. Further, $T_L^* = \lambda_{LN}\delta_{LN}^*$ and $T_K^* = \lambda_{KN}\delta_{KN}^*$. Thus, the two equations in (25) can be written as

$$\hat{Y}_1 = \frac{\lambda_{L2}\lambda_{LN}\delta_{LN}^*(L/K)\big(k_2 - k_N(\delta_{KN}^*/\delta_{LN}^*)\big)}{|\lambda|}$$
$$- \frac{\lambda_{L2}\lambda_{LN}(L/K)(k_2 - k_N)\hat{Y}_N}{|\lambda|} \quad \text{and}$$

$$\hat{Y}_2 = \frac{\lambda_{L1}\lambda_{LN}\delta_{LN}^*(L/K)\big(k_N(\delta_{KN}^*/\delta_{LN}^*) - k_1\big)}{|\lambda|}$$
$$- \frac{\lambda_{L1}\lambda_{LN}(L/K)(k_N - k_1)\hat{Y}_N}{|\lambda|}.$$

As shown in (13), infrastructure aid to the nontraded sector does not affect the factor prices, and hence there are no factor-substitution effects on the traded goods. Therefore, the second terms in the two equations in (25) vanish. This leaves only the factor-saving and nontraded good effects in (31) and (32). The first term on the right-hand side of (31) represents the factor-saving effect on the exportable via the reduction in labor and capital requirement per unit of the nontraded good, and it is positive since the manufacturing good remains capital-intensive relative to the nontraded good after the infrastructure aid, i.e., $k_2 > k_N$ ($\delta_{KN}^*/\delta_{LN}^*$). Similarly, the first term in the right-hand side of (32) denotes the factor-saving effects on the importable via the reduction in labor and capital requirements per unit of the nontraded good, and it is positive since the nontraded good remains capital-intensive relative to the exportable good after the infrastructure aid, i.e., $k_N(\delta^*_{KN}/\delta^*_{LN}) > k_1$.[12]

The second terms in the right-hand side of equations in (30) and (31) represent the nontraded good effects of the infrastructure aid to the nontraded good sector on the outputs of the traded goods via the induced change in nontraded good production. For the nontraded good, $Y_N = X_N$. Recall that since the prices of traded goods (p_1 and p_2) are fixed, $\hat{Y}_N = \hat{X}_N = (\hat{X}_N/\hat{p}_N)\hat{p}_N + (\hat{X}_N/\hat{I})\hat{I}$. In the absence of an inferior good, $\hat{X}_N/\hat{p}_N < 0$ and $\hat{X}_N/\hat{I} > 0$. It has been shown in (13) that the infrastructure aid to the nontraded good sector lowers the price of the nontraded good ($\hat{p}^*_N/T^*_N = -1$). Thus, $(\hat{X}_N/\hat{p}_N)\hat{p}_N > 0$. Further, in (15), it has been shown that infrastructure aid to the nontraded good sector does not affect the national income, $\hat{I}/\hat{T}^*_N = 0$. Thus, $(\hat{X}_N/\hat{I})\hat{I} = 0$, and the net effect of the infrastructure aid to the nontraded good sector on the demand and output of the nontraded good is unambiguously positive, i.e., $\hat{Y}_N = \hat{X}_N = (\hat{X}_N/\hat{p}_N)\hat{p}_N > 0$. Thus, the following proposition can be stated:

PROPOSITION 3. *Infrastructure aid to the nontraded good sector does not cause a deindustrialization in that sector.*

Therefore, the second terms in (31) and (32) are unambiguously negative. That is, infrastructure aid to the nontraded good sector tends to decrease the outputs of both traded goods via an expansion of the nontraded good sector by drawing resources away from the trade sectors.

The net output effect of infrastructure aid to the nontraded good sector on the output of each traded good is the sum of the two component effects. In (31), the first component effect, $(1/|\lambda|)\lambda_{L2}\lambda_{LN}\delta^*_{LN}(L/K)$ $(k_2 - k_N(\delta^*_{KN}/\delta^*_{LN}))$, is positive, while the second component effect, $-(1/|\lambda|)\lambda_{L2}\lambda_{LN}(L/K)(k_2 - k_N)\hat{Y}_N$, is negative. Thus, the net effect of infrastructure aid to the nontraded good sector on the output of the exportable is uncertain. The condition for the Dutch disease to occur in the export sector is:

$$\delta^*_{LN}(k_2 - k_N(\delta^*_{KN}/\delta^*_{LN})) < (k_2 - k_N)\hat{Y}_N.$$

As for the net output effect on the importable, the factor-saving effect in (32), $(1/|\lambda|)\lambda_{L1}\lambda_{LN}\delta^*_{LN}(L/K)(k_N(\delta^*_{KN}/\delta^*_{LN}) - k_1)$, is positive, while the nontraded good effect, $-(1/|\lambda|)\lambda_{L1}\lambda_{LN}(L/K)(k_N - k_1)\hat{Y}_N$, is negative. Thus, the Dutch disease in the import sector occurs when the negative

---

[12] It is notable that if the infrastructure aid is the capital-saving type ($\delta^*_{KN} > \delta^*_{LN}$), the output effect on the exportable (importable) is weaker (stronger) vis-à-vis the neutral case in factor saving. But if the infrastructure aid is the labor-saving type ($\delta^*_{KN} < \delta^*_{LN}$), the output effect on the exportable (importable) is stronger (weaker) vis-à-vis the neutral case in factor saving.

nontraded good effect outweighs the factor-saving effect:

$$\delta_{LN}^* \left(k_N \left(\frac{\delta_{KN}^*}{\delta_{LN}^*} \right) - k_1 \right) < (k_N - k_1) \hat{Y}_N.$$

That is, for the import sector the Dutch disease occurs if the infrastructure aid to the nontraded good sector results in a significant expansion of the nontraded good sector, and the negative nontraded good effect on the output of the importable outweighs the positive factor-saving effect on the output of the importable. However, in reality, for policy makers to invest in the nontraded goods sector, the *initial factor-saving effect* must be dominant. The resources saved through the infrastructure investment in the nontraded goods sector have Rybczynski-type effects on the outputs of the trade sectors, and these factor-saving effects are likely to dominate the subsequent negative nontraded good effects, which are likely to be secondary and subservient to the initial factor-saving effects.

5. Concluding remarks

In this chapter, we have explored the possibility of deindustrialization from infrastructure aid to a developing country by extending the Heckscher–Ohlin model to include the nontraded goods sector. We obtained several significant results from the analysis. Infrastructure aid to either the export or import sector always increases national income and welfare. Infrastructure aid to the nontraded good sector does not affect factor prices or national income, but increases consumer welfare by lowering the price of the nontraded good.

Further, infrastructure aid to either of the two traded good sectors appreciates the foreign exchange rate of the recipient country, while infrastructure aid to the nontraded good industry depreciates it. In the presence of a nontraded good, the signs for the effects of infrastructure aid on the sectoral outputs are indeterminate, with the exception that infrastructure aid to the nontraded good sector necessarily increases the output of that sector. This implies that the Findlay–Grubert type of ultra-biased growth-output effect (obtainable in the 2×2 Heckscher–Ohlin model) does not carry over to the present case in a straightforward manner.

The output effects are generally indeterminate because infrastructure aid creates at least more than two component effects of varying signs on the sectoral outputs via the relative factor-saving effects of the aid, changes in the factor prices and the resulting factor substitution, and the output response of the nontraded good to the aid via price effect and income effect. In particular, if the infrastructure aid results in a strong expansion of the nontraded good sector, the traded good sectors may experience the Dutch disease via the negative effect of resource reallocation for the sectors. These ambiguous output effects are consistent with the varying types of deindustrialization that have been reported by a number of studies in the literature of economic aid.

Since the detailed discussions of the results are in the text, we conclude by noting two omissions in the chapter. First, this study, mainly theoretical in nature, reveals several positive aspects of infrastructure aid, but the task of empirically ascertaining how each of the positive aspects actually operates behind the economic stagnation and the different types of deindustrialization in the developing countries was not undertaken. Second, this chapter considers infrastructure capital as a public input, but it is devoid of analysis of the inter-industrial spillover effects that the infrastructure capital generates to other sectors. We leave these tasks to future research in this area.

References

Adam, C.S., Bevan, D.L. (2003), Aid public expenditures and Dutch disease. Centre for the Study of African Economies Working Paper No. 2003-02, University of Oxford, Oxford.

Bandara, J.S. (1995), The Dutch disease in a developing country: the case of foreign capital inflow to Sri Lanka. *Seoul Journal of Economics* 8 (Fall), 311–329.

Batra, R.N. (1973), *Studies in the pure theory of international trade.* St. Martin's, New York.

Benjamin, N.C., Devarajan, S., Weiner, R.J. (1989), The 'Dutch disease in a developing country: oil reserves in Cameroon. *Journal of Development Economics* 30 (January), 71–92.

Choi, J.-Y., Yu, E.S.H. (1987), Technical progress and outputs under variable returns to scale. *Economica* 54, 249–253.

Choi, J.-Y., Choi, E.K. (2007), Infrastructure aid, deindustrialization and urban unemployment. In: Lahiri S. (Ed.), *Theory and Practice of Foreign Aid, Volume 1 of Frontiers of Economics and Globalization.* Elsevier, Boston, pp. 65–84.

Corden, W.M., Neary, P.J. (1982), Booming sector and de-industrialization in a small economy. *Economic Journal* 92 (December), 825–848.

Ebrahim-zadeh, C. (2003), Dutch disease: too much wealth managed unwisely. *Finance and Development* 40 (March), 50–51.

Elbadawi, I.A. (1999), External aid: help or hindrance to export orientation in Africa? *Journal of African Economies* 8, 578–616.

Findlay, R., Grubert, H. (1959), Factor intensities, technological progress and the terms of trade. *Oxford Economic Papers* 11 (February), 111–121.

Komiya, R. (1967), Nontraded goods and the pure theory of international trade. *International Economic Review* 8 (June), 132–152.

Nkusu, M. (2004), Aid and the Dutch disease in low-income countries: informed diagnosis for prudent prognosis. IMF Working Paper 04/49, International Monetary Fund, Washington, DC.

Nyoni, T.S. (1998), Foreign aid and economic performance in Tanzania. *World Development* 26, 1235–1240.

Prati, A., Sahay, R., Tressel, T. (2003), Is there a case for sterilizing foreign aid? Unpublished manuscript; European Economic Association, Stockholm.

Salter, W.E.G. (1959), Internal and external balance: the role of price and expenditure effects. *Economic Record* 35, 226–238.

Spatafora, N., Warner, A. (1999), Macroeconomic and sectoral effects of terms-of-trade shocks: the experience of oil exporting developing countries. IMF Working Paper 99/134, International Monetary Fund, Washington, DC.

Stijns, J.-P. (2003), An empirical test of the Dutch disease hypothesis using a gravity model of trade. International Trade Working Paper No. 0305001, Washington University, St. Louis, Missouri.

Torvik, R. (2001), Learning by doing and the Dutch disease. *European Economic Review* 45, 285–306.

Vos, R. (1998), Aid flows and 'Dutch Disease' in a general equilibrium framework in Pakistan. *Journal of Policy Modeling* 20, 77–109.

Younger, S.D. (1992), Aid and the Dutch disease: macroeconomic management when everybody loves you. *World Development* 20, 1587–1597.

CHAPTER 16

Environmental Regulations for a Small Open Economy with Tourism

Chi-Chur Chao[a], Bharat R. Hazari[b], Jean-Pierre Laffargue[c] and Eden S.H. Yu[d]

[a]Department of Economics, Chinese University of Hong Kong, Shatin, Hong Kong
E-mail address: ccchao@cuhk.edu.hk
[b]Department of Economics and Finance, City University of Hong Kong, Tat Chee Avenue, Kowloon, Hong Kong
E-mail address: bhazari@gmail.com
[c]PSE-CNRS and CEPREMAP, University of Paris 1, 48 boulevard Jourdan, 75014 Paris, France
E-mail address: Jean-Pierre.Laffargue@orange.fr
[d]Department of Economics and Finance, City University of Hong Kong, Tat Chee Avenue, Kowloon, Hong Kong
E-mail address: efedenyu@cityu.edu.hk

Abstract

Purpose – This chapter shows that in the presence of tourism, the traditional policy prescription, free trade in goods and the standard Pigouvian tax on pollution, is not optimal for a small open economy.
Methodology/approach – The general-equilibrium analysis is employed to study environmental regulations for a small open economy with tourism.
Findings – Foreign tourists consume mainly local non-traded goods in the tourist-receiving economy. Inbound tourism converts formally non-traded goods into tradables, generating a tourism terms-of-trade effect. Owing to this favourable effect, positive tariffs and stricter pollution taxes can actually improve welfare of domestic residents. The optimal rates of tariffs and pollution taxes are derived and explained for the economy with tourism. These positive rates are confirmed by simulations.
Originality/value of chapter – The presence of tourism can alter the welfare implications of the traditional trade policy.

Keywords: Inbound tourism, optimal tariffs, optimal pollution taxes

Paper type: Research paper

Frontiers of Economics and Globalization
Volume 5   ISSN: 1574-8715
DOI: 10.1016/S1574-8715(08)05016-1

1. Introduction

It is well documented in the literature that in a closed economy with pollution, the standard Pigouvian tax, defined by the *direct* marginal damage of pollution, is the optimal prescription for internalizing the pollution externality to the economy. However, in an open economy, this result on environmental regulation needs to be modified. In the case of a large open economy, Krutilla (1991) shows that an import tariff can be used to improve the terms-of-trade and therefore a higher pollution tax, greater than the rate of direct marginal damage, is required for correcting the pollution externality to the consumers. This implies that for a small open economy which cannot affect its terms-of-trade, free trade in goods remains to be the optimal commercial policy and the standard Pigouvian tax is required for regulating the environment to attain a first-best position.[1]

Owing to economic growth and increased globalization, not only trade has surged in goods and factors but also in international tourism. Foreign tourists demand mainly locally produced non-traded goods and services, and thus inbound tourism actually converts non-traded goods into tradables,[2] yielding the so-called *tourism* terms-of-trade effect. We will show that because of the tourism-induced improvement in the terms-of-trade, the optimality of free trade even for a small open economy in commodity trade may be impaired and the standard Pigouvain tax needs to be adjusted accordingly. Our result is analogous to that of Krutilla (1991) except that monopoly power in trade arises from tourism.

Tourism has grown rapidly in the recent years. To explore this important issue, we develop a general-equilibrium trade model by extending Krutilla (1991) to include tourism in the economy. Following the literature on tourism (Hazari and Sgro, 2004), foreign tourists are assumed to only demand local non-traded goods. We examine the welfare effects of tariffs and pollution taxes separately and jointly in this economy. A rise in import tariffs and hence a higher price of the importable creates a consumption substitution effect, as domestic residents switch part of their consumption from the importable to the non-traded good. This gives rise to a higher relative price of the non-traded good, yielding a favourable tourism terms-of-trade effect. In spite of the restrictive effect on imports, tariffs can actually improve welfare of domestic residents even for a small open economy but with inbound tourism. That is, tariffs can serve as an expenditure-inducing policy by raising spending of foreign tourists. Further, assuming the importable-good sector is pollution-emitting, tariffs lead to a greater production of the importable polluting good. Hence, the

---

[1] See Khan (1996) for a related study.

[2] See Komiya (1967) and Batra (1973) for the studies on non-traded goods in general equilibrium. models.

standard Pigouvian tax rate for directly correcting the pollution externality needs to be adjusted by taking into consideration of the tourism terms-of-trade impact. Essentially, the interactions between the tourism-induced terms-of-trade effect and the traditional tariff and pollution effects are highlighted in the analysis.

The chapter is organized as follows. Section 2 sets out a general-equilibrium model for the polluted, small open economy with inbound tourism. Section 3 explores the welfare effects of tariffs and pollution taxes for the economy, and the individually and jointly optimal policies of them are derived and explained. Section 4 provides numerical simulations for optimal tariffs and pollution taxes for the economy with tourism. Conclusions are summarized in Section 5.

2. A model

Consider a small open economy producing three goods: agricultural X, manufacturing Y and non-traded N, in perfectly competitive markets. Assuming constant returns-to-scale technologies, the production functions are: $X = X(L_X) = L_X/a_{LX}$, $Y = Y(L_Y, K)$ and $N = N(L_N, V)$, where a_{LX} is the unit labour requirement for producing good Y. While labour (L_i) is a mobile factor across sectors, capital (K) and land (V) are specific factors to the manufacturing and non-traded sectors, respectively.[3] Letting L be the endowment of labour, full employment requires: $L_X+L_Y+L_N = L$. Moreover, capital and land are fully employed. While manufacturing is the polluting industry, agricultural and non-traded sectors are non-polluting. To simplify the analysis, pollution Z is a by-product in the process of producing good Y with a one-to-one relationship (i.e., $Z = Y$).[4] Since pollution hurts consumers, a pollution tax, s, is imposed on the producers of good Y.

It is assumed that the home country exports good X and imports good Y. Choosing good X as the numeraire, the world price of good Y is given by p^*. The home country imposes a specific tariff, t, on imports so that the domestic price of good Y is p ($= p^* + t$). However, due to the pollution tax on producers, the net producer price of good Y to domestic producers is p–s. Note that the domestic price of the non-traded good N, denoted by q, is determined by its supply and demand. Letting w, r and v be the wage,

---

[3] The discussions of specific factors model are in Jones (1971), Neary (1978), Khan (1982), Batra and Beladi (1990), Beladi (1990), Beladi and Batra (2004), and Marjit *et al.* (2004).
[4] Another approach is to consider environmental elements, such as clean water and trees, as inputs in production. See Yohe (1979) and Yu and Ingene (1982).

rental and rent, unit price equals unit cost in competitive equilibrium:

$$1 = a_{LX}w, \tag{1}$$

$$p - s = \beta(w, r) \quad \text{and} \tag{2}$$

$$q = \gamma(w, v), \tag{3}$$

where $\beta(\cdot)$ and $\gamma(\cdot)$ stand for the unit cost functions of goods Y and N, respectively. By the envelope property, β_w ($\equiv \partial\beta/\partial w$) expresses the unit labour requirement for the production of good Y. Under full employment, the employment conditions for labour, capital and land are given, respectively, in Equations (4)–(6) as follows:

$$a_{LX}X + \beta_w(w, r)Y + \gamma_w(w, v)N = L, \tag{4}$$

$$\beta_r(w, r)Y = K \quad \text{and} \tag{5}$$

$$\gamma_v(w, v)N = V. \tag{6}$$

The endowments of labour, capital and land in this static economy are fixed.

Equations (1)–(6) present the supply side of the economy, which consists of six endogenous variables, w, r, v, X, Y and N, for the given prices p and q and the pollution tax s. The system incorporating the non-traded good is block recursive: w is determined by Equation (1), and hence r is a function of p and s from Equation (2) and v a function of q from Equation (3). Therefore, for given endowments, output Y in Equation (5) depends on p and s while N in Equation (6) depends on q only.

From the above production information, we can define a net revenue function of the economy: $R(p, q, s) = \max \{X(L_X) + pY(L_Y, K) + qN(L_N, V) - sZ: L_X + L_Y + L_N = L\}$ with respect to L_i, $i = X, Y, N$. Using subscripts in $R(\cdot)$ to denote partial derivatives, by the envelope property we have: $R_p = Y$, $R_q = N$ and $R_s = -Z$. Moreover, $R_{pp} > 0$ and $R_{qq} > 0$, as they reflect the positive supply relationship of goods Y and N, and R_{ss} ($\equiv -\partial Z/\partial s$) > 0. It is noted that $R_{pq} = R_{sq} = 0$ because the production of Y and N are dependent on their own prices only. However, the pollution tax dampens the production of good Y by raising its cost, so we have: $R_{ps} < 0$. Furthermore, $R_{ps} = -R_{pp}$ since one unit pollution is generated from per unit production of good Y.

The consumers in the home economy consist of domestic residents and inbound foreign tourists. Domestic residents demand three goods, denoted by C_i, and their utility function is: $u = U(C_X, C_Y, C_N, Z)$, where $\partial U/\partial C_i > 0$ ($i = X, Y, N$) and $\partial U/\partial Z < 0$ because pollution Z generates a direct, negative effect on consumers. The expenditure function of domestic residents is therefore defined as: $E(p, q, Z, u) = \min \{C_X + pC_Y + qC_N: U(C_X, C_Y, C_N, Z) = u\}$. The compensated demand functions for goods Y and N are derived as: $E_p = C_Y$ and $E_q = C_N$, with $E_{pp} < 0$ and $E_{qq} < 0$ for the downward-sloped demand functions. We assume that $E_{qp} > 0$, i.e., goods Y and N are substitutes in consumption. Furthermore, $E_Z > 0$, being the marginal damage to consumers caused by pollution; E_Z represents consumers' willingness to pay for pollution abatements. In addition, $E_{pZ} > 0$ and $E_{qZ} > 0$ express that pollution and goods Y and N are complements in consumption.[5]

As for tourists, they come and consume the unique goods and services produced in the destinations. Following the literature (cf., Hazari and Sgro, 2004), the non-traded good serves as a proxy. Letting T be tourist expenditure, their demand for the non-traded good is $D_N(q, T)$ with $\partial D_N / \partial q < 0$ and $\partial D_N / \partial T > 0$.[6] Since pollution also affects tourists, the utility function of tourists may be expressed as follows: $u^* = U^*(D_N)/h(Z)$, where $dU^*/dD_N > 0$ and $dh/dZ > 0$, capturing the negative pollution effect upon tourists.

Utilizing the above demand and supply information, the equilibrium conditions of the economy can be described by:[7]

$$E(p, q, Z, u) = R(p, q, s) + tM + sZ, \tag{7}$$

$$M = E_p(p, q, Z, u) - R_p(p, q, s), \tag{8}$$

$$Z = -R_s(p, q, s) \quad \text{and} \tag{9}$$

$$E_q(p, q, Z, u) + D_N(q, T) = R_q(p, q, s), \tag{10}$$

where M is the imports of good Y. Assuming that revenues from tariff and pollution tax are rebated to domestic residents, Equation (7) expresses the budget constraint of the economy: domestic residents' expenditure is in turn equal to net income from production plus revenues from tariff and pollution tax. Equation (10) shows the market-clearing condition for the non-traded good N, stating that its total demand by both domestic residents and foreign tourists is met by its supply from domestic production.

Equations (7)–(10), depicting the tourist-receiving home economy, have four unknowns, u, M, Z and q, with the policy instruments of tariffs t and pollution taxes s. We will examine the welfare effects of these two policies for a small open economy with inbound tourism.

---

[5] For example, the expenditure function is: $E = u/\{a^a(b/p)^b(c/q)^c[h/(h+Z)]^d\}$ for a Cobb–Douglas utility function: $U(C_X, C_Y, C_N, Z) = C_X^a C_Y^b C_Z^c[h/(h+Z)]^d$, where $a, b, c, d, h > 0$. We can then obtain: $E_{pZ} = dC_Y/(h+Z) > 0$ and $E_{qZ} = dC_Z/(h+Z) > 0$.

[6] The assumption of substitutability for goods Y and N to residents is consistent with the assumption that tourists consume the non-traded good N only. In addition, this assumption is not too stringent. For instance, visiting museums and watching movies are substitutes to local residents, while foreign tourists may like to visit museums only.

[7] The duality approach for the general-equilibrium model can be found, for example, in Hatzipanayotou and Michael (1995). Also see Hatzipanayotou *et al.* (2002, 2005) for a general-equilibrium model with pollution.

3. Optimal tariff and pollution tax

It is instructive at the outset of this section to determine the set of factors affecting the welfare of domestic residents. This can be obtained by totally differentiating Equation (7) and then using Equations (8)–(10):

$$E_u \mathrm{d}u = t\mathrm{d}M - (E_Z - s)\mathrm{d}Z + D_N \mathrm{d}q, \tag{11}$$

where $E_u > 0$, being the inverse of the marginal utility of income. The first term on the right-hand side of Equation (11) shows the traditional volume-of-trade effect arising from changes in imports. An increase in imports raises welfare of domestic residents in the presence of import restricting tariffs. The second term in (11) captures the conflicting effects of pollution externality: pollution harms consumers as measured by E_Z but it yields revenue from the pollution tax s. The last term in (11) expresses the *tourism*-induced terms-of-trade effect. Tourists' consumption of local non-traded goods leads to a rise in the relative price of good N; this positive terms-of-trade effect contributes to domestic welfare.

To proceed further, we consider the change in imports of good Y obtainable from Equation (8) as:

$$\mathrm{d}M = E_{pu}\mathrm{d}u + (E_{pp} - R_{pp})\mathrm{d}t + E_{pq}\mathrm{d}q - R_{ps}\mathrm{d}s + E_{pZ}\mathrm{d}Z. \tag{12}$$

Imports of good Y are affected by a set of factors underlying its demand and supply. On the demand side, real income (utility) and the prices of goods Y and Z are relevant. In particular, since goods Y and Z are substitutes in consumption (i.e., $E_{pq} > 0$), a rise in the non-tradable price q increases demand for good Y (see the third term on the right-hand side of Equation (12)). As far as the supply side is concerned, the change of the pollution tax affects production of good Y and hence the imports. Further, increases in the pollution level positively affect the demand for good Y, given $E_{pZ} > 0$. Here, the change of pollution can be obtained by differentiating (9):

$$\mathrm{d}Z = -R_{sp}\mathrm{d}t - R_{ss}\mathrm{d}s. \tag{13}$$

Recalling that R_{sp} ($\equiv -\partial Z/\partial p$) < 0 and R_{ss} ($\equiv -\partial Z/\partial s$) > 0, Equation (13) implies that an increase in tariffs for protecting the domestic polluting sector raises the level of pollution, whereas an increase in pollution taxes reduces it.

To determine the change in the relative price q of the non-traded good, we totally differentiate Equation (10):

$$(E_{qq} + \partial D_N/\partial q - R_{qq})\mathrm{d}q = -E_{qu}\mathrm{d}u - E_{qp}\mathrm{d}t - E_{qZ}\mathrm{d}Z, \tag{14}$$

where E_{qu} ($\equiv \partial C_N/\partial u$) > 0 represents the income effect of demand for the non-traded good by domestic residents. As indicated in the first two terms on the right-hand side of (14), the domestic price of the non-traded good positively depends on the income and the tariff-induced substitution effects. In addition, given $E_{qZ}>0$, pollution raises the domestic residents' demand for the non-traded good, generating an upward pressure on the domestic price of the non-traded good, as shown in the last term of (14).

3.1. Tariffs

We consider first the welfare effect of tariffs in the presence of inbound tourism and a given pollution tax. Solving (11)–(14) gives:

$$du/dt$$
$$= [tA + (E_Z - s)R_{sp}(E_{qq} + \partial D_N/\partial q - R_{qq})]/\Delta - D_N(E_{pq} - E_{qZ}R_{sp})/\Delta,$$
$$(15)$$

where $A = H + E_{pq}E_{qZ}R_{sp} - (E_{qq} + \partial D_N/\partial q - R_{qq})(R_{pp} + E_{pZ}R_{sp}) > (<) 0$ and $H = E_{pp}(E_{qq} + \partial D_N/\partial q - R_{qq}) - E_{pq}^2 > 0.$[8] Further, we have $\Delta = (E_u - tE_{pu})$ $(E_{qq} + \partial D_N/\partial q - R_{qq}) + E_{qu}(D_N + tE_{pq}) < 0$ by the stability condition.[9] In the absence of tourism (i.e., $D_N = 0$) in (15), the traditional welfare result on tariffs for a small open economy is obtained: When the pollution tax is set at the standard Pigouvian rate (i.e., $s = E_Z$), free trade in goods ($t = 0$) is optimal. However, in the presence of tourism ($D_N > 0$) in the economy, free trade in goods is no longer optimal even if $s = E_Z$. This can be seen from the last term of (15) that a rise in tariffs can actually improve domestic welfare. Tariffs trigger higher importable price of good Y and hence more pollution emissions. Both the consumption substitution effect ($E_{pq} > 0$) and the pollution-induced consumption ($E_{qZ} > 0$) raise the non-tradable price of good N. This yields a favourable tourism terms-of-trade effect on the welfare of domestic residents.

Setting $du/dt = 0$ in (15), the optimum tariff, t^o, can be derived as

$$t^o = (1/A)[D_N(E_{pq} - E_{qZ}R_{sp}) - (E_Z - s)R_{sp}(E_{qq} + \partial D_N/\partial q - R_{qq})].$$
$$(16)$$

It is noted that t^o is non-zero for $D_N > 0$ even when $s = E_Z$. This shows that free trade in goods is generally not optimal for the economy with inbound tourism.

---

[8] Since the expenditure function is concave in prices, we have: $E_{pp}E_{qq} - E_{pq}^2 > 0$. This gives $H > 0$.

[9] Following Dei (1985), the adjustment for the price q of the non-traded good is: $\dot{q} = \rho G(q)$, where the dot over q is the time derivative, ρ the speed of adjustments and G denotes excess demand for the non-traded good N, i.e., $G = E_q(p, q, Z, u) + D_N(q, T) - R_q(p, q, s)$ in (10). A sufficient condition for stability of the economy is: $dG/dq < 0$. From (11) to (14), we obtain: $dq/dG = E_u(1 - m_Y)/\Delta$, where $m_Y (= pE_{pu}/E_u)$ is the marginal propensity to consume good Y and is less than 1. Hence, the system is stable if $\Delta < 0$.

Figures 1 and 2 provide graphical illustrations for the t^o schedule in the policy space of (t, s) under the case that $A > 0$ in (16). For $A > 0$, the t^o schedule is positively sloped. Domestic welfare is maximized at the corresponding t^o on the schedule for a given s. This can be checked by

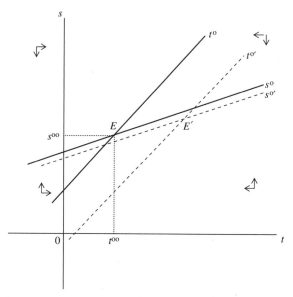

Fig. 1. *Optimal tariff and pollution tax for a smaller pollution externality.*

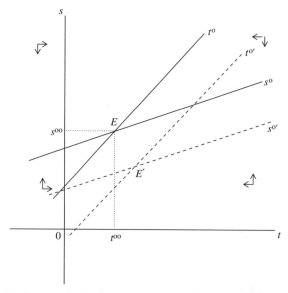

Fig. 2. *Optimal tariff and pollution tax for a larger pollution externality.*

examining the curvature of the domestic welfare function. Following the technique used by Neary (1993, 1998), we substitute the expression of t^o from (16) into (15) to obtain the welfare adjustments for domestic residents:

$$\mathrm{d}u/\mathrm{d}t = A(t - t^o)/\Delta. \tag{17}$$

Since $\Delta < 0$, we have: $\mathrm{d}u/\mathrm{d}t > (<) \, 0$ when $t < (>) \, t^o$. This implies that u is a concave function of t. When t increases as depicted in Figures 1 and 2, domestic welfare increases initially, reaches a maximum at t^o, and then declines. The horizontal arrows indicate these changes in domestic welfare.

3.2. Pollution taxes

We examine next the welfare effect of pollution taxes for a given tariff. From (11)–(14), we obtain:

$$\mathrm{d}u/\mathrm{d}s = [(E_Z - s)(E_{qq} + \partial D_N/\partial q - R_{qq})R_{ss} = tB]/\Delta + D_N E_{qZ} R_{ss}/\Delta, \tag{18}$$

where $B = (E_{qq} + \partial D_N/\partial q - R_{qq})(R_{ps} + E_{pZ}R_{ss}) - E_{pq}E_{qZ}R_{ss} > (<) \, 0$. An increase in pollution taxes immediately raises production cost of good Y, thereby reducing its output and hence pollution emissions. Consequently, damage from pollution decreases but revenue from pollution taxes declines. In addition, due to changes in supply of and demand for the importable good Y, tariff-revenue and tourist-spending alter. These conflicting forces make the welfare effect of pollution taxes indeterminate. By setting $\mathrm{d}u/\mathrm{d}s = 0$ in (18), we can obtain the optimal pollution tax, s^o, as follows:

$$s^o = E_Z - tB/R_{ss}(E_{qq} + \partial D_N/\partial q - R_{qq}) + D_N E_{qZ}/(E_{qq} + \partial D_N/\partial q - R_{qq}). \tag{19}$$

Note that the standard Pigouvian tax ($s^o = E_Z$) is applicable only when $t = 0$ and $D_N = 0$ in (19). For $t > 0$ and $D_N = 0$, a tariff-revenue effect is captured by the second term of (19). As indicated in Krutilla (1991), this effect renders the optimal pollution tax rate to be different from the standard Pigouvian rate, as tariffs promote production of the importable good Y but result in more pollution emissions. Moreover, the presence of tourism ($D_N > 0$) in the last term of (19) gives a tourism terms-of-trade effect. To enhance this effect via the higher non-tradable price q, a smaller pollution tax is needed for raising the demand for the non-traded good via more pollution emissions (i.e., $E_{qZ} > 0$).

For $B > 0$, the s^o schedule in (19), illustrated in Figures 1 and 2, is positively sloped. For a given t, domestic welfare is maximized at s^o. This can be examined by substituting s^o in (19) into (18):

$$\mathrm{d}u/\mathrm{d}s = -(E_{qq} + \partial D_N/\partial q - R_{qq})(s - s^o)/\Delta. \tag{20}$$

Recalling $\varDelta < 0$, we have $du/ds > (<) \, 0$ when $s < (>) \, s^o$ in (20). Hence, vertical movements of the pollution tax s towards its optimal rate s^o are welfare-improving.

3.3. Jointly optimal tariffs and pollution taxes

In the preceding sections, we have derived the individually optimal tariffs t^o for given pollution taxes s and the optimal pollution taxes s^o for given tariffs t. We are now equipped to examine the jointly optimal tariffs and pollution taxes, denoted by t^{oo} and s^{oo}, for the domestic economy with inbound tourism. Solving Equations (16) and (19) yields:

$$t^{oo} = D_N E_{qp}/H \quad \text{and} \tag{21}$$

$$s^{oo} = E_Z + t^{oo} - D_N(E_{pZ}E_{qp} - E_{qZ}E_{pp})/H, \tag{22}$$

where recalling that $H > 0$. This confirms again the traditional wisdom the domestic economy with inbound tourism at in the absence of tourism ($D_N = 0$), free trade in goods, along with the standard Pigouvian tax on pollution, is the first-best policy for the small open economy. However, this policy prescription needs to be revised when tourism is present ($D_N > 0$) in the economy. Since $E_{qp} > 0$, positive tariffs ($t^{oo} > 0$) are warranted in (21). This is due to the favourable tourism terms-of-trade effect induced by the consumption substitution between the importable good Y and the non-traded good N, as measured by E_{qp}.

As for the jointly optimal pollution taxes in (22), the standard Pigouvian tax rate (i.e., $s = E_Z$) needs to be adjusted to reflect the impact of tariffs and the pollution externality effect. Tariffs exaggerate the production of good Y, causing more pollution Z. To mitigate the negatively externality on domestic residents, there is a call for higher pollution taxes expressed in the second term of (22). In addition, more consumption of goods Y and N is needed since $E_{pZ} > 0$ and $E_{qZ} > 0$. This indirectly renders a beneficial tourism terms-of-trade effect via the higher price of the non-traded good. To enhance this effect as captured by the last term in (22), lower pollution taxes are recommended.

We summarize the above results, as follows:

PROPOSITION. *Free trade in goods, together with the standard Pigouvian tax on pollution emissions, is not optimal for a small open economy with inbound tourism. The optimal policies are positive tariffs and pollution taxes. The optimal pollution taxes are greater (less) than the standard Pigouvian rate, if the pollution externality effect is smaller (larger) than the tariff effect.*

For the case of $A>0$ and $B>0$, the jointly optimal tariff and pollution tax, t^{oo} and s^{oo}, are depicted at point E in Figure 1 or 2.[10] From (16) and (19), an increase in tourism via a larger D_N causes a shift of the t^o schedule to the right, while it triggers the s^o schedule to shift downwards. This gives a new equilibrium at E', which gives a higher optimal tariff but with a higher (lower) pollution tax in Figure 1 (2) if the pollution externality effect on demand for goods by domestic residents is relatively small (large) in (22).

4. Simulations

Utilizing the analytical framework above, we simulate optimal tariff and pollution tax rates for the economy. To do so, we need to specify the production and utility functions.

4.1. Specifications

We express the production functions as follows:

$$X = AL_X^\alpha, \tag{23}$$

$$Y = BL_Y^\beta \quad \text{and} \tag{24}$$

$$N = CL_N^\gamma, \tag{25}$$

where A, B, $C>0$ and $0<\alpha$, β, $\gamma<1$. Capital and land do not appear in (24) and (25) because they are specific factors and normalized to 1. Good X is exported and good Y is imported. The domestic price of good Y is p ($=p^*+t$). For pollution, it is assumed that pollution Z emitted in the economy is equal to the output of the manufactured good Y. The unit pollution tax is s and hence the producer's after-tax price of good Y is $p-s$. The marginal conditions of labour in these sectors are therefore:

$$\alpha X = wL_X, \tag{26}$$

$$\beta(p-s)Y = wL_Y, \quad \text{and} \tag{27}$$

$$\gamma qZ = wL_N. \tag{28}$$

---

[10] In the (s, t) space of Figures 1 and 2, the intercepts of the t^o and s^o schedules are: $[E_Z-D_N(E_{qp}-E_{qZ}R_{sp})/R_{sp}(E_{qq}+\partial D_N/\partial q-R_{qq})]|_t$ and $[E_Z+D_N E_{qZ}/(E_{qq}+\partial D_N/\partial q-R_{qq})]|_s$ and the difference of them is: $-D_N E_{qp}/R_{sp}(E_{qq}+\partial D_N/\partial q-R_{qq})<0$. Further, the slopes of the t^o and s^o schedules are: $ds/dt|_t = H+R_{sp}[E_{qZ}E_{pq}-E_{pZ}(E_{qq}+\partial D_N/\partial q-R_{qq})]/R_{sp}(E_{qq}+\partial D_N/\partial q-R_{qq})$ and $ds/dt|_s = -(R_{ps}+R_{ss}E_{pZ})+R_{ss}E_{pq}E_{qZ}/R_{ss}(E_{qq}+\partial D_N/\partial q-R_{qq})$. The difference of the slopes is: $ds/dt|_t-ds/dt|_s = [E_{pp}(E_{qq}+\partial D_N/\partial q-R_{qq})-E_{pq}E_{qp}]/R_{sp}(E_{qq}+\partial D_N/\partial q-R_{qq})>0$. Regarding slopes, the t^o schedule is larger than the s^o schedule in Figures 1 and 2.

Note that the full employment condition for the labour market requires: $L = L_X + L_Y + L_Z$.

The utility of households, depending on the consumptions of goods as well as the quality of the environment, is given by:

$$U(C_X, C_Y, C_N) = V(C_X, C_Y, C_N,)[h/(h + Z)]^d, \tag{29}$$

where $d > 0$ and $h > 0$ represent the parameters of pollution externality to consumers. For the sub-utility $V(C_X, C_Y, C_N)$ in (29), we specify:

$$V(C_X, C_Y, C_N) = \frac{C_X^a \left[b^{1/(1+\sigma)} C_Y^{\sigma/(1+\sigma)} + \bar{b}^{1/(1+\sigma)} C_N^{\sigma/(1+\sigma)} \right]^{\bar{a}(1+\sigma)/\sigma}}{\left[b^{1/(1+\sigma)} + \bar{b}^{1/(1+\sigma)} \right]^{\bar{a}(1+\sigma)/\sigma}},$$

where $a, \bar{a}, b, \bar{b} > 0$ and $\bar{a} = 1 - a$ and $\bar{b} = 1 - b$. In addition, the elasticity of substitution between the non-traded good and the manufacturing good is $1 + \sigma$, and there is an elasticity of substitution of 1 between the aggregate of these two goods and the agricultural good. Given the prices p and q, the marginal conditions of the maximization programme of households are:

$$C_X = (aqC_N/\bar{a})[1 + (b/\bar{b})(q/p)^\sigma] \quad \text{and} \tag{30}$$

$$C_Y = (b/\bar{b})(q/p)^{1+\sigma} C_N. \tag{31}$$

As for the market of the non-traded good N, the tourists' demand is specified as:

$$D_N = Tq^{-\eta}, \tag{32}$$

where $\eta > 0$ is the price elasticity of demand. The equilibrium condition of the non-traded good market in the economy is: $N = C_N + D_N$. In addition, the country's budget constraint is: $C_X + p^* C_Y + qC_N = X + p^* Y + qN$.

4.2. Calibrations

We start by setting the values of the main endogenous variables of the reference equilibrium of the model: $X = 2$, $Y = 2$, $N = 6$, $L_X = 2$, $C_Y = 3.5$, $C_N = 5$, $q = 1$, $p^* = 1$, $t = 0$ and $s = 0$, and the values of the parameters: $\alpha = 0.6$, $\beta = 0.6$, $\gamma = 0.6$, $\eta = 0.5$ and $\sigma = 3$. We then compute the values of the other variables: $p = 1$, $w = 0.6$, $L_Y = 2$, $L_N = 6$, $L = 10$, $Z = 2$, $C_X = 1.5$ and $D_N = 1$, and the values of the other parameters: $a = 0.15$, $b = 0.4118$, $T = 1$, $A = 1.3195$, $B = 1.3195$ and $C = 2.0477$. The value of households' utility, excluding the effect of the quality of the environment in (29), is $V = 3.6476$.

Finally, we assume that, in the reference steady state, pollution reduces households' utility by 2%. If pollution were doubled, households' utility would be reduced by 5%. Then, the parameters h and d in (29) are the solutions of the system of two equations: $h/(h+2) = 0.98$ and $h/(h+4) = 0.95$. Therefore, we get $h = 33.0532$, $d = 0.4262$ and $U = 3.5574$. Note that the Pigouvian tax, which is equal to the direct marginal rate of pollution, is $s^P = d(C_X + pC_Y + qC_N)/(h + Z) = 0.1512$.

4.3. Simulations

We now simulate the model by considering different levels of tourists' spending ($T = 0$, 1 or 1.5) under various price elasticity of demand ($\eta = 3$, 1 or 0.5). We proceed to solve the system (23)–(32) recursively. For given q and w, from (23) to (28), we obtain sectoral outputs: $X = A^{1/(1-\alpha)}(\alpha/w)^{\alpha/(1-\alpha)}$, $Y = B^{1/(1-\beta)}[\beta(p-s)/w]^{\beta/(1-\beta)}$ and $N = C^{1/(1-\gamma)}(\gamma q/w)^{\gamma/(1-\gamma)}$, and employment of labour in three sectors: $L_X = \alpha X/w$, $L_Y = \beta(p - s)Y/w$ and $L_N = \gamma qN/w$. Revenue from production can be set as: $R = X + p^*Y + qN$. Using (30) and (31) and the country's budget constraint, we have: $C_N = \bar{a}\bar{b}R/p\{\bar{b} + b(q/p)^\sigma[(p^* + at)/p]\}$. From the equilibrium conditions of the labour and non-traded good markets, $L = L_X + L_Y + L_N$ and $N = C_N + D_N$, we can solve for w and q. Then, we can obtain C_X and C_Y, and the utility U in (29).

The results are presented in Table 1. In Table 1, $U(0, 0)$ represents utility when the tariff and pollution tax rates are zero. When there is no tourism ($T = 0$), the optimal tariff is zero and the optimal pollution tax is equal to the Pigovian tax rate (s^P). When there is tourism ($T > 0$), the optimal tariff is positive and the optimal pollution tax is larger than the Pigouvian tax rate. The optimal rates of tariffs and pollution taxes increase when the demand by tourists becomes less elastic or when tourists' spending rises. These results support the case illustrated in Figure 1 that the tariff effect dominates the pollution externality effect in determining optimal pollution taxes in (22).

Table 1.   ***Simulations for optimal tariffs and pollution taxes***

T	η	t^{oo} (%)	s^{oo} (%)	s^P	U^{oo}	$U(0, 0)$	Changes in U
0	3	0	11.50	11.50	3.5420	3.5364	0.16
1	3	15.21	16.12	13.34	3.5737	3.5574	0.46
1.5	3	18.55	16.97	13.89	3.5970	3.5731	0.67
0	1	0	11.50	11.50	3.5420	3.5364	0.16
1	1	26.22	18.63	14.36	3.5865	3.5574	0.82
1.5	1	39.25	21.05	15.93	3.6351	3.5772	1.62
0	0.5	0	11.50	11.50	3.5420	3.5364	0.16
1	0.5	34.59	20.28	15.12	3.5951	3.5574	1.06
1.5	0.5	65.49	24.49	18.43	3.6708	3.5786	2.58
0	0.3	0	11.50	11.50	3.5420	3.5364	0.16
1	0.3	41.06	21.40	15.71	3.6008	3.5574	1.22
1.5	0.3	109.2	26.97	22.44	3.7082	3.5792	3.60

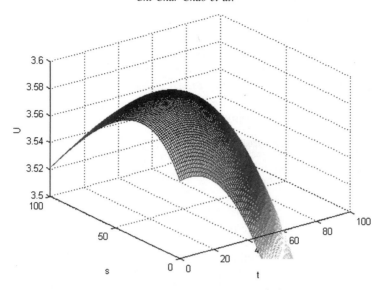

Fig. 3.   Simulation for optimal tariff and pollution tax.

For illustration, we graph the utility of households in Figure 3 in the space of tariff and pollution tax for $T = 1$ and $\eta = 0.5$. The utility function is strictly concave with respects to its two arguments, and the utility optimum is reached for $t^{\circ} = 0.3459$ and $s^{\circ} = 0.2028$.

5. Conclusions

For a small open economy with pollution, the traditional policy prescription is free trade in goods together with the standard Pigouvian tax on pollution. However, this policy prescription must be revised when tourism is present in the economy. Owing to a favourable tourism terms-of-trade effect, we have found that increases in import tariffs and pollution taxes can actually raise welfare of domestic residents. This suggests that for a small open economy with tourism, free trade in goods, along with the standard Pigouvain tax on pollution emissions, is no longer the first-best policy. Hence, caution is warranted in applying the traditional policy prescription for a small open economy with inbound tourism.

Acknowledgements

We thank an anonymous referee for useful comments. The work described in this chapter was supported by a grant from the Research Grants Council of the Hong Kong Special Administration Region, China (Project Code 2120288).

References

Batra, R. (1973), Nontraded goods, factor market distortions, and the gains from trade. *American Economic Review* 63, 706–713.

Batra, R.N., Beladi, H. (1990), Pattern of trade between underemployed economies. *Economica* 57, 485–493.

Beladi, H. (1990), Unemployment and immiserizing transfer. *Journal of Economics* 52, 253–265.

Beladi, H., Batra, R. (2004), Traded and nontraded goods and real wages. *Review of Development Economics* 8, 1–14.

Dei, F. (1985), Voluntary export restraints and foreign investment. *Journal of International Economics* 19, 305–312.

Hatzipanayotou, P., Lahiri, S., Michael, M.S. (2002), Can cross-border pollution reduce pollution? *Canadian Journal of Economics* 35, 805–818.

Hatzipanayotou, P., Lahiri, S., Michael, M.S. (2005), Reforms of environmental policies in the presence of cross-border pollution and public-private clean-up. *Scandinavian Journal of Economics* 107, 315–333.

Hatzipanayotou, P., Michael, M.S. (1995), Tariffs, quotas, and voluntary export restraints with endogenous labor supply. *Journal of Economics* 62, 185–201.

Hazari, B.R., Sgro, P.M. (2004), *Tourism, Trade and National Welfare*. Elsevier, Amsterdam.

Jones, R.W. (1971), A three-factor model in theory, trade and history. In: Bhagwati, J.N., Mundell, R.A., Jones, R.W., Vanek, J. (Eds.), *Trade, Balance of Payments and Growth: Essays in Honor of C. P. Kindleberger*. North-Holland, Amsterdam.

Khan, M.A. (1982), Social opportunity costs and immiserizing growth: some observations on the long run versus the short. *Quarterly Journal of Economics* 97, 353–362.

Khan, M.A. (1996), Free trade and the environment. *Journal of International Trade and Economic Development* 5, 113–136.

Komiya, R. (1967), Non-traded goods and the pure theory of international trade. *International Economic Review* 8, 132–152.

Krutilla, K. (1991), Environmental regulation in an open economy. *Journal of Environmental Economics and Management* 20, 127–142.

Marjit, S., Beladi, H., Chakrabarti, A. (2004), Trade and wage inequality in developing countries. *Economic Inquiry* 42, 295–303.

Neary, J.P. (1978), Short-run capital specificity and the pure theory of international trade. *Economic Journal* 88, 488–510.

Neary, J.P. (1993), Welfare effects of tariffs and investment taxes. In: Ethier, W.J., Helpman, E., Neary, J.P. (Eds.), *Theory, Policy and Dynamics in International Trade*. Cambridge University Press, Cambridge, pp. 131–156.

Neary, J.P. (1998), Pitfalls in the theory of international trade policy: concertina reforms of tariffs, and subsidies to high-technology industries. *Scandinavian Journal of Economics* 100, 187–206.

Yohe, G.W. (1979), The backward incidence of pollution control: some comparative statics in general equilibrium. *Journal of Environmental Economics and Management* 6, 187–198.

Yu, E.S.H., Ingene, C.A. (1982), The backward incidence of pollution control in a rigid-wage economy. *Journal of Environmental Economics and Management* 9, 304–310.

SUBJECT INDEX